# RESEARCH HANDBOOK ON SOCIAL MEDIA AND SOCIETY

# Research Handbook on Social Media and Society

*Edited by*

Marko M. Skoric

*Associate Professor, Department of Media and Communication, City University of Hong Kong, Hong Kong*

Natalie Pang

*Associate Professor, Communications and New Media Department, National University of Singapore, Singapore*

Edward Elgar PUBLISHING

Cheltenham, UK • Northampton, MA, USA

Cover image: Vladimir Todorovic, 'The Snail on the Slope', 2009.



Published by
Edward Elgar Publishing Limited
The Lypiatts
15 Lansdown Road
Cheltenham
Glos GL50 2JA
UK

Edward Elgar Publishing, Inc.
William Pratt House
9 Dewey Court
Northampton
Massachusetts 01060
USA

A catalogue record for this book
is available from the British Library

Library of Congress Control Number: 2023949644

This book is available electronically in the Elgaronline
Sociology, Social Policy and Education subject collection
http://dx.doi.org/10.4337/9781800377059

FSC www.fsc.org MIX Paper | Supporting responsible forestry FSC® C013604

ISBN 978 1 80037 704 2 (cased)
ISBN 978 1 80037 705 9 (eBook)

Printed and bound by CPI Group (UK) Ltd, Croydon, CR0 4YY

# Contents

PART III CIVICS AND POLITICS



PART IV RESEARCH METHODS AND PEDAGOGIES

# Figures

# Tables

# Contributors

**Valerie Albrecht** is a PhD student at the Department for E-Governance and Public Administration at the University for Continuing Education Krems. Her PhD research focuses on the transfer of knowledge in public sector organizations.

**Taylor Annabell** is a Postdoctoral Researcher in the Faculty of Law, Economics and Governance at Utrecht University. Taylor's research interests include the constructions of memory, postfeminist sensibility, everyday digital cultures and social media platforms. Her PhD thesis traced performances of digital memory work by young women on, with and through Instagram and Facebook in 2020. Her research has been published in *Memory Studies*, *Narrative Inquiry* and *Critical Discourse Studies*.

**Emma Baulch** is an Associate Professor of Media and Communications and Director of the Southeast Asia Research Centre for Digital Tech and Society (SEADS) at Monash University Malaysia. Emma researches media and popular culture in Indonesia using cultural studies approaches. She is author of *Making Scenes: Death Metal, Punk and Reggae in 1990s Bali* (Duke University Press, 2007) and *Genre Publics: Popular Music, Technologies and Class in Indonesia* (Wesleyan University Press, 2020), and co-author of the forthcoming *WhatsApp: From a One-to-One Messaging Service to a Global Social Media Platform* (Polity, with Amelia Johns and Ariadna Matamoros-Fernández).

**Márton Bene** is a Senior Research Fellow at the Centre for Social Sciences (Budapest) and an Assistant Professor at ELTE, Eötvös Loránd University. His primary research focus is on political communication and the role social media plays in contemporary politics.

**Annisa R. Beta** is an Australian Research Council Discovery Early Career Researcher Award (DECRA) Fellow (2023–2025) and a Lecturer in Cultural Studies at the School of Culture and Communication, the University of Melbourne. She was a Postdoctoral Fellow at National University of Singapore, where she also completed her PhD. Her research is broadly concerned with youth, new media and political subjectivity in Indonesia and Southeast Asia. She is the co-founder of Anotasi and Jaringan Etnografi Terbuka.

**Andrea Ceron** is an Associate Professor at the University of Milan, where he teaches Italian Political System, Polimetrics and Multivariate Analysis. He has been a Visiting Scholar at Harvard University, and Co-Founder/Board Member of the academic data analytics spinoff Voices from the Blogs. He is currently Principal Investigator of the PRIN project 'DEMOPE: Democracy under Pressure' and Editor of the *Encyclopedia of Technology and Politics*. He has published eight books and 50 articles in international peer-reviewed journals.

**Liang Chen** (PhD, Nanyang Technological University) is an Associate Professor at the School of Journalism and Communication, Tsinghua University. His research interests include health, environmental and risk communication. He is also an Associate Editor at *Environmental Communication*.

**Roei Davidson** is an Associate Professor in the Department of Communication at the University of Haifa, Israel. He studies how the Information Technology industry and the systems it develops – social media, artificial intelligence, digital finance – impact human autonomy and the distribution of capital.

**Noella Edelmann** is Senior Researcher at the Department for E-Governance and Public Administration at the University for Continuing Education Krems. Her research focuses on digital governance and organizational change.

**Manuel Goyanes** (PhD) serves as an Assistant Professor at Carlos III University in Madrid. His research addresses the influence of journalism and new technologies over citizens' daily lives, as well as the effects of news consumption on citizens' political knowledge and participation. He is also interested in global inequalities in academic participation, the systematic biases towards Global South scholars and publication trends in communication.

**Shivani Gupta** is a Lecturer at NUS College (Singapore). She is a feminist anthropologist researching women's everyday lives in non/metropolitan urban settings. She teaches gender and sexuality courses in addition to interdisciplinary social science courses. At NUS College she is curating a special program that focuses on using feminist praxis to benefit marginalized communities in Singapore. In the past, she has worked with women and feminist non-profit organizations in India.

**Michelle Ho** is an Assistant Professor of Feminist and Queer Cultural Studies at the Department of Communications and New Media at the National University of Singapore and on the Steering Committee of the Gender and Sexuality Research Cluster. Coming from an interdisciplinary background, her work has explored gender and sexuality issues in the context of (East) Asia, including (mis)representations of women in the media and gender-based discrimination of transgender women, with a strong emphasis on feminist methodologies, and ethnography.

**Kokil Jaidka** is an Assistant Professor in Computational Communication at the National University of Singapore. Her research interests lie in auditing AI (artificial intelligence) algorithms, developing computational models of persuasive and argumentative language, and building social media platforms that better facilitate constructive conversations. Her research has been published in *Nature Human Behaviour*, the *Journal of Computer-Mediated Communication* and the *Journal of Communication*, among other venues.

**Amelia Johns** is a Senior Lecturer in Digital and Social Media at the University of Technology Sydney. Her work spans digital media and citizenship studies, with a focus on young people's digital media literacy, political participation, activism and safety across networked and closed platforms and publics. She is author of *Battle for the Flag* (Melbourne University Publishing, 2015), co-editor of *Negotiating Digital Citizenship: Control, Contest, Culture* (Rowman & Littlefield, 2016) and co-author of a forthcoming book on WhatsApp (Polity, with Ariadna Matamoros-Fernández and Emma Baulch).

**Juma Kasadha** holds a PhD in Media and Communication from City University of Hong Kong. He was a Postdoc Fellow at the Department of Media and Communication at the same university. He lectures in Communication at the School of Communication, Media and Journalism, Wenzhou-Kean University. His research interests are visual communication, new media technologies and social change with a particular emphasis on citizen political engagement, and civic and political implications of new media technologies in sub-Saharan Africa.

**Jungup Lee** is an Assistant Professor at the Department of Social Work, National University of Singapore, and a social work expert specializing in cyber bullying, violence, safety, and psychological well-being among adolescents and young adults in urban society. Related to this project, she has undertaken online survey research on traditional bullying, cyberbullying and mental health outcomes among Singaporean university students, and evaluation research on an intervention program, 'Digital Mindset', for adolescents' Internet addiction.

**Hai Liang** (PhD, City University of Hong Kong) is an Associate Professor in the School of Journalism and Communication at the Chinese University of Hong Kong. His research interests include computational social science, political communication and digital public health. He has published dozens of journal articles, many of which appeared in the foremost communication journals, such as the *Journal of Communication*, *Communication Research* and *Human Communication Research*. He has published in public health, information science, sociology and other interdisciplinary journals.

**Liew Kai Khiun** has been making scholarly contributions to the topic of the globalization of Korean popular culture, or Hallyu, for close to two decades in the context of the Asia-Pacific region. This has ranged from the early beginnings in the circulation of Korean popular media texts through terrestrial television networks and portable media in the early 2000s to that of social media a decade later. Liew is currently an Assistant Professor at the Hong Kong Metropolitan University.

**Sun Sun Lim** is Vice President, Partnerships & Engagement and Professor of Communication and Technology at Singapore Management University. She has written extensively on the social impact of technology, including *Transcendent Parenting: Raising Children in the Digital Age* (Oxford University Press, 2020). She was a Nominated Member of Parliament from 2018–2020 and an honouree of the inaugural Singapore 100 Women in Tech list in 2020. She frequently offers her expert commentary in leading outlets including *Nature*, the *Guardian* and *Scientific American*.

**Xialing Lin** is an Assistant Professor in the Nicholson School of Communication and Media at the University of Central Florida. She studies risk and crisis communication and communication technology.

**Xiaoming Liu** (Master's, Sun Yat-sen University) is a Research Assistant in the Department of Journalism, School of Communication, Hong Kong Baptist University. Her research interests include health communication, computer-mediated communication and media psychology.

**Michael B. MacKuen** is the Burton Craige Professor of Political Science, Emeritus at the University of North Carolina, Chapel Hill. He received his BA from Virginia and his PhD from the University of Michigan. His research focuses on public opinion, public administration, social psychology, positive economics and the dynamics of persuasion. Among his books is *The Macro Polity* with Robert Erikson and James Stimson (Cambridge University Press, 2001).

**George E. Marcus** is Professor of Political Science, Emeritus at Williams College. His BA is from Columbia and PhD from Northwestern. His field of specialization is political psychology with special interest in the role of emotions in politics. He is lead author of *Affective Intelligence and Political Judgment* (University of Chicago Press, 2000). He was awarded the 2019 Harold D. Lasswell Award from the International Society of Political Psychology for distinguished scientific contributions in the field of political psychology.

**Maria-Jose Masanet** is an Associate Professor from the Serra Húnter programme at the Faculty of Information and Audiovisual Media at the Universitat de Barcelona. She is the Principal Investigator of the projects 'Transmedia Gender & LGBTI+ Literacy' (2021–2024) and 'Youth Street Groups & Media Representations' (2020–2022). Her topics of interest are media literacy, gender, young people and popular media culture. She has been visiting researcher at the New School (Fulbright Fellow), Ghent University, Université Sorbonne Nouvelle and Loughborough University.

**Ariadna Matamoros-Fernández** is a Senior Lecturer in Digital Media at the Queensland University of Technology, Chief Investigator at the Digital Media Research Centre (DMRC) and Associate Investigator at the ARC Centre of Excellence for Automated Decision-Making and Society (ADM+S). Her research focuses on the entanglement between technology and user practices in (re)producing systemic inequality. She is co-author of a forthcoming book on WhatsApp (Polity, with Amelia Johns and Emma Baulch).

**Francis Luis Medado Torres** is currently pursuing his PhD in Cultural Studies in Asia at the Department of Communications and New Media at the National University of Singapore. He received his MA in Comparative Literature from the

University of the Philippines Diliman. His MA study focused on examining the genealogy of the Philippine gay culture in the country's first 350 years. Currently, his research interests revolve around the history of Asian gay/queer criticism, gender studies, modernity and digital technology.

**Sun Meicheng** obtained her doctoral degree in Communication Studies from Nanyang Technological University. Her research interests include transnational popular cultural flows, youth culture and cultural industries. She has published pioneering research focusing on Korean popular music in China. She is currently an Assistant Professor at Beijing Language and Culture University.

**Claire Moran** is a Research Fellow at Action Lab, in the Faculty of IT at Monash University. Claire's research interests include migrant diaspora communities, social media and young people. Her PhD thesis explored the social media practises and experiences of Black African young people in Australia through a critical race lens. Her research has been published in the *Journal of Youth Studies*, *Media, Culture & Society* and *Media International Australia*.

**Sharon Yvette Xiomara Rosamor 'n Doen** is a PhD Candidate in Cultural Studies in Asia at the National University of Singapore. She obtained her BA in Cultural Anthropology and Development Sociology and MA in Indonesian Studies at Leiden University. Her current project focuses on gender propaganda in Indonesian horror films produced during the Suharto era (1966–1998).

**W. Russell Neuman** is Professor of Media Technology at New York University. His PhD is from the UC Berkeley, his BA from Cornell. He served as a Senior Policy Analyst in the White House Office of Science and Technology Policy working in the areas of information technology and international security. He held the John Derby Evans Chair of Media Technology at Michigan, and taught at the University of Pennsylvania, Harvard's Kennedy School, Yale University and the MIT Media Laboratory.

**Natalie Pang** is Associate Professor at the Communications and New Media Department (CNM), as well as Principal Investigator at the Centre for Trusted Internet and Community, both at the National University of Singapore. Her research and teaching focuses on digital citizenship/well-being and digital humanities, and she has published extensively with over 40 journal articles and over 50 conference papers, book chapters, commentaries and encyclopaedia entries. She also works on translation research in the form of policy papers and consultancies with government and intergovernmental agencies, tech companies and non-profits, and serves as a member of the UNESCO Inclusive Policy Lab, and expert in the Pacific Forum Women Experts Directory.

**Peter Parycek** is Professor for E-Governance, heads the Department for E-Governance in Business and Administration and is Vice-Rector for Teaching/ Scientific Continuing Education and Digital Transformation (CDO) at the University for Continuing Education Krems.

**Elianne Renaud** is the Centre Manager at the Australian Centre for Cannabinoid Clinical and Research Excellence at the University of Newcastle, Australia. Her thesis explored queer femme Instagram selfies as an intertextual site for critically imagining alternative femininities and queer subjectivities.

**Brady Robards** is an Associate Professor of Sociology at Monash University. Brady is a sociologist of youth and digital cultures, studying social media use, particularly among young people and LGBTQ+ people, with a focus on identity, belonging and marginalization. Brady's latest book is *Growing Up on Facebook* (Peter Lang, 2020). His research is also published in journals including *New Media & Society*, *Social Media + Society*, *Sexualities*, *Media, Culture & Society*, the *Journal of Youth Studies* and *Qualitative Research*.

**Abdul Rohman** is a Senior Lecturer in the School of Communication and Design at RMIT University Vietnam. He is the author of *Conflict, Continuity, and Change in Social Movements in Southeast Asia* (Routledge, 2022). His research interest revolves around the impact of digital and social media platforms on social change in Indonesia and Vietnam. His latest projects intersect social media and disability movements in the two countries, and Southeast Asian civil society groups' resilience against state oppressions during the COVID-19 pandemic.

**Carlos A. Scolari** is Full Professor at the Department of Communication (Universitat Pompeu Fabra – Barcelona), where he coordinates the PhD Program in Communication. His latest books are *Media Evolution* (with Fernando Rapa; La Marca Editora, 2019), *Cultura Snack* (La Marca Editora, 2020), *La Guerra de las Plataformas* (Editorial Anagrama, 2022) and *On the Evolution of Media* (Routledge, 2023). He was the Principal Investigator of the H2020 Transliteracy project (2015–2018) and now coordinates the PLATCOM project (2020–2024).

**Gabriele de Seta** is a sociologist of technology. He holds a PhD from the Hong Kong Polytechnic University and was a Postdoctoral Fellow at the Institute of Ethnology, Academia Sinica in Taiwan. Gabriele is currently a Postdoctoral Researcher at the University of Bergen, where he is part of the European Research Council-funded project 'Machine Vision in Everyday Life'. His research work, grounded on ethnographic engagement across multiple sites, focuses on digital media practices, sociotechnical entanglements and vernacular creativity in the Chinese-speaking world.

**Marko M. Skoric** is Associate Professor at the Department of Media and Communication, City University of Hong Kong, where he leads the Political Communication and Culture Research Cluster and acts as the PhD Program Coordinator. His research interests are focused on new media and social change, with a particular emphasis on the civic and political implications of digital technologies. He holds a PhD in Communication from the University of Michigan and a BSc in Psychology from University College London.

**Patric R. Spence** is a Professor in the Nicholson School of Communication and Media at the University of Central Florida. He is the Associate Editor of

*Human-Machine Communication* and the *Journal of International Crisis and Risk Communication Research.*

**Tamás Tóth** is an Assistant Professor at the University of Public Service (Budapest). His research interests include populist political communication styles, journalism studies and academic knowledge production. He has been published in journals such as the *International Journal of Communication*, the *Journal of Contemporary European Studies*, *Communications*, the *European Journal of Science and Theology* and *Scientometrics*.

**Bimlesh Wadhwa** is an Associate Professor at the Department of Computer Science, School of Computing, National University of Singapore. Her expertise is in human–computer interaction design and software engineering practices. Her work relevant to this project is in gender in design, data visualization, and development and evaluation of smartphone apps for well-being.

**Yang Wang** is a Research Fellow in Asia Research Institute at the National University of Singapore (NUS). She received her PhD in Communications and New Media from NUS. Her research focuses on information and communications technology domestication, mediated intimacy, transnational householding, mobile parenting and workplace digital transformation, as well as social media and online communities. She has published in leading international journals, including the *Journal of Computer-Mediated Communication*, *New Media and Society* and the *Journal of Children and Media*.

**Barui K. Waruwu** (PhD, City University of Hong Kong) is an Assistant Professor at the Department of Humanities and Creative Writing at Hong Kong Baptist University. His work examines the sociocultural implications of smartphones and social media on transnational family relationships, migrants' community building, and relational stress and communal resilience. His first- and solo-authored research papers have been published in international peer-reviewed journals, including *New Media & Society*, *Mobile Media & Communication*, and *Media, Culture & Society*.

**Fan Yang** is a Research Fellow at the University of Melbourne and ARC Centre of Excellence for Automated Decision-Making Society. She studies technologies and governance in the Global South, migration, innovative digital research methods and postcolonialism.

**Qinfeng Zhu** (PhD, City University of Hong Kong) is an Assistant Professor in the Centre for Media and Journalism Studies at the University of Groningen. Her research examines how social technologies and user practices shape individuals' social and informational environments and their influence on citizens' attitudes, emotions and (dis)engagement in everyday political interactions. Her work has been published in various top journals in the field, such as *New Media & Society*, *Political Communication* and the *International Journal of Press/Politics*.

# Introduction to the *Research Handbook on Social Media and Society*: social media scholarship reaches maturity

*Marko M. Skoric and Natalie Pang*

It was the year 1997 when SixDegrees.com was launched, allowing users to create profiles and connect with others. Named after the concept of the 'six degrees of separation', SixDegrees was perhaps one of the earliest known social media sites. But it was not until the early 2000s that social media platforms became massively popular, with the launch of sites like Friendster (2002), Myspace (2003), Facebook (2004) and YouTube (2005). These early years saw the use of social media sites mostly for socializing, entertainment and informational purposes; two decades on, social media has become ubiquitous and central in many domains of contemporary societies.

In the early years of scholarship on social media, much research focused on understanding the demographics of the users and how they were using these platforms as tools of communication and relationship building and maintenance. Studying and understanding the effects of social media usually involved measures such as frequency of time spent on social media and the platforms used. With the continuing evolution of social media platforms, researchers started recognizing the need to consider different features and affordances that come with various social media platforms. Such considerations included the expansion and inclusion of diverse theoretical concepts used to inform the research, but also the development of methods such as network analysis to better understand the network features of particular platforms.

As social media scholarship grew more diverse, researchers also began to see the importance of context in driving and explaining different effects of social media. For instance, in our meta-analysis of social media impact on citizen engagement in Asia, the effects of social media were observed to be greater in contexts where there are greater controls over legacy media (Skoric, Zhu & Pang, 2016). A good illustration of this would be the role of social media in the Arab Spring, where the use of social media had a significant role in mobilizing and facilitating communications among the protesters. The recognition of context also drove the development of the more qualitative and critical methods of social media scholarship, alongside the quantitative ones.

With the growth and popularity of social media platforms, one of the key challenges that emerged was how to define them as they grew more diverse. A fundamental feature of social media is social networking, exemplified in services such as SixDegrees, Friendster and Facebook that allowed users to connect with people they already know, as well as those that are connected to their friends and acquaintances. Although the number of platforms have grown rapidly in the last decade or so, such social networking features remain central to the design and development of social media. However, the modality of networking has evolved much, with platforms such as Foursquare enabling users to connect with each other via checking in at physical locations, TikTok allowing users to find and follow content and users they like, and Facebook enabling users to connect when a friend request has been accepted. With social media, individuals are able to alter or shape their social networks in very different ways – one can use social media to connect only with people that they already know, but others may prefer to expand their social networks to include people they do not know. In other words, the networks that are facilitated and maintained by social media take on multiple forms, and can be public, semi-public or private. Take WhatsApp and Telegram as examples. While one may see such instant-messaging platforms as newer versions of the short messaging service (SMS) and not social media platforms, we argue that they are essentially part of the social media ecology because there is the possibility to be connected to others as part of a larger social network, even though these ties may be latent. In this context, we agree with O'Sullivan and Carr's (2017) characterization of social media as being *mass-personal*; i.e., at the intersection between mass communication and interpersonal communication.

Other than social networking, social media should also include the ability to support user-generated content (UGC) as well as integrate content generated by other sources such as legacy media, including mainstream news agencies, television and radio. Increasingly, such content comes in various formats and includes images, text, videos and audio. Take, for example, TikTok, which allows users to create short videos, combine different effects available on its platform and draw from its music library through its license agreements with various distributors and labels.

In summary, we defined social media as platforms that: (a) enable users to connect and communicate with others in their social network, (b) allow for mass-personal communication and (c) utilize UGC, as well as content from other media institutions in a variety of formats including but not limited to text, images, videos and audio.

While social media platforms received much positive coverage in their early years, that is no longer the case. Scholars, activists and practitioners alike were optimistic about social media's potential to democratize information flows, address injustices, create opportunities for otherwise unheard and under-resourced communities, and upend oppressive regimes in society. In many ways, these potentials still hold true – social media has become a central feature of many forms of civic participation and mobilization globally. However, many online harms have also been identified, inciting a turn in the scholarship, which now provides more nuanced and often critical views of the impact of social media on individuals and society.

This *Handbook* aims to provide a key resource for students, scholars, media professionals and policy-makers interested in understanding the role that social media platforms play in contemporary societies. The chapters in this *Handbook*, written by a diverse group of international scholars, showcase the academic community's responses to some of the key societal challenges posed by the evolving social media ecologies. The chapters also provide an overview of the emerging methods of social media research and the related pedagogies, and discuss the ethical issues that social media scholars face.

Our contributors, hailing from different intellectual and methodological traditions, showcase that the field is reaching its maturity. Unlike the early phase of research, which was dominated by a rather optimistic agenda regarding the impact of social media on society, the current scholarship paints a more complex and arguably gloomier picture of the role of digital media platforms in our lives. As social media scholarship enters its mature stage, we witness a significant expansion of the research foci and far greater theoretical sophistication paired with more advanced and more interdisciplinary methodological approaches.

The topics and the research locales covered in this *Handbook* demonstrate an increasing internationalization and diversification of social media scholarship, with our contributors offering fresh research perspectives and providing nuanced insights about the role of social media in our societies. The chapters offer scholarly perspectives on a range of social, psychological, cultural and political phenomena, including parenting and family practices, sexual violence, disconnection and avoidance, post-conflict reconciliation, fandom, crowdfunding, classroom pedagogies and participatory governance. Furthermore, our contributors provide valuable methodological guidance to aspiring social media researchers by covering several highly relevant approaches ranging from big data and public opinion analytics to digital ethnography, instant-messaging app research and scroll-back interviewing. Importantly, our chapters provide a balanced coverage of research contexts and locales, featuring scholarship originating from a number of non-Western and Global South countries.

The *Handbook* is organized into four thematic parts:

- Sexuality, gender and family
- Culture and publics
- Civics and politics
- Research methods and pedagogies

The first part of the *Handbook*, on sexuality, gender and family, opens with a chapter by Lim and Wang on the role of social media in parenting. In their chapter, the authors highlight an increasingly public dimension of parenting, in which parents share their joys and trials of childrearing on social media platforms. By showcasing the growth and development of their children, parents invite comments from their audiences, which frequently include praise, social endorsement, emotional support and sympathy. Lim and Wang argue that although 'performative parenting' may offer a sense of community, it may also lead to less desirable consequences such as envy and alienation and it is therefore important to analyse these emerging social media practices more closely.

The second chapter, by Chen and Liu and also focusing on the topic of parenting, provides an empirical examination of the factors predicting parental mediation of adolescents' social media use. Using a survey of parents of teenagers in China, the authors test the predictors of three different mediation strategies: active mediation, restrictive mediation and non-intrusive inspection – all based on the theory of planned behaviour (TPB). They find that while the parents' subjective norms and digital literacy were positively associated with all three forms of mediation, digital literacy in particular made the effect of subjective norms on non-intrusive inspection stronger, but weakened the effect of perceived behavioural control.

In the third chapter of this part, Waruwu examines the emerging practices of digital caregiving; i.e., mediated mothering as performed by migrant mothers in Hong Kong. In this interview-based study, the author pays particular attention to the concept of 'affordances' and how migrant mothers use these actionable potentials of social media to redefine family caregiving rituals. He highlights three affordances of social media, namely visibility, controlled connectivity and persistence, as having the potential to reinforce the emergent practices of mediated mothering while at the same time potentially acting to destabilize the traditional notion of family.

In the closing chapter of this part on sexuality, gender and family, Gupta and colleagues examine a more sinister side of social media use: technology-facilitated sexual violence (TFSV). Their study, conducted in the context of Singapore, uses digital ethnography informed by feminist methodology to bring to fore this under-researched phenomenon. The authors emphasize that such an approach has the potential to provide a roadmap for understanding TFSV and evaluate its implications for social media users, particularly young women.

The part on culture and publics opens with a chapter by Beta, who provides a unique insight into the role of religious social media influencers in the political landscape in Indonesia. The author highlights the role of religion and online displays of piety in the 'attention economy' of contemporary Muslim societies and proposes a method of studying this emerging phenomenon by examining digital platform contexts and affordances. The chapter emphasizes the importance of studying social media-based religious practices for gaining genuine insights into contemporary interpretations of religious orthodoxy.

The second chapter in this part, written by Davidson, offers a new perspective on the emerging social media phenomena of crowdsourcing and crowdfunding. The author provides a collection of historical and contemporary case studies from the United States, Europe and Israel to illustrate the populist nature of many crowdfunding projects. Moreover, Davidson argues that the importance of such projects lies in their poetic dimension rather than in the material outcomes they aim to provide and emphasizes the potential political impact of both successful and failed crowd-based projects.

In the third chapter of this part, Spence and Lin focus on the role of social media in crisis communication. The authors examine the information diffusion and social media uses throughout the crisis lifecycle and offer a useful review of the research methods used in the scholarly literature. They also provide important guidance for future researchers in the field by not only outlining best practices but also by highlighting some noted failures, and discussing challenges and opportunities that lie ahead.

In the fourth chapter in this part, Kasadha provides a unique perspective on the role of social media use in fostering reconciliation in post-conflict societies. The author proposes a new theoretical lens – the Social Media Reconciliation Model – to examine how social media platforms may contribute to conciliatory processes in both developing and developed countries. Kasadha identifies four key approaches in the intervention process – smoke detector, social influencer, reciprocal and deletion – and applies them in the context of the aftermath of the January 6 US Capitol attack.

The last chapter in this part, contributed by Liew and Sun, explores the role of social media platforms in the global diffusion of K-pop and K-pop fandom. An increasingly visible and coordinated socio-political role of K-pop fan communities, the authors argue, has a power to de-centre the predominantly Western music industry and bring new prosumer aesthetics to the fore. Liew and Sun argue that by boosting digital streaming metrics, contributing UGC and mobilizing support for different causes, K-pop fan communities have become a part of the global cyberpublic.

Our part on civics and politics opens with a chapter from Ceron, who examines the role of social media in fostering the reciprocal relationships between different political actors. Using the lens of principal–agent theory, the author argues that social media platforms create new public spaces that could reduce the asymmetry of information between the 'principal' (e.g., leaders, activists, interest groups) and the 'agent' (e.g., politicians, representatives, governments). This is done via the reduction in both the monitoring and the reputation costs, which has the potential to increase government's accountability and responsiveness as well as the transparency within a political system.

The second chapter, written by Zhu, highlights the importance of studying the political implications of disconnective practices on social media such as unfollowing and unfriending. Noting that most of the extant research in political communication has focused on connectivity, the author provides a strong case for re-orienting our research efforts to analysing social media disconnectivity and its consequences for democratic citizenship. Zhu reviews the existing research and provides theoretical guidance for future research on the origins and implications of disconnective practices on social media.

Continuing with a similar theme, Bene, Tóth and Goyanes in Chapter 12 examine why citizens increasingly abstain from participating in social media discussion and debates. Rather than focusing on citizen engagement on social media, a topic that has received significant scholarly attention, the authors advance a novel theoretical concept – Teflonic social media behaviour (TSMB) – to characterize the users' conscious decision to refrain from participating. The chapter identifies several social and political factors behind social media disengagement and discusses why social media can sometimes be unsafe spaces for political discussion.

Chapter four in this part, by Neuman, Marcus and MacKuen, examines people's affective reactions to social media posts related to prominent political issues in the context of the United States. Using an experimental survey design on a sample of American adults, the authors test whether the norm violation rhetoric in the posts raises the levels of anxiety and aversion and also dampens the levels of enthusiasm. The findings support the hypotheses, further indicating the effects of affective responses on the individuals' political information seeking and preparedness to engage in deliberation.

Chapter 14, authored by Rohman, looks into the topic of social media facilitation of social movement activities in the context of Indonesia. The author's analysis emphasizes the emergence of socio-technical and cultural threats to social movements, taking the forms of increasing government surveillance, state-sponsored hacking and trolling, 'cancel' culture, and more. The chapter brings a much-needed realistic assessment of the potential of social media to aid (or deter) social movements in the context of the Global South.

The last chapter in our civics and politics part focuses on social media-based public participation in governance processes from an institutional perspective. In their study, Edelmann, Albrecht and Parycek examine digital public participation in Austria by analysing tools, formats and processes involved, and by reviewing the policy cycle and the impact of digitalization on the design of participatory processes. The chapter explains how this these analyses have informed the development of the new government guidelines for public participation in Austria.

The last part of the *Handbook* features chapters that provide important insights regarding the emerging research methods and pedagogies surrounding social media. In the opening chapter, Liang provides a comprehensive overview of the use of social media data as 'big data' in research, outlining the main analytical methods used and introducing a new typology of social media analytics. Summarizing the extant research, the author proposes that based on the purpose of application in empirical studies, we can divide analytics into (a) measurement, (b) description, (c) causal inference and (d) intervention, and discusses the implications for future research.

Continuing with the topic of social media analytics, in Chapter 17 Jaidka takes a closer look at public opinion analytics, in line with the surging interest from researchers and practitioners in forecasting political climates and events based on social media data. She examines computational approaches used in public opinion predictions based on social media data and engages with the important theoretical and methodological issues that researchers in the field have faced.

In the third chapter of this part, de Seta brings an analytical perspective notably different from the previous chapters', focusing on ethnographic approaches to digital folklore. By digging deep into his own experience of engaging with digital folklore in the Chinese context, the author reveals a rich repertoire of digital creativity, arguing for the usefulness of digital ethnography as a method for studying social media. The chapter provides relevant guidelines and a toolbox for aspiring digital ethnographers for studying vernacular creativity on social media.

Chapter 19, authored by Moran, Renaud, Annabell, Yang and Robards, provides an overview of an important new method of social media research: 'the social media scroll back'. The authors reflect on their individual research experiences with the method and offer four case studies to readers, covering a range of different research topics, participant groups and social media platforms. The authors provide a useful primer for researchers aiming to utilize scroll-back interviews in their studies, and identify a distinct set of opportunities and limitations associated with it.

In Chapter 20, Baulch, Johns and Matamoros-Fernández review the extant scholarship on instant-messaging apps and chronicle methods used for studying them.

The authors look into the societal and historical implications of instant-messaging technologies, geographical contexts and locales that dominate in the field, and the methodological and ethical challenges that researchers face. Their findings indicate the dominance of China-focused studies and those examining WhatsApp, and note the absence of critical studies of messaging apps that pay attention to the increasing platform power.

In the concluding chapter, Masanet and Scolari provide a unique international exploration of the use of social media in the classroom. Unlike most of the chapters in the *Handbook*, the authors focus on understanding the potential of social media to enhance educational outcomes by exploring the acquisition and development of 'transmedia skills' of teenagers. Their data, collected over several years in eight different countries, support an optimistic view of social media as a potential facilitator of innovative, dynamic teaching practices, and they provide the readers with vivid examples of social media uses in the classroom.

By providing this collection of important contemporary research works to our readers, we aim to provide them with both inspiration and guidance in their scholarly journeys and encourage them to pursue their own research studies on social media and society.

## REFERENCES

O'Sullivan, P.B., and Carr, C.T. (2017). Masspersonal communication: A model bridging the mass-interpersonal divide. *New Media & Society*, *20*(3), 1161–80. https://doi.org/10.1177/1461444816686104.

Skoric, M.M., Zhu, Q., and Pang, N. (2016). Social media, political expression, and participation in Confucian Asia. *Chinese Journal of Communication*, *9*(4), 331–47. https://doi.org/10.1080/17544750.2016.1143378.

# PART I

# SEXUALITY, GENDER AND FAMILY

# 1. Social media and performative parenting

*Sun Sun Lim and Yang Wang*

## INTRODUCTION

Social media has become the de facto 'water cooler' for a vast swathe of internet users. Connecting people across geographical areas and time zones, platforms such as TikTok, Instagram, WeChat, Facebook and Twitter provide lively venues for people to connect with others who share common needs, interests and goals. Parents are no exception. With the intensifying use of social media in many realms of everyday life, even parenting is manifesting a decidedly public dimension. Whereas one might understandably assume that parenting is a private activity undertaken within the home, the use of social media to highlight the joys and trials of raising kids has put parenting under the digital spotlight.

Increasingly, parents are keen to showcase their children's growth and development to family and friends through posts on Facebook, photos on Instagram, and videos over WeChat, WhatsApp and TikTok. Significant achievements earn praise and social endorsement, as well as commendations for excellent parenting. At the same time, the sharing of parenting struggles over social media also elicits expressions of commiseration, sympathy and support. The ensuing virtuous cycles of mutual affirmation and validation can create a sense of community, but the competitiveness and envy that could also result may be alienating. The tensions in such social media dynamics that are rooted in performative parenting in our hyper-connected era thus warrant greater scrutiny.

Lying at the intersections of communication, sociology, social psychology, and science and technology studies (STS), we discuss issues associated with performative parenting through an interdisciplinary framework and draw upon fieldwork conducted with families in China's urban areas.

## TRENDS AND MOTIVATIONS IN PERFORMATIVE PARENTING

As technology evolves and assumes growing salience in society, parenting has been both technologically mediated and technologically intensified. Naturally, the parenting remit is sizeable and goes far beyond coordinating schedules, ensuring familial wellbeing and maintaining relationships. Technology is indeed also an invaluable resource for parents in terms of the information they need and the opportunities they seek. A large body of research has thus focused on how parents, especially mothers rather than fathers, appropriate various technological platforms to solicit support and exchange parenting experiences to cope with the tribulations of parenthood. Many such interactions take on a public dimension where people interact with both known and unknown publics, for whom parents engage in some form of performativity, as if under the spotlight of the 'front stage' (Goffman, 1969).

Since the 1990s, mothers have found solace and solidarity on parenting websites and online discussion forums, and more recently parenting blogs and social media, with such online resources complementing the advice of healthcare professionals or trusted family members (Lupton et al., 2016). Notably, online support groups are a potentially valuable resource for new mothers to navigate cultural limitations surrounding more intimate issues such as breastfeeding (Alianmoghaddam et al., 2019), encouraging experience sharing (Hall & Irvine, 2009), offering increased social connections and improving understanding of parenting responsibilities (Brady & Guerin, 2010). These varied online exchanges play critical roles in mitigating depression and enhancing self-esteem, especially among postnatal or young mothers adapting to their new duties and identities (Bragadóttir, 2008).

Similarly, Wilson and Yochim's (2017) study of working- and middle-class stay-at-home mothers in the US found that these women draw heavily upon online resources such as parenting websites, 'mommy blogs' and online communities on Facebook, Instagram and Pinterest for material and emotional support. More recently, there has been a proliferation of pregnancy apps that are connected to wearable devices to facilitate the tracking of conception, foetal growth, heart rate and movements and biometrics, even including taking and sharing photographs of baby bumps (Godwin, 2019). Publicness, performativity and peer support thus go hand in hand and indeed are deeply intertwined in present-day parenting.

Performative parenting may also extend from more instrumental communication, specifically home–school conferencing – referring to parents' communications with teachers that serve to bridge the gap between home and school, such as interacting with teachers via telephone, e-mail or attending parent–teacher meetings (Stright & Yeo, 2014). Such practices have been found to positively influence children's academic performance because they motivate children and offer them a sense of security, while giving parents a closer understanding of their children's educational pursuits and encouraging parental support (Gonzalez-DeHass et al., 2005; Hill & Taylor, 2004). Home-school conferencing via mobile apps is a growing trend that rides on the convenience of digital platforms to facilitate greater communication between parents and teachers. Such apps may push automated messages on routine matters such as homework requirements and deadlines. As well, these apps typically come with private messaging functions where parents and teachers can engage in discussions over specific matters such as more personalized feedback on individual children's learning achievements or difficulties. It is in the latter context that performative parenting can also occur as parents may wish to impress upon teachers their efforts in assisting their children's learning, expressions of support for teachers' efforts, and so on. As we will elaborate on later, this is a salient trend among urban Chinese parents. Strikingly too, besides custom home–school conferencing apps, parents and teachers are increasingly using generic messaging apps and social media platforms such as WhatsApp, Facebook Messenger and WeChat for their interactions (Lim, 2020).

## CHINESE PARENTS AND PERFORMATIVE PARENTING

With China becoming a global AI (artificial intelligence) superpower (Lee, 2018), birthing many technological innovations that have taken the world by storm, it is little wonder that the Chinese are embracing technology in virtually every realm of their everyday lives, including parenting.

Chinese parents regard 'training' their children to subscribe to the right values as key to their positive development (Chao, 1995; Chen & Luster, 2002). Correspondingly, if parents fail to offer effective 'family education' and their children misbehave, parents can be taken to task and criticized for their negligence and indulgence (Kelley & Tseng, 1992). Besides good behaviour, Chinese society has long valorized academic achievement in children (Chao, 1995; Chao & Tseng, 2005). Indeed, contemporary Chinese families have never been more deeply invested in their children's academic endeavours (Lim, 2021) and, therefore, the use of technological applications in education, be it for facilitating, managing, monitoring and boosting children's educational performance, is hardly surprising.

In our research with Chinese parents over the past five years, we have observed increasingly intensive use of mobile apps for education and communication purposes among parents of different socioeconomic brackets. China's technocentric environment encourages unprecedented parental participation in children's school lives and enables extensive and continuous parent–teacher and parent–parent connections. These trends have engendered an interactive and relational culture of parental involvement in children's education. In such a climate, parenting practices that traditionally occurred in private spaces, such as supervising homework, contacting teachers and registering for school activities, have now been brought from 'back stage' to 'front stage' (Goffman, 1969).

We unpack how these previously prosaic activities now necessitate parents' careful and deliberate performance under the gaze of teachers, other parents and children, as well as online networks of weak ties. For contemporary Chinese parents, one important venue for performative parenting is parent–teacher conferencing and class management apps such as *DingTalk* (钉钉), *Yiqixue* (一起学), and *Banji youhua dashi* (班级优化大师). These educational platforms provide a wide range of education-related functions, including children's curriculum schedules, homework management tools, notifications, online courses, parent–teacher communication channels and shared drives for uploading learning resources. They are widely utilized by most primary and secondary school teachers as well as parents in urban China. Intensive use of these apps facilitates efficient, real-time teacher–parent interactions in which teachers provide feedback on children's academic performance at school and disseminate instructions for parental assistance on a daily basis. Parents, in turn, have to respond to these requests while keeping on top of their children's educational progress and outcomes.

While the convenience of real-time parent–school connections enables parents to be actively involved in their children's education, it also escalates parenting responsibilities. The pervasiveness of these educational and communication technologies has extended the criteria for 'good parenting' to include the ability to respond promptly and ably to any request from the school or teachers, be it to upload overdue homework, confirm receipt of notifications or participate in polls. Since the majority of these parenting behaviours are now visible to teachers and other parents, positive responses and active participation help parents leave a 'perfect' impression on all these audiences. Conversely, however, parents' failure to deliver on those tasks will invite disapproval from teachers and other parents and even disadvantage their children at school (as many parents fear). Over time, performativity has become an essential parenting skill and part and parcel of everyday life for these digitally connected parents. As described by a Chinese mother in our research, parenting is 'another full-time job, with endless overtime and the obligation to please everyone except ourselves'.

Besides those formal modes of parent–teacher communication via official school apps, performative parenting is also widely witnessed in day-to-day, casual chats over popular social media platforms such as WeChat, QQ, Weibo, *Xiaohongshu* (小红书), and so on. Parent chat groups on WeChat and QQ are the most common venues for daily parent–teacher and parent–parent chats in China. In these chat groups, teachers usually take on the role of administrators who disseminate education-related information, including school notifications, homework instructions and reports of students' academic performance. They also set and uphold norms of civilized interaction within the chat and answer parents' questions. Parents, who engage in group chats with varying degrees of diligence, are expected to support teachers' educational efforts and provide mutual assistance to other parents by responding to requests, sharing useful information, proposing solutions to others' problems, and so on. These chat groups thus serve a dual purpose. They allow parents to keep abreast of their children's school lives on a daily or even hourly basis and help them build and strengthen relationships with teachers and other parents.

In these interactive parent groups, careful self-presentation and strategic performativity are therefore tacit requirements for every parent, be they openly enthusiastic or grudgingly compliant. Specifically, parents must be prepared to invest considerable attention in all ongoing chats and be unfailingly responsive to all manner of requests. Etiquette-wise, one must express gratitude with words such as 'thank you', 'noted with thanks', 'received', and so on. Parents also have to be cautious about their words and actions in daily chats, including what (not) to say, when (not) to say, to whom (and not), as well as the use of appropriate words, tones and emojis in different contexts. They must frequently engage in 'emotion work' (Hochschild, 1983), where they have to conceal their authentic feelings to maintain a genial, polite and ebullient image in the presence of teachers and other parents. For example, our findings revealed that when parents disagree with each other or take offence during mediated conversations, most of them choose to cloak their negative emotions and forge compromises to avoid direct conflict for fear of sullying their well-cultivated image and adversely affecting their children.

Performative parenting in these parent groups also gives rise to competitiveness and peer pressure. In particular, many parents profess a great desire to become 'opinion leaders' in parent groups through actively participating in discussions and frequently sharing useful information, as well as providing practical and emotional support to fellow members. However, these ostensibly well-intentioned efforts often belie an implicit contest to gain more attention and respect from the teachers and other parents over time. This invisible yet palpable rivalry renders these parents susceptible to unforgiving peer standards and aggravates parental anxiety about 'not doing well enough compared to other parents'.

Similarly, another popular channel for casual parent–teacher and parent–parent connections is through daily posts, comments and likes on social media platforms. Many Chinese parents have the habit of sharing parenting experiences on Moments (a social media platform attached to WeChat) using a combination of text posts, photos and videos, with content about mundane titbits such as children's school and extracurricular activities, new dishes they prepare for their children, family vacation photos, and the like. Aside from personal parenting experiences, parents also share useful information and interesting stories about children, education and parenting that they come across online. These sharing practices are highly interactive since both parents and teachers are active in liking and commenting on these posts, allowing parents to establish and strengthen their relationships via such ancillary yet continual interactions.

In this highly interactive and densely networked environment, while Chinese parents may benefit from more extensive and diverse connections, they also face the perpetual stress of appropriate self-presentation and strategic image management in a state of constant publicness. Since posts on social media are publicly visible to large networks of teachers and parents, as well as other acquaintances and even strangers, they usually feel obliged to share high-quality, carefully curated content that presents a positive, well-groomed and competent image to these audiences. For instance, before sharing photos on social media, many parents spend a lot of time selecting the best-looking photos and embellishing them with editing software. In a similar vein, parents are also careful to avoid potentially controversial topics and disclosure of overly negative emotions in social media posts.

Performative parenting online becomes even more complicated when a parent simultaneously juggles multiple social media platforms. Specifically, they have to develop sharpened awareness of different audiences, preferred topics, and norms of interaction on different platforms, and tactically adjust their online activity to project their best selves (Wang & Lim, 2021). For example, on their own Moments page, parents freely share frivolous and useless personal experiences or have casual conversations with friends using hilarious emojis, jokes and in-group code words. In contrast, in parent chat groups that are typically created for essential teacher–parent communication instead of small talk, parents tend to be more serious and refrain from inundating group members with irrelevant personal issues. Parents may experience 'context collapse' (Davis & Jurgenson, 2014) when they fail to share the 'right' content on the 'right' platform, which could undermine their reputation in certain contexts and even result in misunderstanding and conflicts.

For Chinese parents, therefore, performative parenting over social media is driven by both the symbolic value of gaining recognition and pragmatic purposes of relationship building and information acquisition with teachers and other parents (see also Marwick & boyd, 2010; Turkle, 2011; Vitak et al., 2015). Above all, undergirding these online communities of teachers and parents are inherent rules of reciprocity, mutual support and quid pro quos (Wang & Lim, 2021).

## WHITHER THE DOWNSIDES OF PERFORMATIVE PARENTING

For all of its virtues, technologically mediated performative parenting has significant downsides. The active mobilization of home–school conferencing apps and parent–parent and parent–teacher chat groups underlines how vital these services are for parents who wish to be actively engaged in their children's school lives. Our findings reveal that parents labour under an ever-multiplying variety of channels to communicate with their children's teachers and other parents, compounding their sense of burden. Parents have to diligently manage relentless notifications from these apps and chat groups to keep their children on track in school. Some also lamented that with peer comparisons and peer pressure being galvanized in these public platforms, educational hurdles seem ever more daunting. Social media allows parents to know what other parents are doing on an unprecedented scale. Not only do these parents experience peer pressure from their immediate networks of families and friends or children's classmates' parents, but they are also inundated with perspectives on 'good parenting' from all over the world. Furthermore, with other parents openly flaunting their children's achievements on these platforms and currying favour with teachers to earn preferential treatment, the digitally connected parent must increasingly engage in 'emotion work'.

These public platforms and the interactions they host, little by little, shift the norms around 'ideal parenting'. Just as mothers who interact online via discussion forums and blogs can influence how 'good parenting' is defined (see, for example, Friedman, 2010; Geinger et al., 2014), the mobile-enabled child–parent, parent–parent and parent–teacher communication also helps to set the benchmarks for 'ideal parenting'. Indeed, our findings reveal a kind of 'viral panic' among parents – that they constantly compare their own efforts against those of other parents, evaluate their investment in their children's education, and feel guilty and anxious when they hear about other parents who are doing more or 'better'. And yet, however trying such online interactions are, parents hardly feel ready or willing to extricate themselves from these relational networks because they would be denying themselves vital information and resources that can help their children get ahead in the educational rat race. Therefore, despite the additional psychological burden, parents resolutely bear this weight of exacting parenting norms for the sake of their children.

## CONCLUSION

Parenting in the digital age is replete with both opportunities and challenges – the latter being especially acute in some societies. As we have elaborated earlier, the intensifying use of social media shifts parenting experiences from the private realm into the public spotlight and allows parents to know (with often vivid clarity) what other parents are doing worldwide. During this process, parents' self-perceptions also take on a public dimension and become shaped by the publicness of their own parenting behaviours online. Instead of parenting out of instinct, personal preference and daily trial and error, they choose to accord with 'universally recognized templates' for 'good parenting' for the sake of earning praise, validation and peer support. They also tend to evaluate their success as parents from the viewpoint of spectators, based on 'what others say about me' and 'what impressions I leave on others' rather than simply 'what I have done for my child'. Indeed, our findings show that many parents often feel guilty about their inadequacies and appraise themselves as incompetent just because there are other parents on social media who appear to do even better. Covid-19 and the shift towards working from home around the world stirred considerable individual reflection and social media debate over parenting practices – what to encourage, enhance or eschew. Such discourse, while healthy in some ways, can also amplify parenting anxiety. Future research on perceptions of parenting and de facto norms for good parenting and the role that social media plays in shaping them will help to raise parents' awareness that such 'norms' exist and how these may influence their feelings of self-worth and self-efficacy.

Publicness and performative parenting on social media also have implications for children's development and parent–child relations. Children are omnipresent in their parents' lives via the social media vignettes – text, photos, videos – that showcase and underscore persistent performativity. By the same token, social media and other parental apps serve as a virtual 'umbilical cord' (Ribak, 2009) that allows parents to be omnipresent in children's school lives (Lim, 2020). While such constant connectivity assures parents of children's academic performance and wellbeing, it also extends the boundary of parental surveillance and control and results in parents' over-involvement in children's educational endeavours (see, for example, Caronia, 2008; Lim, 2020; Nelson, 2010). Over time, over-active parental interventions may deprive children of autonomy and space for personal growth, which has negative impacts on children's development and parent–child relationships. Longitudinal interdisciplinary research can be conducted to better apprehend such issues.

Social media and the performative parenting culture that grows out of it have also transformed the normative standards and expectations of being a 'good parent'. In the current technologically mediated environment, parental obligations have expanded far beyond the traditional parenting role of caregiving in the domestic sphere to include complicated education and relationship management in both offline and online realms. Parents now are pressured to live a life of 'transcendent parenting' in which they must constantly transcend the physical distance between them and their children, strategically navigate myriad parental apps and groups, and make connections with all the relevant people and resources that might be helpful to children's education (Lim, 2020). With intense digital connectivity and extensive social networks, norms for 'good parenting' seem increasingly unyielding. Small failures in parenting, such as inappropriate expression of ideas in a parent group or overlooking information from the teacher, can subject parents to scrutiny and judgement that stoke feelings of insecurity and perhaps resentment.

It has been observed that when people encounter transformative technology, it can shape even their inner lives and relationships (Turkle, 2011). The parents who have been bound through their children to these parent–teacher conferencing apps and drawn into these tight digital networks of teachers and peer parents have had to succumb to the publicness and performativity of parenting. And yet, however unwelcome, they soldier on to negotiate these pressures for the benefit of their children in their overriding quest for academic excellence. Fundamentally, therefore, we as a society must pause to consider whether the technological amplification of such social pressures should simply be accepted or whether we can strive consciously towards undoing this undesirable trend. In so doing, parents and children can have a respite from being always on show to taking a breather on the 'back stage'.

## REFERENCES

Alianmoghaddam, N., Phibbs, S., & Benn, C. (2019). 'I did a lot of Googling': A qualitative study of exclusive breastfeeding support through social media. *Women and Birth: Journal of the Australian College of Midwives*, *32*(2), 147–56. https://doi.org/10.1016/j.wombi.2018.05.008.

Brady, E., & Guerin, S. (2010). 'Not the romantic, all happy, coochy coo experience': A qualitative analysis of interactions on an Irish parenting web site. *Family Relations*, *59*(1), 14–27. https://doi.org/10.1111/j.1741-3729.2009.00582.x.

Bragadóttir, H. (2008). Computer-mediated support group intervention for parents. *Journal of Nursing Scholarship*, *40*(1), 32–38. https://doi.org/10.1111/j.1547-5069.2007.00203.x.

Caronia, L. (2008). 'Growing Up Wireless: Being a Parent and Being a Child in the Age of Mobile Communication'. In *Digital Literacy: Tools and Methodologies for Information Society*, edited by P.C. Rivoltella, 99–125. Hershey, PA: IGI Global. https://doi.org/10.4018/978-1-59904-798-0.ch006.

Chao, R., & Tseng, G. (2005). 'Parenting of Asians'. In *Handbook of Parenting, Volume 4: Social Conditions and Applied Parenting*, edited by M.H. Bornstein, 59–94. Mahwah: Lawrence Erlbaum Associates.

Chao, R.K. (1995). Chinese and European American cultural models of the self reflected in mothers' childrearing beliefs. *Ethos*, *23*(3), 328–54. https://doi.org/10.1525/eth.1995.23.3.02a00030.

Chen, F.-M., & Luster, T. (2002). Factors related to parenting practices in Taiwan. *Early Child Development and Care*, *172*(5), 413–30. https://doi.org/10.1080/03004430214549.

Davis, J.L., & Jurgenson, N. (2014). Context collapse: Theorizing context collusions and collisions. *Information, Communication & Society*, *17*(4), 476–85. https://doi.org/10.1080/1369118x.2014.888458.
Friedman, M. (2010). 'It Takes a (Virtual) Village: Mothering on the Internet'. In *Twenty-First Century Motherhood: Experience, Identity, Policy, Agency*, edited by A. O'Reilly, 362–75. New York: Columbia University Press.
Geinger, F., Vandenbroeck, M., & Roets, G. (2014). Parenting as a performance: Parents as consumers and (de)constructors of mythic parenting and childhood ideals. *Childhood*, *21*(4), 488–501. https://doi.org/10.1177/0907568213496657.
Godwin, R. (2019, March 2). 'You can track everything': The parents who digitise their babies' lives. *The Guardian*. https://www.theguardian.com/lifeandstyle/2019/mar/02/apps-that-track-babies-and-give-data-to-tech-firms-parents.
Goffman, E. (1969). *The Presentation of Self in Everyday Life*. London: Penguin Books.
Gonzalez-DeHass, A.R., Willems, P.P., & Holbein, M.F. (2005). Examining the relationship between parental involvement and student motivation. *Educational Psychology Review*, *17*(2), 99–123. https://doi.org/10.1007/s10648-005-3949-7.
Hall, W., & Irvine, V. (2009). E-communication among mothers of infants and toddlers in a community-based cohort: A content analysis. *Journal of Advanced Nursing*, *65*(1), 175–83. https://doi.org/10.1111/j.1365-2648.2008.04856.x.
Hill, N.E., & Taylor, L.C. (2004). Parental school involvement and children's academic achievement. *Current Directions in Psychological Science*, *13*(4), 161–64. https://doi.org/10.1111/j.0963-7214.2004.00298.x.
Hochschild, A.R. (1983). *The Managed Heart: Commercialization of Human Feeling*. Berkeley: University of California Press.
Kelley, M.L., & Tseng, H.-M. (1992). Cultural differences in child rearing: A comparison of immigrant Chinese and Caucasian American mothers. *Journal of Cross-Cultural Psychology*, *23*(4), 444–55. https://doi.org/10.1177/0022022192234002.
Lee, K.F. (2018). *AI Superpowers: China, Silicon Valley, and the New World Order*. Boston: Houghton Mifflin Harcourt.
Lim, S.S. (2020). *Transcendent Parenting: Raising Children in the Digital Age*. Oxford University Press.
Lim, S.S. (2021, July 8). Shedding light on children's digital rights. *AsiaGlobal Online*. https://www.asiaglobalonline.hku.hk/shedding-light-childrens-digital-rights?fbclid=IwAR3LMGK7XxR32l2eKbZvH4TanxJRxL12xbWeSWNfg9lXNfe3y81X_HniIbc.
Lupton, D., Pedersen, S., & Thomas, G.M. (2016). Parenting and digital media: From the early web to contemporary digital society. *Sociology Compass*, *10*(8), 730–743. https://doi.org/10.1111/soc4.12398.
Marwick, A.E., & boyd, d. (2010). I tweet honestly, I tweet passionately: Twitter users, context collapse, and the imagined audience. *New Media & Society*, *13*(1), 114–33. https://doi.org/10.1177/1461444810365313.
Nelson, M.K. (2010). *Parenting Out of Control: Anxious Parents in Uncertain Times*. New York: New York University Press.
Ribak, R. (2009). Remote control, umbilical cord and beyond: The mobile phone as a transitional object. *British Journal of Developmental Psychology*, *27*(1), 183–96. https://doi.org/10.1348/026151008x388413.
Stright, A.D., & Yeo, K.L. (2014). Maternal parenting styles, school involvement, and children's school achievement and conduct in Singapore. *Journal of Educational Psychology*, *106*(1), 301–14. https://doi.org/10.1037/a0033821.
Turkle, S. (2011). *Alone Together: Why We Expect More from Technology and Less from Each Other*. New York: Basic Books.

Vitak, J., Blasiola, S., Patil, S., & Litt, E. (2015). Balancing audience and privacy tensions on social network sites. *International Journal of Communication*, *9*, 20. https://ijoc.org/index.php/ijoc/article/view/3208.
Wang, Y., & Lim, S.S. (2021). Nomadic life archiving across platforms: Hyperlinked storage and compartmentalized sharing. *New Media & Society*, *23*(4), 796–815. https://doi.org/10.1177/1461444820953507.
Wilson, J.A., & Yochim, E.C. (2017). *Mothering through Precarity: Women's Work and Digital Media*. Durham: Duke University Press.

# 2. Factors predicting parental mediation in adolescents' social media use

*Liang Chen and Xiaoming Liu*

## INTRODUCTION

Social media have become an essential part of life for most adolescents, who use them to access an array of information and to improve their social interactivity (Kowalski et al., 2008). At the same time, social media also expose adolescents to a range of online risks, including pornographic and violent content (Fikkers et al., 2017; Staksrud & Livingstone, 2009), unintended privacy disclosure (Chou et al., 2019), and cyberbullying (Ho et al., 2019a). Although parental mediation can reduce such online risks for adolescents (Chen & Shi, 2019), only 10 per cent to 50 per cent of parents employ mediation strategies (Helsper et al., 2013), and few among them use all types of mediation strategies (Barkin et al., 2006; Shin & Li, 2017). In response, examining the antecedents of various parental mediation strategies may be valuable in increasing the rate at which parents mediate their adolescent children's use of social media and, in turn, reduce their encounters with online risks. Therefore, in our study, we examined how attitudes, subjective norms, perceived behavioural control (PBC), and digital literacy affect three kinds of parental mediation – active mediation, restrictive mediation, and nonintrusive inspection – in the context of adolescents' social media use.

The chapter aims to provide a review of the extant research on parental mediation and empirically assess the role of parents' attitudes, subjective norms, PBC, and digital literacy in predicting parents' intention to adopt social media mediation strategies. Through the combination of parental mediation theory and the theory of planned behaviour (TPB), this chapter illustrates the psychological and motivational factors of parental mediation behaviours, which contributes to understanding the intrinsic mechanism of parents and encouraging parents to adopt these behaviours. This chapter examines the explanation power of the TPB which is applied to successfully predict a great variety of health behaviours and also introduces the construct of digital literacy into the TPB under the circumstance of predicting parental mediation strategies.

# LITERATURE REVIEW

## Parental Mediation

*Parental mediation* refers to parents' use of strategies to regulate their children's behaviour, including their use of social media (Shin & Kim, 2019; Warren, 2001). In our study, we focused on three types of parental mediation strategies – active mediation, restrictive mediation, and nonintrusive inspection – commonly used to manage adolescents' social media use. First, in active mediation, parents discuss social media with their adolescent children and guide them in using social media appropriately. Second, in restrictive mediation, parents set rules to limit the time that adolescents spend and the activities that they engage in on social media. Last, in nonintrusive inspection, parents check their adolescents' social media accounts directly and/or follow their children's accounts (e.g., as Facebook friends) to monitor their posts on social media. Although all three mediation strategies can reduce the risks posed by social media (Chang et al., 2016; Ho et al., 2017), parents tend to utilize simpler strategies, not all three (Shin & Li, 2017).

In studies on the antecedents of the use of various parental mediation strategies, researchers have predominantly focused on parents' and children's demographic characteristics (e.g., Lin & Atkin, 1989; Shin & Huh, 2011), household characteristics (e.g., Adigwe, 2021), family communication patterns and family environment (e.g., Fujioka & Austin, 2002; Schaan & Melzer, 2015), media use and media-related perception (e.g., Ho et al., 2019a; Rasmussen et al., 2018), and cultural backgrounds (e.g., Krcmar & Cingel, 2016). Other researchers have evaluated the individual predictive power of variables of using parental mediation strategies, including parental involvement (Martins et al., 2017), self-efficacy (Shin, 2018), and digital literacy (Ho et al., 2019a). Still others have examined determinants of parental mediation strategies with reference to theories such as the resource-based model (Warren, 2003), ecological theory (Warren, 2005), the model of the Big Five personality characteristics (Hwang & Jeong, 2015), protection motivation theory (Hwang et al., 2017), the third-person effect (Ho et al., 2019a), and the socioecological model of parenting (Dedkova & Smahel, 2020). Of all of those studies, the majority have investigated objective factors, including background and media-related perception, whereas few have examined psychological and motivational factors. However, those factors could be useful to consider in designing effective intervention strategies to promote appropriate parental mediation (Shin & Kim, 2019).

## Theory of Planned Behaviour

The TPB, an extension of the theory of reasoned action, theorizes that the intention to perform a behaviour is the most proximal predictor of its actual performance (Shin & Kim, 2019). The TPB proposes three major antecedents of behavioural intention – attitude towards the behaviour, subjective norms, and PBC (Ajzen, 1991) – all of which have been extensively applied to predict behaviour in research in the social sciences and health (Hamilton et al., 2016).

First, *attitude towards the behaviour* refers to the extent to which performing a certain behaviour is positively or negatively evaluated by the person who may engage in the behaviour. When a person has a positive attitude about a behaviour, they are more likely to perform that behaviour, largely because people prefer to maintain consistency between their beliefs and their behaviour (Shin & Kim, 2019). In short, parents with a positive attitude towards parental mediation are likely to engage in it as well.

Second, *subjective norms* refer to one's perception that most people who are important to them think that they should or should not perform a behaviour. According to the TPB, subjective norms relate not only to one's belief about what should be done but also to the perceived social pressure to conform to those norms (Krcmar & Cingel, 2016). Because people tend to fear being rejected by their social group, they are more likely to engage in parental mediation when they perceive supportive social norms (Shin & Kim, 2019). In the context of mediating their children's social media use, important others for parents could be their children, their partner, and/or their good friends.

Last, *perceived behavioural control*, or PBC, refers to one's appraisal of one's ability to perform a behaviour, due to either one's own skill level or the perceived ease of performing the behaviour. Regarding their children's social media use, parents are more likely to engage in parental mediation if they have the skills or perceive that mediation will not be challenging (Krcmar & Cingel, 2016).

Unlike other predictive theories of parental mediation, the TPB explains individuals' behaviour based on informational and motivational factors and can be regarded as a deliberative processing model (Krcmar & Cingel, 2016). As such, it has been applied to successfully predict health behaviours (Bohon et al., 2016; Vanderpool et al., 2013), mostly as a means to understand individuals' decisions about their health. Research has also shown that the TPB can be useful for predicting individuals' decisions affecting others' health, including parents' decisions about their children's health (Hamilton et al., 2016). The theory has additionally been used as a basis for creating theoretically based, empirically driven health intervention messages (Ajzen, 2015; Sundstrom et al., 2018; Vanderpool et al., 2013).

To date, studies have examined variables included in the TPB in the context of children's media use and parental mediation and shown that parents' attitudes, subjective and injunctive norms, and PBC regarding parental mediation were positively associated with their mediation behaviours (Hamilton et al., 2016; Krcmar & Cingel, 2016; Shin & Kim, 2019). By extension, we employed the TPB to predict parents' mediation behaviour in relation to their adolescents' social media use. To that end, our first three hypotheses were:

*H1: Attitude parental mediation is positively related to (a) active mediation, (b) restrictive mediation, and (c) nonintrusive inspection.*

*H2: Subjective norms are positively related to (a) active mediation, (b) restrictive mediation, and (c) nonintrusive inspection.*

*H3: PBC is positively related to (a) active mediation, (b) restrictive mediation, and (c) nonintrusive inspection.*

## Digital Literacy

*Digital literacy* refers to the multiplicity of literacies associated with using digital technology, including desktop computers, mobile devices (e.g., laptops, tablets, smartphones, and game consoles), Web 2.0 technologies, and online resources (e.g., information and multimedia resources, and communication and collaborative resources such as Skype, Blog, and WeChat), for educational, social, and/or entertainment purposes (Ng, 2012). Parental mediation in the context of social media use has been characterized as the enactment of parents' digital literacy and as parents' sharing of their digital literacy skills with their children (Rasmussen et al., 2016). However, parents with low digital literacy are relatively unaware of the negative effects that social media can have on their children, whom they tend to believe are at less risk of being affected by exposure to harmful media messages than other children (Ho et al., 2019a; Rasmussen et al., 2016). Beyond that, research has shown that parental digital literacy is significantly correlated with both active and restrictive mediation (Rasmussen et al., 2016).

Thus, we also hypothesized that:

*H4: Parental digital literacy is positively related to (a) active mediation, (b) restrictive mediation, and (c) nonintrusive inspection.*

Parents with high level of digital literacy are usually well aware of the positive and negative effects of media (Rasmussen et al., 2016) and have enough media skills to regulate their children's media use, which can further help them to mediate their adolescents' social media use more effectively. Moreover, adolescents may consider their parents' mediation as being reasonable if their parents have a high level of digital literacy, which affects the function of parents' subjective norms on their mediation. Therefore, we expected that digital literacy would affect how attitude, PBC, and subjective norms influence parents' mediation behaviours. Although researchers have investigated the primary effects of digital literacy on parental mediation (e.g., Dedkova & Smahel, 2020; Ho et al., 2019a), its moderating effects in the relationship between the TPB's variables on parental mediation strategies remain underexamined. Considering all of the above, we formulated the following research question:

*RQ1: How do digital literacy and the variables of the TPB (i.e., attitude parental mediation, subjective norms, and PBC) interact to affect (a) active mediation, (b) restrictive mediation, and (c) nonintrusive inspection?*

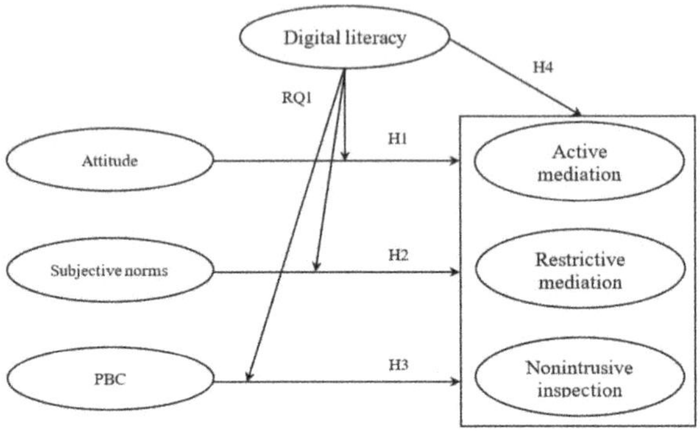


*Figure 2.1* *Conceptual model*

# METHOD

With that question in mind, we conducted an online survey of parents in China with children who were 13–17 years old. We recruited middle school students' parents to participate in this research by sending online questionnaires to students' parents via teachers from targeted middle schools from January to March 2020. Our respondents were mainly from the southern parts of China, including the Guangdong, Hunan, and Fujian provinces. A total of 587 parents ultimately participated in the study. It was approved by our university's institutional review board.

Our sample was 39.7 per cent men and 60.3 per cent women, with a mean age of 43.6 years (*SD*[1] = 7.5). The age range of participants' adolescent children was 13 to 17 years old (*SD* = 1.38, *M* = 15.4), 36.6 per cent of whom were young men. By level of education, 91.0 per cent of the parents had junior high school education (*n* = 378, 64.4 per cent) or senior high school education (*n* = 156, 26.6), while 9 per cent (*n* = 53) had university degrees or more. Most participants' annual household incomes were less than 100,000 RMB (approximately US$13,700 in 2023; *n* = 399, 68.0 per cent), although 21.5 per cent of them were 100,000–200,000 RMB and 10.5 per cent exceeded 200,000 RMB.

## MEASURES

Our questionnaire addressed the demographics of the parents (i.e., age, gender, level of education) and their adolescent children (i.e., age and gender), household income, and parents' social media use as control variables. Meanwhile, our independent variables were attitude, subjective norms, PBC, and digital literacy, which we measured in relation to parental mediation following the procedures and wordings recommended for assessments based on the TPB (Bane et al., 2006; Krcmar & Cingel, 2016). Last, the dependent variables were active mediation, restrictive mediation, and nonintrusive inspection, which we measured with reference to published methods (Ho et al., 2019b; Lwin et al., 2008). Both the independent and dependent variables were scored using a 7-point Likert scale.

*Attitude* was measured using a semantic differential scale in response to the statement 'Mediating my child's social media use would be …,' which respondents completed by selecting either 'harmful' or 'beneficial,' 'useless' or 'useful,' 'unnecessary' or 'essential,' 'inconvenient' or 'convenient,' and 'unhealthy' or 'healthy.' Each of the five pairs of semantic differentials was scored, and higher scores indicated a more positive attitude adopting parental mediation strategies.

*Subjective norms* were assessed with three items: 'My children/partner/good friend think that I should mediate my child's social media use as prescribed,' with response options ranging from 'Definitely do not' to 'Definitely do.' Higher scores indicated more perceived pressure from important others in the participants' lives to use parental mediation strategies as prescribed.

*PBC* was measured with three items regarding the parents' PBC to mediate their children's social media use: 'I am confident that I could mediate my child's social media use as prescribed if I really wanted to' ('Strongly disagree' to 'Strongly agree'), 'For me to mediate my child's social media use as prescribed is …' ('Difficult' to 'Easy'), and 'I feel that I have complete control over mediating my child's social media use as prescribed' ('Strongly disagree' to 'Strongly agree'). Those items were scored and averaged, and higher scores indicating greater PBC.

*Active mediation* was assessed using four items gauging the frequency ('Not at all' to 'Very frequently') at which parents would take certain actions: 'Tell your child about the information they can disclose on social media,' 'Remind your child not to give out personal information on social media,' 'Tell your child to stop any experience on social media if they feel uncomfortable or scared,' and 'Explain to your child about the dangers of social media.'

*Restrictive mediation* was measured using five items, in which respondents were asked about the frequency ('Not at all' to 'Very frequently') at which they took other certain actions: 'Restrict the type of social media platforms your child can visit,' 'Set rules regarding your child's access to social media, including Facebook, Twitter, YouTube, Instagram, WhatsApp, Line, etc.,' 'Limit the kind of activities your child can do on social media,' 'Restrict the amount of time your child can use social media,' and 'Limit your child to using social media only for school work.'

*Nonintrusive inspection* was assessed using three items, in which respondents were asked about the frequency at which they take still other actions: ‘Know your child’s social media account(s),’ ‘Check your child’s social media profile(s),’ and ‘Add your child as a friend on social media to check what he/she posts on social media.’ However, the third item was abandoned because its factor loading was too low (.47 < .70). The correlation coefficient of nonintrusive inspection was .73 ($p < .001$).

Last, *digital literacy* was measured using three items adapted from Ng (2012), in which respondents were asked about how much they agree with the statements ‘I know about a lot of different technologies,’ ‘I have good ICT skills,’ and ‘I am familiar with issues related to web-based activities (e.g., cyber safety, search issues, and plagiarism).’

## RESULTS

We performed confirmatory factor analysis with maximum likelihood parameter estimation in R version 4.0.3. The measurement model was evaluated by several fit indices ($X^2 = 636.14$, $df = 254$, $X^2/df = 2.50$, RMSEA = .05, GFI = .96, TLI = .96). All factor loadings appear in Table 2.1.

Also using R, we tested a moderating regression model. First, attitude ($\beta = .11$, $p < .05$), subjective norms ($\beta = .27$, $p < .001$), and digital literacy ($\beta = 0.48$, $p < .001$) were positively associated with active mediation, which supported H1a, H2a, and H4a. However, PBC was not significantly associated with active mediation. Thus, H3a was not supported. Second, attitude ($\beta = .13$, $p < .05$), subjective norms ($\beta = 0.53$, $p < .001$), PBC ($\beta = 0.20$, $p < .01$), and digital literacy ($\beta = .48$, $p < .001$) were all positively associated with restrictive mediation, which supported H1b, H2b, H3b, and H4b. Third, subjective norms ($\beta = .25$, $p < .001$), PBC ($\beta = .08$, $p < .05$), and digital literacy ($\beta = .20$, $p < .001$) were positively associated with nonintrusive inspection, whereas attitude parental mediation was not. Thus, H2c, H3c, and H4c were supported, but not H1c.

Regarding RQ1, the results showed that the interaction effect between attitude and digital literacy was not significant upon any parental mediation strategy. The interaction between subjective norms and digital literacy was positively associated with nonintrusive inspection ($\beta = .37$, $p < .05$), whereas the interaction between PBC and digital literacy was negatively associated with it ($\beta = -.40$, $p < .01$). Those results indicate that parents with high digital literacy are more likely to perform nonintrusive inspection as their subjective norms increase (see Table 2.1), whereas one with low digital literacy is more likely to perform nonintrusive inspection as their PBC increases (see Table 2.2).

*Table 2.1* *Descriptive statistics and factor loadings for the observed variables (N = 587)*

| Item | Factor loading | *M* | *SD* |
|---|---|---|---|
| ATT1 | .82*** | 3.77 | 1.21 |
| ATT2 | .87*** | 3.79 | 1.24 |
| ATT3 | .88*** | 3.76 | 1.26 |
| ATT4 | .76*** | 3.70 | 1.26 |
| ATT5 | .80*** | 3.72 | 1.23 |
| SN1 | .76*** | 3.91 | 1.84 |
| SN2 | .91*** | 4.43 | 1.80 |
| SN3 | .89*** | 4.15 | 1.79 |
| PBC1 | .88*** | 4.49 | 1.75 |
| PBC2 | .92*** | 4.38 | 1.78 |
| PBC3 | .81*** | 4.01 | 1.74 |
| DL1 | .78*** | 3.52 | 1.61 |
| DL2 | .82*** | 3.95 | 1.63 |
| DL3 | .76*** | 4.17 | 1.66 |
| AM1 | .74*** | 4.49 | 1.83 |
| AM2 | .81*** | 5.15 | 1.75 |
| AM3 | .82*** | 4.71 | 1.90 |
| AM4 | .86*** | 5.10 | 1.73 |
| RM1 | .70*** | 4.81 | 1.70 |
| RM2 | .88*** | 4.33 | 1.82 |
| RM3 | .94*** | 4.18 | 1.84 |
| RM4 | .88*** | 4.11 | 1.86 |
| RM5 | .70*** | 3.98 | 1.88 |
| NI1 | .92*** | 3.59 | 1.95 |
| NI2 | .79*** | 3.38 | 2.01 |

*Notes:*
ATT = attitude; SN = subjective norms; PBC = perceived behavioural control; DL = digital literacy; AM = active mediation; RM = restrictive mediation; NI = nonintrusive inspection.
*** $p < .001$

# DISCUSSION

Our research has made some important contributions to theory on parental mediation and the TPB. With reference to the TPB, we identified psychosocial and motivational factors that guide parental mediation behaviours in the context of their adolescent children's social media use. Beyond that, we introduced the construct of digital literacy into the TPB in order to understand parental mediation behaviours and, in turn, provide a more nuanced view of the TPB.

Our results show that parents' attitude towards parental mediation was a positive predictor of both their active and restrictive mediation, which corroborates published results (Hamilton et al., 2016; Krcmar & Cingel, 2016). Krcmar and Cingel (2016) also found that parents' attitude towards their children's social media control was positively correlated with active and restrictive mediation for Dutch parents. By

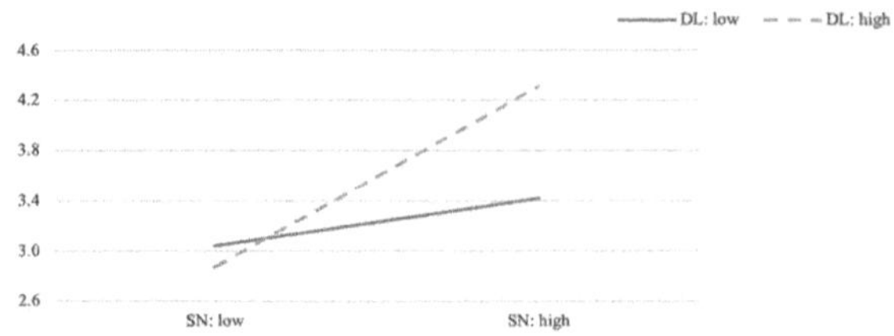


*Figure 2.2* *Interaction effect between subjective norms (SN) and digital literacy (DL) upon nonintrusive inspection*

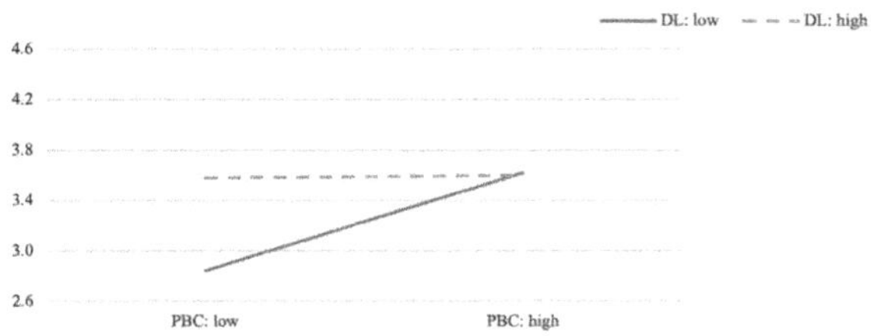


*Figure 2.3* *Interaction effect between perceived behavioural control (PBC) and digital literacy (DL) upon nonintrusive inspection*

*Table 2.2* *Results of the regression model (N = 587)*

| | Active mediation | | Restrictive mediation | | Nonintrusive inspection | |
|---|---|---|---|---|---|---|
| Items | β | *t* | β | *t* | β | *t* |
| Gender (P) | .99* | 2.06 | .72 | 1.25 | –.46 | –1.67 |
| Age (P) | .003 | .09 | –.008 | –.23 | –.02 | –.98 |
| Education (P) | –.23 | –.67 | –.18 | –.43 | –.24 | –1.19 |
| Gender (C) | .80 | 1.67 | .10 | .18 | –.27 | –.96 |
| Age (C) | –.33* | –1.97 | –.44* | –2.21 | –.14 | –1.42 |
| Income | .20 | .79 | –.17 | –.56 | –.08 | –.53 |
| Social media time | .06 | 1.03 | –.04 | –.62 | –.02 | –.52 |
| ATT | .11* | 2.50 | .13* | 2.58 | .003 | .11 |
| SN | .27*** | 4.64 | .53*** | 7.62 | .25*** | 7.42 |
| PBC | .10 | 1.60 | .20** | 2.74 | .08* | 2.37 |
| DL | .48*** | 8.24 | .48*** | 6.88 | .20*** | 6.01 |
| ATT × DL | –.17 | –.75 | .11 | .40 | .02 | .13 |
| SN × DL | –.21 | –.79 | .009 | .03 | .37* | 2.49 |
| PBC × DL | –.02 | –.08 | –.33 | –1.12 | –.40** | –2.75 |
| $R^2$ | .24*** | | .32*** | | .29*** | |

*Notes*:
*** $p < .001$; ** $p < .01$; * $p < .05$.
ATT = attitude; SN = subjective norms; PBC = perceived behavioural control; DL = digital literacy; P = parent; C = children

contrast, parents' attitude was not significantly associated with nonintrusive inspection, a strategy that can involve, for example, adding one's children as friends on social media platforms and observing what they post on social media. Such social behaviour is indeed commonplace among parents who have a high level of digital literacy. However, parents did not consider the specific behaviours of nonintrusive inspection as practical strategies for mediating their children's social media use. Thus, nonintrusive inspection appears to be a function of PBC and digital literacy more than of attitude.

Subjective norms positively predicted all types of parental mediation strategies, which aligns with past findings (Hamilton et al., 2016). Studies have shown that people consider others' judgement when deliberating whether to perform a behaviour, especially in collectivistic cultural environments that prize social harmony circumstances such as China's (Teo et al., 2020). Parents' decision-making for their children has also been shown to be influenced by perceived social pressure from important others (Hamilton et al., 2013), because parents are viewed as being responsible for their children's health behaviours (Andrews et al., 2010). Thus, the finding that subjective norms were a powerful predictor of parental mediation strategies was not surprising.

PBC emerged as a positive predictor of restrictive mediation and nonintrusive inspection but not active mediation. Ajzen (1991) found that the strength of PBC relates to the degree to which it reflects actual control. However, parents tend to over- or underestimate their control over the mediation of their children's behaviour (Hamilton et al., 2016). Active mediation, as a reciprocal interaction, requires interpersonal communication with children and is less determined by parents' PBC (Shin & Kim, 2019). Another reason for that trend is that active mediation is based on parents' greater knowledge of new technologies and the ability to discuss social media use with their children. Thus, digital literacy, which accurately reflects parents' media use ability, is a better predictor of active mediation than PBC.

Beyond that, the findings of our study highlight the significance of digital literacy. Parents with a high level of digital literacy are more likely to engage in parental mediation, which aligns with the results of other studies (Dedkova & Smahel, 2020; Rasmussen et al., 2016). At the same time, the interactions between the TPB's variables and digital literacy did not significantly affect active mediation or restrictive mediation. Unlike nonintrusive inspection, active and restrictive mediation were first adopted in the TV era and later adapted in the Internet era (Staksrud & Livingstone, 2009; Valkenburg et al., 1999). Parents are thus familiar with both strategies and have confidence in executing them. Thus, active mediation and restrictive mediation are primarily influenced by psychological and emotional factors (i.e., TPB variables), and digital literacy cannot be expected to moderate their influence. Nonintrusive inspection, however, as a new type of parental mediation strategy focused on social media, requires a higher level of social media skills. Many parents are unfamiliar with social media and/or do not have enough skills to use social media to monitor their children (Holmes, 2018). Digital literacy can thus affect the influence of psychological factors on nonintrusive inspection. In our study, the higher the parents' digital literacy, the greater the association between subjective norms and nonintrusive inspection, meaning that parents with a high level of digital literacy are more likely to engage in nonintrusive inspection when they perceive high subjective norms. A possible reason is that nonintrusive inspection requires more digital literacy than other parental mediation strategies do; thus, parents with greater digital literacy are more confident in engaging in nonintrusive inspection. In that case, parents who perceive more supportive social norms are more likely to confirm those norms if they have a high level of digital literacy. However, digital literacy decreased the relationship between PBC and nonintrusive inspection, which suggests that PBC's predictive power in relation to nonintrusive inspection lessens when parents have higher digital literacy. A plausible explanation is that parents with higher digital literacy tend to perceive that they have greater control over parental mediation and thus ignore their ability to communicate with their children. PBC thus not only relates to parents' skills with media use but is also associated with their parental communication skills.

Parents play a crucial role in the process of their children's socialization (Maccoby, 1992) and are conducive to mediating negative media effects, especially when adolescents have not yet developed appropriate approaches to use social media and evaluate media content. The key contribution of this chapter is to guide any future efforts to promote parents' participation in behaviours to manage adolescents' social media use by identifying modifiable constructs to target in behavioural interventions. Future research could further examine how to change the determinants of parents' behaviours, including attitude, subjective norms, and PBC (Hamilton et al., 2020). In addition, our study found relatively small-to-medium effect sizes on parental mediation behaviours, which is consistent with the effect sizes observed in extant parental intervention research (e.g., Krcmar & Cingel, 2016). The explanatory power of TPB may be associated with the behaviour type, as the meta-analysis of Hamilton and colleagues (2020) revealed that TPB variables may get a more powerful explanation of physical activity that requires relatively greater social involvement than other behaviour types. Future scholars should further verify parental mediation strategies to manage adolescents' other health behaviours and explore the predictive power of TPB.

## IMPLICATIONS, LIMITATIONS, AND FUTURE RESEARCH

Our study contributes to literature on parental mediation and the TPB in several ways. First, it has advanced prior research on parental mediation by adopting the TPB as a theoretical framework to identify psychosocial and motivational factors associated with parental mediation – namely, active mediation, restrictive mediation, and nonintrusive inspection – moving beyond research that has evaluated only background and/or media-related factors. Second, we examined the effect of digital literacy on parental mediation, along with the interaction effects between digital literacy and the TPB's variables, which afforded useful insights into the TPB. Last, our results provide practical guidance for designing theoretically based and empirically driven health intervention messages.

Even so, several limitations of our study should be addressed in future research. First, we examined only the TPB's variables in relation to parental mediation, not specific mediation strategies. In the future, researchers could explore how those specific variables influence the corresponding behaviours. Second, though driven by theory, our study employed convenience sampling, and as a consequence the results are difficult to generalize to the general population. Third and last, our cross-sectional design could not establish causality. Future research should adopt longitudinal designs in order to validate the assumption of causality inherent in the TPB.

Furthermore, this chapter suggests several possibilities for future research on parental mediation. The explained variance of subjective norms in mediation behaviours is higher than attitude and PBC among Chinese adolescents, which may be attributed to Chinese collective culture. Since various theoretical approaches work better in terms of explaining variance based on cultural differences, future work could explore the explanatory power of TPB variables in other countries. Besides, although a number of scholars have explored the predictive power of attitudes, subjective norms, and PBC, the majority of these studies utilized behavioural intentions as substitutes for actual behaviours. Future scholars should endeavour to carry out theory-based experiments to examine the interventional effects of TPB-based information in parental social media mediation behaviours for adolescents. In addition, future research could also explore other explanatory variables and theoretical mechanisms of parental mediation strategies, such as self-efficacy, the protection motivation theory, and the third-person effect, and try to propose a scientific and complete theoretical framework to understand parental mediation behaviours.

Indeed, most previous studies on parental mediation practices and effectiveness have been conducted in countries with higher rates of digital connectivity and use of digital media by children (Shin & Lwin, 2022), especially in the US and Europe. However, the motivation and effectiveness of parents' behaviours may differ between these countries because of the differences in national cultures. The theoretical research and practical adoption of parental mediation strategies in developing countries in various cultural contexts are still largely unexplored. Future research should therefore endeavour to include more countries and investigate the approaches of parental mediation, and their behavioural motivation, practical effects, and functional mechanisms.

## NOTE

1. *SD* stands for 'standard deviation', *M* stands for 'Mean', and *n* is the number of participants/cases included in the analysis.

## REFERENCES


Adigwe, I. (2021). Identifying the moderating and mediating variables in parental mediation practices in Nigerian families in the digital age. *Social Media+ Society*, *7*(3), 20563051211033817.

Ajzen, I. (1991). The theory of planned behaviour. *Organizational Behaviour and Human Decision Processes*, *50*(2), 179–211.

Ajzen, I. (2015). The theory of planned behaviour is alive and well, and not ready to retire: A commentary on Sniehotta, Presseau, and Araújo-Soares. *Health Psychology Review*, *9*(2), 131–37.

Andrews, K.R., Silk, K.S., & Eneli, I.U. (2010). Parents as health promoters: A theory of planned behaviour perspective on the prevention of childhood obesity. *Journal of Health Communication*, *15*(1), 95–107.

Bane, C., Hughe, C.M., & McElnay, J.C. (2006). Determinants of medication adherence in hypertensive patients: An application of self-efficacy and the theory of planned behaviour. *International Journal of Pharmacy Practice*, *14*(3), 197–204.

Barkin, S., Ip, E., Richardson, I., Klinepeter, S., Finch, S., & Krcmar, M. (2006). Parental media mediation styles for children aged 2 to 11 years. *Archives of Pediatrics & Adolescent Medicine*, *160*(4), 395–401.

Bohon, L.M., Cotter, K.A., Kravitz, R.L., Cello, P.C., Jr, & Fernandez y Garcia, E. (2016). The theory of planned behaviour as it predicts potential intention to seek mental health services for depression among college students. *Journal of American College Health*, *64*(8), 593–603.

Chang, F.C., Miao, N.F., Chiu, C.H., Chen, P.H., Lee, C.M., Chiang, J.T., & Chuang, H.Y. (2016). Urban–rural differences in parental Internet mediation and adolescents' Internet risks in Taiwan. *Health, Risk & Society*, *18*(3–4), 188–204.

Chen, L., & Shi, J. (2019). Reducing harm from media: A meta-analysis of parental mediation. *Journalism & Mass Communication Quarterly*, *96*(1), 173–93.

Chou, H.L., Liu, Y.L., & Chou, C. (2019). Privacy behaviour profiles of underage Facebook users. *Computers & Education*, *128*, 473–85.

Dedkova, L., & Smahel, D. (2020). Online parental mediation: Associations of family members' characteristics to individual engagement in active mediation and monitoring. *Journal of Family Issues*, *41*(8), 1112–36.

Fikkers, K.M., Piotrowski, J.T., & Valkenburg, P.M. (2017). A matter of style? Exploring the effects of parental mediation styles on early adolescents' media violence exposure and aggression. *Computers in Human Behaviour*, *70*, 407–15.

Fujioka, Y., & Austin, E.W. (2002). The relationship of family communication patterns to parental mediation styles. *Communication Research*, *29*(6), 642–65.

Hamilton, K., Spinks, T., White, K.M., Kavanagh, D.J., & Walsh, A.M. (2016). A psychosocial analysis of parents' decisions for limiting their young child's screen time: An examination of attitudes, social norms and roles, and control perceptions. *British Journal of Health Psychology*, *21*(2), 285–301.

Hamilton, K., Thomson, C.E., & White, K.M. (2013). Promoting active lifestyles in young children: Investigating mothers' decisions about their child's physical activity and screen time behaviours. *Maternal and Child Health Journal*, *17*(5), 968–76.

Hamilton, K., Van Dongen, A., & Hagger, M.S. (2020). An extended theory of planned behaviour for parent-for-child health behaviours: A meta-analysis. *Health Psychology*, *39*(10), 863.

Helsper, E.J., Kalmus, V., Hasebrink, U., Sagvari, B., & De Haan, J. (2013). *Country Classification: Opportunities, Risks, Harm and Parental Mediation*. EU Kids Online, The London School of Economics and Political Science.

Ho, S., Lwin, M.O., Chen, L., & Chen, M. (2019b). Development and validation of a parental social media mediation scale across child and parent samples. *Internet Research*, *30*(2), 677–94.

Ho, S.S., Chen, L., & Ng, A.P. (2017). Comparing cyberbullying perpetration on social media between primary and secondary school students. *Computers & Education*, *109*, 74–84.

Ho, S.S., Lwin, M.O., Yee, A.Z., Sng, J.R., & Chen, L. (2019a). Parents' responses to cyberbullying effects: How third-person perception influences support for legislation and parental mediation strategies. *Computers in Human Behaviour*, *92*, 373–80.

Holmes, A.C. (2018). Perception, literacy and confidence in monitoring of Snapchat among parents of adolescents and the creation of a Snapchat educational workshop. *Honors Theses*, *582*.

Hwang, Y., Choi, I., Yum, J.Y., & Jeong, S.H. (2017). Parental mediation regarding children's smartphone use: Role of protection motivation and parenting style. *Cyberpsychology, Behaviour, and Social Networking*, *20*(6), 362–68.

Hwang, Y., & Jeong, S.H. (2015). Predictors of parental mediation regarding children's smartphone use. *Cyberpsychology, Behaviour, and Social Networking*, *18*(12), 737–43.

Kowalski, R.M., Limber, S.P., & Agatston, P.W. (2008). *Cyberbullying: Bullying in the Digital Age*. Blackwell.

Krcmar, M., & Cingel, D.P. (2016). Examining two theoretical models predicting American and Dutch parents' mediation of adolescent social media use. *Journal of Family Communication*, *16*(3), 247–62.

Lin, C.A., & Atkin, D.J. (1989). Parental mediation and rulemaking for adolescent use of television and VCRs. *Journal of Broadcasting & Electronic Media*, *33*(1), 53–67.

Lwin, M.O., Stanaland, A.J., & Miyazaki, A.D. (2008). Protecting children's privacy online: How parental mediation strategies affect website safeguard effectiveness. *Journal of Retailing*, *84*(2), 205–17.

Maccoby, E.E. (1992). The role of parents in the socialization of children: An historical overview. *Developmental Psychology*, *28*, 1006–17.

Martins, N., Matthews, N.L., & Ratan, R.A. (2017). Playing by the rules: Parental mediation of video game play. *Journal of Family Issues*, *38*(9), 1215–38.

Ng, W. (2012). Can we teach digital natives digital literacy? *Computers & Education*, *59*(3), 1065–78.

Rasmussen, E.C., White, S.R., King, A.J., Holiday, S., & Densley, R.L. (2016). Predicting parental mediation behaviours: The direct and indirect influence of parents' critical thinking about media and attitudes about parent-child interactions. *Journal of Media Literacy Education*, *8*(2), 1–21.

Rasmussen, E.E., Coyne, S.M., Martins, N., & Densley, R.L. (2018). Parental mediation of US youths' exposure to televised relational aggression. *Journal of Children and Media*, *12*(2), 192–210.

Schaan, V.K., & Melzer, A. (2015). Parental mediation of children's television and video game use in Germany: Active and embedded in family processes. *Journal of Children and Media*, *9*(1), 58–76.

Shin, W. (2018). Empowered parents: The role of self-efficacy in parental mediation of children's smartphone use in the United States. *Journal of Children and Media*, *12*(4), 465–77.

Shin, W., & Huh, J. (2011). Parental mediation of teenagers' video game playing: Antecedents and consequences. *New Media & Society*, *13*(6), 945–62.

Shin, W., & Kim, H.K. (2019). What motivates parents to mediate children's use of smartphones? An application of the theory of planned behaviour. *Journal of Broadcasting & Electronic Media*, *63*(1), 144–59.

Shin, W., & Li, B. (2017). Parental mediation of children's digital technology use in Singapore. *Journal of Children and Media*, *11*(1), 1–19.

Shin, W., & Lwin, M.O. (2022). Parental mediation of children's digital media use in high digital penetration countries: Perspectives from Singapore and Australia. *Asian Journal of Communication*, *32*(4), 309–26.

Staksrud, E., & Livingstone, S. (2009). Children and online risk: Powerless victims or resourceful participants? *Information, Communication & Society*, *12*(3), 364–87.

Sundstrom, B., Ferrara, M., DeMaria, A.L., Gabel, C., Booth, K., & Cabot, J. (2018). It's your place: Development and evaluation of an evidence-based bystander intervention campaign. *Health Communication*, *33*(9), 1141–50.

Teo, T., Shi, W., Hoi, C.K.W., & Huang, F. (2020). Predicting the intention to use cyber-counseling among Chinese adolescents: An extended theory of planned behaviour. *Cyberpsychology, Behaviour, and Social Networking*, *23*(9), 627–34.

Valkenburg, P.M., Krcmar, M., Peeters, A.L., & Marseille, N.M. (1999). Developing a scale to assess three styles of television mediation: 'Instructive Mediation,' 'Restrictive Mediation,' and 'Social Coviewing.' *Journal of Broadcasting & Electronic Media*, *43*(1), 52–66.

Vanderpool, R.C., Cohen, E.L., Crosby, R.A., Jones, M.G., Bates, W., Casey, B.R., & Collins, T. (2013). '1-2-3 Pap' intervention improves HPV vaccine series completion among Appalachian women. *Journal of Communication*, *63*(1), 95–115.

Warren, R. (2001). In words and deeds: Parental involvement and mediation of children's television viewing. *Journal of Family Communication*, *1*(4), 211–31.

Warren, R. (2003). Parental mediation of preschool children's television viewing. *Journal of Broadcasting & Electronic Media*, *47*(3), 394–417.

Warren, R. (2005). Parental mediation of children's television viewing in low-income families. *Journal of Communication*, *55*(4), 847–63.

# 3. Visible, controlled, and persistent: an affordances approach to understanding social media for transnational parenting among migrant mothers

*Barui K. Waruwu*

## INTRODUCTION

Using an affordances approach, this chapter examines the sociotechnical consequences of social media on the meaning and practices of transnational parenting among Indonesian migrant mothers in Hong Kong. Although much research has examined digital connectivity among migrant families (Abel et al., 2021; Wang & Lim, 2020; Waruwu, 2022), our understanding of parental communicative behaviors in an integrated social media ecosystem is lacking. Social media has steadily become a taken-for-granted part of sociality, altering most aspects of our life, from how we work and express ourselves to how we seek romantic partners and stay in touch with loved ones. It is also increasingly convergent, forming an environment of multiple modes of interaction, known as poly-social-media (Tandoc et al., 2019; based on polymedia by Madianou & Miller, 2012). Hong Kong, the ethnographic site of this study, is one of the world's most technologically saturated societies, where more than 88 per cent of the population is active on social media (Kemp, 2022). Interestingly, the same report shows that these users are active on an average of 7.1 platforms, attesting to the current trend of 'swinging' across platforms to manage social ties (Tandoc et al., 2019).

Although social media boasts an extensive range of uses, most studies agree on its potency in supporting existing close relationships rather than building new ones (Bucher & Helmond, 2018). One such relationship is the family connection among those experiencing a prolonged separation during migration – transnational families. Transnational families are driven to 'display' relationships given the fact that their caring arrangements have breached the traditional, household-bound family norms (Finch, 2007; Share et al., 2018; Waruwu, 2022). According to Finch (2007), displaying family entails the performance of intimacy for 'relevant audiences,' who would then grant their acknowledgment that the relationship being showcased is effective (p. 67). The practice of displaying family in a mediated environment enables migrant families to maintain a sense of validation and connectedness, which in term enhances their resilience in the face of separation and crises (Oktavianus & Lin, 2021). Therefore, understanding how migrant mothers perform family practices in a social media ecosystem is of timely significance.

In this chapter, I analyze social media use for family communication among Indonesian mothers in Hong Kong as part of the emergent repertoire of mediated transnational mothering (Madianou & Miller, 2011; Wang & Lim, 2020; Waruwu, 2022). To this end, I adopted the affordances approach, which recognizes online social practices as being mutually shaped by the technological architecture of a given platform and the user's sociocultural demands (Costa, 2018; Evans et al., 2017). As such, the analysis bypasses the questions of whether social media is inherently good or bad for migrant mothers and how a specific platform facilitates or hinders intimacy. Instead, it looks at how migrant mothers reflexively interpret various actionable potentials of social media – its affordances – to maintain family intimacy during migration. Based on ethnographic evidence, supplemented by narrative interviews with 22 Indonesian mothers in Hong Kong,[1] this chapter reveals three affordances that shape mothering practices on social media: visibility, controlled connectivity, and persistence. It also advances our understanding of social media in close-knit groups by illustrating how affordances give rise to emergent patterns of distant caregiving that destabilize the normative, taken-for-granted idea of family.

## LITERATURE REVIEW

### Feminized Migration and Transnational Mothering: the Indonesian Context

Social media effects are best studied in well-specified sociocultural contexts (Costa, 2018); therefore, an overview of female migration and dominant family values in Indonesian society is necessary to foreground the analysis here. Since the early 1990s, the demand for female migrant workers from the Global South has steadily outstripped that for their male counterparts (Silvey, 2006). These women assist with daily chores such as cleaning, cooking, babysitting, and caring for the elderly. Hong Kong is one of the countries with an insatiable demand for migrant geriatric caregivers, given its rapidly aging society. Current statistics estimate more than 380,000 domestic workers are currently working in Hong Kong, almost equally split between Filipino and Indonesian. The Hong Kong government projects the number to double by 2047 to keep up with the rapidly aging population (ENRICH, 2019). As of the time of writing, the basic monthly salary for a migrant helper in Hong Kong is HKD4,645 (USD596). There is clear evidence of migrant domestic workers' impacts on the economies of Hong Kong and Indonesia (Constable, 2014; Silvey, 2006). However, the understanding of the impacts of migration on their family well-being and sustainability is still growing.

Scholars have begun investigating the impacts of such a feminized migration on family well-being, particularly concerning the performance of maternal duties from afar. Early research tends to characterize transnational mothering as a social cost of migration (Parreñas, 2001), whereas more current studies approach it as a multi-faceted phenomenon with careful attention to the migrants' personal, moral, and emotional motives (Madianou & Miller, 2011; Nguyen et al., 2017). The entrenched feminine values of mothering prevent migrant women from relinquishing maternal obligations during migration, even as they take on a traditionally masculine role as family breadwinners. Indonesian society draws heavily on the Islamic value system in defining women's place in the family. Filial piety is of utmost importance, particularly towards one's mother. Indeed, a local adage says, '*surga berada dibawah telapak kaki ibu*,' which means heaven is beneath a mother's feet, attesting to the mother's place as the light of the house (Faizin, 2018). The golden standard of a Muslim family in Indonesia is composed of three qualities: *sakidah* (contentment), *marwadah* (passion), and *warohmah* (blessing) (Pongoliu, 2017). It is a prevalent belief that a family can achieve these qualities only if the husband and wife commit to their roles as prescribed in Hadith.[2] The desire to adhere to these expectations is an essential driving force behind Indonesian migrant mothers' effort to sustain family ties during migration, as seen in how they use smartphones to socialize children into religious values (Waruwu, 2022).

## Transnational Family and Social Media

For migrant families, long-distance communication is the default means of caregiving. As such, communication technology is not merely a medium of information exchange; it embodies symbolic practices that anchor the meaning and experiences of family relationships (Madianou, 2014). We see this in the stories of a Filipino mother in the UK who leaves her Skype on all day for her daughter in Manila (Kim, 2017), a Jamaican teenage girl who regularly calls her mother abroad for dating advice (Horst, 2006), a wife in Senegal who has to stay home because her husband randomly calls from Ohio to check her whereabouts (Hannaford, 2015), and other examples of how diverse patterns of transnational family interaction reflect the equally diverse patterns of family life (Abel et al., 2021). These observations exemplify the concept of 'doing' family practices, a notion that family is no longer reflected by household configuration but instead by what the members do for/with each other (Morgan, 2011).

Previous research has demonstrated the potential of social media to facilitate family practices among those who live a great distance from each other, allowing them to maintain a sense of belonging, acceptance, and purpose in the face of separation (Abel et al., 2021). Filipino migrants in Australia, for instance, have been observed to use social media to organize and participate in online festivities, a ritual that contributes to their familial bond (Cabalquinto, 2018). In the face of crisis, Indonesian migrant helpers in Hong Kong use social media to share stories with their families as part of their coping strategies, enabling them to articulate their needs and build resilience (Oktavianus & Lin, 2021). On Facebook, individuals do not even need to interact directly to obtain a sense of connectedness, thanks to the multiple connection cues that trigger a sense of ambient co-presence (Bayer et al., 2016). This peripheral awareness of other people's availability and their reciprocal desire to connect offers emotional reassurance for transnationally split families (Madianou, 2016).

Despite these benefits, social media may undermine family cohesion by creating privacy-related conflicts, ambivalence, and coerced intimacy. An ethnography of Asian nannies in France found that migrant mothers' intensive use of social media for transnational communication may increase anxieties and uncertainties about separation (Kim, 2017). This sentiment was also observed among Chinese *peidu mama* in Singapore. These 'study mothers,' who moved to Singapore to accompany their school-going children, confront a growing tension resulting from juggling two sets of expectations, from their home and their current residence, accentuating gender hierarchies in transnational households (Wang & Lim, 2020). Privacy is another critical issue, forcing members to adopt various emotionally effortful strategies to control information and manage expectations during family interactions (Zhao, 2019).

As seen here, the literature on social media for family communication has been dominated by the 'good versus evil' narratives. This is partly due to the tendency to emphasize whether the technical architecture of media strengthens or threatens social order without accounting for the users' agency in manipulating media for their purposes (Hutchby, 2001). This current chapter contributes to the growing research that approaches social media practices as fluid and reflective interactions between technological features and users' social demands. To this end, it adopts an affordances approach.

## Affordances Approach

The term 'affordance' was coined by Gibson (1979) to describe the potentialities of actions in the environment that can be acted upon once perceived by animals. According to Gibson, an object has stable physical properties (e.g., the river is wet, with measurable width and depth), but its affordances are multiple and relative to the animal (e.g., it affords drinking to tigers, wallowing to buffaloes). The concept was introduced into communication media research by Hutchby (2001), who defined media affordances as 'functional and relational aspects, which frame, while not determining, the possibilities for agentic action in relation to an object' (p. 444). Hutchby's chief contribution to the debate was his argument that affordances, while multiple and negotiable, are finite (e.g., one would be hard-pressed to perceive portability in a landline). Therefore, he proposed that it is vital to analyze how media technologies reshape social actions by enabling *and* constraining actions. Immediately, the concept appealed to media researchers because it counterbalances the deterministic views – technological versus constructivist – by recognizing that communication media have stable technical features, but they are acted upon depending on the users' motivation and intention (Nagy & Neff, 2015). As a result, neither media architecture nor users' interpretation can holistically explain media use and consequences. Instead, it is when the two are imbricated – 'interlocked in particular sequence' – that changes in social routines come about (Leonardi, 2011, p. 149).

Another development of affordance is in terms of the reference point that users utilize in defining them. Gibson (1979) claimed that animals perceive the affordances of an object based on its visible features. In a technology context, Norman (1999) proposed that users perceive affordances based on the designers' vision and intended use of the object. This idea proved problematic in light of the observations that users often form new norms and uses around a media technology based on their needs, creating discrepancies between the designer's intention and the actual use (Costa, 2018). Under this circumstance, the affordances arise from the user's direct interaction with the object and social environment (Leonardi, 2011). More recently, Madianou argued that in addition to these points of reference, users also define affordances vertically through comparison among affordances in equally accessible platforms. In this case, the affordance of a text message (e.g., flexible synchronicity) fulfills the user's particular communication needs because it is not a voice call, which in turn is not a video call.

This last point is particularly relevant in today's media-saturated environment, where multiple communication platforms with varying affordances are accessible within one device, such as smartphones. Madianou and Miller (2012) developed the concept of polymedia to characterize this integrated environment of affordances and capture the social, moral, and emotional motives behind media adoption (or avoidance). Tandoc et al. (2019) examined an offshoot of this ecosystem which they called poly-social-media. Their study identified an emergent practice called platform swinging – 'the act of using more than one social media platform and routinely rotating among these platforms, as opposed to switching from one platform and abandoning another' (p. 21). Platform swinging enabled users to sustain gratification by using multiple social media so that other platforms compensate for the limitations of one platform. Interestingly, users also swing around numerous accounts within a platform. A fascinating example is from Costa's (2018) ethnography in southeastern Tukey, where she observed the natives owning up to 12 active Facebook accounts to segregate their social groups.

The ubiquity of social media in everyday life provides a context in which we can understand how specific affordances interact with the users' intentions, designers' visions, and other affordances. Bucher and Helmond (2018) reviewed existing conceptualizations of social media affordances, including perceived, social, and communicative affordances. These varied conceptualizations led to an extensive list of affordances, including visibility, editability, persistence, searchability, controlled connectivity, and many others (boyd, 2011; Treem & Leonardi, 2013; Vanden Abeele et al., 2017). One of the unifying threads across these studies is the idea that objective functionalities of social media interact with users' sociocultural environment. These interactions should be examined in the context of the everyday life of social media users, thus grounding our understanding in what Costa (2018) theorized as affordances-in-practice.

This chapter seeks to contribute to the ongoing debate by investigating how social media implicates family relationships and parenting practices among migrant domestic workers. As such, it illuminates the interplay of social media, parenting demands, and transnational mobility. Based on the literature, the analysis here was guided by these questions: What are the affordances that migrant mothers perceive out of social media for family communication? And how do these affordances influence the meaning and everyday practices of transnational mothering?

## METHOD: ETHNOGRAPHIC APPROACH TO FAMILY INTERACTION ON SOCIAL MEDIA

This study was part of a more extensive multi-sited ethnography to understand the consequences of smartphone and social media technologies on transnational family practices, especially regarding family rituals, resilience, and sustainability during the mother's migration. Ethnography has received renewed appreciation in media research, given the imperative to recognize the subjective experiences of navigating a complex media ecology (Madianou & Miller, 2012). Lorenzana (2016) has demonstrated the value of an ethnographic approach to social media interaction, showing how the desire to obtain recognition shapes Facebook interaction among Filipino middle-class migrants in New Delhi, India. Miller and Venkatraman (2018) adopted a similar method, resulting in rich accounts of how gender and class have differential impacts on relationship management within polymedia in South England and South India. Indeed, based on her extensive fieldwork with Filipino mothers in the UK, Madianou (2019) asserted that ethnography is the most appropriate way to examine polymedia phenomena as it allows the researcher to 'connect the consequences of mediated communication at an interpersonal (micro-)level to a macro-level account of social change' (p. 578).

I conducted the main phase of the fieldwork from July 2019 to June 2021 in conjunction with my volunteering work at various migrant organizations in Hong Kong. Aligned with the principle of ethnographic reciprocity (Fetterman, 1998), I volunteered as an English teacher for the Indonesian Migrant Workers Union (IMWU) and an ad hoc translator. In return, they welcomed me into their community, where we spent many a Sunday celebrating birthdays, religious festivities, cultural events, and casual get-togethers. I am still in touch on Facebook with most respondents I worked with, including those who have returned to Indonesia.

My ethnographic work with the migrant community forms the contextualizing background for the analysis presented here. However, specifically for this study, I also conducted 22 narrative interviews with Indonesian mothers in Hong Kong, half of whom ($n = 11$) had been interviewed by me previously for different projects. This repeated interaction strengthened the rapport, which is essential in studying personal and emotive topics such as family separation and maternal guilt. To increase the variability of participants, I purposefully recruited the remaining 11 mothers based on their non-membership in any social organization. Organization membership was selected as a recruitment criterion following my observation that those active in social organizations tend to have higher exposure to the international community, thus often presenting more liberal views towards family values.

In designing the interview guide and protocol, I drew from the literature on narrative inquiry tradition, which reveals the complexity of articulating an understanding of family reality (Slembrouk, 2015). First, I acknowledged the underlying assumption that I, as the researcher, must take on a role of a co-narrator in the interaction rather than a survey taker. This prompted me to reflect on my values and position in the power relations vis-à-vis the respondents that might have a bearing on the storied accounts emerging from the encounter. Second, I paid attention to the respondents' family stories in addition to the frames of reference with which they form their understanding of maternal identity, social media affordances, and even their political status as temporary workers in Hong Kong. To further contextualize the interaction with my respondents, I adopted the photo-elicitation method, whereby I scrolled through their Facebook page and selected a post related to family life (Miller, 2015). I then asked them to describe the significance of a particular post and invited them to explain the broader patterns of their social media habits. This technique helped ground our interaction and effectively evoked storied accounts of family interactions that would otherwise be obscure.

The data were analyzed using a mix of inductive techniques of constant comparison (Charmaz, 2014) and deductive techniques using several sensitizing themes derived from the literature, especially the social media affordances (Bucher & Helmond, 2018). Given that affordances are finite (Hutchby, 2001), it makes sense to look at existing literature for sensitizing concepts (Birks & Mills, 2015). However, practices associated with specific affordance are contextually bound. This is to say that what mothers do with different affordances depends on their family's social, economic, and cultural circumstances, migration, and identity. Therefore, I also adopted an inductive, thematic analysis to flesh out the behavioral manifestation of affordances.

## FINDINGS AND DISCUSSION

### Platform Swinging and its Limitation

On average, the mothers in this study are active on three social media platforms: Facebook, WhatsApp, and Facebook Messenger. Other platforms mentioned included Telegram, LINE, and WeChat. The average number is significantly lower compared to the general Hong Kong population (7.1 platforms) (Kemp, 2022). The reason for this is twofold. First, working as live-in helpers, the respondents have limited time and privacy to use social media. Judy (24), a mother of one, sleeps on a stow-away futon in a tiny room that doubles as storage. Every night, before she can rest, she must first remove a disused mini refrigerator from the room and unfurl her mattress on the floor. In the morning, she puts the fridge back in the room. This means that Judy does not have private space to use her phone at home other than the time right before bed. The second reason was the lack of interest in increasing digital literacy. The respondents use several social media platforms, but these are often the only ones they know how to use. Judy herself uses three platforms. She is not familiar with Instagram, and she said learning it is not worth the added advantage of using it because her daughter is not on Instagram. Another respondent, Mulyanti (39), said she used two platforms. Interestingly, shortly before wrapping up the interview, she asked me to teach her to use the mobile browser to read the news. When I clicked the application, a welcome message popped up, suggesting she had never used the web browser on her phone. Judy's and Mulyanti's stories show the differential needs and resources to engage in a platform swinging.

The respondents' narratives revealed three affordances that they perceived in social media: visibility, controlled connectivity, and persistence. These affordances shape the way they communicate with their family, especially children. For example, Facebook affords more visibility but is harder to control and more persistent. This makes it a perfect avenue to display family achievements and joyful moments, but inappropriate for disciplining children and risky for airing employer-related grievances.

## Visibility

The first social media affordance that migrant mothers in this study identified was visibility. In narrating the rationales behind their decision to use social media, the mothers referred to the broad reach of social media posts and the joy of having a lot of likes and comments. Social media make visible the mothers' continued involvement in their family's everyday life. Notably, the visibility of mother–children interaction on social media helps ward off the accusation of maternal neglect.

The visibility of social media also supercharges expressive intimacy because the mothers know that others are watching their online interaction. As a result, the mothers become strategic in how they display their family to others. They populate their Facebook walls with photos of their families, accompanied by affectionate captions that highlight their pride in watching their children grow and their hopes and dreams for them. An illustrative case of conspicuous, expressive intimacy can be found in Dianna's (39) Facebook posts, showing her son's birthday party with a birthday cake made of a variety of snacks, stacked in tiers and tied together with a bow.

I used the photo as a visual cue during my interview with Dianna. While looking at it, she explained the significance of posting family photos on social media:

| | |
|---|---|
| Dianna: | I want to show my son that I also celebrate his birthday. |
| Interviewer: | Did you call him directly? |
| Dianna: | Of course. I video-chatted with him. I was on the video chat when they sang "Happy Birthday" to him … Posting on Facebook also reminds my friends and relatives about his birthday so they can wish him a happy birthday … |
| Interviewer: | I don't think I've ever had 100 comments on my Facebook posts. I'm not popular. |
| Dianna: | [*laughing*] Yes, it's mostly from my friends here in Hong Kong and relatives in Indonesia. |

After posting these pictures, Dianna, a mother of three, followed up with another post, this time a video of her singing an Arabic song about birthdays and a slideshow of her son's photos collated by her close friends in Hong Kong. In the same post, Dianna included a short video of her close friend in Hong Kong wishing her son a happy birthday. The caption reveals the painful realization of separation, as she wrote, 'even though he [the son] has been separated from his mom [Dianna] for eight years, he continues to be strong and full of life.' In no time, Dianna's posts received a wave of congratulations and well-wishes, both for her and her son.

By displaying her maternal obligations on social media, Dianna effectively broadens the scope of the audience to whom she showcases her success in raising a healthy son with a thriving social life. It was clear that being *seen* was important for Dianna; she tagged 19 people in her posts, most of whom were not in the posts themselves. Tagging other people, Dianna explained, was a surefire way to ensure people see her posts. By making her mothering visible to the public, Dianna maximizes her chance of obtaining recognition for her unfaltering maternal dedication despite the prolonged separation.

The visibility affordance implicates the concept of displaying family, particularly regarding the contentious notion of audience in family display (Finch, 2007). Finch (2007) initially conceptualized the 'relevant others' as internal to the family. However, I argue that the visibility and publicness of social media activities can obscure the audience–observers boundaries. As evident from Dianna's case, social media affords greater visibility to her mothering display. At the same time, the people Dianna recognizes as the relevant audience have come to include her friends in Hong Kong, her son's teacher, and me as a researcher. Moreover, Dianna's subjective understanding of who constitutes an 'audience' is of great importance; it reflects Rathnayake and Suthers' (2018) assertion that the public on social media is not a given; it is phenomenologically constructed and sustained by the users' action.

Not all family interaction warrants an audience. The mothers were cognizant of the difference in visibility across social media platforms and managed the performance of maternal obligations accordingly. In general, Facebook is considered public, whereas WhatsApp is private. Instagram, on the other hand, was not popular as they thought it redundant since the account could be linked to Facebook. Martina (31), a mother of one, explained that she does on Facebook only what is appropriate in a physical public space. Her Facebook page was populated with posts related to her Islamic faith, congratulatory posts, and the latest development of the COVID-19 pandemic. Martina reserved disciplinarian roles for WhatsApp private chats, including scolding her son when he spent his allowance too fast, and the one time he was suspended from school for smoking. She said, 'I don't like to fight on Facebook. If I have problems, we talk in private, maybe call or WhatsApp … You don't want to "*buka aib sendiri*" [literally, to open one's shame, parallel to the English expression 'to air one's dirty laundry'].'

By swiftly 'swinging' from Facebook to WhatsApp, Martina effectively stayed on top of her son's well-being while respecting what she considered appropriate public/private boundaries.

## Controllable Connectivity

The second affordance that migrant mothers perceived in social media was controllable connectivity – the ability to manage differential degrees of availability for contact with different interactors. Interestingly, this controllability of connection was not necessarily because the platforms differed in technological features. Rather, it was because each platform has specific codes of conduct, limiting what the mothers *believe* they can do on a given platform. One of the commonly honored rules of conduct was not to disclose another's WhatsApp number without first obtaining their permission. However, the same was not true about Facebook usernames. Kamila (32), a mother of one, said: 'I don't think you need permission to disclose someone's Facebook name because people can just google the name anyway. Or, they can just look at close friends' Facebook friends list and search.'

Kamila sorts her potential interactors into different platforms by controlling access to her social media accounts. In doing so, she segments her social media interactors based on how important they are to her. Kamila, like most other respondents, was lenient in deciding whom she befriends on Facebook. However, she reserves WhatsApp for close ties, including her immediate family members and some fellow helpers in Hong Kong, but excluding her distant relatives and most neighbors. This segregation was a pre-emptive measure to curtail incessant requests for money which often come on WhatsApp private chat. Kamila recalled her experience prior to learning the benefit of separating her social contacts into different social media platforms: 'I woke up one morning, and I had five people asking to borrow money [on WhatsApp]. I remember one was my neighbor [in Indonesia], one was my son's [elementary school] teacher, and another one was a relative I had never even met. So I told my mom never to share my WA [WhatsApp] number anymore.'

Another norm that supports controllability is in terms of response expectation. On Facebook, a delayed response was acceptable, even desirable; indeed, a habit of replying to messages or comments on Facebook can immediately signal addiction to social media. However, there was a consensus that one must stay on top of WhatsApp messages. WhatsApp text messaging was the preferred platform for emergency uses; it supports urgency yet is not as intrusive as a voice call, a perfect combination for my respondents who work as live-in helpers in their employers' homes. These platform-specific social norms not only enable migrant mothers to partition different relationships on social media but also give them a justification for ignoring certain people. Hermina (37), a mother of one, explained that she reacts to Facebook notifications much more casually than WhatsApp alerts.

Aside from controlling access and response expectation from their side, the mothers also use social media to control their children's social circle. They do this by routinely checking their children's social media activities and friend lists to make sure their children do not interact with dubious strangers. Mariani (33), a mother of one, controlled her 14-year-old daughter's social media use by limiting the daughter's monthly allowance for the internet data plan. In addition, just like most other mothers I interviewed, Mariani knows her daughter's Facebook password. She regularly checks her daughter's private messages. When asked if this is infringing on her daughter's privacy, she said: 'It was our deal from the beginning. She can have a smartphone and FB [Facebook] account, but I will control it … She doesn't complain. It's scary … there might be bad men asking for pictures from girls on the internet.'

Previous research has discussed controllability as an affordance rooted in the privacy setting that users can manipulate (Evans et al., 2017). This study examines controllability from a different perspective, focusing on the social mechanism that allows users to moderate interactions. These implicit social codes of conduct are the results of the app's socio-economic framework and the user's everyday practices. As such, they can be categorized as social affordances – 'the social structures that take shape in association with a given technical structure' (Postigo, 2016, p. 5). WhatsApp prides itself on its end-to-end encryption, a feature that associates WhatsApp with greater privacy (Santos & Faure, 2018). The ethnographic interaction with migrant mothers teased out how collectively constructed platforms' cultures and norms enable them to segregate audience groups into different platforms and give the mothers a justified rationale for prioritizing certain contacts over others.

**Persistence**

The performance of transnational mothering on social media differs from caregiving on other media in that the materials supporting the performance can be re-accessed at a later time. These materials include family photos, comments, and other posts in which they tag each other. The social media posts and conversations between the mothers and their families function as 'tools for display' (Finch, 2007, p. 77), continuously reaffirming their familial commitment to each other during separation. This also gives a sense of persistence to their display of relationships in a way that pre-paid mobile phones cannot. Some older respondents in this study who have lived through the letter-writing era compared this to the permanence of letters, printed photos, and greeting cards. Hilda (52), a mother of two, said: 'Talking [on the phone] is nice. But with letters, you can save them and look at them again later … I used to hold the letter from my husband whenever I prayed for him. Now we all just keep photos on Facebook for everyone.'

There were cases when the mothers and their families treated Facebook and Instagram as an online photo album and engaged in a 'photo dump' – an act of posting many pictures, often without a clear storyline or relevance among the pictures (Archer, 2022). Dianna, the mother we met earlier, does this frequently on her Facebook account. At one time, she wrote, 'Just put these [the photos] here, so I won't lose them,' as a caption for a post consisting of 24 pictures, ranging from photos of her Sunday activities in Hong Kong, screenshots of her video calls with her son, and images of food. Dianna explained that by posting these pictures on Facebook, she did not have to worry about losing them if she lost her phone. She also said it is her favorite pastime to scroll through these old Facebook posts, helping her cope with homesickness and occasional loneliness.

The persistence of social media posts also means that the mothers can see what their family members in Indonesia post. These posts often function as a prompt for direct conversation. For example, Weti (40), a mother of two, calls her son whenever she sees his Facebook post. The conversation may begin with the post but proceeds into a full-blown phatic conversation that brings them closer together. Even when she sometimes missed her son's post, she would hear about it in her conversation with her daughter. She said, 'It's like updating each other with pictures on Facebook but also become like a topic to talk about ... My daughter would ask me, "Did you see what *abang* [big brother] posted?" And I said, "No, what is it?" She said, "Just look at his Facebook. It's so funny."'

Like other affordances, persistence varies between platforms. The mothers used various social media platforms with different intentions on how permanent they wanted their traces of interaction to be. Facebook and Instagram posts are treated as permanent records of family communication. However, for daily updates, most mothers preferred to use the story function of Instagram and Facebook. Interestingly, aside from sharing quick daily updates, such as pictures of traffic and meals, 'Facebook story' was often used to send a passive-aggressive message that may exacerbate conflicts. Hilda (52) recalled her own Facebook story directed at her daughter-in-law, saying, 'You know what they say, only an evil woman would drive a wedge between her husband and his mother. You will get your karma.' She said this is like a quick warning; you say it, and then it disappears in 24 hours.

## CONCLUSION

The three affordances identified in this study – visibility, controllable connectivity, and persistence – broadly characterize transnational mothering practices on social media among migrant mothers in Hong Kong. By analyzing their social media activities using an affordances lens, this study circumvents the 'technology versus social' theoretical impasse and its associated 'good versus evil' media narrative (Couldry, 2004; Hutchby, 2001). The patterns of communicative behaviors among migrant mothers and their close ties are prompted by their perception of social media functionalities. However, these functionalities are shaped by what they *think* is appropriate to do on each platform, what their employment condition allows, and the image of the family they wish to portray. Notably, the findings suggest that these practices are fluid and negotiable, allowing family members to recalibrate their media habits based on the changing media landscape and relational demands. This observation emerged due to the emphasis on the 'affordances-in-practice,' enabling the analysis to account for the multiple ways that technical functionalities of media materialize across different sociocultural communities (Costa, 2018, p. 3643).

This study advances the literature on mediated communication and transnational family practices by illustrating how social media affordances facilitate the emergence of new patterns of maternal caregiving during an extended separation. It reiterates the idea that transnational mothering via social media is not merely a virtual attempt to reproduce traditional caregiving (Madianou & Miller, 2011); instead, as the mothers interact with their families, with the technical features of social media, and with the designers' intention that forms part of the platform culture, they continuously (re) define the contours and practices of intimacy. Granted, purely 'digitally native' social phenomena are impossible because even the most intensely mediated relationship still occurs within the offline sociocultural environment (Rathnayake & Suthers, 2018). However, I argue that by using the affordances lens, we can broaden the scope of analysis and recognize the emergent interactional dynamics on social media without relentlessly taking reference from co-present family practices.

This study comes with several limitations. First, there is a lack of perspectives from other family members. Future research will benefit from an engagement with family members, especially the left-behind husbands/fathers whose voices are glaringly lacking in the literature on transnational families. Second, while the findings may reflect a broader pattern of family life on social media, we should be cautious against generalizing across migrant populations. Future research may advance the literature by comparing mediated intimacy across nationalities or ethnic groups.

## NOTES

1. All interviewees within this chapter have been anonymized.
2. Hadith is a sacred collection of statements and actions believed to have been said and done by the Prophet Muhammad himself or his followers. It is used as moral guidance and its authority ranks second only to the Quran.

## REFERENCES


Abel, S., Machin, T., & Brownlow, C. (2021). Social media, rituals, and long-distance family relationship maintenance: A mixed-methods systematic review. *New Media & Society*, *23*(3), 632–54. https://doi.org/10.1177%2F1461444820958717.

Archer, H. (2022). The photo dump is more than an Instagram trend – It's a call for authenticity. *Editorialist*. https://editorialist.com/lifestyle/what-is-an-instagram-photo-dump/.

Bayer, J.B., Campbell, S.W., & Ling, R. (2016). Connection cues: Activating the norms and habits of social connectedness. *Communication Theory*, *26*, 128–49. https://doi.org/10.1111/comt.12090.

Birks, M., & Mills, J. (2015). *Grounded Theory: A Practical Guide* (2nd ed.). SAGE.

boyd, d. (2011). Social network sites as networked publics: Affordances, dynamics, and implications. In: Z. Papacharissi (Ed.), *A Networked Self: Identity, Community, and Culture on Social Network Sites* (pp. 39–58). Routledge.

Bucher, T., & Helmond, A. (2018). The affordances of social media platforms. In J. Burgess, A. Marwick & T. Poell (Eds.), *The SAGE Handbook of Social Media* (pp. 233–53). SAGE.

Cabalquinto, E.C. (2018). 'We're not only here, but we're there in spirit': Asymmetrical mobile intimacy and the transnational Filipino family. *Mobile Media and Communication*, *6*(1), 37–52.

Charmaz, K. (2014). *Constructing Grounded Theory* (2nd ed.). SAGE.

Constable, N. (2014). *Born Out of Place: Migrant Mothers and the Politics of International Labor*. Hong Kong University Press.

Costa, E. (2018). Affordances-in-practice: An ethnographic critique of social media logic and context collapse. *New Media & Society*, *20*(10), 3641–56.

Couldry, N. (2004). Theorising media as practice. *Social Semiotics*, *14*(2), 115–32. https://doi.org/10.1080/1035033042000238295.

ENRICH (2019). *The Value of Care: Key Contribution of Migrant Domestic Workers to Economic Growth and Family Well-Being in Asia.* https://enrichhk.org/sites/default/files/2019–09/Final_The-Value-of-Care_Full-Report.pdf.

Evans, S.K., Pearce, K.E., Vitak, J., & Treem, J.W. (2017). Explicating affordances: A conceptual framework for understanding affordances in communication research. *Journal of Computer-Mediated Communication*, *22*(1), 35–52.

Faizin, H. (2018). Apakah sugra berada di bawah telapak kaki ibu: Kontektualisasi *al-Jannatu taḥta aqdām al-Ummahāti*. *Journal Al-Hikmah*, *14*(2), 1–18. http://journal.alhikmahjkt.ac.id/index.php/HIKMAH/article/download/105/80.

Fetterman, D.M. (1998). *Ethnography: Step by Step* (2nd ed.). SAGE.

Finch, J. (2007). Displaying family. *Sociology*, *41*(1), 65–81.

Gibson, J.J. (1979). *The Ecological Approach to Visual Perception*. Houghton Mifflin.

Hannaford, D. (2015). Technologies of the spouses: Intimate surveillance in Senegalese transnational marriages. *Global Networks*, *15*(1), 1470–2266.

Horst, H.A. (2006). The blessings and burdens of communication: Cell phones in Jamaican transnational social. *Global Networks*, *6*(2), 143–59.

Hutchby, I. (2001). Technologies, texts, and affordances. *Sociology*, *35*(2), 441–56.

Kemp, S. (2022). Digital 2022: Hong Kong. https://datareportal.com/reports/digital-2022-hong-kong.

Kim, Y. (2017). Digital media for intimacy? Asian nannies' transnational mothering in Paris. *Journal of International Communication*, *23*(2), 200–217.

Leonardi, P.M. (2011). When flexible routines meet flexible technologies: Affordance, constraint, and the imbrication of human and material agency. *MIS Quarterly*, *35*(1), 147–167.

Lorenzana, J.A. (2016). Mediated recognition: The role of Facebook in identity and social formations of Filipino transnationals in Indian cities. *New Media & Society*, *18*(10), 2189–2206.

Madianou, M. (2014). Smartphones as polymedia. *Journal of Computer-Mediated Communication*, *19*(3), 667–80.

Madianou, M. (2016). Ambient co-presence: Transnational family practices in polymedia environments. *Global Networks*, *16*, 183–201.

Madianou, M. (2019). Migration, transnational families, and new communication technologies. In J. Retis & R. Tsagarousianou (Eds.), *The Handbook of Diasporas, Media, and Culture* (pp. 577–590). John Wiley & Sons.

Madianou, M., & Miller, D. (2011). Mobile phone parenting: Reconfiguring relationships between Filipina migrant mothers and their left-behind children. *New Media & Society*, *13*(3), 457–70.

Madianou, M., & Miller, D. (2012). *Migration and New Media*. Taylor & Francis Group.

Miller, D., & Venkatraman, S. (2018). Facebook interactions: An ethnographic perspective. *Social Media + Society*, *4*(3), 1–11. https://doi.org/10.1177%2F2056305118784776.

Miller, K.E. (2015). Dear critics: Addressing concerns and justifying the benefits of photography as a research method. *Forum Qualitative Sozialforschung/Forum: Qualitative Social Research*, *16*(3), 1–17.

Morgan, D.H.J. (2011). *Rethinking Family Practices*. Palgrave Macmillan.

Nagy, P., & Neff, G. (2015). Imagined affordance: Reconstructing a keyword for communication theory. *Social Media + Society*, *1*(2). https://doi.org/10.1177%2F2056305115603385.

Nguyen, M.T.N., Zavoretti, R., & Tronto, J. (2017). Beyond the global care chain: Boundaries, institution, and ethics of care. *Ethics and Social Welfare*, *11*(3), 199–212.

Norman, D. (1999). Affordances, constraints, and design. *Interactions*, *6*, 38–43. https://doi.org/10.1145/301153.301168.

Oktavianus, J., & Lin, W.-Y. (2021). Soliciting social support from migrant domestic workers' connections to storytelling networks during a public health crisis. *Health Communication*, *38*(6), 1179–88. https://doi.org/10.1080/10410236.2021.1996675.

Parreñas, R.S. (2001). Mothering from a distance: Emotions, gender, and intergeneration relations in Filipino transnational families. *Feminist Studies*, *27*(2), 361–90.

Pongoliu, H. (2017). Family of Sakinah, mawaddah, warahmah in the concept of Islamic marriage. *Al-Mizan: Journal Pemikiran Hukum Islam*, *13*(1), 1–16.

Postigo, H. (2016). The socio-technical architecture of digital labor: Converting play into YouTube money. *New Media & Society*, *18*(2), 332–49.

Rathnayake, C., & Suthers, D.D. (2018). Twitter issue response hashtags as affordances for momentary connectedness. *Social Media + Society*, *4*(3). https://doi.org/10.1177%2F2056305118784780.

Santos, M., & Faure, A. (2018). Affordance is power: Contradictions between communication and technical dimensions of WhatsApp's end-to-end encryption. *Social Media + Society*, *4*(3). https://doi.org/10.1177%2F2056305118795876.

Share, M., Williams, C., & Kerrins, L. (2018). Displaying and performing: Polish transnational families in Ireland Skyping grandparents in Poland. *New Media & Society*, *20*(8), 3011–28.

Silvey, R. (2006). Consuming the transnational family: Indonesian migrant domestic workers to Saudi Arabia. *Global Networks*, *6*(1), 23–40.

Slembrouk, S. (2015). The role of the researcher in interview narratives. In A. De Fina & A. Georgakopoulou (Eds.), *The Handbook of Narrative Analysis* (pp. 2–17). John Wiley & Sons.

Tandoc, E.C., Lou, C., & Min, V.L.H. (2019). Platform-swinging in a poly-social-media context: How and why users navigate multiple social media platforms. *Journal of Computer-Mediated Communication*, *24*(1), 21–35. https://doi.org/10.1093/jcmc/zmy022.

Treem, J.W., & Leonardi, P.M. (2013). Social media use in organizations: Exploring the affordances of visibility, editability, persistence, and association. *Annals of the International Communication Association*, *36*(1), 143–89.

Vanden Abeele, M., Schouten, A.P., & Antheunis, M.L. (2017). Personal, editable, and always accessible: An affordance approach to the relationship between adolescents' mobile messaging behavior and their friendship quality. *Journal of Social and Personal Relationships*, *34*(6), 875–93.

Wang, Y., & Lim, S.S. (2020). Digital asymmetries in transnational communication: Expectation, autonomy, and gender positioning in the household. *Journal of Computer-Mediated Communication*, *25*(6), 365–81.

Waruwu, B.K. (2022). Smartphone mothering and mediated family display: Transnational family practices in a polymedia environment among Indonesian mothers in Hong Kong. *Mobile Media & Communication*, *10*(1), 97–114. https://doi.org/10.1177/2050157921998408.

Zhao, X. (2019). Disconnective intimacies through social media: practices of transnational family among overseas Chinese students in Australia. *Media International Australia*, *173*, 36–52.

# 4. Mapping technology-facilitated sexual violence in Singapore

*Shivani Gupta, Francis Luis Medado Torres, Sharon Yvette Xiomara Rosamor 'n Doen, Jungup Lee, Bimlesh Wadhwa and Michelle Ho*

## INTRODUCTION

In a world where most individuals are tethered to technology, our relationships with technology and each other have been transformed. This vital conduit makes it easy for individuals to work, socialize, conduct day-to-day activities like grocery shopping and buying medicines, and network widely, but it also places them in environments and contexts that are potentially harmful, damaging, and violent (Henry and Powell, 2015). One such phenomenon is technology-facilitated sexual violence (TFSV), which refers to a range of aggressive and harmful sexual behaviors perpetuated through information and communication technologies (ICTs) (Henry and Powell, 2018). Moreover, TFSV is a framework that captures various forms of digital harms experienced by individuals on an everyday basis. TFSV includes online sexual harassment, sexting (non-consensual sexual texting), gender-based hate speech, cyberstalking, and non-consensual distribution of images and sexual images, also known as image-based sexual abuse (IBSA) (Henry and Powell, 2014; Snaychuk and O'Neill, 2020) and sexploitation (Pedersen et al., 2022). TFSV is often targeted at marginalized groups and communities, like women and transgender and gender-nonconforming individuals (Powell and Henry, 2019).

Women are regularly exposed to TFSV on social media and other online platforms, including Instagram, TikTok, Telegram, Twitter, and Facebook (Hill and Johnson, 2020). In light of the #MeToo initiative, coopted as an online movement in 2017 and achieving virality through social media platforms, the topic of sexual violence has become visible in different spheres (Gupta, 2019). Yet, discourses on the role of technology in the perpetuation of sexual violence remain limited, even though there is evidence of sexual violence inhabiting both online and offline spaces and transmuting between the two. In recent times, cases of sexting or revenge pornography can be traced back to the acts of physical abuse and threat and vice versa. In their study, Pedersen et al. (2022) provide evidence of the intersection of digital sexual violence and physical sexual violence among adolescents by arguing that 1.7 per cent of adolescents recognize fluidity in two forms of sexual violence. In our study, a few interlocutors explained the transition between the two forms as they narrated their encounters with sexual violence. One of them narrated that an individual whom she got to know because of a class project cyber-flashed[1] her on WhatsApp before harassing her to go out on a date with him.

Therefore, the misconception that TFSV has limited impact as compared to offline violence (done to 'flesh'), among legal and policy-making institutions, webservice providers, and the public in general, needs to be challenged. This is because in contemporary society, our daily social–spatial interactions are not only mediated by technology but are increasingly dependent on it (Henry and Powell, 2015). Thus, TFSV implies 'gendered harms [are] explicitly or implicitly fixated on the objectification of the feminine body' (Henry and Powell, 2015, p. 768). Examining TFSV on social media and other online platforms makes the gendered aspects of technology apparent and can be used as a weapon to shame victims-survivors. The shame-blame surfaces by placing the onus on the content of violence rather than understanding consent and the crime itself (Hingorani, 2021).

TFSV is a widespread and transnational phenomenon largely impacting women and other marginalized individuals. A study done by Pew Research Center (Duggan, 2017) suggested that one in four Americans has experienced online harassment. Globally, Asia has the largest number of internet users, which suggests a rise in TFSV, although concrete data is not yet available (Carvalho, 2021). TFSV affects many individuals on a daily basis by insidiously entering their lives and shattering the notions of safety and danger by being in a sphere that refuses to be either entirely public or private. In lieu of such digital realities, this chapter develops a methodological approach for examining TFSV as a form of sexual violence in Singapore. Likewise, it gives an insight into the definition of TFSV, forms of TSFV, and ways to study TFSV by deploying digital ethnography as a medium premised on feminist methodology.

In 2020, Singapore had the third highest rate of internet use in Southeast Asia (Müller, 2021). According to a study conducted in 2018, 81.4 per cent (around 4.8 million people) of the population uses the internet on an everyday basis, with an average of 8 hours spent online. The internet's dominance in individuals' lives suggests that Singapore's digital sphere is saturated with online harms, especially TFSV. Data on TFSV in Singapore claims a considerable rise of 36 per cent in 2020 (AWARE, 2021). Recent cases of sexual violence that have come to light in the last few years have carried components of TFSV, such as those of an offensive online poll ranking the most attractive female Muslim teachers (Baharudin, 2021); Telegram (a chat-based platform) groups like SG Nasi Lemak that distributed nude and sexual images of women without their consent (Koh, 2021; *Straits Times*, 2021); and upskirt videos and voyeuristic filming of women (Lam, 2021). In 2022, the Association of Women for Action and Research (AWARE) published a report which stated that 70 per cent of TFSV cases in Singapore, in 2021, were of image-based sexual abuse (Chua, 2022). The age groups that experience TFSV the most are those between 18–24 and 25–34, who constitute 40 per cent and 32 per cent of all victims, respectively (Chan, 2022). Yet, scholars have so far paid scant attention to TFSV. The tendency to dismiss online violence in comparison to offline violence obfuscates

TFSV encounters and minimizes traumatization of victim-survivors, which further hampers articulation and reporting of TFSV.

Therefore, to examine this phenomenon, feminist methodology – a way of conducting research that is rooted in lived and embodied experiences of women by privileging their standpoints – is woven with digital ethnography to understand TFSV in Singapore, as well as alternate ways of conducting research which is influenced by the project as well as external factors. This chapter will establish Singapore's context in relation to TFSV, followed by an explanation of what feminist methodology is and the rationale behind using such sensibility in examination of TFSV. The chapter will then move on to elaborate on digital ethnography as a primary method within which online participant observation and digital interviews were conducted to grasp TFSV as a menacing discourse. Lastly, the chapter provides a comprehensive conclusion on the importance of studying TFSV as a socially debilitating phenomenon. In addition to contributing to the broader literature on TSFV, our aim is to provide a concrete path in mapping TFSV through digital methods that brings forth the entwinement of everyday lives with technology as well as contemporary research approaches to social issues.

## CONTEXT

In 2019, Singapore's population (especially the younger generation) had to come to terms with the prevalence of TFSV when Monica Baey, then an undergraduate at the National University of Singapore (NUS), came forward with her story on Instagram, a visually oriented social media platform. Baey was filmed showering in a campus residence by fellow undergraduate Nicholas Lim. When Baey exposed the act, a mass revelation dawned on the public that TFSV is not only widespread, but also harbors the dangers of uncontrolled distribution, threat, and harm, which further adds to the trauma of the crime itself. Since Baey's story, a lot more cases have come to light and most of them incorporate some form of TFSV (Ang, 2020; Menon, 2020), generating wider discourses on the nature of sexual violence in Singaporean society.

The contemporary discussions on sexual violence in the country have exposed the rising numbers regarding both offline and online cases of violence. Ministry of Home Affairs in Singapore reported 6,988 cases of sexual violence in Singapore of which only 40 per cent were reported to the police (Teng, 2021). In 2021, Ipsos and AWARE found that there remains high prevalence of workplace sexual harassment (Ipsos, 2021). Furthermore, AWARE reported that in 2019, they received 140 cases of TFSV (at their Sexual Assault Care Center) out of 777 sexual violence cases (around 18 per cent); and in 2021, TFSV constituted 19 per cent or 163 cases (AWARE, 2020). On university campuses in Singapore, in the last five years 172 cases of sexual misconduct have occurred (Sin, 2020).

In light of rising cases, Singapore is making a conscious effort to address the 'digital safety gap' and protect girls and women against online harms (Goh, 2021). In 2021, the Ministry of Communication and Information launched an initiative called

Singapore Together Alliance for Action (AfA) to 'encourage Singaporeans to discuss, take action and co-create initiatives to tackle online harms, especially those targeted at women and girls' (Ministry of Communication and Information, 2021). Yet, the worrisome aspect of TFSV is that these digital footprints are permanent; an online post can never be entirely removed. In this regard, Singapore as a digital-technological hub is tackling difficult questions on safety and sexual violence in a sphere that refuses to be contained. Considering TFSV's pervasiveness and its entanglement in the everyday lives of women, this chapter investigates the phenomenon by adopting feminist methodology sustained by digital ethnography.

## METHODOLOGICAL APPROACH: FEMINIST SENSIBILITY

Our research adopts a feminist sensibility as a methodological approach in studying sexual violence in Singapore in the digital age. Feminist methodology is a medium, underscored by feminist principles, where phallocentric knowledge is *shattered* to bring to the surface knowledge and experiences of those on the margins (Hartsock, 1987). Hellen Moore (1988) comments that historically, a male figure is assumed to be an ideal informant, whereas feminist methodology progresses to seek knowledge and perspectives of the marginalized. In this manner, feminist methodologies use the notion of situated knowledge to account for partial realities, grounded in embodied experiences, of those who mainstream society has ignored. The methodology concurrently demands the researcher to be self-reflexive of their positionality, privileges, and biases or, as Haraway (1988) terms it, 'accountable positioning.' In respect to this project, feminist methodology invokes rethinking and reconceptualizing digital spheres that inadvertently are androcentric and brings forth voices by challenging sexist/misogynist assumptions in the virtual world. Thus, feminist methodology gives voice to marginalized individuals' lived and embodied experiences from *their* perspectives, with the emphasis on dismantling structural inequalities, predominantly (hetero)patriarchy (Harding, 1987).

Patriarchy as a social structure that dominates and oppresses (Walby, 1989) is concerned with concepts of gender, power, and relationships between the two. Brubaker (2021) argues that power itself should be understood as a structural oppression, in which intersectionality plays an inherent part. Ergo, patriarchy mutates as a layered system of discrimination – utilizing other forms of structural inequalities – performing insidiously on individuals' minds and bodies (Gilligan and Snider, 2018). In other words, every transgression of patriarchal diktat leads to punishment in a form of violence (Foucault, 1995). Violence as an act, performance, and warning is done by the powerful towards the powerless (hooks, 2015). As Ahmed (2017) comments on the structural and controlling nature of patriarchy, 'violence is directed at some bodies more than others' (p. 34). Therefore, sexual violence is a discourse rooted in the embodied experiences of social-moral order towards the vulnerable. Sexual violence here manifests the anxieties of patriarchal figures who fear the blurring of private and public spheres by perpetuating unwanted sexual behaviors.

Therefore, as the digital sphere lacks the traditional societal boundaries of private and public, sexual violence becomes dominant on social media platforms. Invariably, women, trans, and queer individuals who engage with internet content and platforms in order to raise concerns and make themselves visible, from a supposedly egalitarian stance, encounter violent backlash. Such resistance to and attempts to curtail gender and sexual minorities illustrates heteropatriarchal anxiety through various forms of TFSV. Powell and Henry (2017) therefore stress that sexual violence in the digital age is not new. Rather, they argue that TFSV should be 'better understood simultaneously as a continuation, an elaboration, and an immersion of diverse forms of sexual violence in women's everyday lives' (p. 23) and should be conceptualized consequently as a reproduction of gendered power relations. Therefore, examining TFSV requires an awareness of the differential positions men and women occupy online, predisposed through gender norms and roles offline. In this manner, technology shapes and confirms prevailing gender assumptions and relations (Powell and Henry, 2017).

Digital harms are enacted to limit women's presence, access, and enablement in the online sphere and enhance male dominance through practices of sexual harassment and violence. This is because the patriarchal logic of TFSV rests in its fear of being disassembled by *powerless* bodies whose voices are varied and impassioned in online spaces. Therefore, traditional gender hierarchies and power dynamics of the social everyday world are mirrored in and by digital technologies. Therefore, the skewed ways in which gender regimes occupy the digital sphere validate the need for feminist methodology as it accounts for gendered experiences and situated realities in scope of equality and equity. Relatedly, employing the feminist methodology in study of TFSV brings forth the voices, embodied experiences, and lives that have been neglected in previous scholarship in violence studies, gender and feminist studies, media studies, studies on digital communities, and cultural studies. The digital sphere is where women's experiences and violence are frequently dismissed for not being either 'real' or severe enough, through a ranking system of the acts that are severe versus 'not really harmful' (Healicon, 2016) rendering TFSV a minimized and disembodied problem. Thus, feminist methodology presents the corporeality of TFSV by investigating it through digital ethnography.

## METHODS TO STUDY TECHNOLOGY-FACILITATED SEXUAL VIOLENCE

### Digital Ethnography

Digital ethnography demonstrates the entanglement of everyday life with digital technologies to make sense of the contemporary world individuals inhabit (Pink et al., 2016). In essence, digital ethnography is 'a method for representing real-life cultures through combining the characteristic features of digital media with elements of story' (Underberg and Zorn, 2013, p. 10). Góralska (2020) defines digital ethnography as a *method* used to study societies and culture in the digital space that does not require physical travel. Therefore, digital ethnography drawing on conventional ethnography is a way to tell stories (Murthy, 2008) that exist in the digital sphere but have implications on non-digital worlds as well. Pink et al. (2016) add to this definition by explaining that, like classic ethnographic endeavors, digital ethnography attempts to produce rich narratives that refuse to minimize human experience in any form. Therefore, using feminist methodology in alignment with digital ethnography provides space to conduct inquiry that places victim-survivor and individual voices at the center while paying equal attention to their lives on a continuum of digital and non-digital. Moreover, the final outcome of feminist sensibility is to think through issues of social justice, equality, and equity. Concomitantly, digital ethnography provided us with data and analysis to understand sexual violence, the forms in which it is articulated and interpreted, how individuals want to tackle such issues, and suggestions to minimize TFSV in everyday lives to live a life that is dignified and just. The value of digital ethnography in our study is that we were able to examine a digital phenomenon as we situated and immersed ourselves in digital field sites to gain perspective on the issue of sexual violence.

Relatedly, digital field sites 'comprise anything that the web is made of – texts, videos, images, platform infrastructures, use behaviors, social relations, or an information network' (Góralska, 2020, p. 47). In this manner, digital ethnography comprises the sites and interactions that formulate individuals' worlds by destabilizing binaries of online/offline and public/private. This method enables the theorization of a domain even though it is virtual and has implications for the corporeality of the everyday (Györ, 2017). Ergo, digital ethnography provides insight into how technology and the internet are/can be beneficial for and detrimental to individuals and communities, while proposing changes to policies and demanding social actions to make the internet safe, friendly, and equal for those who occupy digital worlds, and the future generations who will increasingly rely on it.

To invoke digital ethnography as a method is to primarily acknowledge that, as researchers, we continuously rely on predominantly digital communications (Møller and Robards, 2019). The act of contacting interlocutors through emails, texts, and video calls for interviews, surveys, and focus group discussions is to enter the domain of digital technologies where its assistance predominates research endeavors. Therefore, scholars need to reconsider the role digital technologies and platforms play in conducting research – especially in the time of a pandemic. This is to say that we do not only need to accept technology as part of our research but be open to discovering ways to conduct research while physical field sites remain inaccessible. Moreover, Thunberg and Arnell (2021) argue that the ongoing COVID-19 pandemic has led to a digital revolution where online forms of conducting research have found new currency among scholars. Additionally, digital ethnography exposes trends, reconfiguration of social relationships, and knowledge production that is driven by ICTs. Digital ethnography is an adept method that straddles between ethnography (and its family of methods) and digital experiences to seek the meaning-making in people's everyday worlds, especially digital ones. Therefore, digital ethnography premised on principles of feminist methodologies culminated in our study as demonstrated below.

Our project focuses on investigating TFSV on social media, text-based, and video-based platforms. The field site for such an investigation is the internet or, more specifically, Instagram, blogs, Facebook, Twitter, Reddit, and TikTok. A digital field site requires ways of examining that are unique to a traditional site yet complementary, even when methods appear to be the same to tell marginalized narratives and provide partial lived realities of digital existence. Digital ethnography fulfils our project's needs, where data existing in the digital sphere is traced, observed, and collated and the comfort and safety of TFSV victims-survivors are prioritized with an aim of minimizing re-traumatization. The two aims of using digital ethnography are explained through methods of participant observation and digital interviews. Moreover, using the same medium to perpetuate violence and understand its logic, impact, and consequences indicates the tensions, continuities, and comprehension of a digital age that remains gendered.

## ONLINE PARTICIPANT OBSERVATION

We conducted online participant observation on platforms like Reddit, Instagram, and campus-specific blogs, like NUSWhispers.[2] In our preliminary scoping, we uncovered a prominent discussion on sexual abuse, predominantly among young women in Singapore, related to cases that have come to public knowledge. We observed that the anonymity provided by internet platforms encourages survivors of sexual violence to share and discuss their experiences with other users at greater length as compared with known individuals, institutions, and other societal actors. Online participant observation gives insight into public perception – an organic discussion emerges in such a process – where popular opinions and voices surface without the need to be constantly and physically present. Moreover, online participant observation provides an opportunity to archive events and discussion on a given topic even if they are removed. In this way, a substantial research analysis and theory can be derived of the particular phenomenon and its related erasures.

Online participant observation has been vital in understanding specific cases of sexual violence, since the method allows for extensive documentation and collation of data. More importantly, this also enables people to know and reevaluate narratives and struggles without demanding that victims-survivors recount their stories and become retraumatized; and it releases them from immediate victim-shaming and blaming. For instance, we found a particular NUSWhispers post where an individual posted the story of a female friend who was filmed by her partner during an intimate act. Likewise, through online participant observation, we read each comment and documented a myriad of opinions and experiences in the digital sphere. This process means that researchers and observers are no longer bound by real time and physical space, as scrolling and moving through and across website pages produces diverse opinions, discussions, debates, and narratives surrounding an issue – which leads to a simultaneous, yet wholesome, generation of data.

Moreover, doing online participant observation offers a glimpse into how ideologies and cultural norms shape people's perceptions of sexual harassment or violence. Going back to the previous example, some Facebook users posted comments supporting the victim-survivor while others seemingly joked in an adversarial form to support the perpetrator. Even in Baey's and Lim's cases, a lot of comments on Facebook blamed Baey on various fronts, like her clothes, friendliness, bringing men to the hostel floor, and hanging out with men. They supported Lim with comments saying he committed a childish and immature act and should not be punished. Such observations, made on internet forums and platforms, may validate or contradict observers' notions, based on the popular comments and opinions found online. Digital participant observation, through this process, produces concrete data that contributes to the larger academic discussion and theory building.

Furthermore, our online participant observation highlighted multiple incidences of image-based sexual abuse grounded in 'sextortion'[3] and 'revenge pornography'[4] as a part of discussion threads. For example, a short-lived account on Instagram, termed durian.dot, was created to disclose the identities and crimes of sexual perpetrators – an act of doxing[5] that was recently criminalized in Singapore (Khan, 2021). This account received backlash because it was not endorsed by survivors of sexual violence, whom it attempted to support. Durian.dot was shut down within five days of its inception and could not validate the process through which it gathered stories and information on the perpetrators. Another case of TFSV that incited anxious feelings among Singaporean women was the SG Nasi Lemak case. SG Nasi Lemak was a Telegram group where 11,000 mostly explicit pictures of women were non-consensually shared among its 44,000 members (Sun, 2021). This group was discovered in 2020 and resurfaced again in 2021. The exposition of SG Nasi Lemak led to feelings of insecurity, and increased levels of fear, among women who felt uncomfortable maintaining their online profiles in public mode and sharing their pictures even with people they knew (Chua, 2022). This group also highlighted the prevalence of TFSV and the rapid spread of images that are difficult to contain and erase.

Similarly, Monica Baey's case in 2019 led to a dominant discussion on TFSV on various platforms. Aside from Baey's interviews uploaded by the *Straits Times* (Ang, 2019; *Channel News Asia*, 2019), her experience, even after several years, is referred to when talking about campus sexual harassment in Singapore (MothershipSG, 2021; Real Talk by MOSG, 2019). Tracing Baey's case provided insight into the developing discourse on sexual violence on campuses. Online participation observation offers us the benefit of grasping and analyzing the generation and perpetuation of social discourse. This salient feature allows us to follow the topic by ultimately revealing structural, systemic, and institutional inequalities that a survivor and society in general struggle with.

Furthermore, our online participant observation on Monica Baey's episode demonstrated the push universities have received to reevaluate their policies and execution in dealing with cases of sexual violence. More importantly, students have demanded the redrafting of policies at the institutional level and laws at national level. The new policies and social actions should reflect conscious advocacy on consent-based interactions, romantic relationships in institutions, first responder training, bystander training, in-person workshops on sexual violence, and events on reporting systems. These demands are instantly captured in alignment with the emerging discourse on sexual violence, through online participant observation, and in turn giving holistic insight on TFSV as a social problem. This characteristic is difficult to find in traditional participant observation, which would require switching media to comprehend other aspects of the same phenomenon. Therefore, online participant observation sustains the issue's immediacy by providing data capturing multiple dimensions of sexual violence.

## Digital Interviews

Complementary and in parallel to online participant observation was the method of digital interviews. Digital interviews were designed to make sense of individuals' everyday and traumatic experiences of TFSV. Granted, the COVID-19 pandemic encouraged our initial use of digital interviews, but in keeping with the discourse on TFSV, digital interviews became pertinent. This is because digital interviews provide anonymity for victims-survivors to share their experiences without having to completely disclose their identity and become vulnerable to a stranger (the interviewer). The interviews were conducted using Zoom (the video calling platform), where the interviewees were given the option of switching their videos on or off. While the no-video option created a barrier for the interviewer in terms of gauging expressions and reacting to them, it also provided a level of safety that encouraged interviewees to share their traumatic encounters. This process minimized the possibilities of re-traumatization and reduced moments of recognition that generate the fear of victim blaming and shaming. This process is not possible in an in-person interview as the physical meeting creates chances of identification; re-traumatization can be deeper as the person has to engage with the interviewer's physical presence and reactions. This physical distancing provided by digital interviews creates an added advantage in discussing sexual violence.

Digital interviews are empowering for enabling degrees of applied security with no human face attached to narratives, especially in an institutional setting where chances of getting identified are high. Many of the interviewees graphically described their experiences of sexual violence without having to feel anxious about being judged. A major benefit of digital interviews lies in mitigating individuals' victimization. If they had previously experienced image-based sexual abuse, then an image or video of the survivor could become a source of fear. Therefore, using a video calling platform can put the survivors at ease where the requirement to appear physically is not necessary. This way of conducting research would be rather difficult in an in-person interview.

This is further supported by the context in which digital interviews are done in the settings participants are already familiar with; there is a flexibility in digital interviews for them to choose how they want to share – i.e., mute oneself and/or demonstrate certain scenarios through screen-sharing options. Moreover, the option of digital interviews was extremely popular among our participants for multiple reasons. For instance, interviewees did not want to travel, as it costs money and time, which helped them spend more time with the interviewer. Digital interviews also enable individuals with health issues as well as those in different geographical locations to participate. All these factors highlight the benefits of digital interviews, but they are augmented in sexual violence research where interviewees' comfort, security, and well-being are prioritized.

Digital interviews provide a layered and reflexive way to engage with the issue through platforms one is embedded in. A fundamental principle of feminist methodology, to be reflexive and accountable, is fulfilled by digital interviews as a method. The manner in which conversation is conducted within the vulnerability paradigm makes reflexivity a part of the conversation and later in the analysis process. Additionally, by discussing one's own position and experiences with sexual violence, one creates accountability that enables one to break social and communication barriers. Furthermore, constant discussion and traversing digital sites together exposes the violence, which in some cases was repressed. A few survivors intimated to the interviewer that they came to the realization that unwanted texts and sexually explicit images in their inbox and on social media like Instagram, Facebook, and even LinkedIn were acts of TFSV, and not a normalized behavior to be encountered when being online. This was the result of conversing and defining what TFSV means in this day and age – a collaborative approach that supports feminist methodology of making the research interlocutor-centric. In this manner, digital interviews became an exploratory venue where the articulation of TFSV provided a cohesive demonstration, as immediate access to the internet and social media platforms was possible. In some scenarios, interviewees googled certain information and data they wanted to provide to make the case. This process is more complex and difficult than in an in-person interview, where using mobile phones or other forms of technology breaks the flow of the conversation and creates unwanted interruptions.

Quintessentially, digital interviews unearthed people's accounts and in-depth narratives of TFSV that are not easily accessible. There are multiple reasons for this: survivors' dismissal of TFSV as not a 'real' form of violence but a virtual misdemeanor, survivors not finding a space to articulate such virtual forms of violence, survivors' fear of victim blaming and gatekeeping, survivors developing a negative association with social media platforms. Each TFSV experience highlights the everyday nature of the problem and the ease with which it is obscured. Also, the constant fear of being unable to erase non-consensually-posted images, videos, and other media from the internet may lead to denial and certain tactics to keep oneself safe. Powell and Henry (2017) claim that TFSV requires the same attention as in-person sexual violence for it extends the gendered functioning of society and mirrors the power hierarchy rooted in patriarchy. This argument is evident where feminist methodology culminates with digital ethnography to invoke lived realities in digital spheres that refuse to be minimized. At present, where sexual violence narratives are finding space in the public domain, it is imperative to recognize TFSV as a prevailing form of sexual violence.

## CONCLUSION

Contemporarily, to think of sexual violence and its perpetuation, TFSV needs to be taken into account. The negative impact of TFSV can be observed when survivors make their profiles private, quit the medium altogether, or find various strategies like creating fake accounts or disclosing their gender as male (even if they identify with other genders), cover their webcams, and discourage themselves from posting any photo or information. Also, as argued earlier the fluidity between the two forms of sexual violence is undeniable. This is observed with TFSV survivors who suffer greater dilemmas and dismissal as compared to survivors of non-TFSV forms of sexual violence. Numerous cases of cyberstalking materialize themselves physically. Sextortion can lead to rape or other forms of threat. Therefore, placing the onus on survivors-victims for the violation rarely prevents any form of violence other than attacking their self-esteem and confidence. Second, TFSV can damage a person's ordinary life in substantial ways as any other form of violence is conceived to do so. The distribution of nude images without consent to the public (known or unknown) creates shame and trauma that are impossible to reconcile; in the digital sphere, it is notoriously hard to remove and contain data. The distribution of images generates comments, responses, and attitudes towards the victim-survivor's body, thereby producing a cycle of repeated victimization. Similarly, a text blackmailing an individual disallows them to freely move and engage in everyday activities. A few interlocutors remarked that they were cyber-flashed on social media platforms like Instagram by their fellow classmates or acquaintances before getting physically harassed.

Additionally, TFSV cases in Singapore are increasing, which is not only causing concern but increasing fear regarding the ways marginalized groups inhabit digital spaces. SG Nasi Lemak is a case in point that perpetuated image-based sexual abuse at a large scale, making women contemplate their security options online. Moreover, the emergence of the metaverse, by the Meta group, as an immersive digital space driven by augmented and virtual reality poses a serious threat regarding TFSV. A woman was raped in the metaverse as she entered the space to study digital behaviors (Soon, 2022). This is because in digital spaces, cybersecurity is not taken into account, laws are not clearly defined on TFSV, and cyber violence gets dismissed (Pang, 2022). Therefore, the need to bring TFSV into the mainstream discussion is urgent.

Our research began in a COVID-19 era when access to interlocutors was highly limited. We aimed to generate not only data that highlighted TFSV as an emerging phenomenon but also narratives that exposed the deep impact it had on the lives of digital users rendered as victim-survivors. In an attempt to do so, we studied TFSV through digital ethnography methods by privileging voices and experiences that are not given enough attention because their experiences are thought to be virtual and not real. In conducting digital ethnography, to understand and examine TFSV, we are highlighting how digitality is interconnected where digital participant observation and digital interviews create a seamless manner in which TFSV is brought to light. Online participant observation immerses the ethnographer in digital sites, like Instagram, Facebook, and NUSWhispers, among others, to observe and engage with sexual violence content as one can see the comments, posts, videos, photos, and other items that constitute acts of violence. This once again provides depth and incisiveness to the study. Therefore, as the struggle to make TFSV a crucial discourse on sexual violence continues, adopting digital ethnography provides immersive and secure ways of conducting research without jeopardizing the safety and security of the victim-survivor, and experiencing in-depth involvement in the topic being studied.

In this regard, our chapter deploying feminist methodologies calls for the recognition of TFSV as a form of sexual violence alongside non-digital forms of sexual violence as a victim-survivor struggle to narrate their experiences. We have elaborated on the ways in which digital ethnography enables us to showcase the complexities of TFSV by continuing to place the researcher and research participant within digital frameworks, while privileging the survivors' safety and security. Consequently, scholars studying ICTs, sexual violence, the digital sphere, and contemporary feminism should account for TFSV as it is rapidly penetrating individuals' lives and impacting our ways of being and living. In doing so, our methodology and methods provide pathways to study TFSV in sensitive ways and are embedded in the digitality of everyday lives.

## NOTES

1. Sharing of pictures of genitalia to a person non-consensually.
2. NUSWhispers is a website run by NUS students for students where issues, cases, and developments at NUS are discussed anonymously. This space, while encouraging student-centric discussion, has also become a site of bullying, ranting, shaming, and blaming others.
3. Sextortion is 'the non-consensual and coercive obtainment of images, the use of non-nude/non-sexual image[s]' (Vitis, 2020, p. 28).
4. Revenge pornography is a form of image-based sexual abuse. It consists of 'images or video of a sexual nature that is circulated without permission' (Snaychuk and O'Neill, 2020, p. 986).
5. 'Doxing' refers to the act of publishing personal data associated with an individual or organization, usually with malicious intent.

# REFERENCES

Ahmed, S. (2017). *Living a Feminist Life*. Durham: Duke University Press.
Ang, J. (2019, April 26). Exclusive interview: Posting my story on Instagram about NUS peeping Tom was last resort, says Monica Baey. *Straits Times*. https://www.straitstimes.com/singapore/posting-my-story-on-instagram-was-last-resort-monica-baey.
Ang, J. (2020, December 1). NUS political science professor sacked for sexual misconduct against student. *Straits Times*. https://www.straitstimes.com/singapore/parenting-education/nus-political-science-professor-dismissed-for-alleged-misconduct.
AWARE (2020, December 2). AWARE's sexual assault care centre saw 153 cases of technology-facilitated sexual violence in 2019, the most ever in one year. https://www.aware.org.sg/2020/12/awares-sexual-assault-care-centre-saw-cases-of-technology-facilitated-sexual-violence-in-2019-the-most-ever-in-one-year/.
AWARE (2021). AWARE saw 36% increase in cases of technology-facilitated sexual violence in 2020; announces launch of Solid Ground website. Association of Women for Action and Research. https://www.aware.org.sg/2021/07/technology-facilitated-sexual-violence-2020-launch-solid-ground-website-survivors/#:~:text=Gender%2Dequality%20group%20AWARE's%20Sexual,since%20tracking%20began%20in%202016.
Baharudin, H. (2021, May 27). Police investigating offensive poll ranking female Islamic teachers; President Halimah and other leaders criticise poll. *Straits Times*. https://www.straitstimes.com/singapore/mps-and-religious-leaders-speak-out-against-offensive-poll-ranking-female-asatizah.
Brubaker, S.J. (2021). Embracing and expanding feminist theory: (Re)conceptualizing gender and power. *Violence Against Women*, 27(5), 717–26.
Carvalho, R. (2021, May 29). Porn, privacy, and pain: How image-based abuse tears women's lives apart. *South Morning China Post*. https://www.scmp.com/week-asia/long-reads/article/3134719/porn-privacy-and-pain-how-image-based-abuse-tears-womens-lives.
Chan, J. (2022, April 20). 70% of tech-enabled sexual violence cases seen by Aware involved images – highest proportion to date. *TodayOnline*. https://www.todayonline.com/singapore/tech-enabled-sexual-violence-aware-1877546.
*Channel News Asia* (2019, May 1). 'Change has finally come': Monica Baey on NUS handling of sexual misconduct cases. https://www.channelnewsasia.com/news/singapore/monica-baey-sexual-misconduct-nus-university-instagram-11494822.
Chua, N. (2022, April 20). 70% of tech-enabled sexual violence cases in 2021 image-related, including revenge porn. *Straits Times*. https://www.straitstimes.com/singapore/courts-crime/70-of-tech-enabled-sexual-violence-cases-in-2021-image-related-including-revenge-porn.
Duggan, M. (2017). Online Harassment 2017. Pew Research Center. https://www.pewresearch.org/internet/2017/07/11/online-harassment-2017/.
Foucault, M. (1995). *Discipline and Punish: The Birth of the Prison*. New York: Vintage Books.
Gilligan, C., & Snider, N. (2018). *Why Does Patriarchy Persist?* Cambridge: Polity Press.
Goh, T. (2021, June 5). 'Digital safety gap' for women in S'pore must be addressed: Sim Ann. *Straits Times*. https://www.straitstimes.com/singapore/community/digital-safety-gap-for-women-in-spore-must-be-addressed-sim-ann.
Góralska, M. (2020). Anthropology from home: Advice on digital ethnography for the pandemic times. *Anthropology in Action*, 27(1), 46–52.
Gupta, S. (2019). *Mapping Women's Worlds in Contemporary Urban Banaras*. Singapore: National University of Singapore.
Györ, A.F. (2017). *Digital Ethnography: Principles and Practice* by Sarah Pink et al. [Review]. *Corvinus Journal of Sociology and Social Policy*, 8(1), 132–38.

Haraway, D. (1988). Situated knowledges: The science question in feminism and the privilege of partial perspective. *Feminist Studies*, 14(3), 575–99. https://doi.org/10.2307/3178066.
Harding, S. (1987). 'Introduction: Is there a Feminist Method?' in S. Harding (ed.), *Feminism and Methodology: Social Science Issues*. Bloomington: Indiana University Press, pp. 1–15.
Hartsock, N. (1987). 'The Feminist Standpoint: Developing the Ground for a Specifically Feminist Historical Materialism' in S. Harding (ed.), *Feminism and Methodology: Social Science Issues*. Bloomington: Indiana University Press, pp. 157–181.
Healicon, A. (2016). *The Politics of Sexual Violence: Rape, Identity and Feminism*. London: Palgrave Macmillan.
Henry, N., & Powell, A. (2014). 'The Dark Side of the Virtual World: Towards a Digital Sexual Ethics' in N. Henry & A. Powell (eds.), *Preventing Sexual Violence: Interdisciplinary Approaches to Overcoming a Rape Culture*. London: Palgrave Macmillan.
Henry, N., & Powell, A. (2015). Embodied harms: Gender, shame, and technology-facilitated sexual violence. *Violence Against Women*, 21(6), 758–79.
Henry, N., & Powell, A. (2018). Technology-facilitated sexual violence: A literature review of empirical research. *Trauma, Violence, and Abuse*, 19(2), 195–208.
Hill, C., & Johnson, H. (2020). Online interpersonal victimization as a mechanism of social control of women: An empirical examination. *Violence Against Women*, 26(12–13), 1681–1700.
Hingorani, S. (2021, 5 May 2021). Stop asking why she took the nude, start asking why he shared it. *Channel News Asia*. https://www.channelnewsasia.com/commentary/sg-nasi-lemak-telegram-chats-sexual-harassment-singapore-1344236.
hooks, b. (2015). *Feminist Theory: From Margin to Center*. New York: Routledge.
Ipsos (2021, January 14). AWARE-Ipsos survey reveals high prevalence of workplace sexual harassment in Singapore. https://www.ipsos.com/en-sg/aware-ipsos-survey-reveals-high-prevalence-workplace-sexual-harassment-singapore.
Khan, W. (2021, June 4). Durian.dot: The vigilante Instagram account that took the Singaporean cyberspace by storm – for 5 days. *Parrot Review*. https://www.theparrotreview.com/op-ed/duriandot-the-vigilante-instagram-account-that-took-the-singaporean-cyberspace-by-storm-for-5-days.
Koh, W.T. (2021, June 3). SG Nasi Lemak group admin given 1-year mandatory treatment order. *Yahoo! News*. https://sg.news.yahoo.com/sg-nasi-lemak-group-admin-1-year-mandatory-treatment-order-023946242.html.
Lam, L. (2021, June 3). SG Nasi Lemak Telegram chat group administrator sentenced to mandatory treatment. *Channel News Asia*. https://www.channelnewsasia.com/singapore/sg-nasi-lemak-telegram-leonard-teo-treatment-order-1829216.
Menon, M. (2020, October 18). NUS sacks Tembusu College don accused of sexual misconduct. *Straits Times*. https://www.straitstimes.com/singapore/nus-sacks-tembusu-college-don-accused-of-sexual-misconduct.
Ministry of Communication and Information (2021). Alliance for Action to tackle online harms, especially those targeted at women and girls. https://www.mci.gov.sg/pressroom/news-and-stories/pressroom/2021/3/alliance-for-action-to-tackle-online-harms.
Møller, K., & Robards, B. (2019). Walking through, going along and scrolling back. *Nordicom Review*, 40(s1), 95–109.
Moore, H.L. (1988). *Feminism and Anthropology*. Oxford: Polity Press.
MothershipSG (2021, February 28). *What Do Students Think about Sexual Misconduct on Campuses? Mothership Hits the Streets*. https://www.youtube.com/watch?v=6KTNXOUnqt4&ab_channel=MothershipSG.
Müller, J. (2021). Internet usage in Singapore: Statistics & facts. Statista. https://www.statista.com/topics/5852/internet-usage-in-singapore.
Murthy, D. (2008). Digital ethnography: An examination of the use of new technologies for social research. *Sociology*, 42(5), 837–55.

NUSWhispers (2021, July 11). My friend had met an NUS student on a dating app and in early June. https://www.facebook.com/nuswhispers/posts/5716647598405654.
Pang, I. (2022, February 16). Sexual assault in the metaverse: Can victims turn to present-day law for justice? *Home Ground*. https://thehomeground.asia/destinations/singapore/sexual-assault-in-the-metaverse-can-victims-turn-to-present-day-law-for-justice/.
Pedersen, W., Bakken, A., Stefansen, K., & Von Soest, T. (2022). Sexual victimization in the digital age: A population-based study of physical and image-based sexual abuse among adolescents. *Archives of Sexual Behaviour*, 52(1), 399–410.
Pink, S., Horst, H.A., Postill, J., Hjorth, L., Lewis, T., & Tacchi, J. (2016). *Digital Ethnography: Principles and Practice*. London: SAGE.
Powell, A., & Henry, N. (2017). *Sexual Violence in a Digital Age*. London: Palgrave Macmillan.
Powell, A., & Henry, N. (2019). Technology-facilitated sexual violence victimization: Results from an online survey of Australian adults. *Journal of Interpersonal Violence*, 34(17), 3637–65.
Real Talk by MOSG (2019, April 29). *Sexual Harassment: Real Talk Episode 21*. https://www.youtube.com/watch?v=S-qLJvRAxVY&ab_channel=RealTalkbyMOSG.
Sin, Y. (2020, November 3). Parliament: 172 cases of sexual misconduct handled by unis, polys and ITE over past five years. *Straits Times*. https://www.straitstimes.com/singapore/politics/parliament-172-cases-of-sexual-misconduct-handled-by-universities-polytechnics.
Snaychuk, L.A., & O'Neill, M.L. (2020). Technology-facilitated sexual violence: Prevalence, risk, and resiliency in undergraduate students. *Journal of Aggression, Maltreatment & Trauma*, 29(8), 984–99.
Soon, W. (2022, May 30). A researcher's avatar was sexually assaulted on a metaverse platform owned by Meta, making her the latest victim of sexual abuse on Meta's platforms, watchdog says. *Insider*. https://www.businessinsider.com/researcher-claims-her-avatar-was-raped-on-metas-metaverse-platform-2022-5.
*Straits Times* (2021). *SG Nasi Lemak Admin Fined and Jailed*. https://www.youtube.com/watch?v=qVpRkhu_8AI&ab_channel=TheStraitsTimes.
Sun, D. (2021, 9 March 2021). SG Nasi Lemak chat admin jailed and fined; had more than 11,000 obscene photos and videos. *Straits Times*. https://www.straitstimes.com/singapore/courts-crime/sg-nasi-lemak-admin-jailed-and-fined-had-more-than-11000-obscene-photos-and.
Teng, A. (2021, 6 January 2021). About 40% of sexual assault cases from 2017 to 2019 involves victim below 16. *Straits Times*. https://www.straitstimes.com/singapore/courts-crime/about-40-per-cent-of-sexual-assault-cases-from-2017-to-2019-involved-victims.
Thunberg, S., & Arnell, L. (2021). Pioneering the use of technologies in qualitative research: A research review of the use of digital interviews. *International Journal of Social Research Methodology*, 25(6), 757–68.
Underberg, N.M., & Zorn, E. (2013). *Digital Ethnography: Anthropology, Narrative, and New Media*. Austin: University of Texas Press.
Vitis, L. (2020). Private, hidden and obscured: Image-based sexual abuse in Singapore. *Asian Journal of Criminology*, 15(1), 25–43.
Walby, S. (1989). Theorising patriarchy. *Sociology*, 23(2), 213–34.

# PART II

# CULTURE AND PUBLICS

# 5. Religious influencers and socially mediated cultural politics

*Annisa R. Beta*

## INTRODUCTION

'Feel with your heart and ask for His guidance,' writes Ghaida Tsurayya to her more than 400,000 followers in a video post on 16 April 2019, just one day before the 2019 Indonesian general elections. The video shows a series of photos accompanied by the voice of her father, the popular religious teacher Abdullah Gymnastiar. While the voiceover and the caption of the post are posed as religious and somewhat politically neutral, both Tsurayya and her father were ardent supporters of Prabowo Subianto, one of the presidential candidates. Tsurayya is one of many religious influencers in Indonesia, the world's largest Muslim society. How do these kinds of influencers strategically showcase religious virtue and at the same time promote their political interests without sacrificing their own image? This chapter addresses how scholars can understand and examine the growing number of religious influencers, not just in Indonesia but in other parts of the world, to better understand how religion and online representations of piety are significant culturally and politically.

The notion of religious influencer was first conceptualized to address the increasing number of young Muslim women who gained microcelebrity status on social media by deploying online personas founded on a mix of religious, commercial, and political interests (Beta, 2019a). It is an extension to the existing studies on the global influencer industry, especially the ones centred around influencers' microcelebrity status (Abidin, 2015, 2016a, 2016b). A 'microcelebrity,' a term first coined by Theresa M. Senft (2008), bases the idea of the self as a brand on market logics embedded online, especially on social media and the endless iterations of the platform facilitating this contemporary fabulation of the self. A microcelebrity preserves the sense of identity via a coherent presence and publicity online, ready to be circulated and interpreted as a commodity to be produced, distributed, and consumed by other users (Senft, 2013). Influencers extend this notion of microcelebrity. They are the new online public figures in our increasingly socially mediated realities, and they garner a following by sharing intimate details of their lives and personal stories or preferences (Abidin, 2016b). Influencers deploy and gain financial, cultural, and social capitals, and even a sense of self-actualization and interconnectedness with their followers (Abidin, 2015) on popular social media platforms such as Instagram, Twitter, Facebook, YouTube, and TikTok. Instagram's global influencer industry is so successful that it was valued at more than five billion dollars in 2020 (Frolov, 2020). This chapter traces the increasing impact of religious influencers in the

Indonesian political landscape to understand how religion and online representations of piety play important functions in the attention economy of Muslim societies in order to develop an approach to studying religious influencers.

Today, the influencer industry has become so diverse and multifaceted. There are many influencers focusing on different categories of interest, location, gender, sexuality, social class, cultural affiliation, or life stage. I propose religious influencers as a category that represents and articulates the importance of religion, especially religious practices and representations of piety. They are important figures in societies or communities where expressions of religiosity dominate. In societies with large Muslim populations like Indonesia and Malaysia, religious influencers like Dian Pelangi or Jihan Muse represent and articulate the possibilities of creatively fusing Islamic practices, like veiling, and fashion trends. These are not entirely new phenomena. Amongst young Muslim women who consume and aspire to be able to purchase high-end fashion labels and travel globally, the mix of fashion and ideals of modernity and (upper) middle-class lifestyles was first made popular online by the modest fashion bloggers, popularly labelled as 'hijabers' or 'hijabista,' in the first half of the 2010s (Beta, 2014; Lewis, 2015). Visual social media platforms like Instagram intensify the creative forms of empowerment for young Muslims (Bunt, 2009; Nisa, 2018). The religious influencers transform and reconfigure the modest fashion bloggers' earlier interpretations and creative ways of presenting Islamic teachings, making the opportunities to combine commercial, religious, and political interests more pronounced. The speed and convenience afforded by Instagram and Twitter's platform architecture, for instance, change the modes of curating their presentations of the modern pious self and their understanding of involvements in socio-political debates. Religious influencers can also be a popular figure in a society where Muslims are in the minority. Kristin M. Peterson (2020) studies how religious influencer Leah Vernon, who is a black and overweight Muslim woman, can be categorized as a 'social media interrupter' who disrupts the usual white, thin, secular influencer visibility in the United States. In other words, religious influencers can be considered as key opinion leaders in the constantly changing landscapes of lifestyle trends whose interpretations of such trends rely on religious virtues and practices. Their constructions and representations of lifestyle and piety result from the specific socio-political, cultural, and historical contexts they are in and, at the same time, feature transnational cultural flows, resulting in social media posts and personal branding that are highly differentiated but also citing a familiar set of references (Mohamad, 2021; Senft, 2013) – the analytical approach of which will be discussed in the last section of this chapter.

Religious influencers can be individuals or groups of people who combine their interests in religious growth with financial gain *and* socio-political change in a way that is attractive and accessible to their followers. A key distinction between religious influencers and other categories of microcelebrity would be their interests in encouraging their followers and deploying their influence towards an ethical goal. They encourage their followers to undergo self-transformation in order to become ideal and ethical individuals who follow religious injunctions closely. Social, political, and cultural changes are *not* unintended effects of how religious influencers present themselves; rather those are outcomes the influencers consider as part and parcel of their branding and promotion of a way of life. This may be comparable to environmental influencers or eco-influencers who are committed to promoting sustainable lifestyles (Bentley et al., 2021; Ramos & Cownie, 2020). Nevertheless, it is important to remember that the specificities of a society or a community from which the religious influencers come inform the ways they interpret and promote religious virtues, and set specific ethical goals. My research on religious influencers focuses on Indonesia, a predominantly Muslim country. Indonesia's history of Islamic social movements and its specific postcolonial and post-authoritarian political trajectory cannot be detached from how religious influencers understand their roles. The next section explains the religious influencers I have analysed as an example for the analytical approach I am proposing in this chapter.

## RELIGIOUS INFLUENCERS IN INDONESIA

In the Indonesian political landscape, religious influencers articulate religious and online representations of piety, beyond the commercial interests usually attached to the global influencer industry (Abidin & Brown, 2018). The idea of *da'wa* or *dakwah* (Islamic proselytization) is central to how piety and ethical transformation can be interpreted. I have studied young Muslim women's groups and figures with tens of thousands of followers since 2012, observing the transformation of modest fashion bloggers who documented their creative combinations of hijab with the latest fashion trends on their personal blogs and their ongoing engagement with popular visual-based social media platforms like Instagram (Beta, 2014, 2019a, 2019b, 2020).

While the way young Muslim women look (in reference to veiling and modest fashion practices) is central to their regular posts, the religious influencers I followed also emphasize the 'intimate' relationship they have with their followers to justify the importance of reworking the self and the followers' relationship to others around them as well as the socio-political landscape they are a part of. Religious influencers make references to their roles as citizens, but expertly avoid and make blurry expressions and representations that would show their direct interests or connections to formal politics (for instance, their criticisms of the government or their support to certain electoral candidates). They actively organize gatherings with their followers, including large-scale events involving corporate sponsors, and even annual marches on the streets promoting modest dressing. They publish books advocating Islamic lifestyles and produce short web series on YouTube. While they do make money out of those activities, they are also dependent on the voluntary labour and perceived intimate relationship between the individuals behind the social media accounts and the followers. This intimacy is a product of the limited spaces provided in public for young women to teach one another about Islam and society. Here, I refer to cultural theorist Lauren Berlant's concept of the 'intimate public,' which stresses stranger sociability and the sharing of private details in order to celebrate the ethics and aesthetics of perseverance and survival in everyday life (1997, 2008). The intimate public in the age of social media requires the private experiences to be generalizable and shareable enough in order to extract that sense of intimacy and generate a feeling of relatability (Kanai, 2019, pp. 4–6). For religious influencers, their posts and the followers' comments on their social media pages function as an alternative space where they discuss Islamic teachings and their daily life outside the jurisdiction of the usual Islamic authorities. This practice is informed by the architecture of contemporary digital publics and platform societies globally which blur the distinction between public and private spheres (Baym & boyd, 2012; Van Dijck et al., 2018). In addition, it is their reconfiguration of the *da'wa* activism familiar for Indonesians, I suggest, that makes the religious influencers successful.

Indonesia's modern political history is a result of the dynamics, interactions, and tensions between its secular and religious groups. While some were able to mix Islamic teachings with secular, progressive values, most groups distinguished religious state and governance interests from secular ones. The young Muslim women who succeed in their religious influencer careers follow the path of the Islamic study groups formed by university students in their campuses under the authoritarian regime of Suharto (1966–1998). While Indonesia has had a long history of Islamic social movements and modern Muslim organizations (Hefner, 2000), student-led organizations were the first ones to reshape the mode of Islamic activism to avoid government scrutiny and function as an alternative to more visible movements against the regime. Under Suharto's New Order regime, they avoided overtly visible political dissent and instead focused on renewing their members' sense of the pious self. In response to the Javanese-centric cultural politics asserted by Suharto, which at the time was almost synonymous with crooked governance and impure Islam, the students taught and learned from one another a refined version of Islamic 'lifestyle.' This included encouraging modest dressing, discussing Islamic reading materials, and meeting regularly to enhance their knowledge about Islam. They were more interested in encouraging discipline and consciousness amongst fellow Muslim students, which represented a disjuncture from the corrupt and authoritarian regime (Brenner, 1996).

Today, similar sentiments, while not exact copies of previous *da'wa* activists, could be seen in the ways in which the religious influencers run their social media posts and organize events or gatherings. Religious influencers thrived in a digital media landscape supported by the ubiquity of social media and the increasing popularity of Islamic fashion and lifestyle industries (Jones, 2010). In addition, while young Muslim women dominate the religious influencer industry in Indonesia, young male preachers like Felix Siauw and young Muslim men-led groups like Pemuda Hijrah have also gained popularity (Beta, 2020; Hew, 2018; Temby, 2018). They are highly responsive to young people's interests using different formats available in social media, while also offering meaningful engagements to facilitate young Muslims' interests in learning more about Islamic teachings in engaging and relatable ways. This responsiveness and relatability are informed by the specific trajectory of the cultural politics in Indonesia and its current form of socially mediated public life. Most of the time, the religious influencers focus on creating content that encourages their followers to live ethically, for instance, quoting verses from the Qur'an or *hadith* (recorded sayings and actions of the Prophet Muhammad). Everyday conduct is usually their focus. Nevertheless, during intense political moments, they would shift their followers' attention to their candidate of choice.

My analysis of the Indonesian presidential election in 2019 suggests how religious influencers like Dian Pelangi (who has more than five million followers on Instagram) and Ghaida Tsurayya (more than 400,000 followers) strategically placed their interactions with presidential candidate Prabowo Subianto in their Instagram feeds (Beta, 2019b). Against the incumbent president Joko Widodo, Subianto mobilized the support of more conservative Islamist figures and groups (Warburton, 2020). Analyses and coverage of the candidates' political moves often focused on their negative campaigning, further deepening the divide between Indonesia's moderate and conservative Muslims. Meanwhile, Pelangi and Tsurayya took a whole different approach to express their support. For example, Pelangi posted a series of photos on her Instagram account showing her talking to Subianto, and a video of the candidate strolling through her design studio and boutique. The caption of her post detailed her happiness at meeting the candidate. Using a different technique, Tsurayya instead posted a selfie with her adorned in a beautiful long dress. She signed 'number two' or the V sign with her fingers, signalling her support for presidential candidate number two, Subianto. Both religious influencers' posts supporting the candidates received tens of thousands of likes and positive comments. While this might be typical of political performances during elections everywhere, it is important to note that the religious influencers' participation in electoral politics demonstrates how certain appearances and online behaviours work effectively to gain greater following and thus assert more authority. In the case of Indonesia, they are exerting their authority on the majority young and Muslim Indonesians, who account for tens of millions of eligible voters.

All this is to say that religious influencers play important roles in the contemporary cultural politics in Muslim societies. While it could be useful to attend to the obviously political features of social media (big data or hashtag sentiment analysis), a consideration of the mundane and everyday as well as the lifestyles the influencers promote may generate a deeper understanding of how the politics plays out amongst sections of the citizenry rarely considered as influential. The currency of clicks and page views in an attention economy indeed marks the influencer's career success (Marwick, 2015) but it is also a part of the contemporary form of digital political activism (Highfield, 2016; Lim, 2012; Mendes et al., 2019; Tufekci, 2013). And for the religious influencers, their ambitions to encourage their followers to be more pious do not necessarily need to fall between the cracks of the binary of 'political versus apathetic, highly commercialised' online personalities. Rather, it is the task of the researcher to understand the religious influencers' flexibility and capacity to meld their religious, commercial, and political interests.

## AN APPROACH TO STUDYING RELIGIOUS INFLUENCERS

The previous discussion demonstrated the necessity to develop an approach for studying religious influencers without falling into the trap of making exotic or 'Other' Muslims who partake in the industry. In principle, it is important that we do not limit the sites at which the religious influencers play a key part, and we must avoid the tendency to subsume them under *one* specific social or cultural location. Instead, I propose that we analyse religious influencers as the key actors of a conjuncture: a social formation that is 'fractured and conflictual, along multiple axes, planes, and scales, constantly in search of temporary balances or structural stabilities through a variety of practices and processes of struggle and negotiation' (Grossberg, 2010, p. 41). A conjunctural analysis seeks to clarify, while not oversimplifying, the connections that may appear paradoxical between contemporary events and historically-significant moments (Hall et al., 2013, pp. 183–84). That is to say that it is essential to pay close attention to the socio-political history and the constantly changing roles, locations, and the subject positions of religious influencers without assuming that those elements are stable. The study of religious influencers should be mindful of the dynamic configurations of religiosity and piety, gendered dimensions and articulations of the self, the relationship between social media platforms and neoliberal logic, as well as the discourses around political subjectivity, amongst many other elements, scopes, and milieus. To put it simply, my analysis of religious influencers in the second half of the 2010s will be different from analyses of religious influencers in the 2020s. In short, an approach to studying religious influencers needs to be flexible and keenly aware of and responsive to the current conjuncture of contemporary cultural politics within which the influencers are temporarily located.

To do such an analysis, I found Christine Hine's 'ethnography for the internet' (2015) to be a useful framework. While digital ethnography has been adapted into multiple names and iterations, it is essential that we look for an ethnographic approach that is responsive to multiple 'situations' instead of a singular 'situation.' While more conventional ethnographic work benefits from an immersion in a specific location or locality, a study of any internet phenomenon in a hypermediated reality, like microcelebrity or influencer, requires the ethnographer to not only be flexible but also cognizant of the fact that the internet is embedded, embodied, and everyday. The internet's apparent status today as a key infrastructure of our lives and as a significant cultural object requires that we 're-foreground the internet' in our analysis (p. 9). It is obviously embedded in our day-to-day activities. While big internet corporations and their businesses are located in North America, for many people the internet 'sticks' to a specific context and location. The internet is embodied as it is integrated in our sense of being and how we act in the world; the innovations of the internet of things and wearables are the most visible examples of its embodiment. Lastly, it is everyday because its role as an infrastructure in our lives has rendered it banal and unremarkable (pp. 14–15). An ethnography for the internet, in essence, requires the presence and immersion of an ethnographer in(to) not simply the online as a site of study but also the more complex and messy 'offline' sites. An ethnographic work of an internet phenomenon has to be multi-sited, multi-modal, and in pursuit of making sense of different connections and conditions (i.e., a conjuncture) (pp. 19–29). Extending Hine's conceptualization of ethnography for the internet, I have found the following key strategies in studying religious influencers essential.

One key strategy of this approach is the need to be sensitive to socio-cultural context and critical of technological determinism and discourses around 'big data'. This includes addressing the specificities of contexts and affordances of popular social media platforms like Instagram and Twitter *within* a Muslim-majority population. Religion and its practices could be considered as key variables when studying a society, and some works have created generative analysis from this, particularly its impact on politics as it is conventionally defined (Sumaktoyo et al., 2016). Nevertheless, religiosity has long been a part of social struggles; it is multifaceted and not easily measurable. The work of Merlyna Lim on Egyptian online social movements demonstrates the larger historical context of innovative media uses by activists informing the set of repertoires available to them, which involve interpretations of Islamic teachings enmeshed with a localized understanding of liberal and Islamist politics (Lim, 2012). Further, Asef Bayat (2013) shows that, while Islam as a religion obviously is influential in the everyday life of Muslims, especially where they are the majority, it is not the only mobilizing force. Islam itself is a site of struggle for different groups claiming to have the 'right' interpretation of its teachings – a feature I will discuss in the second strategy. This means that while we consider religion as an important part of the lives of Muslims and the content produced and circulated by the religious influencers, we also have to identify the changing social, cultural, political, and economic dynamics surrounding the influencers. An analysis of religious influencers in Indonesia, for example, will be based on a different set of contexts than an analysis of their counterparts in Malaysia, Brunei Darussalam, or Singapore. Of course, there will be some similarities, considering how Islam has historically been used by authorities in those Southeast Asian states. However, the contemporary upsurge of the modest lifestyle industry and creative economy in Indonesia would generate a different kind of pious lifestyle promoted by the influencers. The past and ongoing political dynamics in these spaces would also lead to different representations and expressions of 'appropriate' lifestyles; considering the fact that, for instance, the Indonesian government is turning into increasingly illiberal and conservative governance (Diprose et al., 2019), while in Malaysia, Islam is embedded in the constitution and state administration (Kloos & Berenschot, 2016). The intricacies of social and political contexts also mean that data scraping would not be as useful as an actual immersion into the religious influencers' social media accounts and the media coverage (or perhaps a lack thereof) of their influence. Because of the importance of religiosity in their representations of the self online, its manifestation could take different forms. The convenience of scraping the data from Twitter or Instagram is often proposed as a way to benefit from 'big data,' based on the assumption that it would automatically generate better knowledge (boyd & Crawford, 2012). While hashtag analysis or word clouds are fascinating outputs, the visual representations of what it means to appear pious are coded with many symbols and references that could not simply be quantified. Captions are often used creatively to emphasize or undermine what the images or videos of the posts show. Comments open up a new space to converse between the influencers and followers, and possibly even create new language to further generate relatability value and capital (Kanai, 2019) of the religious influencers. All of which would only make sense to an ethnographer who is keenly aware of the meanings of religious practices made visible by the influencer, the embedded political moment, the current economic dynamics, the absence or intense presence of certain events and issues (most probably due to advertorial commitments but could also be caused by censorship and regulations), and the lifestyle the influencer promotes.

Second, I suggest the importance of understanding how the 'field sites,' when studying religious influencers, may consist of religious institutions and virtues represented on social media posts and embodied in everyday life that require a genuine understanding of rituals, traditions, and critical interpretations of religious orthodoxy. This extends the first strategy to further consider how religious practices are deployed and made visible by the religious influencers. Orthodoxy in Islam pulls certain references of religious practices into a central tenet that appears stable and rarely contestable. In the case of female religious influencers, the veil is a significant feature of their representations of piety. They could creatively interpret the veiling practice and modest dressing – some even had to undergo public questioning of the appropriateness of their veils. However, as Talal Asad suggests, Islamic orthodoxy is based on the idea of 'the correct models' to which practices and rituals have to conform (1986, p. 15). Therefore, while there can be creative and innovative expressions of piety and religiosity, the religious influencers' involvement in Islamic teachings has to be based on genuine interest in learning about Islam. This also means that ethnographers of religious influencers need to understand the different meanings of religious commitment in relation to their economic and commercial interests. Daromir Rudnyckyj aptly argues that amongst Indonesian Muslims, 'the link between corporate success and religious piety is calculated by design' (2010, p. 145). This suggests that while some critical take on the religious influencers' representations of piety may show class inequality, it is also important that they may genuinely understand worldly success and being rich as ways to articulate their religious commitment of Islamic teachings.

Lastly, it is also important to be mindful of the gendered dynamics of the religious influencer market in Indonesia and their impact on what gets to be considered politically influential. While young male religious influencers, like the Pemuda Hijrah group, have started to emerge in Indonesia (Temby, 2018), we have to remember that, for a very long time, social movements that are male-led would be quickly seen as politically significant while women have to enter the formal political stage first (usually by actively participating in the electoral process) before they could be seen as politically active. Ruth Lister, over two decades ago, reminded us that women have long been historically excluded from citizenship, not just in its formal practices (in elections or parliamentary processes) but also in many theoretical considerations, often to justify a universalized definition (2003, pp. 68–70). This is where the role of (new) media becomes important. Young women in different parts of the world have long dedicated 'private' spaces to express their social and political concerns due to the persistence of exclusion perpetuated by their male peers and paternalistic adults (Harris, 2001; McRobbie, 1991). Creativity and do-it-yourself practices facilitated by different forms of media like zines, internet online forums, and social media accounts become a way to express their discontents and their desire to build connections with other young women (Goulding, 2015; Harris, 2008). For young Muslim women, in places where they are the minority, social media has helped shape a public space for them, enacting and reconstructing their identity (Kavakci & Kraeplin, 2017; Pennington, 2018a, 2018b). Clearly, what is politically influential is shaped by the social, cultural, and political contexts that are gendered. An analyst interested in studying religious influencers, therefore, has to be critical of any claims that hide the intricacies of sexual and gender politics.

## CONCLUSION

The emergence of religious influencers as a new kind of influencers and microcelebrities in our already hypermediated sociality marks a moment of intensifying mediated religious expressions; we are witnessing a more complicated picture of Muslim publicity than the one Dale F. Eickelman and John W. Anderson (2003) conceptually ushered in in the late 1990s. The speed and access of technology in addition to the decentralization of religious authority have opened more opportunities for Muslims, old or young, and coming from different socio-economic backgrounds. The ease of travel and migration have also reshaped Muslim communities globally. While in many parts of the world the 'West versus the East' discourse still prevails, religious influencers are more interested in creatively expressing their piety and making sure that their posts are circulating fast and wide enough to convince their followers that becoming (more) religious is exciting. They also cannot be subsumed under one social or cultural location. The connections between female religious influencers in Southeast Asia and in Europe may be built not just because of their religious identity but also class and cosmopolitan lifestyles. Future studies on the cultural politics of religious influencers would find how class distinctions significantly play a part in building the image of creative, successful, and influential Muslims on social media. For upper-middle-class Muslims, social media and digital tools easily facilitate the melding of their commercial, political, and religious interests. The same may not be true for those coming from the lower-middle class with limited financial and cultural capital. In presenting some of my research experiences, I hope that future scholarships and analyses on religious influencers will provide the comprehensive and critical examinations they deserve.

## REFERENCES


Abidin, C. (2015). Communicative intimacies: Influencers and perceived interconnectedness. *Ada: A Journal of Gender, New Media, and Technology*, *8*.

Abidin, C. (2016a). 'Aren't these just young, rich women doing vain things online?' Influencer selfies as subversive frivolity. *Social Media+ Society*, *2*(2), 1–17.

Abidin, C. (2016b). Visibility labour: Engaging with Influencers' fashion brands and #OOTD advertorial campaigns on Instagram. *Media International Australia*, *161*(1), 86–100.

Abidin, C., & Brown, M.L. (2018). *Microcelebrity Around the Globe: Approaches in Cultures of Internet Fame*. Emerald Group.

Asad, T. (1986). *The Idea of an Anthropology of Islam*. Center for Contemporary Arab Studies, Georgetown University.

Bayat, A. (2013). *Life as Politics: How Ordinary People Change the Middle East* (Second Edition). Stanford University Press.

Baym, N.K., & boyd, d. (2012). Socially mediated publicness: An introduction. *Journal of Broadcasting & Electronic Media*, *56*(3), 320–329. https://doi.org/10.1080/08838151.2012.705200.

Bentley, K., Chu, C., Nistor, C., Pehlivan, E., & Yalcin, T. (2021). Social media engagement for global influencers. *Journal of Global Marketing*, *34*(3), 205–19. https://doi.org/10.1080/08911762.2021.1895403.

Berlant, L. (1997). *The Queen of America Goes to Washington City: Essays on Sex and Citizenship*. Duke University Press.

Berlant, L. (2008). *The Female Complaint: The Unfinished Business of Sentimentality in American Culture*. Duke University Press.

Beta, A.R. (2014). Hijabers: How young urban Muslim women redefine themselves in Indonesia. *International Communication Gazette*, *76*(4–5), 377–89. https://doi.org/10.1177/1748048514524103.

Beta, A.R. (2019a). Commerce, piety and politics: Indonesian young Muslim women's groups as religious influencers. *New Media & Society*, *21*(10), 2140–2159. https://doi.org/10.1177/1461444819838774.

Beta, A.R. (2019b). Young Muslim women as digital citizens in Indonesia: Advocating conservative religious outlook. *ISEAS Perspective*, *2019/39*.

Beta, A.R. (2020). The Muslimah intimate public: Re-considering contemporary Da'wa activists in Indonesia. *Asiascape: Digital Asia*, *7*(1–2), 20–41. https://doi.org/10.1163/22142312-BJA10002.

boyd, d., & Crawford, K. (2012). Critical questions for big data. *Information, Communication & Society*, *15*(5), 662–79. https://doi.org/10.1080/1369118X.2012.678878.

Brenner, S. (1996). Reconstructing self and society: Javanese Muslim women and 'the veil.' *American Ethnologist*, *23*(4), 673–97. https://doi.org/10.1525/ae.1996.23.4.02a00010.

Bunt, G.R. (2009). *iMuslims: Rewiring the House of Islam*. Hurst & Co.

Diprose, R., McRae, D., & Hadiz, V.R. (2019). Two decades of reformasi in Indonesia: Its illiberal turn. *Journal of Contemporary Asia*, *49*(5), 691–712.

Eickelman, D.F., & Anderson, J.W. (Eds.) (2003). *New Media in the Muslim World: The Emerging Public Sphere*. Indiana University Press.

Frolov, A. (2020, November 16). Where is influencer marketing heading in 2021? *Talking Influence*. https://talkinginfluence.com/2020/11/16/where-is-influencer-marketing-heading-in-2021/.

Goulding, C. (2015). The spaces in which we appear to each other: The pedagogy of resistance stories in Zines by Asian American riot grrrls. *Journal of Cultural Research in Art Education*, *32*, 161–89.

Grossberg, L. (2010). *Cultural Studies in the Future Tense*. Duke University Press.

Hall, S., Critcher, C., Jefferson, T., Clarke, J., & Roberts, B. (2013). *Policing the Crisis: Mugging, the State and Law and Order* (Second Edition). Red Globe Press.
Harris, A. (2001). Revisiting bedroom culture: New spaces for young women's politics. *Hecate*, *27*(1), 128.
Harris, A. (2008). Young women, late modern politics, and the participatory possibilities of online cultures. *Journal of Youth Studies*, *11*(5), 481–95. https://doi.org/10.1080/13676260802282950.
Hefner, R.W. (2000). *Civil Islam: Muslims and Democratization in Indonesia*. Princeton University Press.
Hew, W.W. (2018). The art of Dakwah: Social media, visual persuasion and the Islamist propagation of Felix Siauw. *Indonesia and the Malay World*, *46*(134), 61–79. https://doi.org/10.1080/13639811.2018.1416757.
Highfield, T. (2016). *Social Media and Everyday Politics*. Polity.
Hine, C. (2015). *Ethnography for the Internet: Embedded, Embodied and Everyday*. Bloomsbury Academic.
Jones, C. (2010). Materializing piety: Gendered anxieties about faithful consumption in contemporary urban Indonesia. *American Ethnologist*, *37*(4), 617–37.
Kanai, A. (2019). *Gender and Relatability in Digital Culture: Managing Affect, Intimacy and Value*. Palgrave Macmillan.
Kavakci, E., & Kraeplin, C.R. (2017). Religious beings in fashionable bodies: The online identity construction of hijabi social media personalities. *Media, Culture & Society*, *39*(6), 850–868. https://doi.org/10.1177/0163443716679031.
Kloos, D., & Berenschot, W. (2016). Citizenship and Islam in Malaysia and Indonesia. In W. Berenschot, H.S. Nordholt & L. Bakker (Eds.), *Citizenship and Democratization in Southeast Asia* (pp. 178–210). Brill.
Lewis, R. (2015). *Muslim Fashion: Contemporary Style Cultures*. Duke University Press.
Lim, M. (2012). Clicks, cabs, and coffee houses: Social media and oppositional movements in Egypt, 2004–2011. *Journal of Communication*, *62*(2), 231–48.
Lister, R. (2003). *Citizenship: Feminist Perspectives* (Second Edition). Palgrave Macmillan.
Marwick, A.E. (2015). Instafame: Luxury selfies in the attention economy. *Public Culture*, *27*(1 (75)), 137–60. https://doi.org/10.1215/08992363-2798379.
McRobbie, A. (1991). *Feminism and Youth Culture: From 'Jackie' to 'Just Seventeen'*. Unwin Hyman.
Mendes, K., Ringrose, J., & Keller, J. (2019). *Digital Feminist Activism: Girls and Women Fight Back against Rape Culture*. Oxford University Press.
Mohamad, S.M. (2021). Micro-celebrity practices in Muslim-majority states in Southeast Asia. *Popular Communication*, *19*(3), 235–49. https://doi.org/10.1080/15405702.2021.1913492.
Nisa, E.F. (2018). Creative and lucrative Daʿwa: The visual culture of Instagram amongst Female Muslim youth in Indonesia. *Asiascape: Digital Asia*, *5*, 1–32. https://doi.org/10.1163/22142312-12340085.
Pennington, R. (2018a). Making space in social media: #MuslimWomensDay in Twitter. *Journal of Communication Inquiry*, *42*(3), 199–217. https://doi.org/10.1177/0196859918768797.
Pennington, R. (2018b). Social media as third spaces? Exploring Muslim identity and connection in Tumblr. *International Communication Gazette*, *80*(7), 620–636. https://doi.org/10.1177/1748048518802208.
Peterson, K.M. (2020). The unruly, loud, and intersectional Muslim woman: Interrupting the aesthetic styles of Islamic fashion images on Instagram. *International Journal of Communication*, *14*, 20.
Ramos, I.Q., & Cownie, F. (2020). Female Environmental Influencers on Instagram. In S. Yesiloglu & J. Costello (Eds.), *Influencer Marketing*. Routledge.

Rudnyckyj, D. (2010). *Spiritual Economies: Islam, Globalization, and the Afterlife of Development*. Cornell University Press.
Senft, T.M. (2008). *Camgirls: Celebrity and Community in the Age of Social Networks*. Peter Lang.
Senft, T.M. (2013). Microcelebrity and the Branded Self. In J. Hartley, J. Burgess & A. Bruns (Eds.), *A Companion to New Media Dynamics* (pp. 346–354). Wiley-Blackwell.
Sumaktoyo, N.G., Ottati, V., & Untoro, V. (2016). The paradoxical religiosity effect: Religion and politics in Indonesia and the United States. *Politics and Religion*, *9*(3), 481–507.
Temby, Q. (2018, June 30). Shariah, dakwah, and rock 'n' roll: Pemuda Hijrah in Bandung—New Mandala. *New Mandala*. https://www.newmandala.org/shariah-dakwah-rock-n-roll-pemuda-hijrah-bandung/.
Tsurayya, G. (2019, April 16). *Rasakan dengan hati dan minta petunjuk Nya* [Instagram post]. https://www.instagram.com/p/BwUOEVWHqek/.
Tufekci, Z. (2013). 'Not this one': Social movements, the attention economy, and microcelebrity networked activism. *American Behavioral Scientist*, *57*(7), 848–70. https://doi.org/10.1177/0002764213479369.
Van Dijck, J., Poell, T., & De Waal, M. (2018). *The Platform Society: Public Values in a Connective World*. Oxford University Press.
Warburton, E. (2020). Deepening Polarization and Democratic Decline in Indonesia. In T. Carothers & A. O'Donohue (Eds.), *Political Polarization in South and Southeast Asia: Old Divisions, New Dangers* (pp. 25–40). Carnegie Endowment for International Peace. http://www.jstor.org/stable/resrep26920.8.

# 6. The populist rhetoric of crowdfunding on digital media

*Roei Davidson*

## INTRODUCTION

The crowd is central to the discourses and practices of populist politicians and political thinkers (Le Bon, 2017). It is also central to contemporary mediated economic practices such as crowdfunding and crowdsourcing (Brabham, 2013; Davidson, 2019). These practices constitute online attempts to harness the resources – money, time, intelligence – of a large group of people to achieve various objectives, including civic ones.

Crowdfunding involves the use of digital networks – dedicated crowdfunding platforms, social media platforms, e-mail – and interpersonal networks to raise financing for a planned project or one that is already underway. Individuals and groups who seek financing (i.e., project founders) craft an online pitch, often combining text and video. In one common model, founders promise rewards tied to a particular level of financial support and set in advance the amount of money they wish to raise from the crowd. There are also platforms that fund projects through the sale of equity, through lending, or by asking for donations with no expectation of a tangible return. Projects involve a vast array of goals, including funding cultural projects (films, videogames, plays, books, news, etc.) and gadgets, as well as the life goals and necessities of individuals (from education to healthcare). More recently some platforms (e.g., Patreon) have emerged to allow funders to support creators repeatedly through a subscription model. Civic crowdfunding (Davies, 2015) involves raising money for, among other things, political campaigns, public facilities, or legal costs. The contemporary projects analyzed here are civic in nature as they putatively aim to fund the debt of a country, the legal costs of a soldier, and the erection of a border barrier. Promoters of these approaches identify pre-digital antecedents. The civic dimension of crowdfunding is central to how crowdfunding platforms present their contemporary activities, as many crowdfunding platforms cite the role Joseph Pulitzer and the *New York World* played, in the nineteenth century, in persuading the public to collectively fund a pedestal for the Statue of Liberty as an antecedent and inspiration (Kazmark, 2013).

I wish to ask: how are populist discourses deployed in mediated crowd mechanisms? To do so, I empirically examine a purposive cross-national set of prominent civic crowdfunding case studies – historical and contemporary – as a means of identifying how mediated crowd practices leverage populist discourses and digital opportunity structures to achieve their ends. I examine four prominent civic crowdfunding projects to consider the ways these projects use populist discourses for instrumental and/or poetic (Larkin, 2013) ends, to instrumentally fund a practical project and/or to poetically raise awareness and support for a political project. The historical project involves a nineteenth-century media effort to fund the Statue of Liberty pedestal and will rely on secondary sources (Berenson, 2012). The three contemporary projects are a European crowdfunding project to create a 'Greek Bailout Fund,' an American project to fund the building of a wall between Mexico and the US, and an Israeli project to create a legal defense fund for an Israeli soldier accused (and later found guilty) of killing a captured terrorist.

## THEORETICAL FRAMEWORK

### Researching Crowdfunding

Just as much political science is traditionally focused on how people vote and for whom,[1] most crowdfunding studies have focused on who people fund. Early seminal work showed that despite its reliance on digital networks, social constraints shape funding patterns, and hence projects physically located in creative cultural hubs (such as New York City or San Francisco) were more likely to experience crowdfunding success (Mollick, 2014). Individuals who have a large network of weak ties are more likely to crowdfund repeatedly (Davidson & Poor, 2015). Successful crowdfunding demands founders labor intensively to promote the project by engaging both online and off with friends, family, and strangers (Hui et al., 2014). A founder's identity also shapes their crowdfunding experiences. Women are under-represented on the prominent crowdfunding platform Kickstarter. However, those women who crowdfund are more successful than men. Moreover, both men and women tend to support projects initiated by entrepreneurs of the same gender (Gafni et al., 2021). Race also shapes crowdfunding experiences as African American men receive less funding than white men. In an experimental study participants rated the same project as lower in quality when they thought the initiator was African American (Younkin & Kuppuswamy, 2018). Clearly, as has been illustrated in general (Schradie, 2020), the use of digital networks does not erase social inequalities in the realm of crowdfunding.

### Populism and the Online Environment

While more research is being conducted and will be conducted in the future on how various characteristics of the founders, the pitches they craft, and the products they wish to fund shape their ability to raise money, I wish in this chapter to briefly consider crowdfunding through a more cultural prism. Crowdfunding is not merely a functional communicative act conducted to raise money for a defined goal. It is also an expressive act: in the process of crowdfunding founders craft elaborate pages and social media posts and sometimes whole websites, and they interact with prospective and existing supporters offline and online. Hence, a project constitutes a meaningful communicative act whether a founder successfully reaches their funding goal or not. Crowdfunding is not only a communicative act of transmission (transmitting a funding message in the hopes of a return transmission of money) but rather a communicative act of ritual as the crowdfunding effort constitutes a means of creating and maintaining a community or movement.[2]

In contemporary politics, populism has gained traction as an ideology that political actors use to celebrate a (sometimes) imagined shared history and identity. I will examine here how populist actors employ crowdfunding as a rhetorical tool for ritual just as much as for transmission. Populist ideology champions 'the people' as the ultimate political sovereigns – 'virtuous, pure or wise' (Engesser et al., 2017, p. 1282). From a populist perspective the people's sovereignty has been usurped by an illegitimate elite in collaboration with 'others' belonging to various out-groups (Engesser et al., 2017; Reinemann et al., 2016). A populist leader is required to reassert the power of the people, often rejecting adherence to accepted procedures while establishing a direct connection with the people (Krämer, 2017).

The online circumvention of established gatekeepers such as news organizations through the use of social media could create an opportunity structure compatible with populism as it allows populist leaders to maintain a direct communication line with followers (Engesser et al., 2017). In many network contexts a minority of actors enjoy the majority of attention (Benkler, 2016; Hindman, 2018; Shaw & Hill, 2014), providing populist leaders with the opportunity to dominate political discourse. For example, on Twitter, increasingly a small proportion of users produce the majority of content consumed and retweeted on the network (Leetaru, 2019). Latin American populist leaders seem to take advantage of this network structure for one-way messaging through social media, often criticizing the mass media and other elites and rarely interacting with the public (Waisbord & Amado, 2017). The tendency for like-minded people to congregate online around partisan media sources (Benkler et al., 2018) can further amplify the populist message. Some have argued that the negative, emotional, and simplistic discursive style characteristic of populism is compatible with an online environment in which content is abundant and attention scarce because such a style could attract attention more easily (Engesser et al., 2017). A prominent populist party (Spain's Podemos) employed internal online plebiscites of party members to gain approval for leadership decisions, suggesting that even parties who espouse an egalitarian rhetoric use digital networks to legitimate hierarchical control (de Nadal, 2021). Whether populist or not political movements around the world have been adept at rapidly mobilizing large numbers of people, often harnessing digital infrastructures to do so, though many movements struggle to develop long-term organizational structures that allow them to consolidate political power and replace governing elites (Tufekci, 2017). Their short-term success could be due to the lower cost of producing and disseminating messages, which allows even materially poor movements to rapidly mobilize large publics. Such low costs are evident in contemporary crowdfunding. While past attempts at raising money from the public demanded access to the costly mass media or to affluent backers, establishing a crowdfunding project page is free (though platforms usually take a commission from successful projects) as is access to social media networks. Hence, some have argued digital crowdfunding could be a promising avenue for raising money and awareness for diverse civic goals.

This chapter's focus on crowdfunding answers the call to study 'how populist actors are exploiting the affordances of digital technology to replace political parties with plebiscites' (de Nadal, 2021, p. 16), examining crowdfunding as an example of a class of socially mediated activities which also includes online petitions that populist actors use to seek political and economic support from the public while circumventing traditional elite gatekeepers.

## The Historical Portrayal and Poetics of Technologies

Emerging media technologies are often presented in patterned ways. 'Founding myths' related to how audiences first encountered a medium or used it are central to these presentations. They provide 'powerful narratives to represent their nature and their role in our society and … [help to] structure early claims about the media effects' (Natale, 2016, p. 437). The developers of novel online mechanisms can instrumentally and ritualistically use the past to clarify the contemporary nature of such mechanisms. The choice crowdfunding entrepreneurs made to relate the funding mechanism to the Pulitzer campaign to fund the Statue of Liberty pedestal (Garber, 2013; Kazmark, 2013) constitutes such a case. In identifying the original campaign's populist dimension and a contemporary crowdfunding platform's adoption of the Pulitzer campaign as its predecessor, I illustrate the populist potential that resides in crowdfunding and similar technologies.

The populist dimension could also be rooted in the poetic aspects of crowdfunding as a socio-technical system. Political actors often construct socio-technical projects – dams, waterways, telecommunication and transportation networks – as a poetic act that projects political power through its sheer existence even when these acts fail to achieve their stated technical goals (Larkin, 2013). The dam need not produce electricity in order for its constructing regime to hail the dam and – by association – the regime's magnificence. Similarly, the act of crowdfunding need not culminate in success in order to make an influential political statement. By its very temporal nature, crowdfunding is future-oriented. In most cases, it promises a project, product, or service that does not yet exist but rather will exist when the crowd funds it. In its focus on the future, crowdfunding explicitly echoes the utopian discourse surrounding information technologies when they emerge (Carey, 1992b), not only in the discourse that surrounds it but in its very grammar, as each crowdfunding project tells a story about a better future. Finally, in most crowdfunding projects there is explicit or implicit criticism of the status quo – an argument that society or the economy as they currently operate do not provide a much-needed service or product that only the project can provide. This denial of the status quo is compatible with the criticism of elites (the guardians of the status quo) that is central to populism.

# POPULISM IN CONTEMPORARY CROWDFUNDING AND ITS ANTECEDENTS

## The Statue of Liberty Campaign

### Early attempts in France

As noted above, the fundraising efforts of *New York World* publisher Joseph Pulitzer serve as a prominent founding myth for contemporary crowdfunding platforms. Secondary sources suggest that the statue's promoters focused at first on gaining political and financial support from elites in France and the US (Berenson, 2012). Only later did its promoters use the media to appeal for popular support.

In France, such an appeal appeared in the lead article in *Le Petit Journal*'s (*LPJ*'s) issue of 29 September 1875, which presented the project and called on readers to financially support it. *LPJ*, founded in 1863, was the first popular newspaper in France. It took advantage of the expansion of literacy following the introduction of compulsory elementary education and the growth of an urban population to serve a popular and newly literate section of French society. In contrast to existing elite papers, *LPJ* was 'ecumenically apolitical' (Charle, 2009, p. 103). Its owner from 1873 was well connected to elites and wished to use its pages to distance the popular classes from revolutionary ideas (Delporte, 1999). The newspaper emphasized coverage of crime, accidents, and other non-political daily developments ('*faits-divers*'), and serialized fiction, and was priced very cheaply, rapidly attaining the highest circulation figures of any newspaper in France (Charle, 2009).

This institutional context suggests the newspaper's coverage of the venture had the potential to position the venture as a populist one. One *LPJ* article (Grimm, 1875) emphasized the nationalist aspects of this project. It noted the statue was planned to be larger than a statue 'the Germans had recently inaugurated' (author's translation), four years after France lost a war to Prussia. It expressed the hope that 'all the French without party distinctions' would subscribe to it, illustrating a populist emphasis on a unitary people. The organizing committee's official call published immediately after the article also emphasized the venture's popular dimensions, stating that 'this monument will be constructed by the two peoples [French and American] … Thus, we will affirm, through this indestructible souvenir, the friendship that the blood shed by our fathers sealed between our two nations' (*Le Petit Journal*, 1875).

Similar patriotic themes were evident in *L'illustration*, an illustrated weekly which catered to the relatively affluent middle class and combined illustrated accounts of politics, entertainment, and literature (Charle, 2009). The magazine included an image of the planned statue (more than ten years before its final completion) towering in the forefront above Manhattan, Brooklyn, and New Jersey, its crown emitting rays of light above the New York harbor. The weekly noted that a group of 'recognized and appreciated' American and French 'friends' thought that the statue would be a way of associating the 'two peoples in a joint expression of friendship' (*L'illustration*, 1875). It added that the statue would be erected close to where blood was first shed in the cause of American independence. 'The monument must be executed by the two people, associated in this fraternal union as they were once [united].' These pronouncements – verbal and visual – illustrate how funding efforts can have a populist poetic dimension: in the very call to readers to fund such a project the newspaper constructs the people as patriotic.

However, this effort took many years to come to fruition. Later, its promoters relied on income from exhibition tickets, gala tickets, merchandising, and the sale of commercial rights to the statue for use in unrelated marketing efforts. Only near the end of the fundraising effort when more money was needed to fund the pedestal did Pulitzer come into the picture (Berenson, 2012; Khan, 2010).

**Later American efforts**

Relying on secondary sources and an analysis of the first week of promotion the *New York World* gave the effort, we find the celebration of the people and the denigration of elites typical of populism in the discourse and practices Joseph Pulitzer deployed through his paper to raise funds from his reading public for the statue pedestal. Pulitzer criticized the moneyed American elites both for their stinginess and for the very idea that they should be the ones to finance a statue that embodied the concept of American liberty. He argued elites opposed republican ideals, including the equality all citizens enjoyed. In the funding appeals he published in the *World*, Pulitzer personalized the statue, presenting it as a concrete popular character in opposition to American elites (Berenson, 2012, p. 83).

The *World* campaign took the voice of its readers (Hall et al., 1978) by selectively weaving letters to the editor into its funding campaign. It also took the voice of other newspapers. It constructed an enthusiastic public for the statue and the newspaper. Simultaneously, it used these voices as testimonials of its commercial and political power as a representative of the popular will. The pedestal campaign doubled as a self-promotional campaign for the newspaper's commercial potential. The coverage included several illustrations of how readers responded directly to the newspaper's appeals. Adjacent to the coverage were self-promotional ads for the advertising effectiveness of the *World* in which the crowd was visually represented as coalesced around the newspaper.

The campaign emphasized the harmonious actions of the people and the newspaper: The *World* quoted a letter to the editor stating that 'the people are behind you [the newspaper]' (*New York World*, 1885c). Although references to elites are less salient, they are mostly negative. The newspaper notes a few times that Congress had failed to appropriate the money needed to fund the pedestal, attributing that failure to the self-interest of parochial politicians. Economic elites are also criticized and contrasted with the common public. In its campaign the newspaper quoted another letter: 'let it not be said that our millionaires should complete the erection of the statue. Let us all contribute a little' (A Patriot, 1885).

Elsewhere, the *New York World* used readers' contributions to orchestrate a populist call and response. It employed the serial nature of the campaign to illustrate the power of the newspaper to shape the behavior of self-interested elites. On 18 March, the *World* quoted a letter to the editor: '"We, as workmen, poor in pocket, but rich in patriotism, contribute our mite in the hope that the example will be followed by workmen generally and shame the close-fisted millionaires" (signed "THE EMPLOYEES")' (The Employees, 1885). A day later, on 19 March, it published a letter sent by an heir to one of the largest commercial fortunes in the US, William Vanderbilt, and the prominent railway tycoon, Jay Gould: 'Please find inclosed $500 (confederate note) as a subscription for the Bartholdi Statue, and don't fail to acknowledge same in your columns. So that we may no longer be called the "close-fisted millionaires"' (Vanderbilt & Gould, 1885).

Several mechanisms evident in the *World*'s campaign presage mechanisms central to modern crowdfunding – rewards (e.g., two double gold eagles promised to the most generous supporter; *New York World*, 1885d), a reliance on and active appeal for use of interpersonal networks, constant updates on funding figures (*New York World*, 1885a), posting the names of supporters, and self-promoting the platform by quoting other intermediaries (as crowdfunding platforms do when boasting about mainstream awards funded projects receive) (Davidson, 2019). The latter is evident, for example, on 20 March when the *New York World* cites the *Trenton Times* writing that 'The New York World has started another boom for the Bartholdi Pedestal' (*New York World*, 1885b).

**The crowdfunding industry retells the Statue of Liberty story**

The prominent crowdfunding platform Kickstarter presents on its corporate blog the Pulitzer campaign as the main source of funding for the Statue of Liberty pedestal: 'the Statue of Liberty had no pedestal on which to stand in New York Harbor. Joseph Pulitzer, publisher of the *New York World*, launched a project for the construction of one … More than 120,000 people from around the world pledged $102,006 to the project' (Kazmark, 2013). Such an account glosses over the fact that the Pulitzer drive provided only a minority of the funds, that a lot of the funds came from elites, that the fundraising effort took over five years, and that a lot of the funds came from tickets to exhibitions and performances, and through the sale of merchandise and commercial rights to use the statue's likeness before Pulitzer adopted the project and helped drive it to completion (Berenson, 2012; Khan, 2010). Emphasizing the role the Pulitzer effort played in funding a globally known landmark, while ignoring the many other efforts involved in raising the funding needed to build the pedestal, frames crowdfunding as an effective popular tool for achieving significant public goals.

The emphasis placed on the Pulitzer effort can also be seen as 'a legitimation tactic' (Natale, 2016, p. 439). The Statue of Liberty has become a floating signifier of nationalism dear to both the political right (the American nation as the exceptional epitome of liberty) and the left (a nation that welcomes immigrants). Such political ecumenism is useful for an internet platform wishing to appeal to a broad audience of entrepreneurs and funders much as it was useful for Pulitzer, who was trying to assemble a lucrative mass audience for advertisers.

## Contemporary Cases of Populist Crowdfunding

The three contemporary projects I examine have very different goals from one another – funding the debt of a European country, financing a border wall, and supporting a soldier's legal defense. In addition, their initiators posted them within different political contexts – the European Union debt crisis, the American immigration debate, and Israel's occupation of the West Bank. Nevertheless, the three projects foreground populist arguments when lionizing the people and criticizing elites. Utilizing these arguments, they all emphasize how a direct private funding mechanism can allow the people to exercise their political will and achieve political goals that politicians have failed to achieve using standard political procedures.

In all three projects the people appear as unitary actors who through their financial support can solve grave political crises. The European project's sub-title is 'CrowdFunding a bailout fund for Greece. By the people, for the people' (Feeney, 2015). The people appear in the American project's title in its earliest publicly archived version: 'We The People BUILT the Wall!' (Kolfage, 2019) and are implicit in the project's trademarked name 'WE BUILD THE WALL.' In the Israeli project's opening paragraph, the project's initiator proclaims: '[we] do not leave the injured behind, full stop. Join us in enlisting in support of Elor Azaria [the on-trial soldier] and his family "because such camaraderie"[3] is not a slogan – it is an essential expression of our strength as a society and a people' (Organization for the Defence of IDF Soldiers, 2016). Following that, the pitch takes on the form of a letter as it addresses the 'Dear people of Israel' and calls on them to contribute to the soldier's defense, echoing the use of letters in the Pulitzer Statue of Liberty campaign.

All three crowdfunding projects criticize elites. The bail-out project contrasts ineffectual self-serving elites with the people: 'European ministers [are] flexing their muscles and posturing over whether they can help the Greek people of [*sic*] not. Why don't we the people just sort it instead?' (Feeney, 2015). This contrast between 'dissolute' elites and the 'worthy' people repeats itself throughout the pitch; for example, when the pitch notes that 'Europeans are pretty generous on the whole, maybe Ms Merkel [the then German Chancellor] and Mr Cameron [the then British Prime Minister] are the exception.' Such a contrast is also prominent in the crowdfunding of the border wall: 'we the people will provide border security for our citizens since Democrats are failing to protect our communities.'

All three projects highlight elite failures when they address the public: 'If you are sick and tired of watching politicians in both parties obstructing President Trump's plan to build a wall on our southern border, then you've come to the right place. We The People are coming together to start building segments of Border wall' (Kolfage, 2019). The Israeli project takes the voice of the public, a discursive strategy common among populist actors (Hall et al., 1978), when it uses the first-person-plural address form to contrast the public and elites: 'We the citizens cannot do nothing and leave Elor and his family defenseless. We the citizens cannot let bureaucracy and politics trump the basic moral and friendship values we were brought up on' (Organization for the Defence of IDF Soldiers, 2016).

Finally, the demonizing of out-groups is explicit in the wall project when it notes 'Democrats are failing to protect our communities from the flow of illegal drugs and criminals.' In an updated version of the project page, it claims that the first section it built 'blocked one of the worst human- and drug-smuggling corridors in the El Paso Sector.' Utilizing an episodic frame, a project update focuses on 'one of America's greatest Border Patrol heroes … [who] was slain while protecting illegal aliens during a shootout with a vicious Mexican Cartel.' Moreover, in the pitch, immigrants are portrayed visually as a mass of dark characters marching on the Mexican side of the United States' southern border. In the other two projects, out-groups are more implicit. However, in both the European and Israeli case, the fate of the Greek economy and the accused soldier was the focus of a highly polarized debate, and therefore by linking support for the bail-out project with 'care' for 'the plight of the Greek people' and by connecting support for the accused soldier with 'basic moral' values the projects implied the opponents' immorality, positioning opponents as a political out-group.

## CONCLUSION

When appealing directly to the public for financial support, all three projects reject the procedural norms common in representative democracy in favor of the potential for direct action. Hence, these projects echo the populist tendency to criticize 'the intermediary institutions that make representative democracy possible' (de Nadal, 2021, p. 16) and replace them with direct action led by a charismatic individual. This rejection of the procedures inherent in 'bureaucracy' and 'politics' while vesting authority and money in the hands of an unelected individual suggests crowdfunding as a socially mediated practice shares the tendency of online peer production to subvert democratic decision-making while elevating charismatic individuals (Kreiss et al., 2011).

In the American project this is evident when the project founder presents himself: 'My name is Brian Kolfage and I'm a triple-amputee war veteran.' As is common on many crowdfunding platforms Kolfage's thumbnail image appears at the top of the project page, in this case with war medals on his chest. Another charismatic individual, Donald Trump, appears at the top of the project page, his right arm raised upwards in a victorious gesture, against the background of a border wall and a 'TRUMP APPROVED' stamp; see Figure 6.1 (Kolfage, 2019). The figure of the project initiator is evident in the European project even though he describes himself more modestly as a former shoe salesman and co-working-space employee. While in the Israeli project, the project founder is identified as being an organization, much of the Israeli news coverage presented the project as the initiative of a well-known right-wing television host and politician who actively promoted the project in the media (Maariv Online, 2017).

The risks involved in replacing bureaucratic politics with ad hoc online initiatives as a means of funding and overseeing massive public projects are illustrated in the

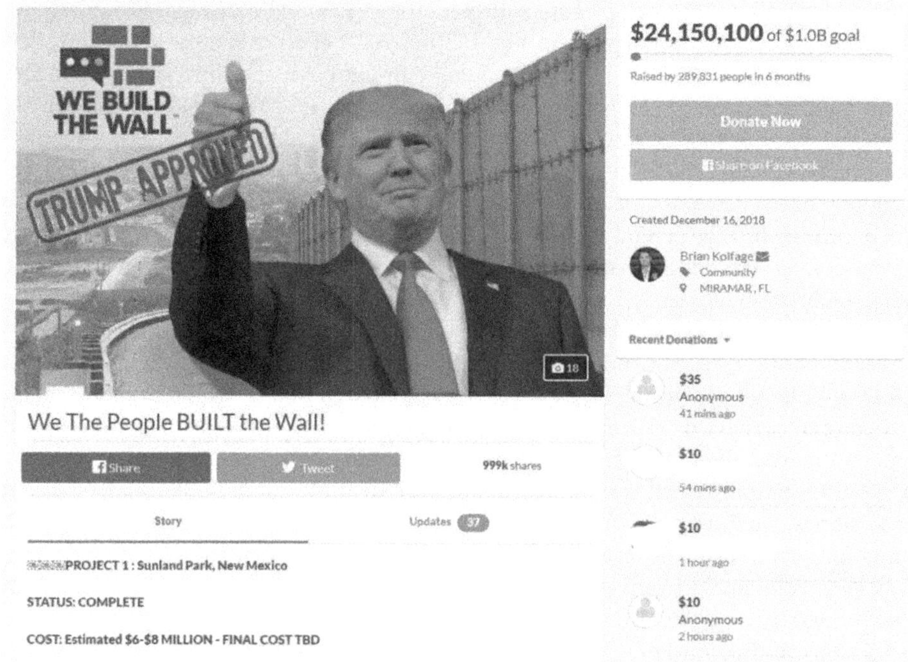


*Figure 6.1* *The top section of the 'We The People BUILT the Wall!' project page*

case of the wall project. In that case, a wall section to which the project contributed 'suffered from major erosion just months after it was finished' (Trevizo et al., 2020), and the project initiator was indicted on tax evasion and wire fraud charges related to the money raised to fund the wall (Theisen, 2021) and later pleaded guilty and sentenced to prison (Offenhartz, 2023).

The poetic nature of these populist projects resides in the fact that their funding goals are often titanic and unattainable – $5 billion in the case of the wall project and 1.6 billion euros in the case of the bail-out project, only a minuscule fraction of which was successfully raised from the crowd. While the Israeli project did achieve its much more modest financial goal, as of 2023 the legal-aid association that had initiated the project was in the process of being dissolved (*be-haliykh'ei m'chiykah*), according to a website operated by the Israeli Corporations Authority in the Israeli Justice Ministry (Guidestar, 2023). Hence, the significance of such populist projects seems to lie more in their discursive weight and the symbolic capital they provide to their initiators than in their concrete achievements. They constitute – as is common in populist politics – the triumph of short-term symbolic gain for the few over long-term collective action benefitting the many. Other digital financial experiments such as Bitcoin and blockchain systems more generally also have a distinct poetic populist dimension. At its inception, many Bitcoin enthusiasts were motivated in a time of financial crisis by the hope of disintermediating financial gatekeepers such as the state and banks, creating a system that did not rely on elites and was therefore less prone to crisis. Hence, Bitcoin is as much a cultural phenomenon as it is a financial one: 'While Bitcoin has not proven to be a practical money form in most circumstances, it has become a staging ground for debate around the cultural role of money in society' (Swartz, 2018, p. 623). Instead of constituting a stable payment system or medium of exchange it constitutes an arena for speculation in which a small minority triumphs. Both Bitcoin and the crowdfunding projects examined here hail the disintermediation of elites but paradoxically rely on the charisma of particular individuals and celebrate their success.

Future research could examine more systematically how political actors deploy crowdfunding for populist ends. It could also consider the degree to which populist discourse boosts projects' capacity to raise funds from the crowd and whether it gains public visibility for the causes it champions and shifts public opinion. More generally, the ritual aspects of crowdfunding could be examined more closely. Crowdfunding a project occurs over a duration of time and includes some standard milestones, including the first announcement of an impending project, its launch, periodic social media posts and the receipt of mass media coverage, the attainment of a project goal, and post-project events. Such standard unfolding over time is likely to have ritual aspects that are pregnant with social and political meaning, and as ritual should be studied further.

## NOTES

1. I wish to thank W. Russell Neuman for this observation. He notes that political research often focuses on voting outcomes because they are easily measurable (and one might add also receive inordinate attention in the press and on social media). Beyond this methodological tendency, from a pragmatic perspective a narrow understanding of politics as focused on voting is normatively suspect because it ignores the importance of community and institutions to the health of democratic societies (Campbell, 2004). By analogy, we should also consider more extensively the communal and institutional aspects of crowdfunding and other online economic practices.
2. On the distinction between a ritual and a transmission view of communication, see Carey (1992a).
3. This is a quote from a poem, 'The Song of Camaraderie' (*shir ha-reut*) (Gouri, 1948), written in the midst of the Israeli War of Independence and identified by its author as commemorating fallen comrades and the principle of not leaving injured comrades behind to perish on the battlefield (Ami-Or, 2018). In the crowdfunding pitch, the project's initiator equates support for the project with the aid soldiers give their injured comrades under fire. Israeli radio stations play a musical version of the poem very frequently on Israel's Memorial Day (Yachin & Tirosh, 2021), and therefore potential Jewish Israeli funders would easily recognize the allusion.

## REFERENCES

A Patriot (1885, 20 March). I send you 25 cents. *New York World*, 5.

Ami-Or, H. (2018, 15 April). Yefei ha-blorit ve-ha-toar: Ha-reut shel Haim Gouri. *Ha-Safranim*. https://blog.nli.org.il/reut/.

Benkler, Y. (2016). Degrees of freedom, dimensions of power. *Daedalus*, *145*(1), 18–32. https://doi.org/10.1162/DAED_a_00362.

Benkler, Y., Faris, R., & Roberts, H. (2018). *Network Propaganda: Manipulation, Disinformation, and Radicalization in American Politics*. Oxford University Press.

Berenson, E. (2012). *The Statue of Liberty: A Transatlantic Story*. Yale University Press.

Brabham, D.C. (2013). *Crowdsourcing*. MIT Press.

Campbell, J. (2004). The Centrality of Community to Democracy. In *Pragmatism and Values* (pp. 99–103). Brill. https://doi.org/10.1163/9789004495869_012.

Carey, J.W. (1992a). A cultural approach to communication. In *Communication as Culture* (pp. 13–36). Routledge.

Carey, J.W. (1992b). Technology and Ideology: The Case of the Telegraph. In *Communication as Culture* (pp. 201–237). Routledge.

Charle, C. (2009). *Le Siècle de la presse (1830–1939)*. Le Seuil.

Davidson, R. (2019). The role of platforms in fulfilling the potential of crowdfunding as an alternative decentralized arena for cultural financing. *Law & Ethics of Human Rights*, *13*(1).

Davidson, R., & Poor, N.D. (2015). The barriers facing artists' use of crowdfunding platforms: Personality, emotional labor, and going to the well one too many times. *New Media & Society*, *17*(2), 289–307.

Davies, R. (2015). Three provocations for civic crowdfunding. *Information, Communication & Society*, *18*(3), 342–55. https://doi.org/10.1080/1369118X.2014.989878.

Delporte, C. (1999). *Les journalistes en France: 1880–1950*. Seuil.

De Nadal, L. (2021). Populism and plebiscitarianism 2.0: How Podemos used digital platforms for organization and decision-making. *New Media & Society*, 146144482110387. https://doi.org/10.1177/14614448211038763.

Engesser, S., Fawzi, N., & Larsson, A.O. (2017). Populist online communication: Introduction to the special issue. *Information, Communication & Society*, *20*(9), 1279–92. https://doi.org/10.1080/1369118X.2017.1328525.

Feeney, T. (2015). Greek Bailout Fund. Indiegogo. https://www.indiegogo.com/projects/1324990.

Gafni, H., Marom, D., Robb, A., & Sade, O. (2021). Gender dynamics in crowdfunding (Kickstarter): Evidence on entrepreneurs, backers, and taste-based discrimination. *Review of Finance*, *25*(2), 235–74. https://doi.org/10.1093/rof/rfaa041.

Garber, M. (2013, 29 June). Kickstarters of Yore: Mozart, Lady Liberty, Alexander Pope. *The Atlantic*. https://www.theatlantic.com/technology/archive/2013/06/kickstarters-of-yore-mozart-lady-liberty-alexander-pope/277389/.

Gouri, H. (1948). Shir Ha-reut. In *The Songs* (Vol. 3, p. 256). Mossad Biyalik & Ha-kibbutz Ha-meuhad.

Grimm, T. (1875, 29 September). La statue de la liberté. *Le Petit Journal*, 1.

Guidestar (2023). The Association for the Protection of Israeli Defense Forces (registered association). https://www.guidestar.org.il/organization/580626620.

Hall, S., Critcher, C., Jefferson, T., Clarke, J., & Robert, B. (1978). *Policing the Crisis: Mugging, the State, and Law and Order*. Macmillan.

Hindman, M. (2018). *The Internet Trap: How the Digital Economy Builds Monopolies and Undermines Democracy*. Princeton University Press.

Hui, J.S., Greenberg, M.D., & Gerber, E.M. (2014). *Understanding the Role of Community in Crowdfunding Work*. ACM. https://doi.org/10.1145/2531602.2531715.

Kazmark, J. (2013). Kickstarter before Kickstarter. Kickstarter Blog. https://www.kickstarter.com/blog/kickstarter-before-kickstarter.
Khan, Y.S. (2010). *Enlightening the World: The Creation of the Statue of Liberty*. Cornell University Press.
Kolfage, B. (2019). Fundraiser by Brian Kolfage: We The People BUILT the Wall! https://web.archive.org/web/20190624113448/https://www.gofundme.com/f/thetrumpwall.
Krämer, B. (2017). Populist online practices: The function of the Internet in right-wing populism. *Information, Communication & Society*, *20*(9), 1293–1309. https://doi.org/10.1080/1369118X.2017.1328520.
Kreiss, D., Finn, M., & Turner, F. (2011). The limits of peer production: Some reminders from Max Weber for the network society. *New Media & Society*, *13*(2), 243–59. https://doi.org/10.1177/1461444810370951.
Larkin, B. (2013). The politics and poetics of infrastructure. *Annual Review of Anthropology*, *42*(1), 327–43. https://doi.org/10.1146/annurev-anthro-092412-155522.
Le Bon, G. (2017). *The Crowd*. Routledge.
Leetaru, K. (2019, 8 March). Twitter users mostly retweet politicians and celebrities. That's a big change. *Washington Post*. https://www.washingtonpost.com/politics/2019/03/08/twitter-users-mostly-retweet-politicians-celebrities-thats-big-change/.
*Le Petit Journal* (1875, 29 September). Souscription, p. 1.
*L'illustration* (1875, 9 October). Monument commémoratif de cintième anniversaire de l'indépendence des Etats-Unis, pp. 229–30.
Maariv Online (2017, 29 May). Sharon Gal is raising money again for Azaria: 'We spent over 600,000 NIS.' https://www.maariv.co.il/news/law/Article-586175.
Mollick, E. (2014). The dynamics of crowdfunding: An exploratory study. *Journal of Business Venturing*, *29*(1), 1–16. http://dx.doi.org/10.1016/j.jbusvent.2013.06.005.
Natale, S. (2016). Unveiling the biographies of media: On the role of narratives, anecdotes, and storytelling in the construction of new media's histories. *Communication Theory*, *26*(4), 431–449.
*New York World* (1885a, 19 March). A boom for the statue, p. 1.
*New York World* (1885b, 20 March). Comments of the press, p. 1.
*New York World* (1885c, 18 March). Helping a good cause, p. 4.
*New York World* (1885d, 20 March). The movement spreads, p. 1.
Offenhartz J. (2023, April 26). We Build the Wall founder sentenced to 4 years in prison. *AP News*. https://apnews.com/article/border-wall-donald-trump-steve-bannon-15db1e18f3cd46a87bc395b14b2bcf15.
Organization for the Defence of IDF Soldiers (2016). Assistance for Elor and needy warriors. https://web.archive.org/web/20160711064601/https://www.headstart.co.il/project.aspx?id=19464.
Reinemann, C., Aalberg, T., Esser, F., Strömbäck, J., & De Vreese, C.H. (2016). Populist Political Communication: Toward a Model of Its Causes, Forms, and Effects. In T. Aalberg, F. Esser, C. Reinemann, J. Strömbäck & C.H. de Vreese (Eds.), *Populist Political Communication in Europe* (pp. 22–36). Routledge.
Schradie, J. (2020). The Great Equalizer Reproduces Inequality: How the Digital Divide Is a Class Power Divide. In B. Eidlin & M. A. McCarthy (Eds.), *Political Power and Social Theory* (pp. 81–101). Emerald Group. https://doi.org/10.1108/S0198-871920200000037005.
Shaw, A., & Hill, B.M. (2014). Laboratories of oligarchy? How the iron law extends to peer production. *Journal of Communication*, *64*(2), 215–38.
Swartz, L. (2018). What was Bitcoin, what will it be? The techno-economic imaginaries of a new money technology. *Cultural Studies*, *32*(4), 623–50. https://doi.org/10.1080/09502386.2017.1416420.
The Employees (1885, 18 March). Please find inclosed $7.25. *New York World*, 5.

Theisen, T. (2021). Florida man who set up GoFundMe for Trump's border wall indicted on tax charges. *Orlando Sentinel*. https://www.orlandosentinel.com/news/florida/os-ne-florida-man-build-a-wall-tax-fraud-20210708-xjzfguiab5bsdm36ittx74tsuy-story.html.

Trevizo, P., Schwartz, J., & Churchill, L. (2020, 20 August). Nonprofit that financed a private border wall is now the focus of a corruption case. *Texas Tribune* and ProPublica. https://www.texastribune.org/2020/08/20/we-build-wall-brian-kolfage/.

Tufekci, Z. (2017). *Twitter and Tear Gas: The Power and Fragility of Networked Protest*. Yale University Press.

Vanderbilt, W.H., & Gould, J.J. (1885, 19 March). Please find inclosed $500. *New York World*, 1.

Waisbord, S., & Amado, A. (2017). Populist communication by digital means: Presidential Twitter in Latin America. *Information, Communication & Society*, *20*(9), 1330–1346. https://doi.org/10.1080/1369118X.2017.1328521.

Yachin, M., & Tirosh, N. (2021). 'A line from a song that punches you in the stomach': Music and the negotiations of cultural memory in Facebook. *Popular Music and Society*, *44*(5), 650–667. https://doi.org/10.1080/03007766.2021.1958444.

Younkin, P., & Kuppuswamy, V. (2018). The colorblind crowd? Founder race and performance in crowdfunding. *Management Science*, *64*(7), 3269–87. https://doi.org/10.1287/mnsc.2017.2774.

# 7. Social media and crisis research

*Patric R. Spence and Xialing Lin*

## INTRODUCTION

Scholars and communication professionals continue to give attention to the potential of social media for risks, crises, and emergencies. To date (April 11, 2022), a Google Scholar search with the keywords of 'social media,' 'crisis,' and 'communication' would generate over 580,000 results. Among these titles, 87.7 percent were published after 2015, and 64.5 percent were within the period 2020–2022. It is promising that more scholarly work from diverse disciplines is analyzing crisis communication on social media. Nevertheless, recommendations for its use in crisis communication and preferred research practices are largely unstructured, untested, and not agreed upon. This chapter reviews the diffusion and use of social media throughout the crisis lifecycle with attention given to different methods for studying social media use. Attention is given to the applications of two particular types of trending research methods, experimental design and big data analysis, in the studies of various risk emergencies and natural disasters. The chapter will outline successful best practices and noted failures in social media studies on the context of crises.

Compared to legacy media, where preferences and usage habits are well known, many of the research and data collection methods regarding social media use in crises are inconsistent, and replicated studies are largely missing from the literature. Moreover, there is a lack of agreement regarding methods to investigate communication and extreme events in social media. Methods are unstructured, and adherence to scientific principles of sampling, analysis, and instrumentation is inconsistent (Spence, Lachlan & Rainear, 2016b; Lin et al., 2017). Part of this comes from the diffusion of social media as a tool for crisis communication with both emergency practitioners and segments of the public. Not only was social media not explicitly designed for crisis communication, but its continual diffusion for risk management and crisis resolution has been rapid and unanticipated. This is what Rogers (2003) outlines as the reinvention process of an innovation. This reinvention and use of social media has become so prevalent that many members of the public anticipate crisis information to be available on any platform and easily accessible at any stage of a crisis. This necessitates that the study and replication of research concerning crisis and social media should be more focused.

## WHAT ASPECT OF COMMUNICATION DO WE EXAMINE?

One potential issue that may impede more standardization of risk and crisis research is how a study is situated and the questions asked. For example, one of the authors of this chapter was provided with a dataset from their doctoral advisor in 2004 (Seeger et al., 2002; Spence et al., 2005; Spence et al., 2006; Lachlan, Spence & Seeger, 2009). The dataset was collected after the 2001 September 11 terrorist attacks in the United States. Generating research questions for the literature review was difficult because there was not an abundance of information in published studies on media use preferences and terrorism in the United States. Moreover, the literature review in one of the published articles from the data examined 'vivid' media; where television was considered 'vivid' media, and radio or print outlets were considered 'non-vivid' media. This distinction was useful until considering how to address the 'internet' in the literature review. Although 2004 was not the first year of the internet, the use and access to this technology were not as saturated as compared to current levels. Moreover, the available literature did not provide much help. A source on the internet could have 'vivid' and 'non-vivid' media, with some being more or less easy to access. Thus, the literature review had disclaimers on the imprecise use of the terms applied.

Social media seems to have created some similar issues in how to best study crisis communication. Many studies have chosen to look at the platform people turn to or the messages and the platform together. This approach to the study of crisis communication and social media has provided many useful findings. For example, scholars have been analyzing the content and framing of YouTube videos in response to organizational crises and public emergencies, such as the 2009 H1N1 flu epidemic (Walton, Seitz & Ragsdale, 2012), the 2015–16 Zika virus pandemic (Bora et al., 2018), and the Huawei controversies (Zhu, Bowen & Lyu, 2022). However, another approach is to look at the affordance available through social media. This approach allows for the unique features of communication to be addressed and helps promote research that focuses more on the communication itself, which should be more timeless than a platform. As noted by Shyam Sundar, a technology 'brings with it a set of affordances or capabilities that can shape the nature of content in a given medium. In addition to dictating content, these affordances also determine the way the content is typically presented via the medium' (2008, p. 75). An advantage of examining affordances of crisis communication and social media is that it helps the generalizability of findings beyond particular platforms, and aids the practitioner in best using social media throughout the crisis lifecycle. A specific example is a study on risk messages looking at the recency of updates on Twitter (Westerman, Spence & Van Der Heide, 2014). Although the study analyzed Twitter as the medium, the examination of message speed and timing is something that is present in most social media sources that assign a timestamp or any form of chronology to a post. Therefore, the finding that a relationship exists between the timing of a message and perceptions of source credibility are useful beyond Twitter.

## EXPERIMENTS AND CRISIS COMMUNICATION

Experiments hold promise for future research in crisis communication and social media, specifically the use of experiments that have unique but underutilized roles. Although social media allows researchers to obtain and analyze actual communication throughout the crisis lifecycle, experiments provide the ability to test the effectiveness of future practices and evaluate existing practices in a controlled environment. Mentioned earlier was a study by Westerman and colleagues that focused on the speed of updates in posting risk-related information (2014). Another study by the same authors examined source credibility and the relationship of followers and follows in the context of a risk (Westerman, Spence & Van Der Heide, 2012). This study helped one better understand how the visualization of networks and the cues present impact the perceptions of message receivers. It has been used to argue the role of opinion leadership in social media and how to identify partners that the government and practitioners can use to retransmit messages.

A similar study by Lin and colleagues examined the promotion of risk messages and retweets (2016b). Specifically, the study focused on differences between messages from a stranger, an expert, and a peer (Lin et al., 2016b). This experiment was helpful because it began to fill a specific gap in the literature surrounding the influence of network ties and proximity. Although researchers have the ability to harvest communication in social media, one thing that method lacks is the ability to look at behaviors or intentions (unless expressly communicated). Experimental designs allow crisis researchers to ask questions around actions beyond reposting or responding and move into behaviors and intentions. Continuing to use the Lin et al. (2016b) study as an example, through social media harvesting a researcher has the ability to see how individuals respond to a message within the social media platform (e.g., Lin, Lachlan & Spence, 2016a); however, the ability to determine if a message causes actions or intentions to act is absent. This is where experiments bring in research that has the potential to fill a gap. Similar research has examined these effects in network size, message content, and other variables (see Lin & Spence, 2018, 2019). Thus, future experimental research can continue to examine behaviors, perceptions, and their relationship with individual networks in crisis and risk response. Moreover, these affordances of a technology can be examined across platforms to better understand if a communication act or response is based on a platform, a specific piece or aspect of the information, or a relationship.

It is also important to remember that experiments can provide us with confidence in the findings concerning communication within social media through the examination of similar features outside of social media. For example, the previously mentioned study concerning the speed of updates on Twitter (Westerman et al., 2014) highlighted the importance of how quickly a message is communicated to the public and its relationship to credibility. In the same year, another study examined what happens when the public learns about a crisis event first through either the media or the organization involved (Spence et al., 2014). In that experiment, a news report about a university shooting was used. Participants either learned about the crisis from a university press release first or the media (with subsequent conditions having more information). The act of receiving a message from an organization first is related to information speed, and the variable examined in that study was the perceived reputation of an organization. Findings from the experiment provided empirical evidence that messages from organizations experiencing crises may offset negative stakeholder responses if those messages are received first and before media accounts. Taken together with the study by Westerman et al. (2014), these experiments provide a unique glimpse into the perceptions and use of communication within a crisis in a form that is unique from other means of inquiry. These studies were extended and replicated in subsequent research (Lachlan et al., 2014a; Spence et al., 2016a).

Specific communication and the crisis lifecycle experiments also afford the opportunity to examine aspects of social media before they are diffused into disaster response. For example, the use of bots in spreading misinformation on social media is criticized (see Shao et al., 2018 for a discussion). However, in a way similar to those used to promote spam, spread misinformation, or create mistrust, bots also have the capacity to enhance crisis response.

After decisions are made concerning messages or actions, the public needs to be informed, educated, and persuaded. Communication to the public consists of a long list of procedures (stated differently, there are tasks involved with communicating to the public). When using social media, some tasks may be best suited for a human to complete, whereas other tasks can be handed off to a machine (see Lachlan et al., 2016; Rainear et al., 2019; Spence et al., 2019a; Spence et al., 2019b; Spence et al., 2021; Rainear et al., 2021). Experiments can better help understand the effectiveness, persuasiveness, and appropriateness of human or machine communication in a crisis before any implementation. A study by Edwards and colleagues (2014) conducted an experiment where participants viewed a Twitter feed by a member of the Centers for Disease Control and Prevention (CDC) or a CDC-programmed Twitterbot. All information was identical except for the source of the Twitter account (human or bot). Their results found that Twitterbots were perceived as credible, attractive, and competent in communication similarly to a human communicating the same risk message. Their study found no differences in the perceptions of source credibility and communication competence between a Twitterbot and human agents. However, the human was rated higher in task and social attraction. These results highlight that if the public is aware that an organization is using a bot for message dissemination, perceptions and reactions can be similar to what would be expected from a human communicator (Spence, 2019a).

Messages and specific sources are not the only areas open for research in crisis communication. Another aspect that experiments allow is the examination of cues within (internal or external) the platform itself and how those cues may relate to perceptions and actions of the public. Much as Twitter provides network information in many forms (followers and follows), other information is also available. For example, until 2018, Klout.com was a website and mobile app that used social media analytics to rate people according to their online influence, and the result was a 'Klout Score.' This was a piece of information immune to any manipulation from the user (DeAndrea, 2014). One study which examined the persuasiveness of the Klout Score found that perceptions of credibility increased with an increase in Klout Score (Edwards et al., 2013). Although Klout Scores no longer exist, this study highlighted the persuasiveness and use of external metrics in social media and provides crisis practitioners with ideas and support for enhancing the credibility of messages and messengers. Experiments that focus on technological affordances may provide results that are more generalizable and are more robust when technology changes.

Twitterbots, Klout Scores, and network characteristics can be studied via social media harvesting or focus groups and other methods throughout the crisis lifecycle. However, experiments offer a unique opportunity for crisis researchers to learn and improve communication. Robust experimental designs avoid threats to internal and external validity and help us have high confidence in findings (see Sawilowsky, 2007; Sawilowsky & Spence, 2007; Spence & Lachlan, 2010; Spence et al., 2016b).

In addition to the ability of experiments to provide results that are more timeless, other aspects of experiments examining social media and crisis communication involve the ability to share data. Experimental designs can take measures to produce deidentified data or be designed and conducted in a way that avoids the collection of any data making the respondent identifiable. Although safeguards can be undertaken with the harvesting of social media data, there are potentially more steps that will need to be taken to protect the identity of the message creators. Through deliberate designs, experimental data can be collected with the intent of making the data publicly available to share. The practice and discussion of open science in crisis communication have not gained much attention, however; with the value of the data collected and subsequent decisions made from that data, opening the data to other interested researchers helps with the corrective aspects of scientific inquiry. With the goal of promoting open science practices, crisis communication research can move to a greater level of transparency (Spence, 2019b). Transparency, in this case, means 'purposeful attempts to make freely available to readers more of the scientific process for a given study, which might include study design documents, stimulus materials, survey metrics, and data analysis and output files' (Bowman & Spence, 2020, pp. 708–9). Moreover, open science practices may lead to increased replication and subsequent extension of studies in crisis communication, a much desired practice.

Many experiments in crisis communication involve the use of stimuli created by the researcher or modified by the researcher for the purpose of exploring the research questions or hypotheses. For these results to be replicated and extended, access to those stimuli should be provided to other researchers. The ability to recreate stimuli in crisis communication studies is dependent on a researcher being able to follow the summary of the stimuli and procedures written up in the methods section of an article or through the original researcher providing the materials when asked. However, if a practice of publishing these materials is more common, replications may also be more common, and this is where open materials are advantageous. The problem with or absence of replication of studies has actually been labeled as 'the replication crisis' (Maxwell, Lau & Howard, 2015), and the arguments promoting the need for replication alongside the challenges are on the rise (McEwan, Carpenter & Westerman,

2018; Spence & Burns, 2020). Because of the impact and applied nature of the results in crisis communication, sharing materials should be highly promoted (for a larger discussion on open science practices, see Bowman & Keene, 2018; Lewis; 2019; Bowman & Spence, 2020; Dienlin et al., 2021).

Although experiments and scientific analysis can be considered the gold standard of research, social media creates a communication context that allows for other methods, measures, and approaches to better help us understand and develop practices for communicating in extreme events (Sawilowsky, 2007; Spence & Lachlan, 2010; Spence et al., 2016b). These methods and their subsequent findings do have the potential to suffer from a reactive measurement effect (Webb et al., 1966). That is, the measurement process used in a specific type of social scientific research may itself affect the outcome or the mere presence of a scientific observer, or the perception of being observed can have an impact on the veracity of research findings. Thus, other means of examination through social media have advantages.

## BIG DATA ANALYSIS FOR CRISIS STUDIES

Scholars from diverse disciplines have gained interest in analyzing social media data for risk and crisis studies. The growing popularity of computational methodologies has benefited from the relentless connectivity of online communities and the development of computational tools and infrastructures. Evident from previous studies (e.g., Lachlan et al., 2014b, 2016), the public and organizations have widely relied on social media for information seeking, community support, or emotional release during disasters and emergencies, leaving those digital traces retrievable for possible future analyses. However, such social media communication data are usually massive and dynamic, and keep evolving as a crisis develops.

Thus, echoing Gerbner's (1983) arguments about the backbone of communication science, in order to contribute to our understanding of new media in risk and crises, the study of crisis communication requires a body of approaches 'that fits its subject matter' (p. 355). Therefore, using computational methodologies to aid the current crisis communication research, especially in the functions of massive data ingestion, organization, calculation, and visualization, seems imperative and advantageous.

To illustrate this, take microblog platforms such as Twitter and Sina Weibo: These microblog network services contain rich crisis communication data. In a series of Twitter content studies, scholars collected 3,577,308 tweets published with the hashtag '#irma' during Hurricane Irma (Lachlan et al., 2019; Xu et al., 2019); as many as 19,442 messages were retrieved for a study of the Tianjin Port Explosion (Deng et al., 2020); more than 1.8 million tweets about COVID-19 were adopted to analyze conspiracy tweet disseminations (Rains et al., 2021). These microblogging messages contain textual information and metadata such as user mentions, references of physical user locations, or cross-topics with hashtags. The scale and complexity of raw data indicate that traditional research methods, such as manual content analysis, are not suitable for carrying out such large-scale data harvesting or cleaning, and would be time-consuming, which calls for the support of computational tools or modeling techniques.

In particular, the rapid advancement of machine learning algorithms further improves the accuracy of automated text categorization in sentiment analysis (Leetaru, 2012; Hasan et al., 2018). Sentiment analysis, an analytical approach using natural language processing techniques, has often been applied to analyzing Twitter conversations during crises to infer the attitudes about certain issues or the organizations these tweets convey (e.g., Hasan et al., 2018; Jin & Spence, 2021; Kwon, Chadha & Wang, 2019; Lachlan, Spence, Lin & del Greco, 2014b; Lin, Lachlan & Spence, 2016a; Stieglitz et al., 2019).

Machine learning techniques could also contribute to better modeling with model selections or shrinkage, providing more valid statistical data or data visualizations (Van Atteveldt & Peng, 2018). In particular, structural topic modeling, an unsupervised learning technique for text analysis, enables researchers to systematically interpret discursive themes from multiple semantic topical clusters (Roberts, Stewart & Airoldi, 2016). Kwon et al. (2019) used this technique to investigate the Twitter network in the aftermath of the Quebec mosque shooting in 2017. Furthermore, the data captured from social media avoid self-report biases that classical surveys or interviews face.

## DATA-DRIVEN RESEARCH HIGHLIGHTS IN CRISIS COMMUNICATION

Computational methodologies allow scholars to inquire about new research questions that traditional quasi-experiments or interviews cannot perform. Such research questions usually consider the possibilities of new media affordances or social network dynamics in real-time crisis communication. For instance, Getchell and Sellnow (2016) conducted a network analysis of national and local official Twitter accounts related to the case of West Virginia water contamination, and examined network density, factions, and the presence of cliques, and suggested several features of the network for effective exchange of information during the crisis. Meanwhile, scholars with structural perspectives have adopted network modeling techniques to explore the real-time sporadic data on social media for entangled relationships among individuals and different levels of social structures. Yang and Veil (2017) combined semantic network analysis with advocacy case study research to investigate how the values of nationalism and animal rights triggered a corporate crisis and how societal values can be exploited to shift media coverage in a crisis.

Big data analysis also makes it possible for scholars to revisit classical crisis communication theories or principles from new perspectives. Many classical theories about crisis communication and management, such as the image repair theory (Benoit, 1997), situational crisis communication theory (Coombs, 2007), and the IDEA model (Sellnow et al., 2017), were built upon classical qualitative and quantitative research inquiries. Utilizing big data confirmatory research helps to test whether the theories of effective crisis communication still hold in the new media contexts. Meanwhile, large-scale exploratory analyses on social media data during crises are also needed to formulate theories that take into consideration new media affordance for effective emergency management. Several studies have applied computational methodologies, such as social network analysis, data-immanent peak analysis, or explanatory data analysis on corporate crisis and disasters, and contributed to crisis communication theory examinations or revisions (e.g., Stieglitz et al., 2019).

## CONCERNS ABOUT COMPUTATIONAL METHODOLOGIES

Although crisis communication scholars have kept pace with and sought to use computational technologies in social media data-driven research, critical methodological issues that impact research validity and reliability are noted. Several significant issues related to sampling and measurement that generated comprehensive discussions related to crisis communication research are addressed below.

First, the validity concern of the large-scale sampling draws the researchers' attention. Large quantities of online data neither necessarily represent the population that research intends to study, nor are its inferences 'with the aura of truth, objectivity, and accuracy' (boyd & Crawford, 2012, p. 663). Despite that, we have been using Twitter conversations to illustrate patterns of crisis responses on a large scale, and the process of data scrawling or algorithm filtering could cause sampling bias (Kwon, Priniski & Chadha, 2018; Van Atteveldt & Peng, 2018). For example, some Twitter public application programming interfaces (APIs) access only a 1 percent sample of the daily stream, and data selection criteria for the 1 percent capture were unavailable for researchers outside Twitter (Kwon et al., 2019), challenging the internal validity of the research.

Also, much online data is messy and unstructured; directly capturing the data without using appropriate data mining or processing could mislead research interpretations. Geolocation cues, for example, are embedded in self-report entities (such as described in messages or photos) or displayed under user authorization; ordinary publics who did not release such cues in their online conversations would be excluded from data ingestion or crisis monitoring (Kwon et al., 2019). Consistently, previous studies indicated that data sampling tends to over-represent opinion leaders who have been active online, such as issue experts or institutional professionals, implying sampling biases in empirical studies (Van Atteveldt & Peng, 2018; Kwon et al., 2019). Moreover, non-organic activities, such as bot-account activities and astroturfing, would contaminate online public discourses and be problematic for studies aiming to explore spontaneous emergent interactions or grass-roots activities (Kwon et al., 2018). Thus, it is also vital to identify and exclude bot activities online when studying crisis communication.

Another primary concern is the validity and reliability of research design and measurement. Global pandemic or large-scale natural disasters mobilize researchers and professionals to offer timely emergency response strategies as well as the rapid discovery of treatments and diagnostics. A recent study pointed out that there are currently around 250,000 listings of COVID-19 related studies in the World Health Organization's global database, including preprints, peer-reviewed literature, published reports, and clinical trial registries (Park et al., 2021). Nevertheless, an overwhelmingly large number of these studies have arguably been inefficient and wasteful without methodological rigor or planning. As a result, those studies are a waste of financial resources and have created confusion 'not only among the scientific community, but also among the public, who are eagerly waiting for the scientific community to make the next breakthrough for COVID-19' (Park et al., 2021, p. e712).

In crisis communication case studies, scholars may consider merely mining textual fragments without considering the social contexts and the meanings of data, such as processing automatic categorization or crowd coding. This might fail to meet the semantic validity criterion if the coding process did not examine the actual test segments and considered texts in contexts (Krippendorff, 2018). The application of computational methodologies and tools challenges conventional inter-coder agreement coefficients and demands updated criteria that are appropriate to judge research reliability.

Recently, Krippendorff (2021) tailored the traditional definition of alpha to extensive data and sketched a quadrilogy of big data reliability. These four measures were proposed, including the replicability and accuracy assessments of the data generation process, the surrogacy of a possible substitute (e.g., proposed theories, coders, formulas, or algorithms to serve as a substitute for human coders), and the decisiveness among several human judgments (Krippendorff, 2021). This set of reliability measurement coefficients aims to serve different methodologies in social research, which crisis communication studies on massive data exploration shall also take into consideration.

The third concern of computational methodology application involves data accessibility and research replication. Most crisis communication studies are generally reliant on limited open sources and single platforms, such as Twitter, or second-hand aggregated reports. Not all crisis datasets are free or available for academic research, except to a small group of researchers with privilege or resources to afford them. This may lead to the problem of generalizability and lack of a holistic understanding of crisis development. In some extreme cases, the lack of data accessibility brings limited situational awareness, posing threats regarding public safety, reputational erosion, financial cost, or community recovery.

In mid-2021, during the COVID-19 pandemic, timely hospitalization and coronavirus data were unavailable or delayed for some US state hospital associations as well as many researchers from community-based healthcare sectors. Such problems contributed to uncertainty and knowledge gaps about statewide crisis management processes (Smith, 2020). It is also noted that several frameworks were using different metrics and measures to perform daily new case reports at local community level, making it impossible to categorize risk levels across the United States in one attempt (Aubrey & Wroth, 2020). Consistently, several studies also indicated the inadequate data sharing for COVID-19 as a significant obstacle; the process of obtaining valid data is ineffective and time-consuming (e.g., Boulware et al., 2020; Park et al., 2021). Data transparency, open accessibility, and standardized measurement metrics help crisis managers and researchers avoid effort duplication or resource-wasting, which is vital in developing crisis-sensing capabilities. Park et al. (2021) suggest coordination and collaboration instead of independent clinical research to effectively facilitate reliable assessment of medical interventions. The premise is making original data retrievable and standardized datasets available for all researchers to share promptly, which is also beneficial for cross-crises studies or future research replications.

## CONCLUSION

This chapter discussed the research methods used over the past decade to study social media communication in emergencies and crises. As we advocate building a holistic understanding of social media use for risk and crisis management, the final notes for future research and practices are provided as follows:

- Consider experimental designs and replications for crisis studies.
- Pay more attention to social media affordances than a particular platform itself.
- Take theory-driven approaches and test classical crisis communication theories on new media affordances.
- Enhance the practices of measurement standardization and methodological rigor.
- Encourage open data accessibility for future cross-crisis comparisons or replication studies.

Controlled by a researcher or harvested from actual communication, social media and the data produced on them tell us much about the communication within crises and other extreme events. It may be argued that humans never before had access to as much communication concerning extreme events as is currently available and continually being produced. Analyzing, using, and applying that data, or, stated differently, learning from the available data is the central challenge to crisis researchers.

## REFERENCES

Aubrey, A., & Wroth, C. (2020, July 1). Green, yellow, orange or red? This new tool shows Covid-19 risk in your county. NPR. https://www.npr.org/sections/health-shots/2020/07/01/885263658/green-yellow-orange-or-red-this-new-tool-shows-covid-19-risk-in-your-county.

Benoit, W.L. (1997). Image repair discourse and crisis communication. *Public Relations Review*, 23(2), 177–86.

Bora, K., Das, D., Barman, B., & Borah, P. (2018). Are internet videos useful sources of information during global public health emergencies? A case study of YouTube videos during the 2015–16 Zika virus pandemic. *Pathogens and Global Health*, *112*(6), 320–328. https://doi.org/10.1080/20477724.2018.1507784.

Boulware, D.R., Pullen, M.F., Bangdiwala, A.S., Pastick, K.A., Lofgren, S.M., Okafor, E.C., … Hullsiek, K.H. (2020). A randomized trial of hydroxychloroquine as postexposure prophylaxis for Covid-19. *New England Journal of Medicine*, 383(6), 517–25.

Bowman, N.D., & Keene, R.J. (2018). A layered framework for considering open science practices. *Communication Research Reports*, 35(4), 363–72. https://doi.org/10.1080/08824096.2018.1513273.

Bowman, N.D., & Spence, P.R. (2020). Challenges and best practices associated with sharing research materials and research data for communication scholars. *Communication Studies*, 71(4), 708–16. https://doi.org/10.1080/10510974.2020.1799488.

boyd, d., & Crawford, K. (2012). Critical questions for big data. *Information, Communication & Society*, 15(5), 662–79.

Coombs, W.T. (2007). Protecting organization reputations during a crisis: The development and application of situational crisis communication theory. *Corporate Reputation Review*, 10(3), 163–76.

DeAndrea, D.C. (2014). Advancing warranting theory. *Communication Theory*, 24(2), 186–204. https://doi.org/10.1111/comt.12033.

Deng, Q., Gao, Y., Wang, C., & Zhang, H. (2020). Detecting information requirements for crisis communication from social media data: An interactive topic modeling approach. *International Journal of Disaster Risk Reduction*, 50, 101692. https://doi.org/10.1016/j.ijdrr.2020.101692.

Dienlin, T., Johannes, N., Bowman, N.D., Masur, P.K., Engesser, S., Kümpel, A.S., … De Vreese, C. (2021). An agenda for open science in communication. *Journal of Communication*, *71*(1), 1–26. https://doi.org/10.1093/joc/jqz052.

Edwards, C., Edwards, A., Spence, P.R., & Shelton, A.K. (2014). Is that a bot running the social media feed? Testing the differences in perceptions of communication quality for a human agent and a bot agent on Twitter. *Computers in Human Behavior*, 33, 372–76. https://doi.org/10.1016/j.chb.2013.08.013.

Edwards, C., Spence, P.R., Gentile, C.J., Edwards, A., & Edwards, A. (2013). How much Klout do you have … A test of system generated cues on source credibility. *Computers in Human Behavior*, 29(5), A12–A16. https://doi.org/10.1016/j.chb.2012.12.034.

Gerbner, G. (1983). The importance of being critical – in one's own fashion. *Journal of Communication*, 33(3), 355–62.

Getchell, M.C., & Sellnow, T.L. (2016). A network analysis of official Twitter accounts during the West Virginia water crisis. *Computers in Human Behavior*, 54, 597–606.

Hasan, A., Moin, S., Karim, A., & Shamshirband, S. (2018). Machine learning-based sentiment analysis for Twitter accounts. *Mathematical and Computational Applications*, 23(1), 11–15.

Jin, X., & Spence, P.R. (2021). Understanding crisis communication on social media with CERC: Topic model analysis of tweets about Hurricane Maria. *Journal of Risk Research*, 24(10), 1266–87. https://doi.org/10.1080/13669877.2020.1848901.

Krippendorff, K. (2018). *Content Analysis: An Introduction to Its Methodology* (4th ed.). Thousand Oaks, CA: SAGE.

Krippendorff, K. (2021). A quadrilogy for (big) data reliabilities. *Communication Methods and Measures*, 15, 165–89.

Kwon, K.H., Chadha, M., & Wang, F. (2019). Proximity and networked news public: Structural topic modeling of global Twitter conversations about the 2017 Quebec mosque shooting. *International Journal of Communication*, 13, 2652–75.

Kwon, K.H., Priniski, J.H., & Chadha, M. (2018). Disentangling user samples: A supervised machine learning approach to proxy-population mismatch in Twitter research. *Communication Methods and Measures*, 12(2–3), 216–37.

Lachlan, K.A., Spence, P.R., Edwards, A., Reno, K.M., & Edwards, C. (2014a). If you are quick enough, I will think about it: Information speed and trust in public health organiza-

tions. *Computers in Human Behavior*, 33, 377–80. https://doi.org/10.1016/j.chb.2013.08.014.
Lachlan, K.A., Spence, P.R., Lin, X., & Del Greco, M. (2014b). Screaming into the wind: Examining the volume and content of tweets associated with Hurricane Sandy. *Communication Studies*, 65(5), 500–518.
Lachlan, K.A., Spence, P.R., Rainear, A., Fishlock, J., Xu, Z., & Vanco, B. (2016). You're my only hope: An initial exploration of the effectiveness of robotic platforms in engendering learning about crises and risks. *Computers in Human Behavior*, *65*, 606–11. https://doi.org/10.1016/j.chb.2016.05.081.
Lachlan, K.A., Spence, P.R., & Seeger, M. (2009). Terrorist attacks and uncertainty reduction: Media use after September 11. *Behavioral Sciences of Terrorism and Political Aggression*, 1(2), 101–10. https://doi.org/10.1080/19434470902771683.
Lachlan, K.A., Xu, Z., Hutter, E.E., Adam, R., & Spence, P.R. (2019). A little goes a long way: Serial transmission of Twitter content associated with Hurricane Irma and implications for crisis communication. *Journal of Strategic Innovation and Sustainability*, 14(1), 16–26.
Leetaru, K. (2012). *Data Mining Methods for the Content Analyst: An Introduction to the Computational Analysis of Content*. New York, NY: Routledge.
Lewis, N.A. (2019). Open communication science. A primer on why and some recommendations for how. *Communication Methods and Measures*, 14(2), 71–82. https://doi.org/10.1080/19312458.2019.1685660.
Lin, X., Lachlan, K.A., & Spence, P.R. (2016a). Exploring extreme events on social media: A comparison of user reposting/retweeting behaviors on Twitter and Weibo. *Computers in Human Behavior*, 65, 576–81. https://doi.org/10.1016/j.chb.2016.04.032.
Lin, X., & Spence, P.R. (2018). Identity on social networks as a cue: Identity, retweets, and credibility. *Communication Studies*, 69(5), 461–82. https://doi.org/10.1080/10510974.2018.1489295.
Lin, X., & Spence, P.R. (2019). Others share this message, so we can trust it? An examination of bandwagon cues on organizational trust in risk. *Information Processing & Management*, 56(4), 1559–64. https://doi.org/10.1016/j.ipm.2018.10.006.
Lin, X., Spence, P.R., & Lachlan, K.A. (2016b). Social media and credibility indicators: The effect of influence cues. *Computers in Human Behavior*, 63, 264–71. https://doi.org/10.1016/j.chb.2016.05.002.
Lin, X., Xu, Z., Rainer, A., Rice, R., Spence, P.R., & Lachlan, K.A. (2017). Research in crises: Data collection suggestions and practices. In S. Elswick (ed.), *Data Collection: Methods, Ethical Issues and Future Directions* (pp. 49–64). Hauppage, NY: Nova Science.
Maxwell, S.E., Lau, M.Y., & Howard, G.S. (2015). Is psychology suffering from a replication crisis? What does 'failure to replicate' really mean? *American Psychologist*, 70(6), 487. https://doi.org/10.1037/a0039400.
McEwan, B., Carpenter, C.J., & Westerman, D. (2018). On replication in communication science. *Communication Studies*, 69(3), 235–41. https://doi.org/10.1080/10510974.2018.1464938.
Park, J.J., Mogg, R., Smith, G.E., Nakimuli-Mpungu, E., Jehan, F., Rayner, C.R., … Mills, E.J. (2021). How COVID-19 has fundamentally changed clinical research in global health. *The Lancet Global Health*, 9(5), e711–e720.
Rainear, A.M., Jin, X., Edwards, A., Edwards, C., & Spence, P.R. (2021). A robot, meteorologist, and amateur forecaster walk into a bar: Examining qualitative responses to a weather forecast delivered via social robot. *Communication Studies*, 72(6), 1129–45. https://doi.org/10.1080/10510974.2021.2011361.
Rainear, A.M., Lachlan, K.A., & Fishlock, J. (2019). Exploring retention and behavioral intentions when using social robotics to communicate a weather risk. *Computers in Human Behavior*, 90, 372–9. https://doi.org/10.1016/j.chb.2018.08.029.

Rains, S.A., Leroy, G., Warner, E.L., & Harber, P. (2021). Psycholinguistic markers of COVID-19 conspiracy tweets and predictors of tweet dissemination. *Health Communication*, 38(1), 21–30.

Roberts, M.E., Stewart, B.M., & Airoldi, E.M. (2016). A model of text for experimentation in the social sciences. *Journal of the American Statistical Association*, 111(515), 988–1003.

Rogers, E.M. (2003). *Diffusion of Innovations* (5th ed.). New York, NY: Free Press.

Sawilowsky, S.S. (2007). ANCOVA and quasi-experimental design: The legacy of Campbell and Stanley. In S.S. Sawilowsky (Ed.), *Real Data Analysis* (pp. 213–38). Charlotte, NC: Information Age.

Sawilowsky, S.S., & Spence, P.R. (2007). Good advice for simultaneous and sequential hypothesis testing. In S.S. Sawilowsky (Ed.), *Real Data Analysis* (pp. 155–62). Charlotte, NC: Information Age.

Seeger, M.W., Venette, S., Ulmer, R.R., & Sellnow, T.L. (2002). Media use, information seeking and reported needs in post crisis contexts. In B.S. Greenberg (Ed.), *Communication and Terrorism* (pp. 53–63). Cresskill, NJ: Hampton Press.

Sellnow, D.D., Lane, D.R., Sellnow, T.L., & Littlefield, R.S. (2017). The IDEA model as a best practice for effective instructional risk and crisis communication. *Communication Studies*, 68(5), 552–67.

Shao, C., Ciampaglia, G.L., Varol, O., Yang, K.C., Flammini, A., & Menczer, F. (2018). The spread of low-credibility content by social bots. *Nature Communications*, 9(1), 1–9. https://doi.org/10.1038/s41467-018-06930-7.

Smith, A. (2020, July 17). With CDC sidelined, some states lose access to timely COVID-19 hospital data. NPR. https://www.npr.org/sections/health-shots/2020/07/17/892357733/with-cdc-pulled-off-data-collection-some-states-lose-access-to-covid-hospital-da.

Spence, P.R. (2019a). Searching for questions, original thoughts, or advancing theory: Human-machine communication. *Computers in Human Behavior*, 90, 285–7. https://doi.org/10.1016/j.chb.2018.09.014.

Spence, P.R. (2019b). Policy, practices and communication studies. The more things change … *Communication Studies*, 70, 129–31, https://doi.org/10.1080/10510974.2019.1570715.

Spence, P.R., & Burns, C.S. (2020). Retrieving arguments and support after publication: Archiving links in communication research. *Communication Studies*, 71(5), 911–4. https://doi.org/10.1080/10510974.2020.1836781.

Spence, P.R., Edwards, A., Edwards, C., & Jin, X. (2019a). 'The bot predicted rain, grab an umbrella': Few perceived differences in communication quality of a weather Twitterbot versus professional and amateur meteorologists. *Behaviour & Information Technology*, 38(1), 101–9. https://doi.org/10.1080/0144929X.2018.1514425.

Spence, P.R., Edwards, C., Edwards, A., & Lin, X. (2019b, March). Testing the machine heuristic: Robots and suspicion in news broadcasts. In *2019 14th ACM/IEEE International Conference on Human-Robot Interaction* (HRI) (pp. 568–9). IEEE. https://doi.org/10.1109/HRI.2019.8673108.

Spence, P.R., Edwards, C., Edwards, A., Rainear A., & Jin, X. (2021). 'They're always wrong anyway': Exploring differences of credibility, attraction, and behavioral intentions in professional, amateur, and robotic-delivered weather forecasts. *Communication Quarterly*, 69, 67–8. https://doi.org/10.1080/01463373.2021.1877164.

Spence, P.R., & Lachlan, K.A. (2010). Disasters, crises, and unique populations: Suggestions for survey research. *New Directions for Evaluation*, 2010(126), 95–106. https://doi.org/10.1002/ev.332.

Spence, P.R., Lachlan, K.A., Edwards, A., & Edwards, C. (2016a). Tweeting fast matters, but only if I think about it: Information updates on social media. *Communication Quarterly*, 64(1), 55–71. https://doi.org/10.1080/01463373.2015.1100644.

Spence, P.R., Lachlan, K.A., Omilion-Hodges, L.M., & Goddard, A.K. (2014). Being first means being credible? Examining the impact of message source on organizational reputation. *Communication Research Reports*, 31(1), 124–30. https://doi.org/10.1080/08824096.2013.846259.

Spence, P.R., Lachlan, K.A., & Rainear, A.M. (2016b). Social media and crisis research: Data collection and directions. *Computers in Human Behavior*, 54, 667–72. https://doi.org/10.1016/j.chb.2015.08.045.

Spence, P.R., Westerman, D., Skalski, P.D., Seeger, M., Sellnow, T.L., & Ulmer, R.R. (2006). Gender and age effects on information-seeking after 9/11. *Communication Research Reports*, 23(3), 217–23. https://doi.org/10.1080/08824090600796435.

Spence, P.R., Westerman, D., Skalski, P.D., Seeger, M., Ulmer, R.R., Venette, S., & Sellnow, T.L. (2005). Proxemic effects on information seeking after the September 11 attacks. *Communication Research Reports*, 22(1), 39–46. https://doi.org/10.1080/0882409052000343507.

Stieglitz, S., Mirbabaie, M., Kroll, T., & Marx, J. (2019). 'Silence' as a strategy during a corporate crisis: The case of Volkswagen's 'dieselgate.' *Internet Research*, 29(4), 921–39.

Sundar, S.S. (2008). The MAIN model: A heuristic approach to understanding technology effects on credibility. In M.J. Metzger & A.J. Flanagin (Eds.), *Digital Media, Youth, and Credibility*. The John D. and Catherine T. MacArthur Foundation Series on Digital Media and Learning (pp. 73–100). Cambridge, MA: MIT Press. https://doi.org/10.1162/dmal.9780262562324.073.

Van Atteveldt, W., & Peng, T.Q. (2018). When communication meets computation: Opportunities, challenges, and pitfalls in computational communication science. *Communication Methods and Measures*, 12(2–3), 81–92.

Walton, L.R., Seitz, H.H., & Ragsdale, K. (2012). Strategic use of YouTube during a national public health crisis: The CDC's response to the 2009 H1N1 flu epidemic. *Case Studies in Strategic Communication*, 1(3), 25–37. http://cssc.web.unc.edu/files/2012/05/art3.pdf.

Webb, E.J., Campbell, D.T., Schwartz, R.D., & Sechrest, L. (1966). *Unobtrusive Measures: Non-Reactive Research in the Social Sciences*. Chicago, IL: Rand McNally.

Westerman, D., Spence, P.R., & Van Der Heide, B. (2012). A social network as information: The effect of system generated reports of connectedness on credibility on Twitter. *Computers in Human Behavior*, 28(1), 199–206. https://doi.org/10.1016/j.chb.2011.09.001.

Westerman, D., Spence, P.R., & Van Der Heide, B. (2014). Social media as information source: Recency of updates and credibility of information. *Journal of Computer-Mediated Communication*, 19(2), 171–83. https://doi.org/10.1111/jcc4.12041.

Xu, Z., Lachlan, K., Ellis, L., & Rainear, A.M. (2019). Understanding public opinion in different disaster stages: A case study of Hurricane Irma. *Internet Research*, *30*(2), 1066–2243.

Yang, A., & Veil, S.R. (2017). Nationalism versus animal rights: A semantic network analysis of value advocacy in corporate crisis. *International Journal of Business Communication*, 54(4), 408–30.

Zhu, Y., Bowen, S.A., & Lyu, X. (2022). Messenger nationality, media skepticism, and crisis communication effectiveness: Huawei's YouTube messages as perceived in the US. *International Journal of Strategic Communication*, *16*(1), 111–26. https://doi.org/10.1080/1553118X.2021.2014499.

# 8. Social media and reconciliation in post-conflict societies

*Juma Kasadha*

## INTRODUCTION

Social media platforms are increasingly criticized for mis/disinformation, with studies showing how misinformation on social media damages societies and democratic institutions (Allcott, Gentzkow & Yu, 2019). However, the same platforms are also argued to have heterogeneous positive uses that range from passive news consumption to active opinion expression (Skoric & Zhu, 2016).

The heterogeneity in how social media platforms are used drives the importance of studying how social media can be used to inform rather than misinform at individual and organizational levels. Scholars have highlighted the importance of social media platforms in boosting knowledge sharing within organizations (Nisar, Prabhakar & Strakova, 2019), and enabling individuals to easily interact and communicate with companies (Cui, Gallino, Moreno & Zhang, 2018). In addition, scholars argue that social media platforms increase interactions between individuals or within organizations, especially through instant messaging – making it a more preferred form of interaction compared to face-to-face interactions (Nardi, Whittaker & Bradner, 2000).

At the individual level, the shared information fosters access to messages that have informational worthiness to impact society – the shared information unites citizens towards a common goal such as conciliatory processes within conflicting and post-conflict regions (Kasadha, 2020a). In addition, Kasadha (2020a) adds that social media platforms provide 'post-conflict communities with new opportunities for interaction across ethnic and tribal divides and help citizens engage in sharing and discussions of reconciliatory messages' (p. 3).

These observations contributed to the development of the Social Media Reconciliation Model (SMRC). According to Kasadha (2022), the SMRC constitutes three dimensions: Interactive Digital Platforms, Information Processing and Intervention.

## SOCIAL MEDIA RECONCILIATION MODEL

The SMRC exemplifies how digital technologies can be used to support reconciliatory idea sharing and discussions using social media. In addition, the three-dimensional model encompasses the use of digital media as means for interaction, as platforms used for information processing and as vehicles through which necessary approaches aimed at resolving a conflict are gradually initiated (Kasadha, 2020b).

First, the SMRC's interactive digital platforms support the notion of deliberative reconciliatory processes in which conflicting parties share and exchange information. In their study, Fishkin and Luskin (2005) suggested the deliberative process as competing considerations in which discussions are based on being informed (supported with appropriate and reasonable accurate factual claims), balanced (meet contrary arguments), conscientious (willingness of participants to talk and listen with civility and respect), substantive (should be considered sincerely on their merits, not how they are made or who is making them) and comprehensive (all points of view held by significant portions of the population should receive attention).

As a result, the use of interactive digital platforms, specifically social media, enables weaker ties in conflicting societies to get connected and take part in deliberations associated with gradual reconciliation. Consequently, the use of interactive digital platforms generates social actors that eventually link the unconnected (also referred to as the weak ties) to the connected.

With the unconnected being connected, the use of interactive digital platforms (social media) enables those affected to deliberate on the issues affecting them at both individual and organizational levels (Fishkin & Luskin, 2005). Furthermore, extant literature suggests that connecting digitally enables citizens to ably engage in collective actions (Bennett & Segerberg, 2012), such as reconciliation (Kasadha, 2020a). Scholars have further urged that the digitally connected are able to generate new relationships – these gradually bolster their online and offline relationships (Ellison, Steinfield & Lampe, 2007, 2011).

In addition, Best et al. (2011) observed that such established relationships thrived based on how much audio-visuals and texts were used and shared to encourage citizens to effectively deal with stressful situations such as conflicts in varying forms. Hoffmann (2013) argued that this is because social media enables people to engage in their own initiatives for peace and engage in interactive dialogue. Therefore, to successfully construct the SMRC, it is presumed that digital platforms have the capacity to facilitate and enable social harmony (Davison, 2017). This is equally based on how recipients of digitally shared or accessed knowledge process it.

Consequently, the Information Processing dimension embodies users of interactive digital platforms to process shared information (un)consciously. This, in due course, results in the shared information contributing to the gradual processes that contribute to problem/conflict solving using distractors. According to psychologists, the use of distractors on unconscious thinkers as a means of avoiding participants from engaging in conscious thoughts helps in creativity and problem solving through both set-shifting and unconscious thought (Zhong, Dijksterhuis & Galinsky, 2008).

The unconscious approach to problem solving may lessen or worsen existing or emerging conflicts – leading to contradictions which are essentially about the incompatibility of aims between involved parties. According to Galtung (1958), the incompatible contradictions result from both attitudinal and behavioral consequences of a conflict. Given that the digital interactive platforms are awash with many distractions depending on the users' existing relationships, social psychologists continue to advocate for measures that use existing or built relationships to unconsciously contribute to gradual reconciliation based on how accessed and shared information is processed among the conflicting parties to lessen the existing conflict-related stress.

However, Davison, Pennebaker and Dickerson (2000) suggest that some people cope with threatening events by using an avoidant or minimizing coping style, whereas others are more likely to use an approach-oriented style that is confronting or at least vigilant, by gathering information or taking direct action. Their suggestion basically embodies a motivational construct – in this information is processed using avoidance measures that are mapped onto broader theories of biobehavioral functioning in which active and approach-oriented coping helps one to problem solve, seek social support and create outlets for emotional expression as a means of dealing with stressors.

In addition, Taylor (2010) encourages those confronted with any situation to primarily focus on shared or accessed information and look out for specific content that can be used to ameliorate the stressor. Using Taylor's deduction that approach-related coping was more successful in managing stress, this chapter incorporates theoretical conventions from Bennett and Segerberg (2012) on the logic of connective action to understand how processed information contributes to reconciliation. In addition, social media users can process the information on social media for reconciliation purposes in two processing stages: resilience and emotional disclosure.

Though scholars opine resilience as a reliable individual difference that boosts one's ability to gradually recover, this varies depending on the different levels of relationship with social media users. More specifically, Tugade and Fredrickson (2004) construed the resilience in a user's ability to adapt flexibility to changing demands of the environment and successfully bounce back from negative emotional experiences. This is because differences in identities contribute to how resilient one becomes and thus define one's adaptability to changing environments in times of conflict.

In their study, Swann and Bosson (2010) connoted that gender identity defined how people of different genders interacted – interactive digital platforms often approve of others who conform to gender roles and penalize those that counter them (Pasterski et al., 2005). Whilst identities differ, there is a need to appreciate how these numerous identities can easily use the interactive digital platforms to process information as a means for fostering gradual reconciliation processes.

For instance, proponents of emotional disclosure as a means of processing information connote that one's ability to share or open up their feelings or sufferings gradually boosts their path to reconciliation. According to Lepore and Smyth (2002), talking or writing about traumatic or stressful events provides an opportunity for an emotional approach to coping. This enables the traumatized to gain insightful information on self-realization and affirm one's personal values (Creswell et al., 2007). Therefore, this chapter's major contribution is expounding on the Intervention dimension – from a perspective of a developed democracy or society compared to initial studies that examined the Intervention dimension primarily focused on developing democracies.

## THE INTERVENTION DIMENSION

The applicability of the SMRC in developed post-conflict societies is based on the notion of the changing global trends that categorize social media as tools that abet conflict rather than lessen its occurrence. More specifically, the Intervention dimension's four approaches – smoke detector, social influencer, reciprocal and deletion – are (re)examined in the context of a developed post-conflict society: the US, following the Capitol attack on January 6, 2021. In addition, the (re)examination of the SMRC's Intervention contributes to the reconceptualization of the SMRC's role in fostering digital reconciliation and generating new theoretical foundations on the importance of digital media in conciliatory processes and initiatives in developed and developing societies.

Preliminary studies have advanced the notion that interactive digital media can be used to intervene in a conflict based on the social media users being able to process accessed or shared information (un)knowingly. This is supported by the (un)conscious decisions social media users make whilst using interactive digital media, as evidenced during the #BlackLivesMatter protests (Jones, 2020). In addition, existing literature supports the notion that social media platforms bolster public engagement and interactive dialogue, which improves relationships and helps in the gradual conciliatory processes where conflicting parties easily access and share information. Such sharing of information and interactions result in deliberations towards conflict-resolution (Kelly & Souter, 2014).

Nonetheless, a user's intervention is often rooted in the unconscious decisions taken to avert or stop a conflict from occurring at both individual and organizational levels. This espouses a theoretical perspective in which social media users are able to connect and collectively respond to any identified conflict (also known as incompatible contradictions) individually or as a group using the SMRC's Intervention dimension's four approaches: smoke detector, social influencer, reciprocal and deletion.

### Smoke Detector Approach

The social media platforms have generated a digital environment that has become a marketplace of extensively accessed and shared information. This information is uncensored and aimed at benefiting a wide range of audiences. Given that anyone can post or share anything on the numerous social media platforms, there is a need for social media users to pay keen attention to what is accessed, as some of it has resulted in socio-political and socio-cultural conflicts. For conflict to be gradually lessened, social media users should act and behave like smoke detectors that are designed to sense smoke which indicates there is fire in a given environment. In the context of social media, the presumed fire is a conflict type that brews in the lives of humans.

The extant literature suggests that smoke detectors are calibrated to minimize (irritating) false positives or to minimize (fatal) false negatives (Neuberg, Kenrick & Schaller, 2010; Nesse, 2005).

In addition, Neuberg et al. (2010) further note that smoke detectors are deliberately calibrated to minimize the costlier false negative error, which inevitably results in the occasional irritating false positive. This helps to shape perceptual, cognitive and emotional systems to minimize the likelihood of making whichever form of error that generates a conflict or delays a conciliatory effort. Therefore, the use of a smoke detector approach at individual or organizational levels helps social media users to share different forms of information, to create social harmony rather than disharmony.

Consequently, the smoke detector highlights the importance of social media users to act as watchdogs of each other – to interact digitally but also keep a keen eye on what is shared or discussed to easily avert any brewing socio-political and socio-cultural conflicts to foster harmony. This notion of social harmony (Davison, 2017) is achieved based on the notion that sources of conflict would be detected and, like a smoke detector, calibrated to minimize conflicts in society either online or offline.

## Social Influencer Approach

Interactive digital media provides users with a wide range of choices, such as whom to become friends with or whom to unfriend (Skoric, Zhu & Lin, 2018). Furthermore, social media users are able to engage or disengage themselves from interacting with or relating to certain activities such as political movements (Zhu, Skoric & Shen, 2017), depending on how the difference in views challenges one's beliefs and opinions. In context, it is argued that the social media users' ability to make friends or unfriend them is not coincidental but rather guided by whom social media users associate with frequently.

This is grounded in the extant literature that individuals are not as independent and free-thinking as they might wish to believe, but subject themselves to behaving or acting like others in the pursuit of social inclusion (Kessler & Cohrs, 2008; Coultas, 2004; Henrich & Boyd, 1998). In their study, Snyder and Fromkin (1980) argue that people are more susceptible to social influence under some situations than others when they risk social exclusion in cases when one's actions or behaviors deviate from the established norms of a group. Such deviations from established norms often pose death threats or physically harm a member of a given group (Gailliot et al., 2008; Griskevicius et al., 2006). For social harmony to prevail, social influencers should exhibit characteristics that inspire others to imitate, obey, conform to or otherwise be influenced by practices of unity (Henrich & Gil-White, 2001).

Therefore, whether a conflict is online or offline, intervention using the social influencer approach lays a foundation for better examples that redefine and set the rules of interaction among different users of the social media platforms in an endeavor to gradually lessen, avert or control a brewing, an emerging or an already existing conflict. According to Hogg (2010), social influencers define our conformity to authority, and they have a persuasive power that defines how we react or respond to given situations in life. For instance, a child will shout at anyone they meet if they see their parents do the same over time. In using social media platforms, those we follow, respect and place in high esteem in our societies often spark off violence, or they contain its occurrence and ensure social harmony prevails.

## Reciprocal Approach

'Do good unto me and I will treat you equally good' is a belief that many inclined to different religious teachings will often preach among their circles or groupings. Nevertheless, an extant body of literature (Kahn, Spencer & Glaser, 2013; Glaser & Kahn, 2005; Kang, 1999) suggests that the decline or lack of appreciation of reciprocal behavior explains the growing trends on online conflicts which escalate into humans' real-world lives. Kahn et al. (2013) elaborate on such assertions in their study that draws conclusions on how online prejudice and discrimination have worsened relationships both online and offline. The absence of reciprocity among parties involved in a relationship resulted in sweet love turning into bickering and hatred.

Neuberg et al. (2010) further reasoned that the exchange of benefits people receive from fellow group members often raises hopes for similar benefits to be reciprocated by each member during interactions. Applying this reasoning, social media users can reciprocate a good deed with a similar good deed or even better. For instance, in the wake of Pittsburgh synagogue attacks in the US, the Muslim community stood in solidarity with the Jewish community and condemned the attack against Jews (Beckett, 2018). In a similar event, Jewish people reciprocated by standing with the Muslim community alongside different religious leaders after the Christchurch killings in New Zealand (Mezzofiore, 2019).

In the same context, the reciprocal approach contributes to the conceptualization of how social media platforms can be used in reconciling conflicting or conflict-prone communities. Griskevicius et al. (2006) observed that it encourages generous sharing, which enhances an individual's status within the group, and such status portends significant benefits of its own, including access to future group resources, and through resource sharing an individual helps other members of the group survive.

This implies that societies or social media users can reciprocate irrespective of their identities. The differences in identities contribute to how resilient one becomes, thus defining one's adaptability to changing environments in situations of conflict. But the same identities also define how humans relate (Swann & Bosson, 2010; Ackerman & Kenrick, 2008; Ackerman et al., 2006).

## Deletion Approach

The deletion approach advances the concept that digital media users accessing such content to avoid conflict in society would delete anything posted in the same way they decide to unfriend or disengage digitally. The deletion approach as an intervention process filters opposing viewpoints from those who have not been exposed to them, preventing any escalation of conflict. Still, some studies (Baldassarri, 2009; Sunstein, 2009; Mutz, 2006) contend that those differences in opinions often enhance the democratic process and help modify political attitudes.

It is also vital to note that the suggested deletion approach differs from moderation as suggested in other studies. For instance, many online news and media sites delete comments on stories that are deemed inappropriate (Sherrick & Hoewe, 2018). However, Sunstein (2009) observes that conversations among like-minded individuals often breed extreme opinions compared to those who often disagree in their conversations, which acts as a safeguard against those advancing extreme opinions (Mutz, 2006). Although the act of online news and media sites deleting content deemed inappropriate would qualify to constitute the earlier arguments on deletion, especially the inappropriateness, it should be observed that the suggested deletion approach cuts across all digital media users and not just a few, such as the online news and media sites.

Whilst the social media interactions generate extreme political positions that gradually brew into a conflict, it is equally important to appreciate that the same interactions generate moderating influences on a polarized digital community (Harris, Morgan & Gibbs, 2014). As a result, contentious topics or discussions can be deleted instantly to avoid the spread or to limit access to any information that would result in or escalate a conflict. The process of deleting such content deemed harmful to the rest results in deleterious consequences that can be personal and social in nature (Ross, Lepper & Ward, 2010). In addition, social media users can individually or collectively delete any accessed information. Ross and colleagues note that deleting a source whose information is not forthcoming would be an appropriate decision to avoid taking decisions on incomplete or unsatisfactory pieces of shared information.

Though Judd and Kenny (2010) argue that deletion of information could result in the loss of data, it is vital to comprehend that deletion would save countless social media users from accessing incorrect or misleading information. In context, the deletion approach aims at creating a situation in which social media users delete content to avoid the spread of dis/misinformation and delete based on the notion that exposure to certain information can increase conflicts.

As a measure that can help in gradually avoiding anything extreme that could result in conflict, this chapter advances a deletion approach as a means of intervening to gradually reduce the occurrence of a conflict in a conflict-prone environment (Kasadha, 2022). Whilst deletion of content curtails social media users' free speech and discussions, it bolsters their ability to avoid the deleterious real-life consequences faced when everything read is acted upon at individual or group level (Baldassarri, 2009).

As a result, individuals or organizations gradually disengage from radicalized activities after deletion of shared and accessed content. For instance, the deletion of over 70,000 QAnon accounts disengaged many social media users from radicalized beliefs and conspiracies that 'can lead some individuals and groups to engage in violent behavior' (Lane, McCaffree & Shults, 2021). Even in politically sensitive societies such as China, the deletion of politically sensitive content enables it to lessen access to information that can result in conflict in Tibet and Qinghai areas (Bamman, O'Connor & Smith, 2012). Notwithstanding that deletion curbs social media users' exposure to alternative viewpoints in places like China, it encourages gradual conciliatory processes in conflicting and conflict-prone societies.

The delayed deletion of QAnon social media accounts in the US fostered radicalization of social media users at individual and organizational level leading to the January 6 Capitol attack. This calls for a collective effort for social media users at individual and organizational level (Bennett & Segerberg, 2012) to delete accessed or shared content deemed to cause or contribute to a conflict or any related traumatic exposure (Kasadha, 2022). Whilst any existing or emerging conflict can be traumatic and culminate in stressful events, the deletion approach would help victims of a conflict to successfully cope with the stress in their efforts to reconcile with the faced reality. Through the deletion approach, victims of a conflict would manage to tolerate stress in their lives primarily because they develop effective ways of coping through which others have been able to lessen or avoid a given conflict (Neuberg et al., 2010). Contrary to the existing literature that advances internet censorship or moderation, the suggested deletion approach advances the use of digital media to prevent the consumption of any such content that results in or escalates a conflict.

## (RE)CONCEPTUALIZING THE SMRC'S INTERVENTION DIMENSION DURING THE CAPITOL ATTACK

On January 6, 2021, the world was shocked when thousands of American citizens gathered to attack the Capitol Building in Washington DC in a bid to disrupt a Congress session to formalize President Joe Biden's victory over former President Donald Trump. Much has been discussed about the Capitol attack, but this chapter will focus on the gradual post-election reconciliation through the SMRC's Intervention dimension applicability.

First, a mere mention of Trump resonates with a personality that social media users easily label as the American President who defied conventional governance standards in the US. Trump(ism) can be characterized as the effect of populist/populism in parties that disrupts societal politics. In their study, Inglehart and Norris (2016) observed that citizens who supported populism were driven by varying factors. First was the economic insecurity that accentuated the effects of profound changes transforming the workforce and society in post-industrial economies. The second was the cultural backlash, which suggests that support can be explained as a retro reaction by once-predominant sectors of the population to progressive value change.

According to Moran (2017), Trump's policies or enacted decisions were sheer political rhetoric statements that were chaotic and lacked specific objectives. Moreover, all decisions taken by the Trump administration are increasingly being revoked, stopped, halted, whilst some are undergoing review by the Biden administration. Ironically, the undoing of Trump(ism) policies would reposition the US as the apex of democracy rather than what Trump had turned it into, a place of unconventionality and a place some, especially neoconservatives, even compared to a shelter for 'Frankenstein's monster' (Kagan, 2016).

Given that Trump's avant-garde policy remarks alarmed the US and the world at large (Cha, 2016), scholars asserted that Trump's presidency was one that symptomized 'manipulative infotainment and cultural decline' (Ouellette, 2016, p. 647). As a result, psychologists deduced that Trump's supporters exhibited 'authoritarianism, social dominance orientation, prejudice, relative deprivation, and intergroup contact' (Pettigrew, 2017, p. 107). Hence the scholarly need to examine the applicability of the SMRC's Intervention dimension in fostering gradual post-election reconciliation.

## Intervention Dimension during the Capitol Attack

Whilst the attack on the US Capitol continues to generate global debate on the level of unpreparedness for the events that unfolded, the four approaches of the Intervention dimension are (re)examined considering the attack to discuss how it contributes to the ongoing reconciliatory processes within the US at large.

The smoke detector approach is based on the notion that social media users are able to detect negative messages and avoid false narratives they construe (Neuberg et al., 2010). However, the failure of the US social media giants, individual social media users and the different democratic institutions to rise to the task of cautioning then President Trump's erratic behavior resulted in tweets that put America's 'democratic processes and institutions' to the test (Kasadha, Zhang, Mpoza & Alli, 2020). Although Trump's tweets posed a greater threat to the US, these were smoke detected and calibrated against false narratives, especially the tweet that rallied millions of supporters to Washington DC, aimed at stopping the '#Steal' of his purported presidential 'victory'. Similarly, a follow-up tweet alleging there were more votes in the US than people who voted was also smoked – a disclaimer was added to it.

Notwithstanding, the disclaimer did not stop the tweet from being retweeted or liked by the Trump supporters – an indicator that the intended message was and remained circulating. A lack of scrutiny of Trump's 'tweet politics' (Kreis, 2017) emboldened him to use his tweets to allege that the US elections were fraudulent. As a result, social media users, in particular Trump's supporters, joined the '#StopTheSteal' campaign. The Atlantic Council's Digital Forensic Research Lab (DFRLab) notes that Trump's false narrative tweets on election fraud encouraged many of his supporters, who posted and reshared the false narrative and rallied to join the protest in Washington DC on January 6 (Holt, 2021).

In reconceptualizing the SMRC's Intervention approaches, the messages deemed to foster false narratives should be deleted once they are smoke detected. This is based on studies that discuss the ability of social media users to engage in or disengage from political activities (Zhu et al., 2017). Thus, the adoption of a deletion approach comes second rather than the social influencer approach.

The deletion approach, which highlights the importance of deleting content deemed to cause or result in a conflict, bolsters the SMRC's intervention approach by (in)directly cutting off social media users from 'tweet politics' (Kreis, 2017) which results in conflicts such as the Capitol attack.

The deletion of content can be done at either individual or organization levels. In the US, Facebook and Twitter have deleted over 70,000 QAnon group accounts related to right-wing conspiracy theories (Frenkel, 2020), or were used to share content celebrating violence, show intent to use weapons and attract followers with patterns of violent behavior (Menn, 2020). Whilst the US continues to grapple with the post-election violence and false Trump election fraud narratives, deleting QAnon accounts shows that the social media platforms can be used in fostering the gradual conciliatory processes – this equally creates scholarly opportunities to devise means in which such social media users are banned from using or accessing alternative social media platforms.

The social influencer approach is vital in maintaining a status quo within conflicting and post-conflict communities. In the context of the US after the Capitol attack, different social media users exhibited leadership and guided social media discussions fostering the need for justice to prevail and to hold the culprits accountable. The social influencer approach is focused on the ability of social media users to influence other users into activities that bolster peacebuilding and not those that foster violence. Though those who responded to Trump's rally calls sought what scholars have termed as 'striving for social inclusion' (Kessler & Cohrs, 2008) their breach of the US Capitol instead labeled them as the enemy of the American peaceful transfer of power. Therefore, individuals and organizations that stood the test of time are those that repeatedly condemned the act – as the advocates of social harmony (Davison, 2017).

Social influencers who usually have many followers connect otherwise disconnected people within their respective digital networks in fostering gradual reconciliatory processes on what affects society, using the platforms to 'be influential and exhibit leadership' (Hogg, 2010). For instance, before and after the Capitol attack, American singer and actress Selena Gomez, with over 245 million followers, called out social media executives for having contributed to the Capitol attack since they did not delete accounts or content from social media users who propagated hate or violence.

In addition, social influencers that speak against violence, and encourage harmonious coexistence, exhibit leadership traits that are advocated by Hogg (2010). At both individual and organizational levels, speaking out increases the levels of connectedness among social media users and impacts how other users respond in more reconciliatory ways to situations of conflict, and it boosts users' socialization. As a result, socialization enables citizens to easily connect and engage (White, 2010), and share reconciliatory messages (Kasadha, 2020a).

Lastly, the reciprocal approach. The post-election violence in the US suggests the importance of affected communities or persons reciprocating. For instance, the US Capitol officers who testified before the House Select Committee echoed the importance of investigating who ignited the attack on the Capitol as a truth process to ensure justice is served. Reciprocally, Liz Cheney, a US House Representative for

Wyoming, echoed the importance of holding those responsible for the Capitol attack accountable.

Americans used their different social media platforms to applaud the Capitol Police officers who defended America's democracy. As a result, numerous social media interactions about the officers' testimony before the House Select Committee re-energized their spirits with love, care and hope for a better America. This constitutes exchanging benefits from fellow group members, such as a moment of silence for those who died in the line of duty. The universality in messages of hope to the officers emboldens the affected who are able to access additional resources to boost recovery from a conflict (Griskevicius et al., 2006).

# CONCLUSION

Technological improvements, particularly interactive digital platforms, pose numerous challenges to and opportunities for humanity. However, these developments have resulted in numerous debates on how social media can be used to foster reconciliation, yet they remain accused of polarization and causing numerous societal conflicts in the developed and developing democracies. Therefore, it is important for governments to vigorously invest in scholarly studies that examine the effects of social media mis/disinformation and equally explore how social media platforms are being used to gradually reconcile those affected in conflicting and conflict-prone regions. The SMRC creates scholarly opportunities to examine its applicability across different types of conflicts such as the Russia–Ukraine conflict and the Palestine–Israel conflict. Whilst the SMRC Intervention dimension's deletion approach generates debate on internet censorship, it is of scholarly importance to examine how digital technologies can be used in fostering gradual conciliatory processes for lessening or averting conflicts resulting from the relationships at the individual, organization or state level or the socio-economic, socio-cultural and socio-political incongruities.

# REFERENCES

Ackerman, J.M., & Kenrick, D.T. (2008). The costs of benefits: Help-refusals highlight key trade-offs of social life. *Personality and Social Psychology Review*, *12*(2), 118–40.

Ackerman, J.M., Shapiro, J.R., Neuberg, S.L., Kenrick, D.T., Becker, D.V., Griskevicius, V., … Schaller, M. (2006). They all look the same to me (unless they're angry): From out-group homogeneity to out-group heterogeneity. *Psychological Science*, *17*(10), 836–40.

Allcott, H., Gentzkow, M., & Yu, C. (2019). Trends in the diffusion of misinformation on social media. *Research & Politics*, *6*(2), 2053168019848554.

Baldassarri, D. (2009, May). *Social Networks, Political Heterogeneity, and Interpersonal Influence: Evidence from the 2006 Italian Elections*. Paper prepared for the Political Networks Workshop at the University of California, Davis.

Bamman, D., O'Connor, B., & Smith, N. (2012). Censorship and deletion practices in Chinese social media. *First Monday*, *17*(3). https://doi.org/10.5210/fm.v17i3.3943.

Beckett, L. (2018, October 27). Pittsburgh shooting: Suspect railed against Jews and Muslims on site used by alt-right. *The Guardian*. https://www.theguardian.com/us-news/2018/oct/27/pittsburgh-shooting-suspect-antisemitism.

Bennett, W.L., & Segerberg, A. (2012). The logic of connective action: Digital media and the personalization of contentious politics. *Information, Communication & Society*, *15*(5), 739–68.

Best, M.L., Long, W.J., Etherton, J., & Smyth, T. (2011). Rich digital media as a tool in post-conflict truth and reconciliation. *Media, War & Conflict*, *4*(3), 231–49.

Cha, T. (2016). The return of Jacksonianism: The international implications of the Trump phenomenon. *Washington Quarterly*, *39*(4), 83–97.

Coultas, J.C. (2004). When in Rome … An evolutionary perspective on conformity. *Group Processes & Intergroup Relations*, *7*(4), 317–31.

Creswell, J.D., Lam, S., Stanton, A.L., Taylor, S.E., Bower, J.E., & Sherman, D.K. (2007). Does self-affirmation, cognitive processing, or discovery of meaning explain cancer-related health benefits of expressive writing? *Personality and Social Psychology Bulletin*, *33*(2), 238–50.

Cui, R., Gallino, S., Moreno, A., & Zhang, D. J. (2018). The operational value of social media information. *Production and Operations Management*, *27*(10), 1749–69.

Davison, K.P., Pennebaker, J.W., & Dickerson, S.S. (2000). Who talks? The social psychology of illness support groups. *American Psychologist*, *55*(2), 205.

Davison, R.M. (2017, May). 'Facilitating Social Harmony through ICTs' in *International Conference on Social Implications of Computers in Developing Countries*, 3–9. Cham: Springer.

Ellison, N.B., Steinfield, C., & Lampe, C. (2007). The benefits of Facebook 'friends': Social capital and college students' use of online social network sites. *Journal of Computer-Mediated Communication*, *12*(4), 1143–68.

Ellison, N.B., Steinfield, C., & Lampe, C. (2011). Connection strategies: Social capital implications of Facebook-enabled communication practices. *New Media & Society*, *13*(6), 873–92.

Fishkin, J.S., & Luskin, R.C. (2005). Experimenting with a democratic ideal: Deliberative polling and public opinion. *Acta Politica*, *40*(3), 284–98.

Frenkel, S. (2020, August 19). Facebook removes 790 QAnon groups to fight conspiracy theory. *New York Times*. https://www.nytimes.com/2020/08/19/technology/facebook-qanon-groups-takedown.html.

Gailliot, M.T., Stillman, T.F., Schmeichel, B.J., Maner, J.K., & Plant, E.A. (2008). Mortality salience increases adherence to salient norms and values. *Personality and Social Psychology Bulletin*, *34*(7), 993–1003.

Galtung, J. (1958). *Theories of Conflict: Definitions, Dimensions, Negations*. New York, NY: Columbia University Press.

Glaser, J., & Kahn, K. (2005). 'Online Prejudice and Discrimination: From Dating to Hating' in Y. Amichai-Hamburger (ed.), *The Social Net: Understanding Our Online Behavior*, 247–74. Oxford: Oxford University Press.

Griskevicius, V., Goldstein, N.J., Mortensen, C.R., Cialdini, R.B., & Kenrick, D.T. (2006). Going along versus going alone: When fundamental motives facilitate strategic (non)conformity. *Journal of Personality and Social Psychology*, *91*(2), 281.

Harris, B.D., Morgan, C.V., & Gibbs, B.G. (2014). Evidence of political moderation over time: Utah's immigration debate online. *New Media & Society*, *16*(8), 1309–31.

Henrich, J., & Boyd, R. (1998). The evolution of conformist transmission and the emergence of between-group differences. *Evolution and Human Behavior*, *19*(4), 215–41.

Henrich, J., & Gil-White, F.J. (2001). The evolution of prestige: Freely conferred deference as a mechanism for enhancing the benefits of cultural transmission. *Evolution and Human Behavior*, *22*(3), 165–96.

Hoffmann, J. (2013). *Conceptualizing 'Communication for Peace'* (UNPEACE Open Knowledge Network Occasional Working Papers No. 1). University for Peace. http://www.upeace.org/OKN/working%20papers/Conceptualizing%20Communicationpercentage20for%20Peace%20OKN.pdf.
Hogg, M.A. (2010). 'Influence and Leadership' in S.T. Fiske, D.T. Gilbert & G. Lindzey (eds.), *Handbook of Social Psychology*. 5th ed. Vol. 2, 1166–1207. Hoboken, NJ: John Wiley & Sons.
Holt, J. (2021, February 10). #StopTheSteal: Timeline of Social Media and Extremist Activities Leading to 1/6 Insurrection. *Just Security*. https://www.justsecurity.org/74622/stopthesteal-timeline-of-social-media-and-extremist-activities-leading-to-1-6-insurrection/.
Inglehart, R.F., & Norris, P. (2016). *Trump, Brexit, and the Rise of Populism: Economic Have-Nots and Cultural Backlash* (HKS Faculty Research Working Paper Series RWP16-026). Harvard Kennedy School. https://www.hks.harvard.edu/publications/trump-brexit-and-rise-populism-economic-have-nots-and-cultural-backlash.
Jones, L.K. (2020). # BlackLivesMatter: An analysis of the movement as social drama. *Humanity & Society*, *44*(1), 92–110.
Judd, C.M., & Kenny, D.A. (2010). 'Data Analysis in Social Psychology: Recent and Recurring Issues' in S.T. Fiske, D.T. Gilbert & G. Lindzey (eds.), *Handbook of Social Psychology*. 5th ed. Vol. 2, 115–42. Hoboken, NJ: John Wiley & Sons.
Kagan, R. (2016, February 25). Trump is the GOP's Frankenstein monster. Now he's strong enough to destroy the party. *Washington Post*. https://www.washingtonpost.com/opinions/trump-is-the-gops-frankenstein-monster-now-hes-strong-enough-to-destroy-the-party/2016/02/25/3e443f28-dbc1-11e5-925f-1d10062cc82d_story.html.
Kahn, K.B., Spencer, K., & Glaser, J. (2013). 'Online Prejudice and Discrimination: From Dating to Hating' in Y. Amichai-Hamburger (ed.), *The Social Net: Understanding Our Online Behavior*, 201–19. Oxford: Oxford University Press.
Kang, J. (1999). Cyber-race. *Harv. L. Rev.*, *113*, 1130.
Kasadha, J. (2020a). Digitizing community building and reconciliation in post-conflict communities: A case of #Let'sTalkUganda in Northern Uganda. *Social Media + Society*, *6*(2), 2056305120924785.
Kasadha, J. (2020b). *Social Media and Civic Engagement: Reconciliation, Inclusion and Community Building* (Doctoral dissertation, City University of Hong Kong).
Kasadha, J. (2022). Digital reconciliation: A social media reconciliation model (SMRC). *Peace Review*, *34*(3), 431–9.
Kasadha, J., Zhang, N., Mpoza, A., & Alli, A.A. (2020). The 2020 US presidential election: A litmus test. *Journal of Public Affairs*, *20*(1), e1994.
Kelly, T., & Souter, D. (2014). *The Role of Information and Communication Technologies in Postconflict Reconstruction*. Washington DC: World Bank Publications.
Kessler, T., & Cohrs, J.C. (2008). The evolution of authoritarian processes: Fostering cooperation in large-scale groups. *Group Dynamics: Theory, Research, and Practice*, *12*(1), 73–84.
Kreis, R. (2017). The 'tweet politics' of President Trump. *Journal of Language and Politics*, *16*(4), 607–18.
Lane, J.E., McCaffree, K., & Shults, F.L. (2021). Is radicalization reinforced by social media censorship? arXiv preprint. arXiv:2103.12842.
Lepore, S.J., & Smyth, J. (2002). *The Writing Cure: How Expressive Writing Influences Health and Well-Being*. Washington DC: American Psychological Association.
Menn, J. (2020, August 20). Facebook removes hundreds of QAnon groups, citing public safety risks. Reuters. https://www.reuters.com/article/us-facebook-content/facebook-removes-hundreds-of-qanon-groups-citing-public-safety-risks-idUSKCN25F2HY.
Mezzofiore, G. (2019, March 15). Within hours of the Christchurch mosque attacks, people of various faiths rallied around Muslims. CNN. https://edition.cnn.com/2019/03/15/asia/christchurch-world-helping-muslimcommunity-trnd/index.html.

Moran, C.F. (2017). Crystallising the international rule of law: Trump's accidental contribution to international law. *Washburn LJ*, *56*, 491.

Mutz, D.C. (2006). *Hearing the Other Side: Deliberative Versus Participatory Democracy*. Cambridge: Cambridge University Press.

Nardi, B.A., Whittaker, S., & Bradner, E. (2000, December). 'Interaction and Outeraction: Instant Messaging in Action' in *Proceedings of the 2000 ACM Conference on Computer Supported Cooperative Work*, 79–88. New York, NY: Association for Computing Machinery.

Nesse, R.M. (2005). Natural selection and the regulation of defenses: A signal detection analysis of the smoke detector principle. *Evolution and Human Behavior*, *26*(1), 88–105.

Neuberg, S.L., Kenrick, D.T., & Schaller, M. (2010). 'Evolutionary Social Psychology' in S.T. Fiske, D.T. Gilbert & G. Lindzey (eds.), *Handbook of Social Psychology*. 5th ed. Vol. 2, 761–96. Hoboken, NJ: John Wiley & Sons.

Nisar, T.M., Prabhakar, G., & Strakova, L. (2019). Social media information benefits, knowledge management and smart organizations. *Journal of Business Research*, *94*, 264–72.

Ouellette, L. (2016). The Trump Show. *Television & New Media*, *17*(7), 647–50.

Pasterski, V.L., Geffner, M.E., Brain, C., Hindmarsh, P., Brook, C., & Hines, M. (2005). Prenatal hormones and postnatal socialization by parents as determinants of male-typical toy play in girls with congenital adrenal hyperplasia. *Child Development*, *76*(1), 264–78.

Pettigrew, T.F. (2017). Social psychological perspectives on Trump supporters. *Journal of Social and Political Psychology*, *5*(1), 107–16.

Ross, L., Lepper, M., & Ward, A. (2010). 'History of Social Psychology: Insights, Challenges, and Contributions to Theory and Application' in S.T. Fiske, D.T. Gilbert & G. Lindzey (eds.), *Handbook of Social Psychology*. 5th ed. Vol. 2, 3–50. Hoboken, NJ: John Wiley & Sons.

Sherrick, B., & Hoewe, J. (2018). The effect of explicit online comment moderation on three spiral of silence outcomes. *New Media & Society*, *20*(2), 453–74.

Skoric, M.M., & Zhu, Q. (2016). Social media and offline political participation: Uncovering the paths from digital to physical. *International Journal of Public Opinion Research*, *28*(3), 415–27.

Skoric, M.M., Zhu, Q., & Lin, J.H.T. (2018). What predicts selective avoidance on social media? A study of political unfriending in Hong Kong and Taiwan. *American Behavioral Scientist*, *62*(8), 1097–1115.

Snyder, C.R., & Fromkin, H.L (1980). *Uniqueness: The Human Pursuit of Difference*. New York, NY: Plenum Press.

Sunstein, C.R. (2009). *Going to Extremes: How Like Minds Unite and Divide*. Oxford: Oxford University Press.

Swann, W.B., & Bosson, J.K. (2010). 'Self and Identity' in S.T. Fiske, D.T. Gilbert & G. Lindzey (eds.), *Handbook of Social Psychology*. 5th ed. Vol. 2, 589–628. Hoboken, NJ: John Wiley & Sons.

Taylor, S.E. (2010). 'Health' in S.T. Fiske, D.T. Gilbert & G. Lindzey (eds.), *Handbook of Social Psychology*. 5th ed. Vol. 2, 698–723. Hoboken, NJ: John Wiley & Sons.

Tugade, M.M., & Fredrickson, B.L. (2004). Resilient individuals use positive emotions to bounce back from negative emotional experiences. *Journal of Personality and Social Psychology*, *86*(2), 320.

White, S.K. (2010). 'Ethos and Late-Modern Democracy' in A. Finlayson (ed.), *Democracy and Pluralism: The Political Thought of William E. Connolly*, 46–67. Abingdon: Routledge.

Zhong, C.B., Dijksterhuis, A., & Galinsky, A.D. (2008). The merits of unconscious thought in creativity. *Psychological Science*, *19*(9), 912–18.

Zhu, Q., Skoric, M., & Shen, F. (2017). I shield myself from thee: Selective avoidance on social media during political protests. *Political Communication*, *34*(1), 112–31.

# 9. Capital, commons, collectives: K-pop's digital corps de ballet

*Liew Kai Khiun and Sun Meicheng*

## INTRODUCTION: K-POP'S NEW CYBERPUBLICS

This chapter seeks to position social media cultures within contemporary Korean popular music or K-pop in engendering new global cyberpublics. Initially making regional headways in the early 2000s, its globalizing momentum significantly intensified alongside the advent of social media (Min et al., 2018). From making their presence felt everywhere from global *Billboard* charts to the US presidential elections, the transformative potentials of youth-based K-pop fandom are often synonymous with those of social media.

As prominent cyberpublics, the K-pop fan communities will here be termed 'digital corps de ballet', in reference to groups of dancers supporting and synchronizing those of the principal solo leads. Building from more democratic sharing economies of cultural and creative commons, this chapter seeks to frame the digital corps de ballet within a more dynamically interactive mediascape. In turn, such practices have the transformative potential to push social mediascapes to new digital frontiers.

## BACKGROUND: K-POP'S GLOBALIZATION FROM ANALOGUE TO SOCIAL MEDIA

Previously confined to the boundaries of South Korea and its diaspora, K-pop has evolved to assume broader global identities within the last three decades. Beginning in China in the late 1990s, the globalization of Korean popular music straddles several transitions in media cultures from the early portal digital media of CDs/DVDs and internet 1.0 to that of social and mobile media (Jin, 2014; Sun & Liew, 2019). Accompanying these transitions have been the evolution of K-pop towards greater musical hybridity, visuality and kinesthetics in highly synchronized dance choreographies performed by intensively trained artistes organized along the lines of predominately gendered 'idol' groups. In contrast to the images of authenticity emphasized in American-based pop music where talent is 'found', the K-pop music industry prides itself on 'training'. Common amongst the main industry labels – SM, YG, JYPE and HYPE – are the vertically integrated management practices covering artiste training from the start to production, distribution and marketing (Shin & Kim, 2013).

What distinguishes K-pop are its dedicated and organized fan practices and communities that are critical in globalizing the genre's digital presence in particular. Characterized by groups of uniformly attired youths shouting fan chants in unison in public venues, vibrant organized fan communities were already prevalent in South Korea in the 1990s amongst then trendier boy-groups like Seo Taiji and Boys, HOT and SechKies. Such organized fandom probably expanded to other countries alongside the broadening of K-pop's influence from the early 2000s. However, with communications and exchanges limited to snail mail and subsequently electronic-mail correspondence, K-pop fandom remained largely confined to national contexts for much of the early 2000s.

The new groups, like Big Bang, 2NE1, Girls Generation and T-ara, that emerged during this period expanded the regional fanbase significantly. Coinciding with the popularization of social media by the mid-2000s, as platforms like YouTube, Twitter and Facebook were being gradually introduced, these groups started to gain more international traction on these platforms (Oh & Lee, 2013). It was the historic reception of Psy's 'Gangnam Style' on YouTube in 2012 that heralded the presence of the genre in the global imagination (Jung & Li, 2014). With more than two billion views registered on the then six-year-old platform shortly after its release, the song was the historic first upload to exceed the maximum limit of the portal. What started as more of a sporadic hit became more concerted efforts of K-pop fandom in channelling their networks into augmenting their groups' social media presence.

It is the new affordances of social media that have given K-pop fandom new cyberpublics that will here be termed the digital corps de ballet. The transformative impacts of this corps through social media will be addressed here through its unique K-pop digital ecosystem triangulated in three areas: 'Capital', 'Commons' and 'Collectives'.

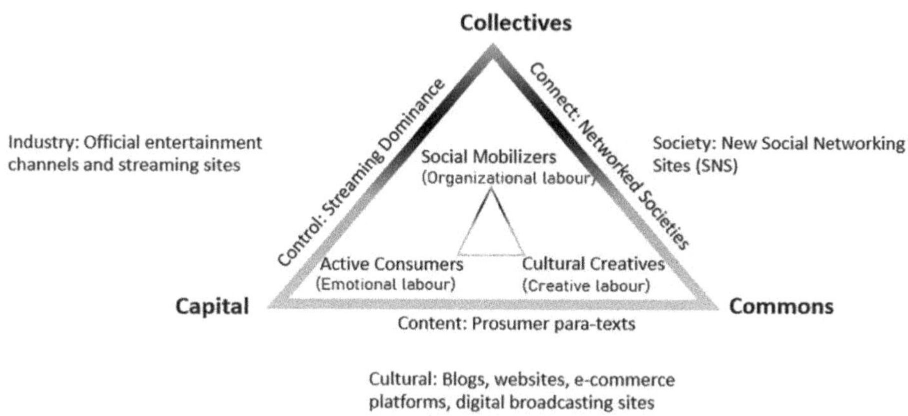


*Figure 9.1* *K-pop's digital ecosystem*

Figure 9.1 shows the dynamically fluid triangular movement of the K-pop digital ecosystem that serves to create a more interactive framework connecting otherwise separate discourses on the extent of the enlargement of social agencies against corporate and political control. In the case of 'Capital', the recurrent power dynamics are surfaced once again on the digital sphere between consumers and the music industry transiting from record sales to streaming sites (Hesmondhalgh & Meier, 2018; Fleischer, 2017). Offering the impression of abundant choices within the area of 'Commons' have been the trends of cultural and creative commons, entailing the shared ownership and public circulation of grassroots-initiated knowledge bases and products (Bilgrami, 2021; Dalla Chiesa, 2020; Ossewaarde & Reijers, 2017). Against the tide of especially jealously guarded legalistic notions of individual intellectual property, through both digital products and information, cyberspace has been offering UGC, often in parallel with official corporate narratives. Such trends are especially evident in more participatory hobbyist and fandom DIY undertakings.

Lastly, 'Collectives' connote the publics that social media platforms have provided for broader social mobilizations of previously latent publics into social movements and political protests (Velasquez & LaRose, 2015). Distinguished from the more formalized hierarchical traditional social movements, the collectives generated from the social mediascapes have often been observed to be more youth-oriented spontaneous and autonomous fluid formations (Aim, 2021; Kim & Hutt, 2021).

At each bisector of the triangle are K-pop fan practices, from the emotional labour of active consumers in gaining streaming dominance or control of the global music charts to the UGC of K-pop-inspired prosumer activities like dancers copying K-pop choreography and fan art posted on social media platforms. At the apex of this digital corps de ballet are highly networked societies readily mobilizable and pivotable towards collective actions in the broader political realm.

Powering this triangulation from within are the interrelated forms of Emotional, Creative and Organizational labour in the inner triangle in Figure 9.1, which defines the affective Active Consumers, the Cultural Creatives and the Social Mobilizers in the K-pop digital ecosystem. To be elaborated further in the following sections, it is the multiple levels of financial, emotional, aesthetic and political investments towards community engagements and political involvement that characterizes K-pop's digital corps de ballet.

## CAPITAL: ACTIVE CONSUMER

In the early 2010s, it was unthinkable for a K-pop music video (MV) to be released or 'dropped' and reach a million views on YouTube within a day. A decade later, the benchmark was raised to a million per hour, with an MV achieving a hundred thousand views in the opening minutes after its release. Compared to the MVs of earlier generations of K-pop groups, like Big Bang, Girls Generation and 2NE1, the views of which have not exceeded 700 million even after a decade, crossing the billion mark on YouTube is now expected of BTS and Blackpink, with the latter setting the precedent with the song 'Ddu-Du Ddu-Du' in 2019 (Kpop Radar, n.d.). Debuted in 2016 under the YG Entertainment label associated with globalizing rising groups like Big Bang and 2NE1, the quartet of female performers saw instant fame within a year. Until now, the newest pinnacle is the MV 'Lalisa', from Lalisa (Lisa) Manoban of Blackpink. Released on September 17, 2021, 'Lalisa' garnered a record YouTube viewership of 74 million within 24 hours (Guinness World Records, n.d.).

Contemporary global popular music has been synonymous with British- and American-based genres, and this has been the case since the 1950s, whereby industry rankings and acknowledgements like the *Billboard* charts and Grammy Awards have often been considered as being 'international'.

Principally, the new digital data yardsticks of social media are part of the disruptions to the otherwise established musical hierarchies. Starting in the 1950s, *Billboard* rankings were, until the recent decade, based on record sales from portable media of vinyl, cassette tapes and compact discs produced and distributed via predominately American-based record labels, retail outlets and broadcasting networks. Although *Billboard* has been expanding its ranks to include emerging genres from hip hop and Afro-Caribbean music to electronic dance music, the representations of Asian selections for the platform have been scant. In 1963, the Japanese song 'Sukiyaki' gained popularity in the US and was listed in *Billboard*, and remained the only Asian-based song that topped the charts until K-pop songs made more concerted inroads in the late 2000s (*Billboard*, n.d.).

Beginning with the 2008 song 'Nobody' by Wonder Girls of JYPE, the presence of K-pop songs gradually increased in *Billboard* charts. The trend was intensified and sustained with the albums of BTS and Blackpink a decade later (Fu, 2021). Media observers have attributed this phenomenon to creative strategies deployed by the K-pop industry for songs to be performed in the English language and for collaborations with American pop artistes (*South China Morning Post*, 2020). On their own, these attributes are not sufficient to account for the breakthroughs, given that similar arrangements had also been made by other Asian entertainment industries. Even before producing English-language songs, the current generation of K-pop groups were already popular in the Western markets.

Having bumped them to the top of social media algorithms, the role of K-pop fandom in sending their groups into *Billboard* rankings is critical where the traditional analogue media networks are no longer the main gatekeepers. Watchful of the vestigial metrics of CD sales, K-pop fans have also been buying in bulk the physical stocks of newly released albums to strengthen the digital indicators of the popularity of their groups (Dong, 2020). Collectively, just for K-pop alone, these activities have even been instrumental in reversing the rapidly and universally declining sales of CDs.

Social media outlets like YouTube and, more recently, streaming sites like Spotify have provided the platforms for more dynamic ranking structures with immediacy and transparency. The inroads of K-pop songs into *Billboard* rankings reflect a more deliberate and conscious form of active consumption practices that require significantly more emotional and financial commitments (Frater, 2021; Lee & Nguyen,

2020). With monitoring mechanisms of streaming sites being tooled to detect 'fake engagement' and 'view-botting' to inflate view counts, the fan labour required in meeting the streaming target remains largely individual manual acts of attentive viewing of new MVs and songs repeatedly (Sun, 2020; Zhang & Negus, 2020). Encouraging this process are constant social media posts containing instructions and reminders for joining organized streaming activities for K-pop artistes (Blackpink Stats, 2021). Routine and structured with measurable goals towards streaming dominance, the labour of the active consumer becomes the affective capital within the K-pop digital ecosystem.

*Figure 9.2 K-pop fandom and streaming dominance*

Figure 9.2 shows the various digital and traditional analogue media networks that the K-pop digital corps de ballet has to control in gaining streaming dominance to springboard their artistes into both the national and global charts. With only low digital literacy skills being required, plus moderate organizational management and varying levels of financial expenditure, active consumption forms the basic level of K-pop social media fandom. With the K-pop industry being the biggest commercial beneficiary of this 'earned media', the phenomenon comes as a double-edged sword. It exhibits the capitalistic extraction of youth's emotional and financial resources. However, it has also cultivated a broader pop-cultural citizenry built upon digital community networks and cultural resources from such affiliations that are now distinct in K-pop's digital corps de ballet.

## COMMONS: CULTURAL CREATIVES

It is in this area of the 'Commons' that the multiverse of K-pop fandom starts the radical expansion afforded by digital media tools, social media platforms and the proliferation of prosumer UGC. The presence of cultural creatives, which started with the desktop computer about two decades ago, has intensified with the availability of once significantly expensive and complex production and post-production mechanical editing tools even in the mobile media. Extracting and appropriating from official materials, K-pop prosumer para-texts represent more subjective re-interpretative cultural creatives in responding, diversifying and economizing the industry-centred pop entertainment texts.

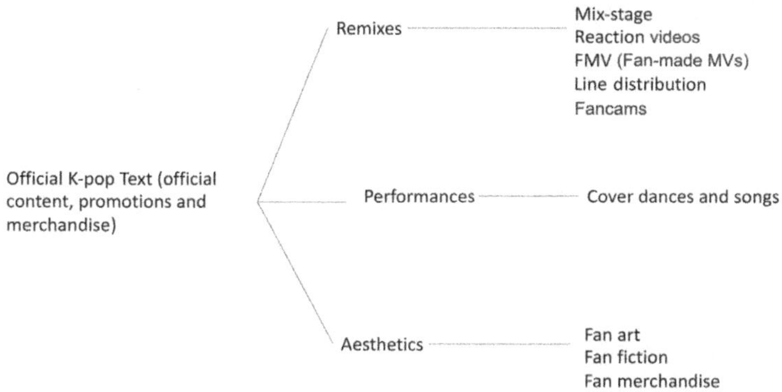


*Figure 9.3* *K-pop fandom UGC and Creative Commons (created by Liew Kai Khiun)*

Figure 9.3 categorizes three main areas of such fan-creative labour based on official content of the K-pop industry: 'Remixes', 'Performances' and 'Aesthetics'. In terms of frequency and volume, content from 'Remixes' in the area of fan-made videos (FMVs) is often at the forefront of social media trends (Kim, 2017; Oh, 2017). Some of the UGC under this category includes 'mix-stages' (compilations of live performances); 'line distribution', which maps out the various translations of lyrics as well as the proportion of a song allocated to each artiste within the group; 'fancams', which focus on specific individual artistes; and 'reaction videos' entailing the recording of emotional responses to the first viewing of new MVs. In the Performances category will be the fan renditions of original scores and choreography in K-pop cover dances and songs (Liew, 2013; Oh, 2020). With the uploads of the first cover dance songs coming less than a day after the official release, complete versions and accompanying tutorials would follow after the choreography is demonstrated via official stage performances and dance practices (Ellen and Brian, 2018; Spice Team, 2021). Within a week, cover dance groups would be able to stage public performances in their own localities, dressed in costumes similar to those of the K-pop artistes they are referring to.

In Aesthetics come fan fiction, art and merchandise, which are critical in framing more autonomous imaginations and even more economical alternatives, especially in independent fan merchandise (Bimbim, 2020). Departing from the bisector of Capital represented by the K-pop industry, K-pop-based digital literature and materials are often made accessible for exhibition as well as trade in the more conventional blogs and websites (Fluffpuffwuff, n.d.; Kpop Celeb, 2018). For marketable merchandise, such offers are becoming ubiquitous in e-commerce platforms, generating their own parallel economy. As digitally accessible cultural resources and subsequently vernacular archival texts, such UGC becomes part of the creative commons for K-pop fandom.

## COLLECTIVES

K-pop fans form a uniformed presence in concerts and other public engagements through organized displays of support, including exhibiting custom-made paraphernalia like placards, clothing and light sticks, and specifically practicing chants in unison. These are perhaps some of the common practices that have been associated with fandom cultures. What became unexpectedly more novel in the K-pop scene was fan activism. Beginning in the late 2000s, with public protests by fan communities against what fans highlighted as industry malpractice regarding unfair labour contracts for their artistes (Lee, 2015), the momentum of K-pop fan activism expanded radically beyond the entertainment arena.

A decade later, from American politics (BBC News, 2020) to civil protests in Southeast Asia, K-pop fan activism was pivoted to new precedence in taking the political centre stage. To show their opposition to the former US President Donald Trump, TikTok users and K-pop fans registered for his rally in Tulsa without any intention to show up, which left a large number of empty seats at the venue (McCurry, 2020). At almost the same time, Thai K-pop fans supported Thailand's youth protests through fundraising, trending Twitter hashtags and other common K-pop fan practices (Tanakasempipat, 2020). Developments in mobile communications as well as the advent of newer social media platforms like TikTok and Amino have engendered new networked societies for the current generation of youths. Networks and communities built from K-pop activities smoothly flipped and pivoted into social movements, taking officialdoms off guard regarding what is commonly dismissed as obsessive teenage girls.

From 'Reaction' to 'Action' and 'Activism' in 'collective trajectories', Figure 9.4 charts the pivoting of K-pop's digital corps de ballet from often defensive reactions to any perceived criticisms of their artistes' reputations towards social movements in the broader public arena. At the left end of the spectrum of the K-pop fandom mobilizations are the acts of social surveillance of fans in monitoring the activities, images and reputations of K-pop artistes. Often played out via social media exchanges in rivalries and 'fan wars', reactions are commonly confined to the K-pop entertainment circles (Tinaliga, 2018). However, revelations of the negative pasts of some K-pop

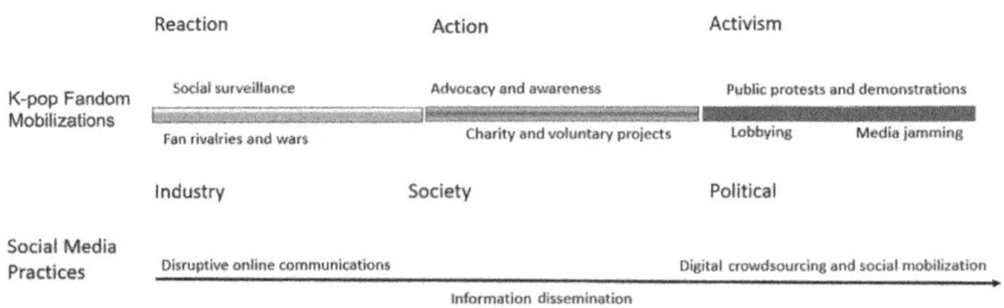


*Figure 9.4* *K-pop collective trajectories*

artistes – such as a record of bullying behaviour – industry malpractices and exploitation often gained broader public attention. This is where the digital corps de ballet moves towards 'Action' in the fields of advocacy. This area is also characterized by often publicly visible community and charity projects carried out by K-pop fan clubs as part of enhancing the reputation of their artistes (Fedorenko, 2021; Ohandjanian, 2018). The third and final stage of this pivot comes in the political activism of 'Action', in the radicalization of otherwise apolitical K-pop fandom into the forefront of national and international politics (Lee et al., 2021).

Accompanying this trajectory are social media practices that range from the disruptive online communications in the digitally combative practices of trolling and spamming to the more constructive efforts of information dissemination, digital crowdsourcing and other online activities in social mobilizations. Cyberspace has given K-pop's digital corps de ballet a platform to repurpose otherwise routine fan activities to boost their idols' digital presence as well as other related prosumer K-pop-inspired artworks and materials into political spearheads.

In contrast to the more institutionalized political parties, trade unions and non-governmental organizations, K-pop's organizational labour comes across as more diffused and levelled, without formal hierarchies and structures. Often flooding the political establishments' social media platforms with posts of K-pop idols, digital crowdfunding and recruitment, as well as using otherwise innocuous K-pop social media forums and networks to direct public protests, K-pop activism manifests new digital guerrilla practices (Chen & Pang, 2020; Herman, 2020). Built on the networks and resources in the bisections of Capital and Commons, the Collectives represent, in some ways, the apex of the practices of K-pop's digital corps de ballet.

## CONCLUSION: VIRALITY TO ENDEMICITY IN K-POP'S DIGITAL CORPS DE BALLET

Previously confined largely to its national borders and diaspora, K-pop's influence is now global, de-centring the otherwise Eurocentric dominance of the circulation of contemporary popular music. Coinciding with the rapid adoption of social media in the past decade, the rise of digital fandom, described here as the digital corps de ballet, can be attributed to K-pop's phenomenal global ascent. As discussed in this chapter, K-pop fandom has been critical in intensifying and accelerating the spreadability of media cultures.

K-pop fans concertedly boost K-pop groups under newly emphasized digital metrics into once American-dominated charts, proliferate prosumer UGCs referencing closely with the latest productions and mobilize existing social networks to impact public politics. The digital corps de ballet pushed the creative frontiers of social media possibilities in terms of social networking, building cultural resources and, be it either for *Billboard* rankings or joining protest movements, engaging in acts of public lobbying. These practices have been generally termed as 'Capital', 'Commons' and 'Collectives' in this chapter. Often treated as separate scholarly topics, these practices are contextualized in this discussion as dynamically triangulating within the digital K-pop ecosystem powered by the more affective emotional, creative and organizational labour of the genre's fandom.

Nonetheless, we identify several limitations of our conceptual framework. Although there is now more transparency with digital streaming processes and data mining tools extracting information about social media activities, official data on revenue figures and other indicators from the music industry are still largely publicly unavailable. At the other end of the consumer base, our model would not capture the category of 'passive consumers'. With consumption patterns largely confined to individual reception of K-pop media texts, any participatory activities reflected on social media from this audience base would be low. As the silent majority, these passive consumers would not be detected in this K-pop digital ecosystem meant for showcasing the digital corps de ballet.

Given the increasing predictability of the intensity and speed of the media spreadability of K-pop texts, virality is expected of the impacts made by its digital corps de ballet. Since the crossing of the billionth mark in YouTube viewership for K-pop MVs, the proliferation of fan art and cover dances of new releases, as well as involvement of fan communities in any political flashpoint, become expected. A new endemicity can perhaps describe K-pop in the social mediascape.

Such potentials would be crucial to the sustainability and currency of the scholarship on K-pop and social media for at least the next five years. Within this period, K-pop's corps de ballet may take on posthuman identities with the deployment of new affordances from the increasingly accessibility of artificial intelligence (AI) technologies of machines and bots automating and augmenting the affective labour of K-pop fandom. On the broader societal level, as its transformative potential becomes increasingly recognized, the now relatively autonomous K-pop digital ecosystem can also be co-opted and appropriated as a hegemonic apparatus. With the production of virtual AI K-pop artistes as well as disinformation campaigns from actors/entities masquerading as K-pop artistes (Javier, 2022; Dong, 2021; Abidin, 2019), a more abstracted and cynical dystopian K-pop digital ecosystem will run parallel to the agencies and solidarities cultivated by the digital corps de ballet. The challenge of scholarship will come in critically flagging these general trends.

## REFERENCES

Abidin, C. (2019, April 11). K-pop social media, (anti-)fan labour, and networks of (mis)information. *Society Pages*. https://thesocietypages.org/cyborgology/2019/04/11/k-pop-social-media-anti-fan-labour-and-networks-of-misinformation/.

Aim, S. (2021). Hashtag activism: social media and the #FreeYouth protests in Thailand. *Critical Asian Studies*, 53(2), 192–205. https://doi.org/10.1080/14672715.2021.1882866.

BBC News (2020, June 8). BTS Black Lives Matter: Fans match band's $1m donation. https://www.bbc.co.uk/news/world-asia-52960617.

Bilgrami, A (2021). The cultural commons: A philosophical analysis – Part 1. *Economic and Political Weekly*, 56(26). https://www.epw.in/journal/2021/26–27/perspectives/cultural-commons.html.

*Billboard* (n.d.). Kyu Sakamoto. https://www.billboard.com/artist/kyu-sakamoto/.

Bimbim [@7abimabima7] (2020, December 9). [Stock sale] Worldwide shipping [Tweet]. Twitter. https://twitter.com/7abimabima7/status/1336340689731211264.

Blackpink Stats [@Blackpinkstats5] (2021, October 1). Join my streaming party for #Money to Top 10 Spotify Chart on Renaissance! @BLACKPINK [Tweet]. Twitter. https://twitter.com/BLACKPINKSTATS5/status/1443832189397835779.

Chen, M.Y., & Pang, T.H. (2020, December 1). Technology is fuelling fandoms into a force beyond entertainment. Wunderman Thompson. https://www.wundermanthompson.com/insight/mobilizing-fandoms.

Dalla Chiesa, C. (2020). From digitalisation to crowdfunding platforms: Fomenting the cultural commons. In: E. Macrì, V. Morea & M. Trimarchi (eds) *Cultural Commons and Urban Dynamics* (pp. 173–86). Cham: Springer. https://doi.org/10.1007/978-3-030-54418-8_11.

Dong, S.-h. (2021, 8 December). Will AI-powered groups take over K-pop? *Korean Herald.* https://www.koreatimes.co.kr/www/art/2021/06/398_310095.html.

Dong, S.-h. (2020, November 24). K-pop defies digital trend with growing physical album sales. *Korea Times*. https://www.koreatimes.co.kr/www/art/2020/11/732_299809.html.

Ellen and Brian (2018, June 15). *Blackpink- Ddu-Dd Ddu-Du (뚜두뚜두) Dance tutorial (mirrored) | Ellen and Brian* [Video]. YouTube. https://www.youtube.com/watch?v=js9InLDV2X8.

Fedorenko, O. (2021). Idol ads in the Seoul Metro: K-pop fandom, appropriation of subway space, and the right to the city. *City & Society*, 33(3), 492–517. https://doi.org/10.1111/ciso.12415.

Fleischer, R. (2017). If a song has no price, is it still a commodity? Rethinking the commodification of digital music. *Culture Unbound: Journal of Current Cultural Research*, 9(2), 146–62. http://www.cultureunbound.ep.liu.se.

Fluffpuffwuff (n.d.). Fluffpuffwuff. https://fluffpuffwuff.bigcartel.com/.

Frater, P. (2021, July 5). K-pop propels YouTube to streaming dominance in Korea, study finds. *Variety*. https://variety.com/2021/digital/asia/k-pop-youtube-streaming-dominance-in-korea-1235011868/.

Fu, Y. (2021, July 22). 11 Asian acts who broke into the Billboard Hot 100: BTS, CL, PSY, Wonder Girls, BLACKPINK, Pinkfong, and more. *Bandwagonasia*. https://www.bandwagon.asia/articles/11-asian-artists-billboard-hot-100-bts-blackpink-psy-cl-wonder-girls-suga-jhope-rose-red-velvet-pinkfong-agust-d-kyu-sakamoto-butter-permission-to-dance-how-you-like-that-baby-shark-list-2021.

Guinness World Records (n.d.). Most viewed YouTube music video in 24 hours by a solo K-pop artist. https://www.guinnessworldrecords.com/world-records/654268-most-viewed-youtube-music-video-in-24-hours-by-a-solo-k-pop-artist.

Herman, T. (2020, June 22). Digitally-savvy and passionate, K-pop fans' Trump activism should come as no surprise. *The Guardian.* https://www.theguardian.com/commentisfree/2020/jun/22/digitally-savvy-and-passionate-k-pop-fans-trump-activism-should-come-as-no-surprise.

Hesmondhalgh, D., & Meier, L. (2018). What the digitalisation of music tells us about capitalism, culture and the power of the information technology sector. *Information, Communication & Society*, 21(11), 1555–70. https://doi.org/10.1080/1369118X.2017.1340498.

Javier, P. (2022, April 21). K-pop stan strategies are being used in political campaigns. *CNN.* https://www.cnnphilippines.com/life/culture/politics/2022/4/21/k-pop-strategies-political-campaigns.html.

Jin, D.Y. (2014). The power of the nation-state amid neo-liberal reform: Shifting cultural politics in the new Korean Wave. *Pacific Affairs*, *87*(1), 71–92. https://doi.org/10.5509/201487171.
Jung, S., & Li, H. (2014). Global production, circulation, and consumption of Gangnam Style. *International Journal of Communication*, *8*, 2790–2810. https://ijoc.org/index.php/ijoc/article/view/2966.
Kim, J. (2017). *K-Popping: Korean Women, K-Pop, and Fandom*. [Doctoral dissertation, University of California, Riverside]. https://escholarship.org/uc/item/5pj4n52q.
Kim, P., & Hutt, E. (2021). K-pop as a social movement: Case study of BTS and their fandom ARMY. *Journal of Student Research*, 10(3). https://doi.org/10.47611/jsrhs.v10i3.1772.
Kpop Celeb [@Kpopceleb] (2018, November 29). Even in Mexico 'BTS (BTS) boom'! [Tweet]. Twitter. https://twitter.com/kpopceleb/status/1068006330739224576.
Kpop Radar [kpop-radar] (n.d.). Youtube Viewcount. https://www.kpop-radar.com/viewcount?type=2&date=1&gender=1.
Lee, J., & Nguyen, A.T. (2020). How Music Fans Shape Commercial Music Services: A Case Study of BTS and ARMY. ISMIR. https://archives.ismir.net/ismir2020/paper/000147.pdf.
Lee, J., Oh, C., & Kim, Y.-C. (Eds.) (2021). *The Candlelight Movement, Democracy, and Communication in Korea*. London: Routledge.
Lee, S.-A. (2015). Of the Fans, by the Fans, for the Fans: The JYJ Republic. In S. Lee & A. M. Nornes (Eds.), *Hallyu 2.0: The Korean Wave in the Age of Social Media* (pp. 108–29). Ann Arbor: University of Michigan Press.
Liew, K.K. (2013). K-Pop Dance Trackers and Cover Dancers: Global Cosmopolitanization and Local Spatialization. In Y. Kim (Ed.), *The Korean Wave: Korean Media Go Global* (pp. 165–82). London: Routledge.
McCurry, J. (2020, June 24). How US K-pop fans became a political force to be reckoned with. *The Guardian*. https://www.theguardian.com/music/2020/jun/24/how-us-k-pop-fans-became-a-political-force-to-be-reckoned-with-blm-donald-trump.
Min, W., Jin, D.Y., & Han, B. (2018). Transcultural fandom of the Korean Wave in Latin America: Through the lens of cultural intimacy and affinity space. *Media, Culture & Society*, 41(5), 604–19. https://doi.org/10.1177/0163443718799403.
Oh, C. (2020). From Seoul to Copenhagen: Migrating K-pop cover dance and performing diasporic youth in social media. *Dance Research Journal*, 52(1), 20–32. https://doi.org/10.1017/S0149767720000030.
Oh, D.C. (2017). K-pop fans react: Hybridity and the white celebrity-fan on YouTube. *International Journal of Communication*, 11, 2270–2287. https://ijoc.org/index.php/ijoc/article/view/6307.
Oh, I., & Lee, H.-J. (2013). Mass media technologies and popular music: K-pop and YouTube. *Korea Journal*, 53(4), 34–58.
Ohandjanian, S. (2018, May 8). The giving power of K-pop fandoms. *SBS*. https://www.sbs.com.au/popasia/blog/2018/05/08/giving-power-k-pop-fandoms.
Ossewaarde, M., & Reijers, W. (2017). The illusion of the digital commons: 'False consciousness' in online alternative economies. *Organisation*, 24, 609–28. https://doi.org/10.1177/1350508417713217.
Shin, S.I., & Kim, L. (2013). Organizing K-pop: Emergence and market making of large Korean entertainment houses, 1980–2010. *East Asia*, 30, 255–72. https://doi.org/10.1007/s12140-013-9200-0.
*South China Morning Post* (2020, March 24). From BTS and Halsey to Dua Lipa and Hwasa: Western and K-pop collaborations on the increase. https://www.scmp.com/lifestyle/entertainment/article/3076665/bts-and-halsey-dua-lipa-and-hwasa-western-and-k-pop.
Spice Team (2021, October 9). *[K-pop in Public | One Take] Twice - The Feels | Dance Cover by Spice from Russia* [Video]. YouTube. https://www.youtube.com/watch?v=HVeURJ2Raqs.

Sun, M. (2020). K-pop fan labor and an alternative creative industry: A case study of GOT7 Chinese fans. *Global Media and China*, 5(4), 389–406. https://doi.org/10.1177/2059436420954588.

Sun, M., & Liew, K.K. (2019). Analog Hallyu: Historicizing K-pop formations in China. *Global Media and China*, 4(4), 419–36. https://doi.org/10.1177/2059436419881915.

Tanakasempipat, P. (2020, November 3). K-pop's social media power spurs Thailand's youth protests. *Reuters*. https://www.reuters.com/article/us-thailand-protests-k-pop-idUSKBN27I23K.

Tinaliga, B. (2018). *'At War for OPPA and Identity': Competitive Performativity among Korean-Pop Fandoms*. [Master's Projects and Capstones. University of San Francisco]. https://repository.usfca.edu/capstone/768.

Velasquez, A., & LaRose, R. (2015). Youth collective activism through social media: The role of collective efficacy. *New Media & Society*, 17(6), 899–918. https://doi.org/10.1177/1461444813518391.

Zhang, Q., & Negus, K. (2020). East Asian pop music idol production and the emergence of data fandom in China. *International Journal of Cultural Studies*, 23(4). https://doi.org/10.1177/1367877920904064.

# PART III

# CIVICS AND POLITICS

# 10. Monitoring and reputation: principal–agent relationships and the role of social media in political representation

*Andrea Ceron*

## INTRODUCTION: HOW MANY ONLINE PUBLIC SPHERES?

For a long time, academics, journalists and political analysts have debated on the risks and the opportunities provided by new communication technologies, namely the Internet and social media, in terms of deliberation and diffusion of news, trends and opinions. The debate was generally focused on the Web as a kind of unitary environment, and social networking sites (SNS) were often considered as a single body to which blame can be attributed. Over the years, Facebook, Twitter and other SNS (e.g., Telegram, more recently) became the 'usual suspects,' repeatedly deemed responsible for allowing hate speech and spreading fake news (Salo, Mäntymäki & Islam, 2018), helping undesirable candidates (especially populist parties; see Flew & Iosifidis, 2020) to manipulate and win elections or even for boosting terrorists' proselytism (e.g., Johnson et al., 2016).

Actually, rather than being a unified monolithic actor with its own traits, able to influence social and political outcomes (based on specific collective opinions), social media look more like 'Matryoshka dolls': they are a layered environment composed of distinct subsets and nested subgroups; each of them retains peculiar features that portray the different faces of each 'doll' and expresses different opinions.

Separating online conversations into multiple subsamples makes perfect sense in light of the idea that social media are composed of 'echo chambers' (e.g., Bright et al., 2020; for a different view, see Dubois & Blank, 2018). In these echo chambers the most similar users gather together, being exposed to similar stimuli that reciprocally reinforce their beliefs and confirm their pre-existing opinions.

The idea of splitting social media into smaller communities seems particularly reasonable on SNS such as Telegram (with its own segregated, or even secret, groups and channels) or Facebook (given its wide penetration rate and the heterogeneity of its users); however, differences can also be found on Twitter despite the fact that only a minority of users is active on it. In fact, Twitter seems mostly populated by socio-political elites. Nevertheless, even in such narrower and elitist social media, one can find multiple Twitterspheres disconnected from each other, some of them reflecting the views of the 'mainstream,' being dominated by media consumers and socio-political elites, while others can lie away from the major centers of decision-making (Ceron & Splendore, 2019; see also Vargo, Basilaia & Shaw, 2015).

Summing up, instead of talking about the Web as a single online public sphere, it seems more reasonable to discuss the existence (and the effects) of multiple online blogospheres/Twitterspheres.

## SOCIAL MEDIA AS NEW (COMPETING) PRINCIPALS?

Notwithstanding the real nature of social media, there is currently an ongoing debate about their potential impact on a range of political actors, including parties or governments and parliaments during the policymaking process.

As is well known, in political systems, politicians and political agents (e.g., party officers, members of parliament, ministers, prime ministers) have to deal with the requests and meet the demands of several actors, such as: citizens/voters, party members and activists, colleagues from the same party/coalition, party leaders, interest groups and mass media, to name just a few. As long as each actor can raise conflicting requests, politicians and political agents will face the pressure of these 'competing principals' (Carey, 2007).

In light of the non-monolithic and layered structure of social media, we may wonder whether the different subgroups and blogospheres that express their voices online can really influence politics, acting like additional 'principals' that political 'agents' must satisfy (Ceron, 2016).

While politicians can use social media with a 'top-down' approach, spreading the party line (with messages tailored to their supporters) or generating personalized contents that can even differ from the official party position, they are also exposed to the opinions expressed 'bottom-up' on social media (Graham, Jackson & Broersma, 2016). In a study on members of the lower legislative houses in the Netherlands, United Kingdom, and United States (October 2013), Tromble (2018) found evidence of interactions between elected politicians and citizens from their constituency on concrete policy issues. Consequently, politicians can feel a pressure to conform to such opinions in order to make their followers and voters happy.

Despite the fact that the relationships between citizens and politicians online could be asymmetrical, as politicians mostly care about broadcasting their messages rather than interacting with citizens, the interactive nature of social media makes it hard to ignore someone else's opinions, especially those of their 'friends' and 'followers,' who can try to interact with politicians and speak back, commenting on texts posted by politicians or sending them direct messages (Ceron, 2016; Scarrow, 2015). As such, social media can allow parties to gather feedback, not only from their core membership base, but also from larger subsets of citizens interested and engaged in politics (and perhaps not committed to a political party yet).

It could be argued that some of these new sympathizers, which are primarily active online, could retain policy preferences and express opinions that partially differ compared to the traditional party line and to the viewpoints of the ordinary rank-and-file members and traditional core party voters.

If this is the case, parties will be exposed to such a new environment composed of 'competing networks of supporters' (Chadwick & Stromer-Galley, 2016, p. 287) and social media can be considered as a new 'competing principal' that politicians must take into account. If such different social media audiences are indeed becoming new competing principals, this should boost the responsiveness of political parties and politicians toward the wills of these new principals, especially during the policymaking process.

In view of that, academic studies and practical applications have investigated to what extent social media data are used to inform policymakers across the whole policy cycle, from the planning phase to the *ex post* evaluation (Poel, Meyer & Schroeder, 2018; Suominen & Hajikhani, 2021). For instance, from 2014 to 2018 no less than 120 academic articles were published on this topic (Studinkaa & Guenduez, 2018). Social media are mostly deemed useful in the agenda-setting and planning phase (empowering and engaging citizens and stakeholders). For instance, by analyzing Twitter data to monitor public opinion on space policy in the United States, Whitman Cobb (2015) found that Twitter can represent a new measure of public interest available to policymakers and policy analysts. As such, 'policy entrepreneurs in both the space community and political community could find this type of data valuable as they endeavor to lobby Congress and the executive branch to support further activities or spending for NASA' (Whitman Cobb, 2015, p. 16).

However, there is some room for the use of social media even in the formulation, implementation and *ex post* evaluation of public policies (Ceron & Negri, 2016). In this regard, the main prospective improvement seems the opportunity to perform a continuous evaluation and the use of social media data seems markedly linked with the idea of evidence-based data-driven policymaking. So far, however, the preferences expressed online are not fully taken into account by governments and parliaments. The degree of responsiveness of political actors toward the demands of the social media audiences in the field of policymaking seems still limited and driven by other contextual factors. Previous research, including a meta-analytical review of existing studies (Dekker & Bekkers, 2015), indicates that several elements contribute to explaining why in some cases governments follow social media's suggestions while in others they do not. In particular, three elements seem to play a role: (1) the policy preferences of policymakers (compared to those of social media users and to those of their constituency), (2) government openness to online opinions and (3) the strength of the online protest.

As such, rather than becoming responsive toward these new online principals (per se), policymakers seem to follow the requests of social media users only when their demands match those of more traditional principals; e.g., core voters, activists or ideologically leaning interest groups (Ceron & Negri, 2016). If this is the case, we should move away from the idea of social media communities as new isolated actors and provide a different interpretation of their role.

## SOCIAL MEDIA AS A NEW TOOL FOR DECREASING AGENCY COSTS

Here we provide an alternative explanation concerning the role and the impact of social media on political choices and policy outcomes. In fact, technological innovation can provide parties with new means to communicate directly with voters and to recruit local support (also in the inter-election period), offering to parties 'a chance to rebuild deeper offline connections into their local communities' (Gibson, 2015, p. 191). In addition, political conversations online '[deepen] party-related engagement by offering new avenues by which party members can provide parties with support, feedback, and resources' (Vaccari & Valeriani, 2016, p. 295). Apart from reinforcing the connection between politicians and party members or voters, social media can also strengthen politicians' link with their leader and the party elites, allowing them to interact together (also) online. In the same vein, social media can help to establish close and more direct relationships with interest groups, both at the local and at the national level. For instance, in Sweden the union for industrial workers (IF Metall), which is closely connected to the Social Democratic Party, successfully exploited digital communication to attract attention and to 'amplify personal, prestigious, and established contacts' with key political actors (Johansson & Scaramuzzino, 2019, p. 1536).

In this regard, far from adding new actors to the list of competing principals (Carey, 2007), social media can represent a new tool available to traditional principals, providing them with a new public space suitable for reducing the 'agency costs,' decreasing the asymmetry of information between each traditional principal (citizens/voters, party members and activists, party leaders, interest groups, etc.) and the agent (which can be, in turn, a backbencher or local politician, a member of parliament as well as a minister, or the prime minister). On the one hand, social media can decrease the 'monitoring costs,' paid by the principal to monitor and orient the activity of the agent; on the other hand, they can reduce the 'reputation costs,' paid by the agent to prove the willingness to comply with the principal's interests and demands.

First, given that they reduce monitoring costs, social media can foster accountability and responsiveness as the principal can more easily observe the behavior of its agent. However, this is more likely to happen in some contexts: the individual behavior of politicians can be more easily shaped in candidate-centered electoral systems, when intra-party rules promote decentralization, or when the media system amplifies their message; in addition, responsiveness can take place when the stakes raised on social media match the interests of the party leadership or pose a real threat to parties' strength, so that the party cannot ignore social media comments without losing support.

For instance, in March 2018, the leadership of the Italian Democratic Party (PD) was negotiating a coalition agreement with the Five Star Movement (M5S), a rival (populist) party. This negotiation was stopped by a 'tweet bombing,' promoted by the former PD leader Matteo Renzi, which suddenly revealed the disagreement of many PD voters and elected representatives, who expressed on Twitter their aversion for this alliance through the hashtag '#senzadime' (#WithoutMe). The massive disagreement of party activists and representatives (which threatened the strength and the unity of the party) prevented the PD from reaching a compromise with the M5S.[1]

To sum up, politicians and parties can be more easily monitored thanks to social media, but they will become more accountable and more responsive only when there is an incentive to do so (for instance, an electoral incentive, or incentives linked with career advancements); beside this, accountability and responsiveness can be strengthened when the asymmetry of information between the agent and the principal gets erased (perhaps thanks to the interaction of social media and mass media), so that the agent cannot hide its misconduct and he or she will be sanctioned by the principal.

Second, given that they reduce reputation costs, social media can increase the transparency of politicians and the whole political system. For instance, during the television debate between Emmanuel Macron and Marine Le Pen, which took place before the runoff of the 2022 French presidential elections, Le Pen answered a question about her views on the war between Russia and Ukraine, showing to the cameras a 2014 tweet in which she supported the independence of Ukraine. Such a dated tweet was used by Le Pen as an attempt to prove the transparency and the consistency of her thought, boosting her reputation.

In turn, the usage of social media to promote personal reputation can be more evident for the backbenchers compared to prominent politicians belonging to the party leadership or for some types of parties and not for others (according to the different intra-party rules and the degree of intra-party discipline within each party). Nevertheless, as long as backbenchers can use social media to build their reputation (either showing their loyalty toward the leadership or boosting their popularity among party activists and voters), social media can trigger some degree of 'equalization' (Jacobs & Spierings, 2016),[2] at least at the intra-party level, though the party leadership still retains control (Ceron, 2017a).

In a nutshell, politicians have to deal with a number of competing principals, including the party leadership. Consequently, they should remain partially loyal to the party and social media can certainly provide an opportunity to publicly display such loyalty; this opportunity can be more crucial for backbenchers who can gain more visibility (and maybe get career advancements) thanks to these tools, given that usually they do not have an easy access to traditional media or to higher offices within traditional party structures (for instance, they might not be allowed to speak, or to get their voices heard by the leadership, during offline internal party meetings).

Alternatively, social media can also allow politicians to distinguish themselves from the official party line. This can be a fruitful strategy in some contexts, being rewarding in terms of votes and office payoffs (especially in candidate-centered electoral systems); this choice can be reasonable also in other contexts – i.e., to express dissent when the policy view of the leadership is too distant from the views of the politician or to express dissatisfaction when the perspectives of career advancement within the party are null. In such cases, politicians can criticize the leadership on social media, using their online voice to appear responsive toward other principals:

their factional leader or a challenger leader (a politician challenging the current leader), as well as toward their local constituency or interest groups, provided that these political actors will help the politician supporting his or her rebellious behavior.

Anyway, the opportunity to express a voice on social media can increase the transparency, allowing individual politicians to shed light on their preferences (Ceron, 2017b; Sältzer, 2022). In detail, Sältzer (2022) analyzed more than 800,000 tweets from 498 members of the German Bundestag through correspondence analysis and managed to reproduce the policy positions of politicians (within and across parties) on the economic and cultural left–right scales. Analogously, Ceron (2017b) proved that text analysis of contents posted online can be informative on the ideological preferences of politicians, allowing one to understand their actual behavior and several political outcomes concerning: (1) a politician's choice to endorse one or another party leader, (2) a politician's likelihood of switching off from his or her parliamentary party group and (3) a politician's probability of being appointed as a minister.

To sum up, according to this alternative approach social media are not becoming a new competing principal that politicians must satisfy; nevertheless, by increasing politicians' incentives to respond to their traditional principals (among them: leaders, activists and voters), social media can strengthen the circuit of representation and the chain of responsiveness that goes from voters to political parties and elected members of parliament, and from them to governments and bureaucrats (Ceron, 2017a). Therefore, they can still help build a bridge between citizens and political elites, reinforcing the processes behind representative democracy.

## TOWARD A SENTIMENT DEMOCRACY?

In recent years, a wide academic debate addressed the role of the Internet and social media and their democratic potential, trying to assess whether they can represent a virtual public sphere (Dahlgren, 2005) in Habermasian terms (Habermas, 1989). Social media do not seem suitable to provide the space for an idealized form of democratic deliberation (Habermas, 1989), even though they allow the different layered communities and the different groups of activated public opinion (Ceron & Negri, 2016) to express their voices and get in touch with other political actors. Indeed, the fact that politicians and voters can potentially interact online looks like a confirmation for the democratic potential of communication on social media (Tromble, 2018).

Due to the limited representativeness of social media users active online (who do not mimic the socio-demographic traits of the whole population of voters), the usage of social media to make a guess about public opinion is currently limited. While national governments still collect information on the sentiment expressed online toward public policies, so far this information is deemed less relevant than that provided by traditional survey polls and elected officials are not 'governing with the sentiment' yet.

Having said that, there are reasons to believe that governments and political actors will become more responsive toward the pressure of social media communities, when such pressure will thoroughly correspond to the viewpoints of citizens, voters and interest groups, even more so if in the future all the citizens will exploit the opportunity to be active and comment online, with their own verified digital identities.

Although some voices expressed online are still ignored, some steps have been taken in the direction of a 'sentiment democracy.' This concept refers to the idea of embedding the role of online opinions in the different spheres of the society and in all the bodies of political institutions, including political parties and legislatures.

In light of the role of social media as tools that facilitate principal–agent relationships, a sentiment democracy also involves the use of social media by politicians to express their political preferences. As discussed above, this can produce higher levels of accountability and transparency, no matter whether such preferences are sincere or expressed for instrumentally strategic purposes, given that the opinions expressed online remain visible and, based on that, politicians can be held accountable by their principals, namely voters, party activists, leaders and interest groups. Indeed, democratic accountability is all about communicating policy preferences (Proksch & Slapin, 2015), and social media can certainly play a role in this process.

## CONCLUSION AND DIRECTIONS FOR FUTURE RESEARCH

This chapter highlighted several features of political communication on social media, focusing in particular on: (1) the existence of multiple and layered public spaces; (2) the role of social media in decreasing the agency costs, thereby making principal–agent relationships easier (rather than creating new principals); and (3) the democratic potential and the road toward a sentiment democracy, despite the current non-representativeness of (active) social media users compared to the whole population of citizens/voters.

All these elements open the way to new avenues of research that require a deeper reflection by social scientists interested in political communication on social media.

To start with, given that social media do not represent a monolithic actor, scholars working with social media data should be warned of the variety of online communities that might express conflicting opinions and display divergent reactions over time. There is no unique online public sphere and there is not a single blogosphere/Twittersphere or social media body that we can investigate and to which we can attribute effects on political relevant outcomes. This has implications, for instance, on agenda-setting studies. The current research is often limited to observing whether social media do anticipate or follow the agenda of traditional media (or that of other political actors). Instead, given the nature of social media, agenda-setting processes could be better identified by splitting the online public space into multiple pieces. There are plenty of options to do so; for instance, distinguishing some authors/accounts from others, or discriminating between political elites (such as official accounts of parties and politicians), cultural elites of news producers (traditional media or individual journalists and bloggers), so-called influencers (highly active and popular accounts, no matter their field of expertise, from make-up to high-tech) and the average user.

Alternatively, filter bubbles can be exploited to cluster together members that usually share similar contents (and therefore can be potentially exposed to similar news inputs) or that interact more often together in an echo chamber (community-detection tools offered by social network analysis can be particularly useful for this). Another choice could be to isolate 'communities of conversations,' using keywords or hashtags to identify peculiar groups of people that comment on the same topic. Taking into account the variety of subsets existing online is a choice suitable also for other subfields of political communication.

Beside this, future studies should dig more in depth into the differences between alternative social media to account for the fact that different platforms are used by different users for different purposes. As such, studies could compare political communication on Facebook, Twitter and Telegram, just to name a few.

Future research should also compare the strategies of political communication (and their effects in terms of engagement and responsiveness) under different political systems (Bene et al., 2022), with an eye to the differences between party- and candidate-centered electoral systems, which can give rise to crucial differences in terms of reputation costs, as discussed above. Analogously, the communication strategies of politicians can be investigated to shed light on their individual behavior and to analyze the development of their political careers. Lastly, while scholars have made attempts to analyze social media comments by weighting them (according to the socio-demographic traits of the users) or combining them with traditional survey polls, the current peculiar structure of social media conversations calls for the development of new concepts of public opinion. Scholars should acknowledge that the object of social media analysis is generally different from the concept of public opinion as the sum of individual preferences, which is usually caught through survey polls (even though the findings from these different data sources can align).

Time will tell whether the evolution of social media and big data analysis in our society, in the long run, will close the gap between these two different concepts of public opinion, paving the way to new institutional structures, to new types of political communication and to new forms of (sentiment) democracy.

## NOTES

1. https://www.reuters.com/article/us-italy-politics-idUSKBN1HV1TA.
2. In a study on the Netherlands, Jacobs and Spierings (2016) found that several backbenchers manage to use social media at a high-quality level, better than their political leaders, and generate more engagement (obtaining higher 'Klout Scores'). This can equalize intra-party relationships as some of the politicians more active online also got a higher number of preference votes in the elections.

# REFERENCES

Bene, M., Ceron, A., Fenoll, V., Haßler, J., Kruschinski, S., Larsson, A.O., Magin, M., Schlosser, K., & Wurst, A.-K. (2022). Keep them engaged! Investigating the effects of self-centered social media communication style on user engagement in 12 European countries. *Political Communication*, *39*(4), 429–53. https://doi.org/10.1080/10584609.2022.2042435.

Bright, J., Marchal, N., Ganesh, B., & Rudinac S. (2020). Echo chambers exist! (but they're full of opposing views). *arVix.org*. https://arxiv.org/abs/2001.11461.

Carey, J.M. (2007). Competing principals, political institutions, and party unity in legislative voting. *American Journal of Political Science*, *51*(1), 92–107. https://doi.org/10.1111/j.1540–5907.2007.00239.x.

Ceron, A. (2016). Competing Principals 2.0? The impact of Facebook in the 2013 selection of the Italian head of state. *Italian Political Science Review*, *46*(3), 313–33. https://doi.org/10.1017/ipo.2016.14.

Ceron, A. (2017a). *Social Media and Political Accountability: Bridging the Gap between Citizens and Politicians*. Palgrave Macmillan.

Ceron, A. (2017b). Intra-party politics in 140 characters. *Party Politics*, *23*(1), 7–17. https://doi.org/10.1177/1354068816654325.

Ceron, A., & Negri, F. (2016). The 'social side' of public policy: Monitoring online public opinion and its mobilization during the policy cycle. *Policy & Internet*, *8*(1), 131–47. https://doi.org/10.1002/poi3.117.

Ceron, A., & Splendore, S. (2019). 'Cheap talk'? Second screening and the irrelevance of TV political debates. *Journalism*, *20*(8), 1108–23. https://doi.org/10.1177/1464884919845443.

Chadwick, A., & Stromer-Galley, J. (2016). Digital media, power, and democracy in parties and election campaigns: Party decline or party renewal? *International Journal of Press/Politics*, *21*(3), 283–93. https://doi.org/10.1177/1940161216646731.

Dahlgren, P. (2005). The internet, public spheres and political communication: Dispersion and deliberation. *Political Communication*, *22*(2), 147–62. https://doi.org/10.1080/10584600590933160.

Dekker, R., & Bekkers, V. (2015). The contingency of governments' responsiveness to the virtual public sphere: A systematic literature review and metasynthesis. *Government Information Quarterly*, *32*(4), 496–505. https://doi.org/10.1016/j.giq.2015.09.007.

Dubois, E., & Blank, G. (2018). The echo chamber is overstated: The moderating effect of political interest and diverse media. *Information, Communication & Society*, *21*(5), 729–45. https://doi.org/10.1080/1369118X.2018.1428656.

Flew, T., & Iosifidis, P. (2020). Populism, globalisation and social media. *International Communication Gazette*, *82*(1), 7–25. https://doi.org/10.1177/1748048519880721.

Gibson, R.K. (2015). Party change, social media and the rise of 'citizen-initiated' campaigning. *Party Politics*, *21*(2), 183–97. https://doi.org/10.1177/1354068812472575.

Graham, T., Jackson, D., & Broersma, M. (2016). New platform, old habits? Candidates' use of Twitter during the 2010 British and Dutch general election campaigns. *New Media & Society*, *18*(5), 765–83. https://doi.org/10.1177/1461444814546728.

Habermas, J. (1989). *The Structural Transformation of the Public Sphere: An Inquiry into a Category of Bourgeois Society*. MIT Press.

Jacobs, K., & Spierings, N. (2016). *Social Media, Parties and Political Inequalities*. Palgrave Macmillan.

Johansson, H., & Scaramuzzino, G. (2019). The logics of digital advocacy: Between acts of political influence and presence. *New Media & Society*, *21*(7), 1528–45. https://doi.org/10.1177/1461444818822488.

Johnson, N.F., Zheng, M., Vorobyeva, Y., Gabriel, A., Qi, H., Velasquez, N., … Wuchty, S. (2016). New online ecology of adversarial aggregates: ISIS and beyond. *Science*, *352*(6292), 1459–63. https://doi.org/10.1126/science.aaf0675.

Poel, M., Meyer, E.T., & Schroeder, R. (2018). Big data for policymaking: Great expectations, but with limited progress? *Policy & Internet*, *10*(3), 347–67. https://doi.org/10.1002/poi3.176.

Proksch, S.-O., & Slapin, J.B. (2015). *The Politics of Parliamentary Debate: Parties, Rebels and Representation*. Cambridge University Press.

Salo, J., Mäntymäki, M., & Islam, A.K.M.N. (2018). The dark side of social media – and *Fifty Shades of Grey* introduction to the special issue: the dark side of social media. *Internet Research*, *28*(5), 1166–8. https://doi.org/10.1108/IntR-10-2018-442.

Sältzer, M. (2022). Finding the bird's wings: Dimensions of factional conflict on Twitter. *Party Politics*, *28*(1), 61–70. https://doi.org/10.1177/1354068820957960.

Scarrow, S.E. (2015). *Beyond Party Members: Changing Approaches to Partisan Mobilization*. Oxford University Press.

Studinkaa, J., & Guenduez, A.A. (2018). The Use of Big Data in the Public Policy Process: Paving the Way for Evidence-Based Governance. European Group for Public Administration (EGPA) Conference, Lausanne, 5–7 September 2018. https://www.alexandria.unisg.ch/255680/.

Suominen, A., & Hajikhani, A. (2021). Research themes in big data analytics for policymaking: Insights from a mixed-methods systematic literature review. *Policy & Internet*, *13*(4), 464–84. https://doi.org/10.1002/poi3.258.

Tromble, R. (2018). Thanks for (actually) responding! How citizen demand shapes politicians' interactive practices on Twitter. *New Media & Society*, *20*(2), 676–97. https://doi.org/10.1177/1461444816669158.

Vaccari, C., & Valeriani, A. (2016). Party campaigners or citizen campaigners? How social media deepen and broaden party-related engagement. *International Journal of Press/Politics*, *21*(3), 294–312. https://doi.org/10.1177/1940161216642152.

Vargo, C.J., Basilaia, E., & Shaw, D.L. (2015). Event versus issue: Twitter reflections of major news – A case study. *Communication and Information Technologies Annual: Studies in Media and Communications*, *9*, 215–39. https://doi.org/10.1108/S2050-206020150000009009.

Whitman Cobb, W.N. (2015). Trending now: Using big data to examine public opinion of space policy. *Space Policy*, *32*(1), 11–16. http://dx.doi.org/10.1016/j.spacepol.2015.02.008.

# 11. Political implications of disconnective practices on social media: unfriending, unfollowing, and blocking

*Qinfeng Zhu*

## INTRODUCTION

Since the early days of social media, scholars and pundits have been fascinated with the communication technologies that could strengthen the social fabric, collapse geographic and demographic boundaries, and form large, decentralized social networks. This burgeoning interest could be traced to the socio-historical conditions of declining group memberships and associational lives, conditions thought to be vital to a vibrant democratic society (Bennett & Iyengar, 2008; Putnam, 2000; Putnam et al., 1994). Against this background, a large body of research has focused on the functioning of social media through the lens of connectivity, arguing that by promoting a more open and accessible form of communication, social media are able to revive citizen engagement in public life.

To be sure, social media afford users the ability to easily extend their social circles beyond milieus of family and close friends and maintain a large repertoire of new, weak, and diverse ties (Ellison et al., 2007, 2011). The expansion of online social networks not only facilitates information cascades, providing more learning and participation opportunities, but also exposes people to a more diverse array of political views than other communication channels (Barnidge, 2016; Goel et al., 2010; González-Bailón et al., 2011). It also holds the key to 'connective action'; in the process of forming large online social networks individuals' self-expressions are recognized, shared, and amplified, mobilizing others and oneself to join political campaigns and social movements (Bennett & Segerberg, 2012). A meta-analytic study further confirms that using social media to connect with others is one of the most important predictors of engagement in civic and political life (Boulianne, 2019).

Overall, this bulk of literature presents an optimistic view that social media harbor the potential for cultivating an informed and participatory citizenry. More importantly, it highlights that this democratic potential rests on the affordance of connectivity. But what the digital architects have envisioned does not necessarily resemble people's lived experiences. On the contrary, the expansion of online social networks has led to social fatigue and information saturation, depleting individuals' social batteries and decimating cognitive capacities (Dunbar, 2016; Metzger et al., 2010). Post hoc filtration thus becomes a necessity, and people can do so by terminating or suspending previously established digital ties, such as unfriending, unfollowing, and blocking (Sibona, 2014; Yang et al., 2017). These *disconnective* practices allow people to prune their online social networks and curate newsfeeds to their liking. In times of heightened political conflicts, they serve to exclude those one disagrees with, filter undesirable content and challenging views, regulate the boundaries of 'personal public spheres,' and build socially supportive and emotionally 'safe' spaces (John & Agbarya, 2020; John & Gal, 2018; Zhu & Skoric, 2021a, 2021b).

The question thus arises: since connectivity is essential to an informed and engaged citizenry, how would the rise of disconnectivity shape individuals' political worldviews and behaviors and impact the democratic potential of social media? To shed light on this, the current chapter will delineate the politics of disconnective practices, review the existing theoretical and empirical evidence to explain and discuss the underlying mechanisms and political implications, and suggest directions for future research.

## THE POLITICS OF DISCONNECTIVE PRACTICES

Digital tie dissolution on social media (often studied under the broad term of 'unfriending' or 'defriending') is 'a conscious act by a person to end the dyadic relationship and manifests itself through the removal of a link between the dyad' (Sibona, 2014, p. 1677). Though it can be easily achieved with a click of a button, it is socially costly in the sense that unfriending naturally reduces social capital associated with social media use (Ellison et al., 2011). It is often considered socially undesirable as well, as it can reflect on one's image negatively (Bryant & Marmo, 2012). Disconnective practices are also deliberate and explicit. Different from gradual relationship decay common in the 'offline' world, they resemble deliberate withdrawal that is often caused by interpersonal conflicts or actions perceived as relational transgressions (Bryant & Marmo, 2012).

Early research suggests that people usually refrain from dissolving ties once they have been established on social media, even when categorized as dispensable (Karr-Wisniewski et al., 2011; Krämer et al., 2015). A national survey conducted by the Pew Research Center in 2014 showed that only between 18 and 26 percent of the American social media users reported unfriending or unfollowing others in their entire social media lives. The major deterrent to unfriending is the fear of losing a social contact forever (Krämer et al., 2015). Indeed, the primary goal of many people is to get along with one another on a day-to-day basis; they value the social resources embedded in the new, weak, and diverse ties, project their own beliefs and values onto others, and downplay the importance of politics in their social interactions (Goel et al., 2010; Grevet et al., 2014; Messing & Westwood, 2014; Mutz, 2006).

While people are able to live in a politically diverse social environment in the apolitical everyday life, in times of heightened political conflicts people tend to become more eager to display political badges and sort themselves into like-minded enclaves (Iyengar et al., 2012). It is also a time when many openly express their strongly held political beliefs and are confronted with disagreeable or questionable views within their online social networks (John & Gal, 2018; Schwarz & Shani, 2016). These views are often taken as heuristic cues or boundary markers to categorize others, especially strangers and distant acquaintances, into in- and out-groups (Tajfel, 1982). Interactions across the ideological lines, when they occur, tend to be confrontational (Yardi & boyd, 2010). While the social currency depreciates and the defensive mindset prevails, politics becomes a prominent motivator in individuals' unfriending decisions.

A string of studies utilizing the survey method has gauged the scope of disconnective practices in a series of high-profile political conflicts, commonly termed 'politically motivated unfriending.' For example, during the Israel–Gaza armed conflict in 2014, around 16 percent of the Jewish Israeli Facebook users reported having unfriended or unfollowed someone because of Operation 'Protective Edge' (John & Dvir-Gvirsman, 2015). During the pro-democracy Umbrella Movement in Hong Kong 2014, a survey of university students showed that 15.6 percent of the young Facebook users reported hiding others' comments and posts or unfriending someone because of protest-related disagreement (Zhu et al., 2017). In a multi-country survey study conducted in 2017 (Skoric et al., 2021), 16.97 percent of the social media users in the UK after the Brexit referendum reported having unfriended or unfollowed others over their support for a candidate or issue they disagreed with. The US sample had the highest percentage of politically motivated unfriending: 29.75 percent, arguably due to the highly divisive 2016 presidential election that 'normalized the use of personal attacks, incendiary comments, and distorted facts as rhetorical devices on social media' (Skoric et al., 2021, p. 12). This was a sharp increase compared to the result based on the Pew survey in 2012, where only about 7 percent of American social media users reported having blocked, unfriended, or hidden someone for political reasons (Bode, 2017).

Needless to say, the variation in the extent of politically motivated unfriending is partially due to different method designs and questionnaire specifics. However, these findings together indicate an emerging trend of network pruning and cleansing during political conflicts. The larger political environment may well shape individuals' behaviors, as the extent of political unfriending seems to correspond to the level of political polarization on the ground. At the same time, we also note that overall political unfriending is not a dominant tendency, given that the majority of social media users do not remove social ties. While this may be true at the individual level, one can also argue that since people are most likely to drop weak ties that bridge otherwise disconnected groups (John & Dvir-Gvirsman, 2015; Zhu & Skoric, 2021a), disconnective practices will likely result in something akin to online gated communities at the aggregate level.

So, what are the political implications of disconnective practices? Although a relatively nascent program, empirical research in the past seven years has examined some antecedents of political unfriending and its influence on political engagement. One stream of findings shows that political disagreement is generally a consistent predictor of politically motivated unfriending, especially fundamental disagreement among weak ties that is deemed polarizing or uncivil (Bode, 2016; John & Dvir-Gvirsman, 2015; Neubaum et al., 2021a, 2021b; Zhu & Skoric, 2021a), although with some exceptions (Yang et al., 2017). In line with the theory of cognitive dissonance, these findings suggest that disconnective practices can function as a means of selective avoidance (Zhu et al., 2017). It serves to re-establish the social and informational homogeneity within individuals' online social networks, shielding people from opposing views. The other stream of research takes the larger social structure into consideration, specifically the minority–majority power dynamics. It emphasizes that for those feeling marginalized, disconnective practices are an expression and exercise of power. They are a means to protest against the hegemony of a dominant majority (John & Agbarya, 2020), and to create online safe spaces where minorities can express themselves and pursue their causes more freely (Zhu & Skoric, 2021a, 2021b). In the following two sections, I will review and discuss these two streams of research in more detail.

## SELECTIVE AVOIDANCE THROUGH DISCONNECTION

Since social media newsfeeds are largely curated by social contacts (Thorson & Wells, 2015), removing or suspending a digital tie with someone will also consequently filter out posts and comments made by that person. It can further feed into the platform's algorithmic decisions and reduce the chance of similar encounters in the future. In other words, disconnective practices are mechanisms for content filtration. Together with other means (e.g., friending/following, liking/hiding posts), they enable social media users to proactively control and personalize their news consumption (Lee et al., 2019; Lu, 2020). The question is thus *who* is more likely to be unfriended, in *which topical and relational context*, and for *what reasons*.

Based on a survey study conducted in Hong Kong shortly before the 2017 Chief Executive election, we found that encountering disagreement about the election coming from distant others (e.g., strangers, distant acquaintances) on social media is associated a higher likelihood of unfriending (Zhu & Skoric, 2021a). This is consistent with studies conducted in other political contexts, such as the 2016 Taiwanese presidential election, Israel–Gaza conflict of 2014, post-Brexit-referendum UK, and 2016 US presidential election. Together, this body of research suggests that discussing politics with disagreeing or distant others, frequency of encountering political disagreement, and perceived ideological and topical incongruence in online networks are all consistent predictors (Bode, 2016; John & Dvir-Gvirsman, 2015; Skoric et al., 2018, 2021). In brief, political disagreement plays a key role in unfriending.

This is in line with the theory of cognitive dissonance. It stipulates that people naturally gravitate toward information congenial to their prior beliefs and away from discordant messages (Festinger, 1957), as dissonance elicits negative arousal and people tend to judge counter-attitudinal information to be less credible or impartial (Metzger et al., 2015; Zanna & Cooper, 1974). This pattern has been consistently observed in individuals' news consumption and other information-seeking behaviors across media platforms; i.e., a tendency to selectively approach pro-attitudinal information, also known as selective exposure (Garrett, 2009; Hart et al., 2009; Stroud, 2008). Weighing in on the debate regarding whether the internet is facilitating a turn toward avoidance (Bennett & Iyengar, 2008; Garrett et al., 2013), the above-mentioned findings suggest that disconnective practices like unfriending constitute a means to selective avoidance; they allow people to deliberately and actively avoid counter-attitudinal information following initial exposure by cutting ties with the sources. Compared to selective exposure motivated by dissonance reduction, selective avoidance is likely driven by a state of defensive aversion (Garrett et al., 2013). Kim and colleagues (2022) further specified that it is due to the cognitive burden and emotional stress arising from the conflicting needs to defend one's political stance and to process information accurately.

Recent studies further identified the boundary conditions. First of all, not all social ties are susceptible to dissolution or suspension in the face of political disagreement. Weak ties are more likely to be broken than strong ties (John & Dvir-Gvirsman, 2015; Neubaum et al., 2021a; Zhu & Skoric, 2021a), and relational closeness and social support inhibits people from doing so (Neubaum et al., 2021a). This is arguably because, as a salient political event collapses the imaged homogeneity in online social networks, weak ties are likely the main source of major disagreements that are perceived as relational transgressions, trigger the feelings of shock and anger, and indicate fundamental incongruence (Grevet et al., 2014; John & Gal, 2018; Schwarz & Shani, 2016). We highlight here that, different from Mutz's (2006) vision of cross-cutting weak ties that are bounded by obligations and involve regular interactions (e.g., a family dentist), most of the weak ties on social media stand idle and involve little prior relational history or knowledge (e.g., a high-school classmate one has not spoken to for many years, or a person whom one met once at a conference). Since people are less constrained by the need to preserve these ties, they tend to be brittle when confronted with (perceived) conflicts.

Moreover, not all political disagreements lead to disconnection. Disagreements that violate moral codes; are deemed unresolvable, polarizing, disrespectful or uncivil; or indicate discrepancies in fundamental values are culpable (John & Agbarya, 2020; Neubaum et al., 2021a, 2021b). It thus suggests that unfriending decisions likely reflect the divide between groups subscribing to different moral foundations and value systems (e.g., the left vs. right in Germany, Democrats vs. Republicans in the US). Consequently, it may foster tribalism in the online environment. Of course, not everyone shields themselves from the other side; those who are politically interested and hold strong ideologies are more likely to do so (Bode, 2016; John & Dvir-Gvirsman, 2015; Skoric et al., 2018). Interview studies also reported instances where people accepted those holding opposing views through tolerance and understanding and engaged with them in order to change their opinions; nevertheless, this seems to happen mostly in close relationships, and people tend to see persuasive attempts among weak ties as futile (Grevet et al., 2014; Neubaum et al., 2021a).

Overall, disconnective practices enable people to shape their social media information exposure to their liking; it constitutes a form of selective avoidance, which 'cleanses' newsfeeds of discordant political views previously introduced by the expansion of online social networks. In line with the echo chamber concern, this is troubling given the long-standing normative expectation that exposure to political disagreement will moderate political attitudes and feelings. On the other hand, however, since unfriending targets those with fundamentally different worldviews, it can create an overall congruent environment and yet still leave room for issue disagreement to be aired in a more supportive and friendlier social setting. Since discussing politics is uncomfortable for many (Warren, 1996), one may thus ask: will disconnective practices be able to create a safer environment that is conducive to political expression and engagement? To answer the question, I proposed a more nuanced view of disconnective practices, which I call the 'safe space' thesis.

## DISCONNECTED BUT SAFE SPACES

When cutting someone off from our online networks, we are not only filtering content from that person, but also denying that person's access to view or comment on our (private) posts. This is a means to curate our audiences and manage discussion partners by regulating the boundaries of online social networks. The notion of disconnectivity as a form of boundary regulation is not new; previous research suggests that it is in response to the context collapse and increased socio-technical mediation brought about by social media platforms (Frederic & Woodrow, 2012; Sibona, 2014). John and Gal (2018) further argue that people engage in this kind of boundary regulation because they see their social media space as a 'personal public sphere'; they have both power in controlling it and responsibility for what other people may encounter there. Disconnectivity is thus 'the exercise of sovereignty over the personal public sphere, and specifically as a form of social exclusion' (p. 2982).

Following this stream of research, I argue that through social exclusion, disconnective practices can help create a psychologically, socially, and emotionally safe space, especially among those feeling marginalized. Emerging from the women's movement in the late twentieth century and advocated in the activist communities, the concept of 'safe space' is understood as a protected space that keeps marginalized groups free from violence and harassment (Roestone Collective, 2014). Feminist research highlights that for sexual and racial minorities, safety is not only about the absence of violence or danger, but often experienced as comfort – 'the emotional experience of retreat, sanctuary and being in place' (Moran & Skeggs, 2014, p. 88). Hence the ability to inhabit a space comfortably is an effect of power relations; those who can are protected by the comfort of the norm (Boulila, 2015). Similarly, according to the 'spiral of silence' theory, opinion minorities tend to experience an elevated fear of negative social sanctions and are hence inclined to self-censor or conform to the majority view (Hayes, 2007; Noelle-Neumann, 1974, 1979).

Thus, for marginalized groups, there is a heightened need to make their surroundings safe, and it is achieved through separation and control due to social norms and sanctions that are rooted in unequal power relations. In online spaces, cutting or suspending digital ties can be a means to this; it excludes those who may criticize or ridicule, prevents disapproval and confrontations, removes oneself from negative and sometimes toxic interactions, and curates a congenial audience and a supportive norm. These are important elements of a safe space that can empower the minorities to acquire 'a certain license to speak and act freely, form collective strength, and generate strategies for resistance' (Kenney, 2001, p. 24).

Existing research has offered some evidence in support of the safe space thesis. In a survey study conducted during the 2017 Hong Kong Chief Executive election period, we found that people who perceived themselves as opinion minorities had a stronger propensity than their majority counterparts to unfriend those holding challenging views. This is arguably because minorities generally have a clearer self-concept, are more likely to consider oppositions provocative or threatening, and have stronger needs to belong and to be validated (Zhu & Skoric, 2021a). In the context of Hong Kong politics, while the general public has experienced increasing polarization during and since the Umbrella Movement civic protests in 2014, people on both sides of the divide felt like a minority in their own home. The pro-democracy side felt marginalized as the Hong Kong government disqualified pro-democracy legislators and prosecuted prominent activists. As the state sanctions increased, they began to see people who disagreed with them with suspicion. On the other side, the pro-establishment supporters largely remained quiet, as their preference for economic prosperity over political reform and Chinese identity was often deemed illegitimate and dismissed amid the prevailing pro-democracy public discourse. In a political climate like this, the mounting fear of social and state sanctions can prompt people to reinstall the previously collapsed boundaries on social media. This is consistent with findings from in-depth interview studies that Arab Israelis reported unfriending Jewish Israeli Facebook friends during the Israel–Gaza conflict in order to avoid getting abusive messages, and turning away from confrontations and circumventing social surveillance that could lead to real-life sanctions (John & Agbarya, 2020; John & Gal, 2018).

Moreover, these online safe spaces created through disconnection can empower minorities to express otherwise suppressed opinions and marginalized identities. Using data from a two-wave panel survey conducted in Hong Kong, we found that politically motivated unfriending at Time 1 predicted an increase in political expression on social media at Time 2, but it was only statistically significant among those who saw themselves on the minority side (Zhu & Skoric, 2021b). This is corroborated by findings from semi-structured in-depth interviews. For example, a central theme that emerged from Arab Israelis' stories of unfriending is that, as minority members with a deficit of rights, unfriending allowed them to express their views and identities more freely without worrying about potential risks and repercussions (John & Agbarya, 2020). Some also saw unfriending as a way to 'punch up,' to protest against the hegemony of a dominant majority, and to return the provocative assault on their marginalized identity (John & Agbarya, 2020). In a way, to unfriend someone is also to strike a political statement. According to the notion of self-effects (Valkenburg,

2017), it can produce a self-mobilizing effect, motivating the 'unfrienders' to be more outspoken.

In sum, unfriending can be understood as practices to curate digital safe spaces for minorities. To be sure, this is democratically desirable as the disconnective practices empower the disenfranchised and potentially prepare them to acquire the courage and skills necessary to face challenges in the public arena. We found that during the Umbrella Movement in Hong Kong, politically motivated unfriending predicted participation in street protests, and this pattern was more pronounced among those who perceived a high level of out-group threat (Zhu et al., 2017). It is also consistent with the recent trend that people are migrating conversations from open social network sites (SNS) to the private and controlled environment of instant messaging (IM) platforms, and that this is particularly appealing to those who tend to otherwise self-censor or belong to minority groups (Valeriani & Vaccari, 2018; Velasquez et al., 2021).

Nevertheless, this also poses a democratic dilemma. As John and Agbarya (2020) pointed out, 'when a member of the minority unfriends someone from the majority group – even if they are punching up – they are distancing themselves from the centers of power' (p. 1075). Thus, unfriending may limit one's ability to persuade and mobilize others, which is crucial for advancing one's claim in a political contest. Moreover, this kind of digital activism is based on social exclusion and empowered by acts that could signal the silencing of fellow citizens (Tsfati & Dvir-Gvirsman, 2018). It may thus facilitate political participation at the expense of hearing the other side, deliberation, and associated benefits (Zhu & Skoric, 2021b). Essentially, it is engaging and disengaging at the same time.

## CONCLUSION AND DIRECTION FOR FUTURE RESEARCH

Going back to the initial question posted at the beginning of the chapter: since connectivity holds the key to an informed and engaged citizenry, how would the rising trend of disconnectivity shape the democratic potential of social media? So far, we have learned that disconnective practices in times of political conflicts are a means for the politically interested, opinionated, and marginalized to shield their eyes from opposing views, distance themselves from the other side, re-establish socio-informational homogeneity of their online social networks, reclaim the sovereignty of their online personal public spheres, and build safe spaces where minority views and identities can be freely expressed. They are driven by defensive goals, fueled by moral conflicts, and rooted in the existing power structures. Overall, the outcome presents a democratic paradox that disconnectivity can make people more engaged but not necessarily more informed, and more active in pursuing group interests while disengaging from those holding opposing views. It empowers political expressions of the marginalized, but also adds fuel to identity politics and runs counter to the ideal of political diversity. It can reverse the spiral of silence but distance the minorities further away from the center of power. It is simultaneously inclusive and exclusive, integrated and separatist, engaging and disengaging. As the norms of connectivity continue to decline in the digital media landscape, it may be the time again for us to revisit the nature of digital activism and rethink the virtue of participation that is often uncritically accepted as normative.

During the past seven years, the phenomenon of disconnectivity on social media has attracted a growing scholarly interest. However, this is still a nascent program, and there are many unresolved questions that beg further investigations. First of all, most of the studies so far have focused on political unfriending as terminating a previously established social tie. But disconnective practices vary in their sociability and different social media platforms have different regimes of disconnectivity, which may have distinct political implications. Future research should thus broaden the repertoire of disconnective practices, provide a more detailed anatomy of each practice, and conduct cross-platform comparisons.

Second, existing research has mostly focused on the cognitive and relational aspects of disagreement when explaining politically motivated unfriending. And yet in practice, it can be a deeply emotional experience, especially for those on the margins of a society. Thus, I encourage future research to shift its focus from the normative lenses of publics and counterpublics to the metaphor of 'safe spaces' that captures the emotional and discursive power struggles in people's everyday lives.

Furthermore, existing research has mostly approached disconnectivity as an individual decision and focused on the micro-level factors such as political orientations, cognitive traits, and network characteristics in its explanation. However, the characters and conduct of individuals are not only situated in the immediate social milieu but also enacted within a larger institutional context. For instance, two cross-country comparative studies indicate that the predictive power of the individual factors on politically motivated unfriending may vary across political landscapes and cultures (Skoric et al., 2018, 2021). Future research thus needs to further identify which and how institutional factors shape individuals' disconnective practices and condition their political impact.

Last but not least, we need to examine digital disconnectivity in a contemporary social media landscape that continues to evolve. For example, people are migrating conversations from open SNS to closed IM platforms that are end-to-end encrypted and without publicly visible profiles. Research suggests that IM platforms are conducive to political talk and have a depolarizing potential, arguably because they create a private and safe environment (Kligler-Vilenchik et al., 2020; Valeriani & Vaccari, 2018; Velasquez et al., 2021). Future research can thus draw on users' lived experiences to provide a more nuanced understanding of how people navigate the changing social-technological affordances to disconnect and (re)connect in responding to what they imagine and experience as a safe or insecure world.

## REFERENCES

Barnidge, M. (2016). Exposure to political disagreement in social media versus face-to-face and anonymous online settings. *Political Communication*, *34*(2), 302–21. doi:10.1080/10584609.2016.1235639.

Bennett, W.L., & Iyengar, S. (2008). A new era of minimal effects? The changing foundations of political communication. *Journal of Communication*, *58*(4), 707–31. doi:10.1111/j.1460-2466.2008.00410.x.

Bennett, W.L., & Segerberg, A. (2012). The logic of connective action: Digital media and the personalization of contentious politics. *Information, Communication & Society*, *15*(5), 739–68. doi:10.1080/1369118X.2012.670661.

Bode, L. (2016). Pruning the news feed: Unfriending and unfollowing political content on social media. *Research & Politics*, *3*(3), 1–8. doi:10.1177/2053168016661873.

Bode, L. (2017). Closing the gap: Gender parity in political engagement on social media. *Information Communication and Society*, *20*(4), 587–603. doi:10.1080/1369118X.2016.1202302.

Boulianne, S. (2019). Revolution in the making? Social media effects across the globe. *Information, Communication & Society*, *22*(1), 39–54. doi:10.1080/1369118X.2017.1353641.

Boulila, S.C. (2015). What makes a lesbian salsa space comfortable? Reconceptualising safety and homophobia. In K. Browne & E. Ferreira (Eds.), *Lesbian Geographies: Gender, Place and Power* (pp. 133–52). London: Ashgate.

Bryant, E.M., & Marmo, J. (2012). The rules of Facebook friendship: A two-stage examination of interaction rules in close, casual, and acquaintance friendships. *Journal of Social and Personal Relationships*, *29*(8), 1013–35. doi:10.1177/0265407512443616.

Dunbar, R.I.M. (2016). Do online social media cut through the constraints that limit the size of offline social networks ? *Royal Society Open Science*, *3*(1), 1–9. doi:10.1098/rsos.150292.

Ellison, N.B., Steinfeld, C., & Lampe, C. (2007). The benefits of Facebook 'friends': Social capital and college students' use of online social network sites. *Journal of Computer-Mediated Communication*, *12*(4), 1143–68. doi:10.1111/j.1083-6101.2007.00367.x.

Ellison, N.B., Steinfield, C., & Lampe, C. (2011). Connection strategies: Social capital implications of Facebook-enabled communication practices. *New Media & Society*, *13*(6), 873–92. doi:10.1177/1461444810385389.

Festinger, L. (1957). *A Theory of Cognitive Dissonance*. Stanford, CA: Stanford University Press.

Frederic, S., & Woodrow, H. (2012). Boundary regulation in social media. In *Proceedings of the ACM Conference on Computer Supported Cooperative Work, CSCW* (pp. 769–78). New York, NY: Association for Computing Machinery. doi:10.1145/2145204.2145320.

Garrett, R.K. (2009). Echo chambers online? Politically motivated selective exposure among Internet news users. *Journal of Computer-Mediated Communication*, *14*(2), 265–85. doi:10.1111/j.1083-6101.2009.01440.x.

Garrett, R.K., Carnahan, D., & Lynch, E.K. (2013). A turn toward avoidance? Selective exposure to online political information, 2004–2008. *Political Behavior*, *35*(1), 113–34. doi:10.1007/s11109-011-9185-6.

Goel, S., Mason, W., & Watts, D.J. (2010). Real and perceived attitude agreement in social networks. *Journal of Personality and Social Psychology*, *99*(4), 611–21. doi:10.1037/a0020697.

González-Bailón, S., Borge-Holthoefer, J., Rivero, A., & Moreno, Y. (2011). The dynamics of protest recruitment through an online network. *Scientific Reports*, *1*, 1–7. doi:10.1038/srep00197.

Grevet, C., Terveen, L., & Gilbert, E. (2014). Managing political differences in social media. In *Proceedings of the 17th ACM conference on Computer Supported Cooperative*

*Work & Social Computing* (pp. 1400–1408). New York, NY: Association for Computing Machinery.

Hart, W., Albarracín, D., Eagly, A.H., Brechan, I., Lindberg, M.J., & Merrill, L. (2009). Feeling validated versus being correct: A meta-analysis of selective exposure to information. *Psychological Bulletin*, *135*(4), 555–88. doi:10.1037/a0015701.

Hayes, A.F. (2007). Exploring the forms of self-censorship: On the spiral of silence and the use of opinion expression avoidance strategies. *Journal of Communication*, *57*(4), 785–802. doi:10.1111/j.1460-2466.2007.00368.x.

Iyengar, S., Sood, G., & Lelkes, Y. (2012). Affect, not ideology: A social identity perspective on polarization. *Public Opinion Quarterly*, *76*(3), 405–31. doi:10.1093/poq/nfs038.

John, N., & Agbarya, A. (2020). Punching up or turning away? Palestinians unfriending Jewish Israelis on Facebook. *New Media and Society*, *23*(5), 1063–79. doi:10.1177/1461444820908256.

John, N., & Dvir-Gvirsman, S. (2015). I don't like you anymore: Facebook unfriending by Israelis during the Israel-Gaza conflict of 2014. *Journal of Communication*, *65*(6), 953–74. doi:10.1111/jcom.12188.

John, N., & Gal, N. (2018). 'He's got his own sea': Political Facebook unfriending in the personal public sphere. *International Journal of Communication*, *12*, 2971–88.

Karr-Wisniewski, P., Wilson, D.C., & Richter-Lipford, H. (2011). A new social order: Mechanisms for social network site boundary regulation. *Proceedings of the Seventeenth Americas Conference on Information Systems, Detroit, Michigan, August 4–8*.

Kenney, M. (2001). *Mapping Gay LA: The Intersection of Place and Politics*. Philadelphia, PA: Temple University Press.

Kim, D.H., Jones-Jang, S.M., & Kenski, K. (2022). Unfriending and muting during elections: The antecedents and consequences. *Mass Communication and Society*, *25*(2), 161–84. doi: 10.1080/15205436.2021.1942494.

Kligler-Vilenchik, N., Baden, C., & Yarchi, M. (2020). Interpretative polarization across platforms: How political disagreement develops over time on Facebook, Twitter, and WhatsApp. *Social Media and Society*, *6*(3). doi:10.1177/2056305120944393.

Krämer, N., Hoffmann, L., & Eimler, S. (2015). Not breaking bonds on Facebook: Mixed-methods research on the influence of individuals' need to belong on 'unfriending' behavior on Facebook. *International Journal of Developmental Sciences*, *9*(2), 61–74. doi:10.3233/DEV-150161.

Lee, F.L.F., Chan, M.C.M., Chen, H.T., Nielsen, R., & Fletcher, R. (2019). Consumptive news feed curation on social media as proactive personalization: A study of six East Asian markets. *Journalism Studies*, *20*(15), 2277–92. doi:10.1080/1461670X.2019.1586567.

Lu, S. (2020). Taming the news feed on Facebook: Understanding consumptive news feed curation through a social cognitive perspective. *Digital Journalism*, *8*(9), 1163–80. doi:10.1080/21670811.2020.1837639.

Messing, S., & Westwood, S.J. (2014). Selective exposure in the age of social media: Endorsements trump partisan source affiliation when selecting news online. *Communication Research*, *41*(8), 1042–63. doi:10.1177/0093650212466406.

Metzger, M.J., Flanagin, A.J., & Medders, R.B. (2010). Social and heuristic approaches to credibility evaluation online. *Journal of Communication*, *60*(3), 413–39. doi:10.1111/j.1460-2466.2010.01488.x.

Metzger, M.J., Hartsell, E.H., & Flanagin, A.J. (2015). Cognitive dissonance or credibility? A comparison of two theoretical explanations for selective exposure to partisan news. *Communication Research*, *47*(1), 3–28. doi:10.1177/0093650215613136.

Moran, L., & Skeggs, B. (2014). *Sexuality and the Politics of Violence and Safety*. Abingdon: Routledge.

Mutz, D.C. (2006). *Hearing the Other Side: Deliberative Versus Participatory Democracy*. London: Cambridge University Press.

Neubaum, G., Cargnino, M., & Maleszka, J. (2021a). How Facebook users experience political disagreements and make decisions about the political homogenization of their online network. *International Journal of Communication*, *15*, 187–206.
Neubaum, G., Cargnino, M., Winter, S., & Dvir-Gvirsman, S. (2021b). 'You're still worth it': The moral and relational context of politically motivated unfriending decisions in online networks. *PLoS ONE*, *16*(1), 1–3. doi:10.1371/journal.pone.0243049.
Noelle-Neumann, E. (1974). The spiral of silence: A theory of public opinion. *Journal of Communication*, *24*(2), 43–51. doi:10.1111/j.1460-2466.1974.tb00367.x.
Noelle-Neumann, E. (1979). Public opinion and the classical tradition: A re-evaluation. *Public Opinion Quarterly*, *43*(2), 143–56. doi:10.1086/268507.
Putnam, R.D. (2000). *Bowling Alone: The Collapse and Revival of American Community*. New York, NY: Simon & Schuster.
Putnam, R.D., Leonardi, R., & Nanetti, R.Y. (1994). *Making Democracy Work*. Princeton, NJ: Princeton University Press.
Roestone Collective (2014). Safe space: Towards a reconceptualization. *Antipode*, *46*(5), 1346–65. doi:10.1111/anti.12089.
Schwarz, O., & Shani, G. (2016). Culture in mediated interaction: Political defriending on Facebook and the limits of networked individualism. *American Journal of Cultural Sociology*, *4*(3), 385–421. doi:10.1057/s41290-016-0006-6.
Sibona, C. (2014). Unfriending on Facebook: Context collapse and unfriending behaviors. In *47th Hawaii International Conference on System Sciences* (pp. 1676–85). doi:10.1109/HICSS.2014.214.
Skoric, M.M., Zhu, Q., Koc-Michalska, K., Boulianne, S., & Bimber, B. (2021). Selective avoidance on social media: A comparative study of Western democracies. *Social Science Computer Review*, *40*(5), 1241–58. doi:10.1177/08944393211005468.
Skoric, M.M., Zhu, Q., & Lin, J.-H.T. (2018). What predicts selective avoidance on social media? A study of political unfriending in Hong Kong and Taiwan. *American Behavioral Scientist*, *62*(8), 1097–1115. doi:10.1177/0002764218764251.
Stroud, N.J. (2008). Media use and political predispositions: Revisiting the concept of selective exposure. *Political Behavior*, *30*(3), 341–66. doi:10.1007/s11109-007-9050-9.
Tajfel, H. (1982). Social psychology of intergroup relations. *Annual Review of Psychology*, *33*(1), 1–39. doi:10.1146/annurev.ps.33.020182.000245.
Thorson, K., & Wells, C. (2015). Curated flows: A framework for mapping media exposure in the digital age. *Communication Theory*, *26*(3), 309–28. doi:10.1111/comt.12087.
Tsfati, Y., & Dvir-Gvirsman, S. (2018). Silencing fellow citizens: Conceptualization, measurement, and validation of a scale for measuring the belief in the importance of actively silencing others. *International Journal of Public Opinion Research*, *30*(3), 391–419. doi:10.1093/ijpor/edw038.
Valeriani, A., & Vaccari, C. (2018). Political talk on mobile instant messaging services: A comparative analysis of Germany, Italy, and the UK. *Information Communication and Society*, *21*(11), 1715–31. doi:10.1080/1369118X.2017.1350730.
Valkenburg, P.M. (2017). Understanding self-effects in social media. *Human Communication Research*, *43*(4), 477–90. doi:10.1111/hcre.12113.
Velasquez, A., Quenette, A.M., & Rojas, H. (2021). WhatsApp political expression and political participation: The role of ethnic minorities' group solidarity and political talk ethnic heterogeneity. *International Journal of Communication*, *15*, 2743–64.
Warren, M.E. (1996). What should we expect from more democracy? Radically democratic responses to politics. *Political Theory*, *24*(2), 241–70. doi:10.1177/0090591796024002004.
Yang, J., Barnidge, M., & Rojas, H. (2017). The politics of 'unfriending': User filtration in response to political disagreement on social media. *Computers in Human Behavior*, *70*, 22–9. doi:10.1016/j.chb.2016.12.079.

Yardi, S., & boyd, d. (2010). Dynamic debates: An analysis of group polarization over time on Twitter. *Bulletin of Science, Technology & Society*, *30*(5), 316–27. doi:10.1177/0270467610380011.

Zanna, M.P., & Cooper, J. (1974). Dissonance and the pill: An attribution approach to studying the arousal properties of dissonance. *Journal of Personality and Social Psychology*, *29*(5), 703–9. doi:10.1037/h0036651.

Zhu, Q., & Skoric, M.M. (2021a). From context collapse to 'safe spaces': Selective avoidance through tie dissolution on social media. *Mass Communication and Society*, *24*(6), 892–917. doi:10.1080/15205436.2021.1883671.

Zhu, Q., & Skoric, M.M. (2021b). Political implications of disconnection on social media: A study of politically motivated unfriending. *New Media & Society*, 24(12), 2659–79. doi:10.1177/1461444821999994.

Zhu, Q., Skoric, M.M., & Shen, F. (2017). I shield myself from thee: Selective avoidance on social media during political protests. *Political Communication*, *34*(1), 112–31. doi:10.1080/10584609.2016.1222471.

# 12. Teflonic social media behavior: why users refrain from participating in political discussions and why it matters[1]

*Márton Bene, Tamás Tóth and Manuel Goyanes*

## INTRODUCTION

The concept of 'Teflonic social media behavior' (TSMB; Goyanes & Skoric, 2021) was developed to capture intentional withdrawal from political activities on social media platforms in the context of the Catalan referendum on independence. Specifically, the metaphor of 'Teflonic' aims to link two related scenarios: (1) the behavior of a typical social media user when exposed to contentious discussions, and (2) Teflon's effect when cooking in a pan – the food slides, and does not get stuck. A related concept is the lurking attitude, but unlike the quantitative measurement based on a set of given and taken-for-granted items, the TSMB aims to problematize the attitudinal and behavioral trade-offs of partaking in political discussions.

Scholarship examining the impact of social media on politics has largely demonstrated the antecedents and effects on political participation (Skoric et al., 2016). Previous studies suggest that consuming news and expressing political views via social media significantly predict future political actions (Gil de Zúñiga et al., 2012). However, findings also suggest that many users remain passive (e.g., Vaccari, 2017), and refrain from expressing their political opinions in public because they intend to avoid online harassment, endless arguments, and tensions within their families (Goyanes & Skoric, 2021). While many are inactive because they are simply not interested in politics, research shows that there are other deterring factors beyond political (dis)interest (Pitcan et al., 2018, Vraga et al., 2015). We explicate one of them in this chapter: Teflonic social media behavior (Goyanes & Skoric, 2021). Therefore, we first problematize this concept's theoretical complexity and its main implications for political communication theory. Then, we discuss the challenges that social media platforms face as spaces for political discussion and action. Last, we summarize the existing findings to describe the social and psychological characteristics of the 'passive' users who engage in TSMB.

# TEFLONIC SOCIAL MEDIA BEHAVIOR: CONCEPT EXPLICATION AND THEORETICAL IMPLICATIONS

Recently, the initially positive view of social media as fostering democratic ideals associated with protest engagement and other forms of political participation has been systematically challenged (Goyanes et al., 2021). Recent scholarship has indeed documented that social media expand a fertile soil for a myriad of deleterious outcomes, such as the massive circulation of fabricated content (Goyanes and Lavin, 2018), ideological segregation (Bright, 2018) and polarization (Barberá et al., 2015; Vraga et al., 2015). While prior studies have mainly focused on the main antecedents that activate social media political discussions and participation (Huber et al., 2021), there is a surprising lack of knowledge on why people, despite being relatively active in these ecologies, shield themselves from the (un)civil noise and decide to avoid politics. The Teflonic social media behavior is a recent metaphorical concept that tries to explain this phenomenon. Although the original idea was aimed at explaining Catalan citizens' avoiding tactics during the referendum on independence in 2017, we believe this concept may also speak to other broader realities faced in our everyday lives.

Briefly, the TSMB is a construct that encompasses different motivational explanations that transpire into a consequential behavior: avoiding political discussions on social media. Specifically, it was defined as social media users' conscious abstention from political discussions on social media to avoid polemics and let social media political discussion 'slide' (Goyanes & Skoric, 2021, p. 11). Although the motivational antecedents are different in nature, the main rationale for their activation is that many citizens find political discussions in such ecologies unnecessary and bothersome, or they simply try to avoid heated polemics. TSMB thus implies a conscious effort to avoid political discussion in public spaces (i.e., social media), and a consequential retreat to more private spheres of instant messaging platforms (i.e., WhatsApp) and face-to-face interactions, usually with strong ties (Treré et al., 2017). In the original text, the TSMB is described as motivations through which refraining from political discussions is possible (Goyanes & Skoric, 2021, p. 11):

> "In social media opinions are taken out of context and therefore I preferred not to defend anything."
> "I didn't participate on social networks because it's useless and it ends up disrespecting each other."
> "I didn't take part because it creates conflicts, and I don't want conflicts."

Beyond voluntary behavior, the TSMB is also influenced by external factors, such as having public responsibilities, working in the public sector or having family in other regions of Spain (in the context of the Catalan referendum on independence). 'If I show what I really think about the Catalan referendum I will lose some of my clientele,' said Susana, the owner of a clothing store in Barcelona. Likewise, Rosalía, a caretaker from Barcelona, explained that she has family in Aragon and, accordingly, she 'preferred not to bother them and generate polemics' (Goyanes & Skoric, 2021, p. 11).

Altogether, the TSMB is important for understanding the interplay of social media discussion and democratic deliberation, as it challenges prior assumptions regarding the presumed relevance of these ecologies in activating civic deliberations among peers (see Goyanes & Demeter, 2020). Contrarily, the TSMB aims to theorize one of the most common tactics employed when witnessing political disputes in public spaces: the idea of 'seeing, while not being seen,' due to the presumed retaliatory actions. Like lurking, the contentious effects that political discussions may trigger provide the justification for the TSMB, ensuring that controversies and potential political problems do not 'stick.' Broadly speaking, this concept suggests the idea that social media are growingly turning into information hubs rather than spaces for public discussions (Swart et al., 2018), in which many citizens are just lurking, not participating.

## SOCIAL MEDIA IS AN UNSAFE SPACE FOR POLITICAL INTERACTION

It has been widely demonstrated that social contexts shape the ways in which political interactions happen (Goffman, 1959; Eliasoph, 1998). Social media platforms, however, create unique contexts for political talk. Thorson (2014) argues that they amplify the 'social groundlessness' (Warren, 1996) of political interaction as they are characterized by heightened uncertainty and ambiguity where users have no effective control over the situation. While there are some people who can overcome this challenge, and act as 'entrepreneurs of political talk' (Thorson, 2014, p. 204), many are deterred from engaging in political activity. In the next section, we will discuss factors that make social media platforms unattractive for political interactions, and which restrain their users from expressing political views in this context.

One of the main challenges of self-expression on social media platforms is the collapse of contexts (Marwick & boyd, 2011). As an expressive act, people's communication is largely shaped by the situation where they occur as people behave differently in front of different audiences (see Goffmann, 1959). In the offline environment, the different contexts people come across during their everyday lives are more or less separated: their public faces can be varied in front of their friends, colleagues or family members. On social media sites, however, the cost of creating connections is negligible, and the norms widely shared on most platforms also encourage people to translate even their weakest ties into social media friendships (boyd, 2014). As a result, the different contexts separated offline are collapsed into one large online network. By default, people's connections are the potential audience(s) for all their activities on these platforms. While most platforms offer extended options to change default settings and enable users to define the audiences in a more sophisticated way, studies found that most people hardly use these opportunities and let their activities be seen by all of their contacts (Wisniewski et al., 2017). However, it is important to emphasize that studies show there are cross-country differences in the usage of these affordances, and in certain cultures people more carefully separate their multiple contexts from each other (Costa, 2018; Skoric et al., 2021). But still, people generally need to manage their social media presence in front of an extremely diverse audience consisting of family members, friends, colleagues, old classmates, etc.

In an offline context, when contexts are collapsing, frequent responses are embarrassment (Goffman, 1959) or silence (boyd, 2014). These reactions are often seen on social media platforms too. Several studies demonstrate that many users cannot manage this tension, and decide to stay away from any visible activity, especially when it comes to politics (Mascheroni & Murru, 2017; Marder, 2018). Their main concern is that their honest expressions may pose a risk to the public image they have in certain contexts. This is especially true for younger people, whose public behavior can be very different among peers versus among family members (boyd, 2014). However, there is some evidence for the opposite pattern as well. Beam and colleagues (2018) argue that the collapsed contexts indirectly motivate some users to engage in political activities on these platforms as the more diverse environment leads to more frequent news reading, which then increases their willingness to share news content. However, this is true only for users who are less concerned about privacy issues, and their findings also showed that people are mostly careful about it.

While the experience of collapsed contexts frequently leads to self-censorship, a complete retreat is not the only possibility. Research has identified several individual strategies that enable users to express political opinions in a limited way. People could follow the 'lowest common denominator' approach, and post only content that could be acceptable in front of all their contexts (Hogan, 2010). This strategy requires them to be selective and moderate when expressing a political opinion, but still enables them to voice some political views. While in practice this strategy means that users adjust their behavior to the 'strictest audience,' a competing strategy can be to consider the 'strongest audience' (Marder et al., 2016). In this case, users' social media behavior is conditioned by the expectations of the audience which is the most important for them for any social or economic reason: users will avoid any political expression that would risk their image in front of this specific audience, but be less reluctant to express views that are unpopular for less important audiences.

A related challenge is the uncertainty or invisibility of the audience on these platforms (boyd, 2014; Thorson, 2014). First, people usually have a large number of connections on these platforms, and therefore it is cognitively impossible to keep all friends in mind (Hogan, 2010; Litt & Hargittai, 2016). Second, the audience is never fixed on social media sites. On the one hand, friends' interactions can make posts visible to their own friends by default, and if users do not apply specific privacy options, their posts could reach many people indirectly. On the other hand, posts are not ephemeral on these platforms, but archived and searchable, and this way they can appear at a later point for new audiences (boyd, 2014; Litt & Hargittai, 2016). This can collapse the contexts of users as well, but this is less intentional and controllable than the collapse of contexts resulting from connection-making activity (see Davis & Jurgenson, 2014).

This uncertainty of the communication context can be mitigated by creating a mental construct of a presumed audience (Marwick & boyd, 2011). Research, however, shows that these imagined audiences are a highly inaccurate representation of reality as there is a major discrepancy between the imagined and actual recipients of the posts. On the one hand, users largely underestimate the size of the audience: Bernstein and colleagues (2013) found that the imagined audience is just 27 percent of its true size. On the other hand, strong connections and more active and interactive friends are significantly overrepresented in this imagined audience (Bazarova & Choi, 2014) even if most friends on these platforms are less visible with weak ties (Kim & Chen, 2015). This misalignment between the imagined and the actual audience may sometimes have tangible and unpleasant consequences in the form of unexpected comments (Sveningsson, 2014) or even in the offline context when someone who was not part of the imagined recipients makes some remarks about posted content (Mor et al., 2015).

This uncertainty of the audience and the negative experiences resulting from the biased imagined audience lead several users to withdraw, especially when it comes to the more 'risky' topic of politics (Sveningsson, 2014; Mascheroni & Murru, 2017). Others exercise self-censorship in the form of being more careful and selective in what they post, and in which form they express their own opinion (Bazarova & Choi, 2014).

Another challenge is that social media platforms are built upon the idea of interactivity, and all expressions can be interacted with by any connection in a variety of ways. In these contexts, feedback is instant, direct and quantifiable, a fact which implies several risks from the users' perspective. First, feedback on these platforms represents a type of popularity cue (Van Dijck, 2013; Porten-Cheé et al., 2018) that users care about (Thorson, 2014). For many people, the fear of being ignored can be a deterring force from activities that are perceived to be less popular among friends (Bäck et al., 2019). On social media platforms, political content is not particularly popular among users (Larsson, 2016; Bode et al., 2017); thus, posting on political matters involves the risk of getting less feedback (Mor et al., 2015). Naturally, people are not equally affected by this concern. Bäck and colleagues (2019) showed that people with a higher level of rejection sensitivity are the ones who are less likely to post political content on social media. Second, the opportunity for instant and direct feedback involves the risk that conflicts will emerge. Like in the offline sphere (see Eliasoph, 1998), the fear of conflict is one of the major deterrents to political discourse (Vraga et al., 2015). People feel that politics is an especially divisive and conflict-burdened area. On social media, this is even amplified by the fact that due to the preponderance of weak ties, networks are rather heterogeneous (Diehl et al., 2016), and people usually have friends from all sides of the political spectrum. Interview research shows that it is a recurrent experience that political content provokes harsh online clashes in the comment sections (Vraga et al., 2015; Goyanes & Skoric, 2021). However, it is not the disagreement in itself that disturbs users, but the style of these conflicts: social dramas (Vraga et al., 2015); incivility (Pang et al., 2016; Goyanes & Skoric, 2021; Jordá et al., 2021); heated, offensive debates (Mascheroni & Murru, 2017); and 'wild card' commenters and provocateurs (Thorson, 2014) made people stay away from political activity. At the same time, individual differences matter as well: people differ in their conflict sensitivity and this plays a role in affecting who goes passive due to the conflicting nature of the political activity (Jang et al., 2014; Vraga et al., 2015; Beam et al., 2018).

Last, the well-known 'spiral of silence' is also a factor behind passivity on these platforms. The spiral of silence is one of the leading theories accounting for the withdrawal from political conversion in the offline sphere (Noelle-Neumann, 1974). In a nutshell, it refers to a situation in which people refrain from expressing political opinions that are perceived to be in the minority in their social context, which consequently leads to the overrepresentation of the majority opinion. This theory is extensively tested in the online sphere as well, and studies have found that it is valid on social media platforms too (Miyata et al., 2015; Chan, 2018; Liu et al., 2017). Moreover, Neubaum and Krämer (2018) found that the spiral of silence is the strongest in social media compared to other communication contexts. For the reasons discussed above it is too difficult to have control over the situation and thereby minority opinion needs to be expressed in front of a large, diverse and invisible audience. Also, on social media sites, there is no 'involvement obligation,' often perceived in the face-to-face situation, as it is much easier to opt out and remain silent (Neubaum and Krämer, 2018).

However, the spiral of silence may be amplified not only because it is more difficult to express minority opinions on these platforms, but also because the perceived opinion climate is different here. People on these platforms are more frequently exposed to cross-cutting content compared to other communication contexts (Barnidge, 2017). Seeing content on social network sites largely affects people's agendas (Feezell, 2018) and their perception of the climate of opinion (Morales, 2020). Therefore, people often believe that social media reflect the general public's opinion. As a result, larger exposure to cross-cutting content may decrease the perceived popularity of one's own political stance. Indeed, Chan (2018) showed that larger exposure to disagreement leads to heightened willingness to self-censor on social media. Individual differences, naturally, are important in this case, too. Willingness to suppress political views that are perceived to be a minority opinion is more specific to people who have a strong fear of isolation (Pang et al., 2016; Chan, 2018) and whose contingency of self-worth is approval-based as their self-esteem is built upon others' recognition (Liu et al., 2017).

## WHO ARE THE DISENGAGED? TEFLONIC SOCIAL MEDIA BEHAVIOR IN PRACTICE

Even though many people utilize social media to express their political views or comment on political events, there are many people who do not articulate their political perspectives there, thus fitting the TSMB approach. Therefore, in this section we summarize research findings by which we might depict user characteristics related to political passivity on social media. It is important to note, however, that most studies focus on passivity in an undifferentiated way as they do not make a difference between passivity resulting from a more general political apathy or disengagement and TSMB applied only to the specific context of social media. Therefore, we discuss here the more general roots of political passivity on social media rather than those that are exclusively specific to TSMB.

Based on the discussion above, it is not surprising that network characteristics matter when it comes to passivity on social media platforms. Jang and colleagues (2014) argued that the more extended one's Facebook network is, the less likely it is that the individual tends to talk about politics on his or her personal profile page. In other words, they suggest that smaller online communities are more effective for political deliberation than an extended circle. On the other hand, Barnidge and colleagues (2018) find that users tend to be politically inactive on social media if their social networks are homogeneous. An explanation for this surprising outcome might be that heterogeneous social networks might indicate discussions via social media, and the so-called 'corrective action' (Barnidge & Rojas, 2014) can kick in because several individuals are inclined to correct biased or wrong claims (Sun et al., 2008). It is demonstrated that false claims can provoke activities even from otherwise passive users (Goyanes & Skoric, 2021). Also, the heterogeneous network can widen the circle of users who are exposed to political information, and this can have a further engagement-triggering effect (Beam et al., 2018).

Social capital is also a network feature that is found to play a role in social media passivity. Scholars analyzed the possible relationships between social capital and political expression on Facebook. Bridging social capital, which is based on heterogeneous groups of individuals but lacking close relationships, does not affect political expressions on Facebook, but bonding social capital, defined as strong and close ties to more homogeneous groups such as family, friends and colleagues, is a positive predictor of passivity among Facebook users (Ferrucci et al., 2020). This is in line with the findings discussed above, but the concept of social capital is more about the quality of personal connections rather than the political composition of network members. Last, when it comes to social capital, a non-networked user type should be also mentioned. Studies found that the less an individual utilizes social media to be informed, the higher the chance that they will not be familiar with political issues, and thus he or she might not participate in discussions or express political views and comments (Gil de Zúñiga et al., 2014). The lack of knowledge will thus reduce people's propensity to be active in the semi-public context of social media.

In the previous sections, it was mentioned that certain psychological and motivational factors can help overcome the challenges of social media interactions, while others make people more sensitive to these difficulties. Findings suggest that Facebook users who avoid conflict are less likely to post political content (Vraga et al., 2015). Similarly, scholars argue that these individuals might disregard expressing political views online if they believe that their opinion may create disagreement between users (Chen, 2018). This is especially true for individuals considering themselves conservatives as they are found to be more likely to avert political discussions on social media if they perceive them to be on 'liberal' topics (Jang et al., 2014). Motivation *for* online political talk might also decrease if the user aims to protect relationships, and thus researchers conclude that many people prioritize personal connections over politics (Pennington & Winfrey, 2020). Pennington and Winfrey (2020) argue that when there is a potential conflict between social relationships and political views, people with high relationship goals will prioritize the social aspects over the political expression. Even though numerous studies suggest that prioritizing relationships over political expression on social media is a common practice, relationship goals do not automatically exclude political discussions; moreover, in some cases, social motivation can promote political activity: Lane and colleagues (2017) show that individuals focusing primarily on relationship maintenance might be more willing to listen to others' diverse political views and join the conversation because they aim to put extra effort to preserve the connection (Lane et al., 2017).

Emotional states might also influence the extent to which people are able to overcome the barriers of social media interactions: enthusiasm, anxiety and anger may increase the probability of claiming political views on social media if political motivation reaches a minimum threshold to utilize social media for political activity (Heiss, 2021). In addition, Heiss argues (2021) that anxiety might lessen the intensity of expressing political views among politically motivated people if individuals have a more profound knowledge of politics. Individuals who do not lack political knowledge might not seek feedback on political issues attracting anxiety. In contrast, a two-wave panel survey study examining adults living in the United States suggests that anger and anxiety are not associated significantly with online political expressions (Tian et al., 2020). The researchers also highlight that enthusiasm and political cynicism are negatively related, with the former being a trigger for online political expression. Therefore, the less enthusiastic one becomes due to political cynicism, the higher the chance that the person avoids online political expressions (Tian et al., 2020). Scholars also argue that emotions might intensify when identity-related issues are raised in political discussions; consequently, digital friendships might cease (Bode, 2016; Pennington, 2020). To sum up, although the findings related to the role of specific emotions seem to be rather mixed, they also indicate that the heightened emotional state is able to provoke activity, while the more emotionless condition decreases the chances of being involved in political discussions.

Lastly, it is important to mention that there is a slight gender gap between the levels of political expressions on social media. Studies show that men tend to seek online information more often as they read political, financial or sports news and look for jobs while women more frequently go online to maintain social interaction and relationships (Colley & Maltby, 2008). Experts also concluded that these factors might affect the idea that females tend to share less content online than their male peers (Hargittai & Walejko, 2008; Hargittai & Shaw, 2015), but they also emphasize that the aforementioned gap is shrinking (Bode, 2017). One study has shown that women post less about politics than men do, especially when they feel that their posts might offend some users in their network (Bode, 2017). Yet, females are more likely to unfriend users for political reasons, and thereby adjust their news feed to their own political preferences (Bode, 2017).

## CONCLUSION

All forms of political participation are characterized by certain kinds of inequalities as there are several factors that prevent some segments of society from participating in political actions. However, the context and forms of these activities affect these determining factors, and this way the nature of participation inequalities differs across political activity forms. Social media platforms are unique contexts which result in specific obstacles to political activities.

While the literature primarily focuses on the factors enabling political activities on these sites, we argued that it is important to theorize the phenomenon of when people withdraw intentionally from any public political expression on social media platforms. This is what we labeled as Teflonic social media behavior, and we demonstrated its presence on social media platforms using interview-based methods.[2] Our overview discussed the factors that often make social media sites an unsafe and uncertain context of political interaction for many users. Collapsed contexts, invisible audiences, expanded interaction opportunities and the resulting risk of conflicts, as well as the stronger presence of the spiral of silence, are all factors that decrease the perceived individual control over the context of political interaction.

As in any context of political activities, individual differences matter regarding to what extent one can overcome the challenges of the interaction situation. Based on our literature review, it seems that people with a larger and more homogeneous network, and with more binding social ties, are more likely to opt out. Also, people who are more sensitive to conflict and more motivated by relationship maintenance are more careful when it comes to social media political activity. Emotional states also matter, and lower emotional intensity discourages digital participation. Female users are also often more passive and careful due to motivational and psychological reasons.

It is important to note, however, that our knowledge is still very limited regarding TSMB. Research addressing factors behind political activity in social media usually does not differentiate between the different motivational bases for political passivity. However, the concept suggests that not all forms of passivity are the same. There are people who generally avoid participating in any political activities due to their lack of interest or motivation. Their social media passivity is not substantially different from their offline political disengagement. However, political passivity of people characterized by TSMB is specific to and caused by the unique communication context of social media platforms. They may be politically active citizens, but are not able to participate in these digital spaces. To describe this social group in a more detailed way, future studies should differentiate between the different types of political passivity on social media.

# NOTES

1. Regarding Márton Bene, the study was supported by his Bolyai János Research Fellowship awarded by the Hungarian Academy of Sciences (BO/334_20).
2. All interviewees within this chapter have been anonymized.

# REFERENCES


Bäck, E.A., Bäck, H., Fredén, A., & Gustafsson, N. (2019). A social safety net? Rejection sensitivity and political opinion sharing among young people in social media. *New Media & Society*, *21*(2), 298–316. https://doi.org/10.1177/1461444818795487.

Barberá, P., Jost, J.T., Nagler, J., Tucker, J.A., & Bonneau, R. (2015). Tweeting from left to right: Is online political communication more than an echo chamber? *Psychological Science*, *26*(10), 1531–42.

Barnidge, M. (2017). Exposure to political disagreement in social media versus face-to-face and anonymous online settings. *Political Communication*, *34*(2), 302–21. https://doi.org/10.1080/10584609.2016.1235639.

Barnidge, M., Huber, B., Gil de Zúñiga, H., & Liu, J.H. (2018). Social media as a sphere for 'risky' political expression: A twenty-country multilevel comparative analysis. *International Journal of Press/Politics*, *23*(2), 161–82.

Barnidge, M., & Rojas, H. (2014). Hostile media perceptions, presumed media influence, and political talk: Expanding the corrective action hypothesis. *International Journal of Public Opinion Research*, *26*(2), 135–56.

Bazarova, N., & Choi, Y. (2014). Self-disclosure in social media: Extending the functional approach to disclosure motivations and characteristics on social network sites. *Journal of Communication*, *64*(4), 635–57. https://doi.org/10.1111/jcom.12106.

Beam, M.A., Child, J.T., Hutchens, M.J., & Hmielowski, J.D. (2018). Context collapse and privacy management: Diversity in Facebook friends increases online news reading and sharing. *New Media & Society*, 20(7), 2296–2314. https://doi.org/10.1177/1461444817714790.

Bernstein, M.S., Bakshy, E., Burke, M., & Karrer, B. (2013). Quantifying the invisible audience in social networks. *Proceedings of the SIGCHI Conference on Human Factors in Computing Systems*, 21–30. https://doi.org/10.1145/2470654.2470658.

Bode, L. (2016). Pruning the news feed: Unfriending and unfollowing political content on social media. *Research & Politics*, *3*(3), 2053168016661873.

Bode, L. (2017). Closing the gap: Gender parity in political engagement on social media. *Information, Communication & Society*, *20*(4), 587–603.

Bode, L., Vraga, E.K., & Troller-Renfree, S. (2017). Skipping politics: Measuring avoidance of political content in social media. *Research & Politics*, *4*(2), 2053168017702990. https://doi.org/10.1177/2053168017702990.

boyd, d. (2014). *It's Complicated: The Social Lives of Networked Teens*. Yale University Press.

Bright, J. (2018). Explaining the emergence of political fragmentation on social media: The role of ideology and extremism. *Journal of Computer-Mediated Communication*, *23*(1), 17–33.

Chan, M. (2018). Reluctance to talk about politics in face-to-face and Facebook settings: Examining the impact of fear of isolation, willingness to self-censor, and peer network characteristics. *Mass Communication and Society*, *21*(1), 1–23. https://doi.org/10.1080/15205436.2017.1358819.

Chen, H.-T. (2018). Spiral of silence on social media and the moderating role of disagreement and publicness in the network: Analyzing expressive and withdrawal behaviors. *New Media & Society*, *20*(10), 3917–36.

Colley, A., & Maltby, J. (2008). Impact of the Internet on our lives: Male and female personal perspectives. *Computers in Human Behavior*, *24*(5), 2005–13.

Costa, E. (2018). Affordances-in-practice: An ethnographic critique of social media logic and context collapse. *New Media & Society*, *20*(10), 3641–56.

Davis, J.L., & Jurgenson, N. (2014). Context collapse: Theorizing context collusions and collisions. *Information, Communication & Society*, *17*(4), 476–85.

Diehl, T., Weeks, B.E., & Gil de Zúñiga, H. (2016). Political persuasion on social media: Tracing direct and indirect effects of news use and social interaction. *New Media & Society*, *18*(9), 1875–95. https://doi.org/10.1177/1461444815616224.

Eliasoph, N. (1998). *Avoiding Politics: How Americans Produce Apathy in Everyday Life*. Cambridge University Press.

Feezell, J.T. (2018). Agenda setting through social media: The importance of incidental news exposure and social filtering in the digital era. *Political Research Quarterly*, *71*(2), 482–94. https://doi.org/10.1177/1065912917744895.

Ferrucci, P., Hopp, T., & Vargo, C.J. (2020). Civic engagement, social capital, and ideological extremity: Exploring online political engagement and political expression on Facebook. *New Media & Society*, *22*(6), 1095–1115.

Gil de Zúñiga, H., Jung, N., & Valenzuela, S. (2012). Social media use for news and individuals' social capital, civic engagement and political participation. *Journal of Computer-Mediated Communication*, *17*(3), 319–36.

Gil de Zúñiga, H., Molyneux, L., & Zheng, P. (2014). Social media, political expression, and political participation: Panel analysis of lagged and concurrent relationships. *Journal of Communication*, *64*(4), 612–34.

Goffman, E. (1959). *The Presentation of Self in Everyday Life*. Doubleday.

Goyanes, M., Borah, P., & Gil de Zúñiga, H. (2021). Social media filtering and democracy: Effects of social media news use and uncivil political discussions on social media unfriending. *Computers in Human Behavior*, *120*, 1–9.

Goyanes, M., & Demeter, M. (2020). Beyond positive or negative: Understanding the phenomenology, typologies and impact of incidental news exposure on citizens' daily lives. *New Media & Society*, *24*(3), 760–777.

Goyanes, M., & Lavin, A. (2018). *The Sociology of Fake News: Factors Affecting the Probability of Sharing Political Fake News Online*. Media @LSE Working Paper Series.

Goyanes, M., & Skoric, M. (2021). Citizen (dis)engagement on social media: How the Catalan referendum crisis fostered a Teflonic social media behaviour. *Mediterranean Politics*, *28*(1), 27–48.

Hargittai, E., & Shaw, A. (2015). Mind the skills gap: The role of Internet know-how and gender in differentiated contributions to Wikipedia. *Information, Communication & Society*, *18*(4), 424–42.

Hargittai, E., & Walejko, G. (2008). The participation divide: Content creation and sharing in the digital age. *Information, Community and Society*, *11*(2), 239–56.

Heiss, R. (2021). The affective foundation of political opinion expression on social media: A panel analysis. *International Journal of Public Opinion Research*, *33*(1), 57–75.

Hogan, B. (2010). The presentation of self in the age of social media: Distinguishing performances and exhibitions online. *Bulletin of Science, Technology & Society*, *30*(6), 377–86. https://doi.org/10.1177/0270467610385893.

Huber, B., Goyanes, M., & Gil de Zúñiga, H. (2021). Linking extraversion to collective and individual forms of political participation: The mediating role of political discussion. *Social Science Quarterly*, *102*(4), 1289–1310.

Jang, S.M., Lee, H., & Park, Y.J. (2014). The more friends, the less political talk? Predictors of Facebook discussions among college students. *Cyberpsychology, Behavior, and Social Networking*, *17*(5), 271–5. https://doi.org/10.1089/cyber.2013.0477.
Jordá, B., Cañedo, A., Bene, M., & Goyanes, M. (2021). Out-of-place content: How repetitive, offensive, and opinion-challenging social media posts shape users' unfriending strategies in Spain. *Social Sciences*, *10*(12), 460.
Kim, Y., & Chen, H.-T. (2015). Discussion network heterogeneity matters: Examining a moderated mediation model of social media use and civic engagement. *International Journal of Communication*, *9*, 22.
Lane, D.S., Kim, D.H., Lee, S.S., Weeks, B.E., & Kwak, N. (2017). From online disagreement to offline action: How diverse motivations for using social media can increase political information sharing and catalyze offline political participation. *Social Media + Society*, *3*(3), 2056305117716274.
Larsson, A.O. (2016). 'I shared the news today, oh boy.' *Journalism Studies*, *19*(1), 43–61. https://doi.org/10.1080/1461670X.2016.1154797.
Litt, E., & Hargittai, E. (2016). The imagined audience on social network sites. *Social Media + Society*, *2*(1), 2056305116633482.
Liu, Y., Rui, J.R., & Cui, X. (2017). Are people willing to share their political opinions on Facebook? Exploring roles of self-presentational concern in spiral of silence. *Computers in Human Behavior*, *76*, 294–302. https://doi.org/10.1016/j.chb.2017.07.029.
Marder, B. (2018). Trumped by context collapse: Examination of 'Liking' political candidates in the presence of audience diversity. *Computers in Human Behavior*, *79*, 169–80. https://doi.org/10.1016/j.chb.2017.10.025.
Marder, B., Joinson, A., Shankar, A., & Thirlaway, K. (2016). Strength matters: Self-presentation to the strongest audience rather than lowest common denominator when faced with multiple audiences in social network sites. *Computers in Human Behavior*, *61*, 56–62. https://doi.org/10.1016/j.chb.2016.03.005.
Marwick, A.E., & boyd, d. (2011). I tweet honestly, I tweet passionately: Twitter users, context collapse, and the imagined audience. *New Media & Society*, *13*(1), 114–33. https://doi.org/10.1177/1461444810365313.
Mascheroni, G., & Murru, M.F. (2017). 'I can share politics but I don't discuss it': Everyday practices of political talk on Facebook. *Social Media + Society*, *3*(4), 2056305117747849. https://doi.org/10.1177/2056305117747849.
Miyata, K., Yamamoto, H., & Ogawa, Y. (2015). What affects the spiral of silence and the hard core on Twitter? An analysis of the nuclear power issue in Japan. *American Behavioral Scientist*, *59*(9), 1129–41. https://doi.org/10.1177/0002764215580618.
Mor, Y., Kligler-Vilenchik, N., & Maoz, I. (2015). Political expression on Facebook in a context of conflict: Dilemmas and coping strategies of Jewish-Israeli youth. *Social Media + Society*, *1*(2), 2056305115606750.
Morales, J.S. (2020). Perceived popularity and online political dissent: Evidence from Twitter in Venezuela. *International Journal of Press/Politics*, *25*(1), 5–27. https://doi.org/10.1177/1940161219872942.
Neubaum, G., & Krämer, N.C. (2018). What do we fear? Expected sanctions for expressing minority opinions in offline and online communication. *Communication Research*, *45*(2), 139–64. https://doi.org/10.1177/0093650215623837.
Noelle-Neumann, E. (1974). The spiral of silence: A theory of public opinion. *Journal of Communication*, *24*(2), 43–51. https://doi.org/10.1111/j.1460-2466.1974.tb00367.x.
Pang, N., Ho, S.S., Zhang, A.M.R., Ko, J.S.W., Low, W.X., & Tan, K.S.Y. (2016). Can spiral of silence and civility predict click speech on Facebook? *Computers in Human Behavior*, *64*, 898–905. https://doi.org/10.1016/j.chb.2016.07.066.
Pennington, N. (2020). An examination of relational maintenance and dissolution through social networking sites. *Computers in Human Behavior*, *105*, 106196.

Pennington, N., & Winfrey, K.L. (2020). Engaging in political talk on Facebook: Investigating the role of interpersonal goals and cognitive engagement. *Communication Studies*, *72*(1), 100–114.
Pitcan, M., Marwick, A.E., & boyd, d. (2018). Performing a vanilla self: Respectability politics, social class, and the digital world. *Journal of Computer-Mediated Communication*, *23*(3), 163–79.
Porten-Cheé, P., Haßler, J., Jost, P., Eilders, C., & Maurer, M. (2018). Popularity cues in online media: Theoretical and methodological perspectives. *Studies in Communication and Media*, *7*(2), 208–30. https://doi.org/10.5771/2192-4007-2018-2-80.
Skoric, M.M., Zhu, Q., Goh, D., & Pang, N. (2016). Social media and citizen engagement: A meta-analytic review. *New Media & Society*, *18*(9), 1817–39.
Skoric, M.M., Zhu, Q., Koc-Michalska, K., Boulianne, S., & Bimber, B. (2021). Selective avoidance on social media: A comparative study of Western democracies. *Social Science Computer Review*, *40*(5), 08944393211005468.
Sun, Y., Shen, L., & Pan, Z. (2008). On the behavioral component of the third-person effect. *Communication Research*, *35*(2), 257–78.
Sveningsson, M. (2014). 'I don't like it and I think it's useless, people discussing politics on Facebook': Young Swedes' understandings of social media use for political discussion. *Cyberpsychology: Journal of Psychosocial Research on Cyberspace*, *8*(3), Article 3. https://doi.org/10.5817/CP2014-3-8.
Swart, J., Peters, C., & Broersma, M. (2018). Shedding light on the dark social: The connective role of news and journalism in social media communities. *New Media & Society*, *20*(11), 4329–45.
Thorson, K. (2014). Facing an uncertain reception: Young citizens and political interaction on Facebook. *Information, Communication & Society*, *17*(2), 203–16. https://doi.org/10.1080/1369118X.2013.862563.
Tian, Y., Zhang, X., Yamamoto, M., & Morey, A.C. (2020). Cynicism, insults, and emotions in the 2016 US presidential election: An affective intelligence framework. *Journal of Information Technology & Politics*, *17*(4), 321–36.
Treré, E., Jeppesen, S., & Mattoni, A. (2017). Comparing digital protest media imaginaries: anti-austerity movements in Greece, Italy & Spain. *tripleC: Communication, Capitalism & Critique. Open Access Journal for a Global Sustainable Information Society*, *15*(2), 404–22.
Vaccari, C. (2017). Online mobilization in comparative perspective: Digital appeals and political engagement in Germany, Italy, and the United Kingdom. *Political Communication*, *34*(1), 69–88.
Van Dijck, J. (2013). *The Culture of Connectivity: A Critical History of Social Media*. Oxford University Press.
Vraga, E.K., Thorson, K., Kligler-Vilenchik, N., & Gee, E. (2015). How individual sensitivities to disagreement shape youth political expression on Facebook. *Computers in Human Behavior*, *45*, 281–9.
Warren, M.E. (1996). What should we expect from more democracy? Radically democratic responses to politics. *Political Theory*, *24*(2), 241–70. https://doi.org/10.1177/0090591796024002004.
Wisniewski, P.J., Knijnenburg, B.P., & Lipford, H.R. (2017). Making privacy personal: Profiling social network users to inform privacy education and nudging. *International Journal of Human-Computer Studies*, *98*, 95–108. https://doi.org/10.1016/j.ijhcs.2016.09.006.

# 13. The affective resonance of norm-violation rhetoric in social media

*W. Russell Neuman, George E. Marcus and Michael B. MacKuen*

## INTRODUCTION

In recent years, the research literature addressing political communication has become increasingly and appropriately concerned with the phenomenon of polarization (Druckman, Peterson & Slothuus, 2013; Iyengar, 2016; Iyengar & Westwood, 2015; Lee, 2015; Mutz, 2015; Peterson & Kagalwala, 2021; Prior, 2013; Westfall et al., 2015; Yarchi, Baden & Kligler-Vilenchik, 2021). There is indeed dramatic evidence of elite polarization along ideological lines. But issue polarization within the mass electorate is more ambiguous and has been most evident within the relatively small stratum of political activists both on the left and on the right (Ahler, 2014; Fiorina, Abrams & Pope, 2010; Levendusky & Malhotra, 2016). A key issue in mass polarization is the possible role of social media (Persily & Tucker, 2020; Sampson, Maddison & Ellis, 2018; Tucker et al., 2018; Yarchi et al., 2021).

The rhetorical flourishes of the 2015–16 American presidential campaign, perhaps most notably those of Donald Trump, appear to be drawing an even larger number of citizens into the fray (Bazelon, 2017; Denby, 2015; Tomasky, 2015). It is not clear that we are witnessing a dramatic and abrupt shift as Republican voters veer to the right while Democrats swerve left on fundamental political beliefs, although there is some modest and gradual sorting and ideological alignment underway (Levendusky, 2013).

The recent political drama may be most appropriately characterized as a shift of mood and language, a political zeitgeist reinforced by turbulent changes in the American media and patterns of media use. Iyengar and associates make the case that the:

> explanation of intensified inter-party animus lies in the rhetoric of political campaigns. Virtually every study of campaign advertising documents the steep increase in the frequency of attacks and counterattacks … The tendency of the media to recycle the candidates' negative messages only confirms partisans' suspicions about those on the other side … [They conclude] Our principal goal has been to reframe the debate over polarization in terms of affect rather than ideology. (Iyengar, Sood & Lelkes, 2012, 427–8)

We agree, but argue that we may be confronting more than just emotional negativity (Boller, 2004; Mattes & Redlawsk, 2014; Miller & Conover, 2015).

## NORM-VIOLATION RHETORIC

Norm-violation rhetoric is a unique style of political discourse that identifies the opposition as illegitimate, devious, disingenuous, and not playing by the rules rather than simply uninformed or wrong-headed. It characteristically makes the case that the violations are historic, unprecedented, and decidedly not 'politics as usual.' We have developed a series of hypotheses about emotional responses to this variant of political rhetoric. We tested our hypotheses with two representative samples of American adults. The initial and most broadly framed prediction is this: when a group in a political conflict perceives the other side is violating the norms of procedural fair play, the emotions of anxiety, enthusiasm, and aversion are engaged. We anticipate further that each emotional dimension will be differentially moved by norm-violation rhetoric and that, in turn, each emotional response will have unique 'downstream' effects in terms of information seeking and political engagement.

Our interest in this rhetorical style draws together two related theoretical traditions in the study of political communication – incivility and negativity. Each of these literatures is currently actively pursued and each addresses the question of how elite rhetoric affects the level and quality of mass participation in the electoral process. Each indirectly touches on a notion of norm violation, but each focuses on different qualities of the rhetoric involved. We will address each literature in turn and attempt to make the case that attention to the impact of perceived procedural norm violations strengthens the theoretical basis of each tradition.

## THE STUDY OF RHETORICAL INCIVILITY

In reviewing the incivility literature, Brooks and Geer (2007) note that a precise definition of incivility has proven to be quite elusive. Their conclusion cites Sapiro (1999, p. 2): 'Any scholarly treatment of civility and politics must start with the recognition that civility, while widely discussed and argued, does not really have full conceptual standing as a "keyword" in scholarship on democratic politics.' In their own experimental design, Brooks and Geer operationalize incivility as a mixture of ad hominem commentary focusing on an opposing candidate's personal life and personal qualities rather than their policy positions or administrative competencies. In addition, Brooks and Geer characterize incivility as impoliteness and a lack of courtesy or mutual respect. Words such as 'insensitive,' 'heartless,' and 'cowardly' were added to otherwise negative but civil critiques to generate the uncivil condition. They take pains to distinguish incivility from negative comments legitimately critical of an opponent's issue positions, which are essential to the electoral process. They conclude that, so defined, the incivility condition in the random assignment does not appear to result in significant declines in levels of political trust or participation.

In contrast, Mutz and Reeves (2005) find that incivility in televised public discourse, although it may raise levels of interest and attention, does adversely affect trust in government. They used professional actors in simulated television debates and emphasized alternative versions of a debate – one involving polite respect and the other involving rude remarks, frequent interruptions, raised voices, rolled eyes, and head shaking. Mutz (2007) extends this experimental protocol by demonstrating that close-up camera angles exaggerate these effects, leading her to characterize this rhetorical style of incivility as 'in-your-face' politics. In her summative analysis of these studies, Mutz (2015) fleshes out the argument about why televised incivility can be politically important. She argues it is significant because such incivility contributes to a sense among the public that the 'other side' is illegitimate – that the opponent is not trustworthy, not playing by the rules. We believe this is particularly important. It corresponds to our conception of the violation of procedural norms. It draws attention to a rhetorical dimension beyond simple interpersonal rudeness. More recently, Kenski, Coe, and Rains (2017) and Muddiman (2017) have explored multidimensional measures of incivility, drawing particular attention to the significance of perceptions of name-calling and vulgarity among the mass public.

Susan Herbst takes the long view in her book *Rude Democracy* (2010). She emphasizes that cycles of political incivility come and go and that, because incivility tends to attract interest, it will remain a strategic asset for issue proponents vying for public attention. The interaction of incivility and public attentiveness is also emphasized by Papacharissi (2004), Ryan (2012), Anderson et al. (2014), and Sydnor (2017). Our study attempts to explore the emotional mechanisms that link incivility and attentiveness.

## POLITICAL NEGATIVITY

Ansolabehere and Iyengar (1995, pp. 147–8) make the case that:

> Negative politics generates disillusionment and distrust among the public. Attack advertisements resonate with the popular beliefs that the government fails, that elected officials are out of touch and quite corrupt, and that voting is a hollow act. The end result: lower turnout and lower trust in government, regardless of which party rules.

The ensuing and growing literature continues to debate conflicting findings on whether negativity actually helps candidates and whether it might inadvertently result in lower levels of political participation and general political trust. Fridkin and Kenney (2004) argue that, under some circumstances, negative messages can be very effective. Lau and colleagues (2007) conclude from a meta-analysis that there is little evidence of a net gain in electoral power because of the negative backlash against the negative campaigners themselves. The backlash phenomenon will prove to be an important element in our analysis.

The telling argument for us is Sigelman and Kugler's 2003 assertion that the various measures of negative campaigning (typically content analyses of ads) may not actually be interpreted by the electorate as 'negative' because of various partisan biases and selective attention. Geer (2006) points out that negative campaigning when directed at the policy positions of opponents is essential to the electoral process. In reviewing this literature, we conclude that because one person's negativity can be another's legitimate critique of an opponent's policies, the concept of negativity is itself overly broad and is of limited theoretical use without further specification and theoretical elaboration.

## VIOLATION OF NORMS IN RELATED LITERATURE

Our principal hypothesis is derived from these two extensive pieces of literature. The study of behavioral responses to explicit norm violation, however, has a relatively small presence in the research literature and is often identified by varying terminologies. The violation of norms of fairness is reflected in legal and institutional scholarship under the terminology of procedural justice (Lind & Tyler, 1988; Ng & Allen, 2005). In this tradition, there is a strong distinction between distributive justice (fairness of outcome) and procedural justice (transparency and openness of decisional processes), and our focus here is on this latter dimension, particularly the perception of unfairness (Tyler & Lind, 1992). Most of this research literature focuses on the procedural openness of the criminal justice system. Only more recently has the connection been made to generalized political trust and political participation (Ulbig, 2008) and to the perception of rigged elections (Stephenson & Kahn, 2016). Since the 1960s, scholars have studied political cynicism in American public opinion, often measuring the public's concern about secret decisions made in 'smoke-filled rooms.' A debate has emerged over whether such cynicism results from anger over political policy outcomes or a perception of unfairness in the political process (Agger, Goldstein & Pearl, 1961; Citrin, 1974; Miller, 1974).

Violations of norms of equity and fairness are also part of the psychological literature that addresses prejudice and intergroup relations (De Ridder & Tripathi, 1992; Sidanius & Pratto, 1999). Notions of norm violation appear in international relations research, most often focusing on elite behavior (Shannon, 2000). Interestingly, neuropsychologists have found evidence that suggests that humans may be hardwired to detect norm violations (Tabibnia, Satpute & Lieberman, 2008). In a similar vein, behavioral economists have been working with the notion of a 'fairness equilibrium' as a fundamental tenet of game theory (Camerer, Loewenstein & Rabin, 2004). Psychologists working in the tradition of appraisal theory have found a link between the perception of norm violation and anger, but the work to date is limited to interpersonal relations rather than social and political concerns (Checkroun & Brauer, 2002; Nelissen & Zeelenberg, 2009).

The most politically oriented research drawing on the psychology of norm violation involves studies of political tolerance. Sullivan, Piereson and Marcus (1982), for example, note: 'tolerance is closely associated with the idea of procedural fairness. An important element of liberal political theory is its emphasis on the distinction between the substantive issues of political conflicts and the procedural rules by which conflicts are resolved' (1982, p. 2). What makes the notion of procedural or fair-play norm violation particularly important is the reciprocity implication – if the other guys are going to cheat and break the rules, so should we (Levitsky & Ziblatt, 2018). The question arises in an analysis of American political polarization in the Trump era – to what extent does public opinion reflect increased policy differences as opposed to an increased belief that the political process has broken down and traditional procedural means of political competition are no longer tenable (Bermeo, 2019; Huq & Ginsburg, 2018).

These three related grounding concepts under review are summarized in Table 13.1.

*Table 13.1 Key conceptual distinctions between analytic concepts*

| Analytic concept | Key elements | Contradistinction | Predicted outcome for electorate |
|---|---|---|---|
| Incivility | Interpersonal rudeness | Interpersonal respectfulness | Disengagement |
| Negativity | Negative characterization of opponent | Positive characterization of self | Disengagement |
| Fair-play norm violation | Illegitimate, devious, dishonest, not playing by the rules | Playing by the rules | Engagement? |

## AFFECTIVE INTELLIGENCE THEORY

The affective intelligence literature suggests a potential mechanism to explain the connection between elite rhetorical styles and mass political behavior (Marcus, Neuman & MacKuen, 2000). Much of the psychologically oriented literature on emotion and attention takes on a valence-based approach, contrasting the effects of positive versus negative feelings (Lodge & Taber, 2013). But the insight of affective intelligence research, as Ryan puts it, 'is that political actors would want to evoke emotions not just of a particular valence – e.g., warmth for the speaker and coldness toward an opponent – but to switch voters to different modes of processing – e.g., one in which the audience would be more or less attentive' (Ryan, 2012, p. 1140; see also Lerner & Keltner, 2000). Ryan proceeds to review what he characterized as a 'substantial base of evidence confirming that emotions do activate different styles of thinking about politics' in the literature, citing particularly Lerner et al. (2003) and Valentino et al. (2011).

Affective intelligence research reinforces the position that the widely used term 'negative' is problematic as it confounds two distinct emotional states – anxiety and aversion. The distinction between anxiety and aversion is a critical element of this theoretical tradition. Each of these two emotional states has distinct antecedents, distinct underlying neural structures, and distinct roles to play in initiating the expression of affect and behavior. The evaluation of novelty requires a neural system that can compare incoming sensory data to what is anticipated – a simple comparison system but with many 'outputs.' The amygdala is one element in the neural system that supports attention to novelty. In contrast, the marshaling of extant resources is served by a different neural array that, in part, uses the insula to assess and execute so that norm violations are identified and addressed (Moretti et al., 2012). The terms 'anxiety' and 'aversion' in the affective intelligence tradition correspond to the terms 'fear' and 'anger' typically used in the cognitive-appraisal/discrete-emotion tradition in social psychology.

Drawing on the theoretical propositions of the affective intelligence tradition, we designed an instrument that focused on the violation of procedural norms of fairness – focusing on accusations of self-serving duplicity, dishonesty, and related concepts. The reaction of aversion to oppositional political views and enthusiasm for conforming political views as reflected in Hypothesis 1 is well established in the literature (Marcus, Neuman & MacKuen, 2000). Notably, the instrument does not attempt to invoke simple interpersonal rudeness or incivility. As noted above, we posit that all three emotional dimensions emphasized in the affective intelligence model are predicted to respond to the perception of norm violation.

*H1: When a group in a political conflict perceives the other side is violating the norms of procedural fair play, the emotions of anxiety, enthusiasm, and aversion are impacted – the perception of norm-violating rhetoric will cause anxiety and aversion to be elevated, while enthusiasm will be depressed.*

The perception of norm violation in the political sphere represents the sense that one has not been treated fairly – an actor has lied, broken the rules, cheated. We have noted that the concept of fairness in our social interactions may be 'hard wired' from social evolution (André & Baumard, 2011; Tabibnia, Satpute & Lieberman, 2008). If the threat is novel, anxiety is predicted to be the dominant response. In contrast, if the threat is familiar, an aversive, angry response is likely to be the result. Characteristically, when anxiety and aversion are elevated, enthusiasm is depressed (Marcus, Neuman & MacKuen, 2000). Such posited affective dynamics are likely to set off attentional alarms of novel threats, notably distinct from the widely recognized dynamics of motivated reasoning, which would serve to minimize cognitive dissonance and attentional alarm (Epley & Gilovich, 2016; Kunda, 1990).

In terms of behavioral outcomes, we predict that these affective responses to the rhetorical environment will impact information seeking. More specifically, we hypothesize that the mobilization of anxiety in response to uncertainty is the likely route. Anxiety is more often associated with a fresh and deliberative appraisal of political alternatives, while aversion as a negative reaction to familiar negative elements in the political environment prompts a digging-in-of-the-heels and partisan resolve rather than seeking the new (MacKuen et al., 2010). So, although anxiety and aversion are typically correlated indicators, they have potentially distinctive behavioral outcomes.

*H2: Elevated anxiety will increase information seeking, particularly from those information sources which are not in agreement with the respondent.*

*H3: Elevated aversion will reinforce steadfastness as against openness to new information and ideas.*

The basic structure of our expectations is summarized in Figure 13.1. We will also have the opportunity to explore related dependent variables to test the unique correlates of these three emotional states.

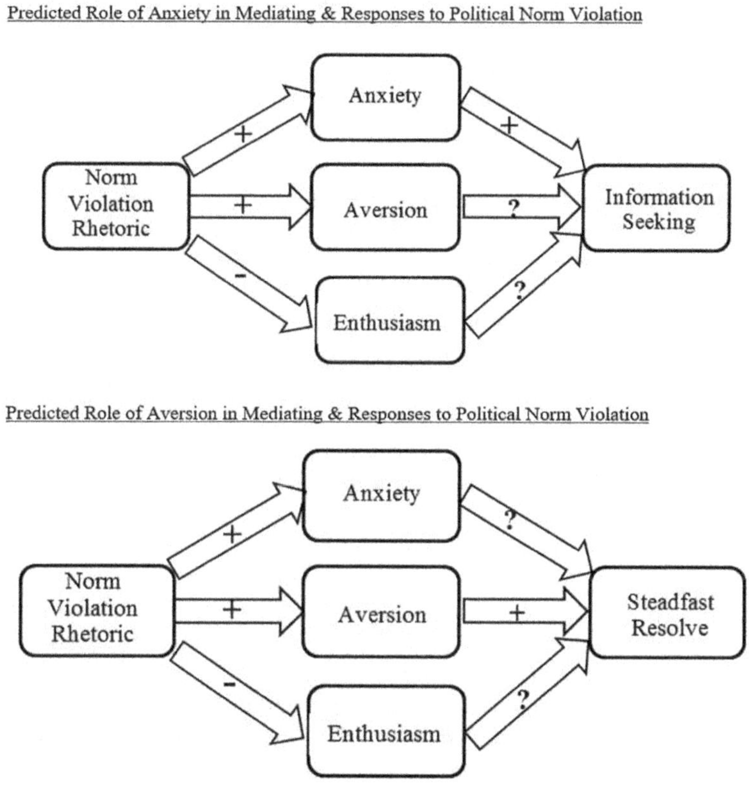


*Figure 13.1* *Prediction roles of anxiety and aversion in mediating and responses to political norm violation*

To test these hypotheses, we randomly expose respondents to negative rhetoric, which varies only in the presence or absence of norm-violation references, and assess the resulting affective responses. If the treatment is successfully operationalized and then fails to generate a unique emotional response, then our thesis would stand unsupported.

## RESEARCH DESIGN

Our research strategy for studying social media dynamics was to take three prominent political issues in modern American politics – the health care debate, global climate change, and immigration policy – and randomly present our respondents with either (1) a strong conservative critique of the liberal views or (2) a strong liberal critique of conservative views on these three issues, which are presented simultaneously. The key to our design was to randomly present each of these critiques with one of two contrasting rhetorical styles – either characterization of the political opposition as reasonable and fair (norm-compliant) or alternatively as devious, self-serving, and dishonest (norm-violating). Thus, our basic design is a 2 x 2 experiment.

Additionally, for a subset of our respondents (labeled Study II), we replicated the original design, drawing attention to the rhetorical critic rather than the object of the criticism to sort out which element of the complex political stimulus may be generating the most distinct emotional resonance. We were particularly interested in how both liberals and conservatives would react emotionally to a critique that characterized their own views in contrast to opposing views as devious and dishonest.

The critiques were presented as blog posts from, correspondingly, a 'thoughtful' or 'flaming' liberal or a 'thoughtful' or 'flaming' conservative blogger. Thus, for example, the norm-compliant/thoughtful critique of the liberal position on health care reform notes simply that 'Obamacare may be an honest attempt to respond to the health problems of the poor and unemployed, but it cannot avoid inserting government bureaucrats into medical decisions. Why not rely on an open, competitive marketplace for health insurance?' The flaming/norm-violation version makes the same basic point as follows: 'Obamacare is an unbelievably devious plan to insert government bureaucrats into medical decisions. Instead of an open competitive marketplace for health insurance, liberals cynically cite the health problems of the poor and unemployed to further their big-government agenda.'

The four rhetorical manipulations are summarized in Table 13.2. We utilized a set of 10 survey items (measured in this online survey with a 'slider' response format) to assess the three fundamental dimensions of emotional response identified by affective intelligence theory – Anxiety, Aversion and Enthusiasm.

Our online survey was conducted by Knowledge Networks (now GfK) in the spring of 2011, utilizing their representative panel of American adults. The use of an online panel is appropriate for our research design as we are focusing on relationships among variables rather than estimating population parameters (Baker et al., 2010; Scherpenzeel & Toepoel, 2012). Respondents were recruited to participate in a study of 'news and public affairs,' so there is little reason to expect participants in this sample to self-select into this particular survey or to be particularly ideological or intensely political, and that is confirmed by self-reports of party identification

*Table 13.2 Four versions of political rhetoric*

| | Rhetoric emphasizing norm violation | Rhetoric without norm violation |
|---|---|---|
| Right | Flaming Conservative Speaks Out ...<br>Critique of Obamacare; climate change as a hoax; immigration policy as pandering to Latino voters | Thoughtful Conservative Asks ...<br>Liberal healthcare policy overly bureaucratic; environmentalists may have overreacted; amnesty for illegal aliens is inappropriate |
| Left | Flaming Liberal Speaks Out ...<br>Opposition to health care reform is a devious effort to choke off health care for the poor; junk science on climate change; and shameless manipulation of racist fear on immigration | Thoughtful Liberal Asks ...<br>Reasonable concern about bureaucratization of health care; growing scientific consensus on global warming; immigration issue is complex |

and ideology. The respondents' ethnicities, educational levels, and geography were representative of national demographics. Party identification was 37 percent Republican, 41 percent Democratic, and 21 percent Independent. Ideology was 42 percent Conservative, 32 percent Moderate, and 26 percent Liberal. Our study is based on two related but independent survey-experiments – Survey I ($N = 516$) and Survey II ($N = 518$). Each survey experiment varied the way in which the rhetorical stimuli were presented to respondents. Survey I simply presented the randomized norm-violating or norm-compliant stimulus materials. In Survey I, no particular attention was drawn to the blogger or the policy issues the blogger critiqued. In Survey II, each participant was explicitly asked to focus attention on the blogger's rhetorical style.

## RESULTS

Our first analysis is an examination of the emotional responses to our stimulus conditions. Did the addition of norm-violation rhetoric make a difference? Table 13.3 reports the index means for the stimulus conditions across both survey-experiments. It also tests the statistical significance of the difference in means in response to the presence and absence of norm-violation rhetoric, using t-tests to compare norm-violation and the absence of norm-violation rhetoric within each type of political critique. Higher scores on the index represent a higher level of emotional intensity on each dimension. To simplify the analysis and make comparisons among variables expedient, all variables and indices have been recoded to a range of 0–1.

Our hypotheses predict straightforwardly (H1) that emotions will be more dramatically engaged by exposure to norm-violation rhetoric and specifically that Anxiety and Aversion will be elevated and that Enthusiasm will be depressed by the inclusion of norm-violation rhetoric. The this-is-historic/this-is-out-of-the-ordinary flavor of norm-violation rhetoric emphasizes the unusual and unknown, and thus we expect higher levels of anxiety. The prediction of a decline in enthusiasm and an increase in aversion draws on the literature on negativity, incivility, and affective intelligence

*Table 13.3* *Emotion index means and standard deviations for different stimulus conditions*

| | Anxiety | | Aversion | | Enthusiasm | |
|---|---|---|---|---|---|---|
| Political Critique | *M* | *SD* | *M* | *SD* | *M* | *SD* |
| Overall[a] | | | | | | |
| Norm-Violation Rhetoric | .48 | .26 | .48*** | .24 | .35*** | .23 |
| No Norm Violation | .47 | .25 | .41*** | .24 | .40*** | .23 |
| From Right[b] | | | | | | |
| Norm-Violation Rhetoric | .51 | .26 | .49** | .24 | .34** | .22 |
| No Norm-Violation Rhetoric | .48 | .25 | .43** | .25 | .40** | .24 |
| From Left[c] | | | | | | |
| Norm-Violation Rhetoric | .46 | .26 | .47*** | .25 | .35* | .24 |
| No Norm-Violation Rhetoric | .45 | .25 | .39*** | .24 | .40* | .23 |

*Notes:*
Mean comparisons can be made vertically (within columns) between Norm and No Norm Violation for both types of political critique. Results from surveys I and II combined.
[a] $n = 1034$, [b] $n = 531$, [c] $n = 503$. $^{*}p < .05$, $^{**}p < .01$, $^{***}p < .001$

noted above, which reports numerous empirical examples of such findings (Kahn & Kenney, 1999; Mutz & Reeves, 2005; Ryan, 2012).

As expected, the norm-violation rhetoric dramatically depresses enthusiasm and heightens aversion. But there was no systematic difference in levels of anxiety in response to our experimental manipulations. Our initial test of Hypothesis 1 resulted in a mixed result. Has rhetoric of this sort become so commonplace that most citizens slough it off as routine and hardly a cause for anxiety? Perhaps the undifferentiated response to anxiety is a function of the prominence of the particular issues we used in the manipulation. The next step was to dig a little deeper and explore the affective responses separately for liberals, conservatives, and moderates.

Table 13.4 provides us with some answers, but the puzzle deepens. The expected heightened anxiety among the more liberal and more conservative respondents is not evident. And the expected strengthening of the effect of the norm-violation manipulation on aversion and depressed enthusiasm is only evident in some of the six tests in each emotional dimension. The middle-of-the-road folks who might be expected to react equally to the hyperventilated rhetoric of both the left and right did not appear to do so consistently. Something more complicated appears to be at work.

Are our hypotheses simply disconfirmed or is it possible some cognitive mechanism is masking the expected effects?

Elements of the emotional reaction to norm-violation rhetoric may have been diffused because of the complexity of the stimulus. This, of course, echoes the problematics in negativity research of attempting to parse out the effects on the source of and on the object of negative political advertising. Our political blog stimulus in each case contains two elements to which our subjects may be responding – (1) the rhetorical critics themselves and (2) the actual policies and ‘policy problems’ that are correspondingly the object of the various critics’ scorn.

*Table 13.4* *Emotional response index means for different stimulus conditions by respondent ideology*

| Respondent ideology | Political critique condition | Anxiety *M* | Anxiety *SD* | Aversion *M* | Aversion *SD* | Enthusiasm *M* | Enthusiasm *SD* |
|---|---|---|---|---|---|---|---|
| Conservative[a] | Rhetoric from Right | | | | | | |
| | Norm Violation | .56 | .25 | .51 | .24 | .27** | .19 |
| | No Norm Violation | .51 | .21 | .46 | .23 | .41** | .25 |
| | Rhetoric from Left | | | | | | |
| | Norm Violation | .47 | .28 | .45 | .26 | .32 | .23 |
| | No Norm Violation | .46 | .23 | .43 | .24 | .40 | .21 |
| Middle of the Road[b] | Rhetoric from Right | | | | | | |
| | Norm Violation | .54* | .22 | .47 | .19 | .40 | .19 |
| | No Norm Violation | .41* | .21 | .38 | .23 | .42 | .22 |
| | Rhetoric from Left | | | | | | |
| | Norm Violation | .49 | .27 | .48 | .24 | .37 | .22 |
| | No Norm Violation | .53 | .21 | .45 | .18 | .45 | .23 |
| Liberal[c] | Rhetoric from Right | | | | | | |
| | Norm Violation | .54** | .26 | .54* | .22 | .33 | .23 |
| | No Norm Violation | .38** | .24 | .41* | .22 | .36 | .18 |
| | Rhetoric from Left | | | | | | |
| | Norm Violation | .39 | .24 | .48** | .25 | .35 | .23 |
| | No Norm Violation | .40 | .22 | .32** | .24 | .43 | .20 |

*Notes:*
Mean comparisons can be made vertically (within columns) between Norm and No Norm Violation.
Survey I [a] $n = 214$, [b] $n = 165$, [c] $n = 124$. $^{*}p < .05$, $^{**}p < .01$, $^{***}p < .001$

In order to sort this out, we took advantage of the manipulation in Survey II that asked our study participants to focus their attention on the blogger-critic's rhetoric and to ignore for the moment the policy agenda being targeted by that rhetoric. Thus, for those exposed, for example, to the conservative critique of liberal policies using norm-violation rhetoric, our battery of 10 affective items was formatted: 'How does the blogger in this commentary 'Flaming Conservative' make you feel?'

The result of this analysis is presented in Table 13.5. The bottom panel shows rhetoric's impact across all individuals. The outcome remains the same for Aversion (norm violation increases an aversive response) and the same for Enthusiasm (norm violation decreases an enthusiastic response). But this time, by focusing on the speaker and not the policy position being critiqued, we find the predicted response for Anxiety – norm violation increases anxiety. The effect is largely driven by self-described conservative respondents, which raises interesting questions about the interaction of ideology and affective resonance in various rhetorical strategies (Jost, 2009).

It is also interesting to note what is not in evidence in Table 13.4. Given that moderates are less likely to have a horse in the race, politically speaking, they might be expected both to exhibit lower overall levels of emotional response to our various

*Table 13.5* *Emotional reactions to 'Blogger-Critic' with and without norm-violation rhetoric by ideology of respondent and ideology of Blogger-Critic*

| | | | Anxiety | | | Aversion | | | Enthusiasm | | |
|---|---|---|---|---|---|---|---|---|---|---|---|
| Respondent ideology | Blogger-Critic ideology | Norm-violation condition | *M* | | *SD* | *M* | | *SD* | *M* | | *SD* |
| Conservative[a] | Conservative | Violation | .57 | ** | .28 | .48 | ** | .22 | .31 | ** | .20 |
| | | No Violation | .42 | ** | .19 | .34 | ** | .22 | .45 | ** | .21 |
| | Liberal | Violation | .44 | ** | .24 | .48 | *** | .23 | .28 | | .20 |
| | | No Violation | .30 | ** | .28 | .27 | *** | .27 | .24 | | .22 |
| Middle of the Road[b] | Conservative | Violation | .40 | | .24 | .45 | | .25 | .38 | | .21 |
| | | No Violation | .47 | | .24 | .48 | | .27 | .41 | | .26 |
| | Liberal | Violation | .48 | | .20 | .53 | *** | .17 | .35 | ** | .17 |
| | | No Violation | .41 | | .25 | .34 | *** | .23 | .46 | ** | .18 |
| Liberal[c] | Conservative | Violation | .43 | | .30 | .69 | *** | .22 | .20 | *** | .19 |
| | | No Violation | .42 | | .24 | .36 | *** | .27 | .45 | *** | .22 |
| | Liberal | Violation | .42 | | .26 | .51 | *** | .26 | .30 | | .22 |
| | | No Violation | .37 | | .24 | .29 | *** | .27 | .32 | | .24 |
| Total | | Violation | .46 | * | | .52 | *** | | .30 | *** | |
| | | No Violation | .40 | * | | .35 | *** | | .39 | *** | |

*Notes:*
Mean comparisons can be made vertically (within columns) between Norm and No Norm Violation.
Data are from Survey II (focus attention on blogger). $^a$ $n = 68$, $^b$ $n = 161$, $^c$ $n = 31$. $^*p < .05$, $^{**}p < .01$, $^{***}p < .001$

rhetorical exemplars and to be less responsive to norm-violation rhetoric itself. But in Study II, as in Study I, we find that moderates display roughly equivalent levels of Anxiety, Aversion and Enthusiasm and respond in similar patterns to the norm-violation manipulation. Further, we do not see evidence of liberals or conservatives rooting for their teams and, in effect, displaying higher Enthusiasm and lower Anxiety and Aversion when a blogger-critic of their persuasion critiques their traditional political adversaries. The negative response to norm violation remains in evidence regardless of ideological sympathies.

We turn now to the second hypothesis (H2), which predicts that Anxiety will have the strongest association with reported further political engagement and the seeking of additional political information. We shift from difference of means to linear regression at this stage of the analysis. The reason for this is that our focal point is an analysis of the unique contribution of each emotional dimension to the various political behaviors and orientations of interest. As indicated in Figure 13.1, the analytic focus is on affective resonance as the key mechanism (Marcus et al., 2019). Because indicators of Anxiety and Aversion are usually correlated and often substantially so, we invoke multiple regression's characteristic strengths in parsing the potential impacts of related variables.

The following tables address the question of whether the emotional resonances provoked by our stimulus conditions replicate the previous findings in the literature

*Table 13.6* *Regression analyses predicting more information seeking and different information seeking from emotions*

| | Information seeking | | | |
|---|---|---|---|---|
| | More information[a] | | Different information[b] | |
| Variable | | | | |
| Constant | .139 | .036 | .095 | .032 |
| Anxiety | .149** | .055 | .127** | .048 |
| Aversion | .028 | .057 | .031 | .049 |
| Enthusiasm | .098** | .052 | .101* | .046 |

*Notes:*
All variables have been recoded to range of 0 to 1 so B's can be interpreted as roughly equivalent to Betas.
*$p < .05$, **$p < .01$. [a] alpha = .80; [b] alpha = .80 Survey I (attention to blogger and policy) [a] $n = 501$; [b] $n = 505$

on the unique contributions of Aversion and Anxiety to deliberative information seeking as against steadfastness. In short, we find that the affective intelligence hypotheses are largely confirmed. We construct a two-item index measuring the likelihood the respondent reports an inclination to seek further information on the political issues at hand in response to our various stimulus conditions and call it 'More Information.' Table 13.6 then regresses that 'More Information' index on the three emotional indices. We find that Enthusiasm and particularly, as predicted, Anxiety are positively correlated with the deliberative response to seek out further political information. An Aversive response to these rhetorical manipulations, interestingly, makes no difference one way or another. Anxiety and Enthusiasm are also moderately correlated with our index of seeking out websites or opinions likely to contain information contrary to our political views under the heading 'Different Information' in Table 13.6. Again, Aversion is not a significant factor.

In Table 13.7, we address H3 and the Aversive response comes to the fore. Our Steadfast Index is composed of four items which assess the respondents' inclination, given the stimulus at hand, to 'provide no room for compromise' and to assert that 'listening to everyone is going to get us entangled and produce endless debate.' Some old hands may recognize these items as reminiscent of F-Scale (Adorno et al., 1950). Here, Aversion resonates with steadfastness while neither Anxiety nor Enthusiasm appear to be relevant (Valentino et al., 2011).

Our Cooperate Index is not exactly the opposite of Steadfastness; it assesses the respondents' agreement with four statements like 'These sorts of issues and events should be resolved so that everybody's needs are met.' The right half of Table 13.7 under the heading 'Cooperation' reports these results. Interestingly, Aversion, which one might expect to be negatively correlated with a cooperative orientation, is not related at all. This suggests a functional specificity to each affective route: Anxiety modulates interest while Aversion modulates steadfastness. There remains the prospect, however, of a more complex interaction of Aversion and Cooperation as more

*Table 13.7* *Regression analyses predicting more steadfastness and cooperation from emotions*

| | Steadfastness[a] | | Cooperation[b] | |
|---|---|---|---|---|
| Variable | | | | |
| Constant | .326 | .028 | .477 | .031 |
| Anxiety | .026 | .042 | .116** | .047 |
| Aversion | .159*** | .043 | -.001 | .049 |
| Enthusiasm | .028 | .040 | .027 | .045 |

*Notes:*
All variables coded from 0 to 1.
$^{*}p < .05$, $^{**}p < .01$, $^{***}p < .001$ [a] alpha = .53; Cooperation Index [b] alpha = 74. Survey I (attention to blogger and policy) [a] $n = 500$; [b] $n = 495$

cooperatively oriented individuals respond more dramatically to norm-violation rhetoric or a related reciprocal interaction (Slater, 2007).

Finally, we included a two-item index of the respondents' inclination to get politically involved and 'do something about these issues' or 'talk to others and get people involved.' Here again, Anxiety appears to be the key factor; see Table 13.8. We might expect that the style of political engagement would be quite different if it were motivated by Anxiety as opposed to Aversion. Perhaps this is further evidence of the frequently observed phenomenon in political behavior – the existence of multiple and independent paths to political engagement (Verba, Schlozman & Brady, 1995).

*Table 13.8* *Regression analyses predicting political engagement*

| | Political engagement |
|---|---|
| Variable | |
| Constant | .037 |
| Anxiety | .056 |
| Aversion | .058 |
| Enthusiasm | .053 |

*Notes:*
All variables coded from 0 to 1.
$^{*}p < .05$, $^{**}p < .01$, $^{***}p < .001$. Survey I (attention to blogger and policy) $n = 506$

## DISCUSSION

The concept of norm violation, we assert, adds a new and important psychologically grounded element to theorizing the process of political communication. Polarization is a distributional attribute of the array of policy positions, not a characteristic of individual citizens. Variation in incivility and negativity refers to rhetorical styles but focuses on characteristics of interpersonal communication such as rudeness and ad hominem critiques. Sobieraj and Berry (2011), for example, provide an expansive list of the components of incivility in their analysis, reproduced here as Table 13.9.

*Table 13.9 Components of incivility, from Sobieraj & Berry (2011)*

| | | |
|---|---|---|
| Insulting language | Verbal fighting/sparring | Conflagration |
| Name-calling | Character assassination | Extremizing lang. |
| Emotional display (visual) | Misrepresentative exaggeration | Slippery slope |
| Emotional language | Mockery | Obscene lang. |

It is notable that the list includes concepts of emotion and emotional intensity but not norm violation. Norm violation, however, is a central component of Pamela Shoemaker's approach to understanding communicative dynamics. She proclaims we are 'hardwired for news' and a central element in her model for attracting public attention is *social deviance* – the breaking of accepted norms and traditions (Shoemaker, 1996). The evolved human cognitive system emphasizes the importance of the social, the collaborative, and, of course, the tribal in processing information from our environment. Perhaps we should not be surprised that, despite dramatic changes in the technologies of interpersonal and mass communication, the dynamics of selective attention and selective perception are deeply rooted and unchanging (Grabe & Kamhawi, 2006; Haidt, 2012; Kalmoe, 2014).

These results, of course, should be viewed as preliminary. There are important limitations in our research design. All of our measures are simple self-reports and it is well known that individuals have a limited capacity to discern their feelings and to predict future behavior. Further, we have relied on a single operationalization of norm-violation rhetoric. Because this implementation of the liberal and conservative critiques used different phrases, we cannot be sure some other element in the stimulus materials, such as a passing reference to Obamacare, or gas-guzzling pick-up trucks, may not have triggered a particular emotional resonance with our respondents. The manipulation that asks respondents to pay attention to the blogger rather than to the policy position in question is, of course, unnatural and unlikely to correspond to real-world conditions.

Furthermore, we chose to focus on political issues rather than on candidates in this study. It may be that emotional dynamics play out somewhat differently when an actual individual standing for public office is the focal point of norm-violation or ad hominen critique. Finally, in research like this, where many variables are analyzed simultaneously, cell sizes shrink perilously. So, stronger confidence in these patterns would benefit from multiple and diverse replications.

But these results are provocative and raise interesting theoretical issues. We have reviewed the affective dynamics of public response to the rhetoric of illegitimacy and norm violation. The broadly defined patterns predicted by affective intelligence theory are largely confirmed. The affective intelligence literature demonstrates that novel negative stimuli invoke anxiety while familiar negative stimuli invoke heightened aversion and depressed enthusiasm (MacKuen et al., 2010). A key finding here was that the anxiety response was not immediately evident in the data. It was masked by the contrasting emotional responses to the critic and to the focus of the critic's indignation. It was not until we directed the respondent's attention explicitly to the critic that the anxiety effect was evident. This finding resonates with the literature on campaign negativity – both negative campaigners and their targets are diminished in voters' perceptions by the negativity.

Unfortunately, and not surprisingly, the affective response to norm-violation rhetoric in social media is not necessarily resonant with the democratic ideal of thoughtful deliberation and negotiated compromise (Achen & Bartels, 2016; Caplan, 2008; Miller & Conover, 2015; Schreiner, Fischer & Riedl, 2021; Weismueller et al., 2022). Spatial models of issue voting, rational choice calculations, and even so-called rational ignorance do not anticipate that perceptions of unfairness and norm violation can motivate political involvement and information seeking. Perhaps they should. It may be that a little anxiety can go a long way in getting citizens to give fresh thought to political options. Unfortunately, as voices are raised and the perception of disingenuousness pervades, the reinforcement of established aversions may outweigh the prospect of a little thought-provoking anxiety. The politics of affect in social media, it appears, represents a double-edged sword.

## REFERENCES

Achen, C.H., & Bartels, L.M. (2016). *Democracy for Realists: Why Elections Do Not Produce Responsive Government*. Princeton: Princeton University Press.

Adorno, T.W., Frenkel-Brunswik, E., Levinson, D.J., & Sanford, R.N. (1950). *The Authoritarian Personality*. New York: Harper and Row.

Agger, R.E., Goldstein, M.N., & Pearl, S.A. (1961). Political Cynicism: Measurement and Meaning. *Journal of Politics*, *23*(August), 477–506.

Ahler, D.J. (2014). Self-Fulfilling Misperceptions of Public Polarization. *Journal of Politics*, *76*(3), 607–20. doi:10.1017/S0022381614000085.

Anderson, A.A., Brossard, D., Scheufele, D.A., Xenos, M.A., & Ladwig, P. (2014). The 'Nasty Effect': Online Incivility and Risk Perceptions of Emerging Technologies. *Journal of Computer-Mediated Communication*, *19*(3), 373–87. doi:10.1111/jcc4.12009.

André, J.-B., & Baumard, N. (2011). Social Opportunities and the Evolution of Fairness. *Journal of Theoretical Biology*, *289*, 128–35. doi:10.1016/j.jtbi.2011.07.031.

Ansolabehere, S., & Iyengar, S. (1995). *Going Negative: How Attack Ads Shrink and Polarize the Electorate*. New York: Free Press.

Baker, R., Blumberg, S.J., Brick, J.M., Couper, M.P., Courtright, M., Dennis, J.M., … Zahs, D. (2010). Research Synthesis: AAPOR Report on Online Panels. *Public Opinion Quarterly*, *74*(4), 711–81. doi:10.1093/poq/nfq048.

Bazelon, E. (2017). How Do We Contend with Trump's Defiance of 'Norms'? *New York Times Magazine* (July 11).

Bermeo, N. (2019). Reflections: Can American Democracy Still Be Saved? *Annals of the American Academy of Political and Social Science*, *681*(1), 228–33. doi:10.1177/0002716218818083.

Boller, P.F. (2004). *Presidential Campaigns: From George Washington to George W. Bush*. New York: Oxford University Press.

Brooks, D.J., & Geer, J.G. (2007). Beyond Negativity: The Effects of Incivility on the Electorate. *American Journal of Political Science*, *51*(1), 1–16. http://www.jstor.org/stable/4122902.

Camerer, C.F., Loewenstein, G., & Rabin, M. (Eds.). (2004). *Advances in Behavioral Economics*. Princeton: Princeton University Press.

Caplan, B. (2008). *The Myth of the Rational Voter: Why Democracies Choose Bad Policies*. Princeton: Princeton University Press.
Checkroun, P., & Brauer, M. (2002). The Bystander Effect and Social Control Behavior: The Effect of the Presence of Others on People's Reactions to Norm Violations. *European Journal of Social Psychology*, *32*, 853–67.
Citrin, J. (1974). Comment: The Political Relevance of Trust in Government. *American Political Science Review*, *68*(September), 973–88.
De Ridder, R., & Tripathi, R.C. (1992). *Norm Violation and Intergroup Relations*. New York: Oxford University Press.
Denby, D. (2015). The Plot Against America: Donald Trump's Rhetoric. *New Yorker* (December 15).
Druckman, J.N., Peterson, E., & Slothuus, R. (2013). How Elite Partisan Polarization Affects Public Opinion Formation. *American Political Science Review*, *107*(1), 57–79. doi:10.1017/S0003055412000500.
Epley, N., & Gilovich, T. (2016). The Mechanics of Motivated Reasoning. *Journal of Economic Perspectives*, *30*(3), 133–40. doi:10.1257/jep.30.3.133.
Fiorina, M.P., Abrams, S.J., & Pope, J.C. (2010). *Culture War? The Myth of a Polarized America*. New York: Longman.
Fridkin, K.L., & Kenney, P.J. (2004). Do Negative Messages Work? The Impact of Negativity on Citizens' Evaluations of Candidates. *American Politics Research*, *32*, 571–605.
Geer, J. (2006). *In Defense of Negativity*. Chicago: University of Chicago Press.
Grabe, M.E., & Kamhawi, R. (2006). Hard Wired for Negative News? Gender Differences in Processing Broadcast News. *Communication Research*, *33*(5), 346–69. doi:10.1177/0093650206291479.
Haidt, J. (2012). *The Righteous Mind: Why Good People Are Divided by Politics and Religion*. New York: Random House.
Herbst, S. (2010). *Rude Democracy: Civility and Incivility in American Politics*. Philadelphia: Temple University Press.
Huq, A., & Ginsburg, T. (2018). How to Lose a Constitutional Democracy. 65 *UCLA Law Review* 78.
Iyengar, S. (2016). E Pluribus Pluribus, or Divided We Stand. *Public Opinion Quarterly*, *80*(S1), 219–24. doi:10.1093/poq/nfv084.
Iyengar, S., Sood, G., & Lelkes, Y. (2012). Affect, Not Ideology: A Social Identity Perspective on Polarization. *Public Opinion Quarterly*, *76*(3), 405–31. doi:10.1093/poq/nfs038.
Iyengar, S., & Westwood, S.J. (2015). Fear and Loathing across Party Lines: New Evidence on Group Polarization. *American Journal of Political Science*, *59*(3), 690–707. doi:10.1111/ajps.12152.
Jost, J.T. (2009). 'Elective Affinities': On the Psychological Bases of Left–Right Differences. *Psychological Inquiry*, *20*, 129–41. doi:10.1080/10478400903028599.
Kahn, K.F., & Kenney, P.J. (1999). Do Negative Campaigns Mobilize or Suppress Turnout? Clarifying the Relationship between Negativity and Participation. *American Political Science Review*, *93*(4), 877–89. doi:10.2307/2586118.
Kalmoe, N.P. (2014). Fueling the Fire: Violent Metaphors, Trait Aggression, and Support for Political Violence. *Political Communication*, *31*(4), 545–63. doi:10.1080/10584609.2013.852642.
Kenski, K., Coe, K., & Rains, S. A. (2017). Perceptions of Uncivil Discourse Online: An Examination of Types and Predictors. *Communication Research*. Pre-published April 3. doi:10.1177/0093650217699933.
Kunda, Z. (1990). The Case for Motivated Reasoning. *Psychological Bulletin*, *108* (3), 480–498. doi:10.1037/0033-2909.108.3.480.

Lau, R.R., Sigelman, L., & Rovner, I.B. (2007). The Effects of Negative Political Campaigns: A Meta-Analytic Reassessment. *Journal of Politics*, *69*(4), 1176–1209. doi:10.1111/j.1468-2508.2007.00618.x.

Lee, F.E. (2015). How Party Polarization Affects Governance. *Annual Review of Political Science*, *18*(1), 261–82. doi:10.1146/annurev-polisci-072012-113747.

Lerner, J.S., Gonzalez, R.M., Small, D.A., & Fischhoff, B. (2003). Effects of Fear and Anger on Perceived Risks of Terrorism: A National Field Experiment *Psychological Science*, *14*(2), 144–50. doi:10.1111/1467-9280.01433.

Lerner, J.S., & Keltner, D. (2000). Beyond Valence: Toward a Model of Emotion-Specific Influences on Judgement and Choice. *Cognition and Emotion*, *14*(4), 473–93. doi:10.1080/026999300402763.

Levendusky, M. (2013). *How Partisan Media Polarize America*. Chicago: University of Chicago Press.

Levendusky, M.S., & Malhotra, N. (2016). (Mis)perceptions of Partisan Polarization in the American Public. *Public Opinion Quarterly*, *80*(S1), 378–91. doi:10.1093/poq/nfv045

Levitsky, S., & Ziblatt, D. (2018). *How Democracies Die*. New York: Crown.

Lind, E.A., & Tyler, T.R. (1988). *The Social Psychology of Procedural Justice*. New York: Plenum Press.

Lodge, M., & Taber, C.S. (2013). *The Rationalizing Voter*. New York: Cambridge University Press.

MacKuen, M., Wolak, J., Keele, L., & Marcus, G.E. (2010). Civic Engagements: Resolute Partisanship or Reflective Deliberation. *American Journal of Political Science*, *54*(2), 440–458. doi:10.1111/j.1540-5907.2010.00440.x.

Marcus, G.E., Neuman, W.R., & MacKuen, M. (2000). *Affective Intelligence and Political Judgment*. Chicago: University of Chicago Press.

Marcus, G.E., Valentino, N.A., Vasilopoulos, P., & Foucault, M. (2019). Applying the Theory of Affective Intelligence to Support for Authoritarian Policies and Parties. *Political Psychology*, *40*(S1), 109–39. doi:10.1111/pops.12571.

Mattes, K., & Redlawsk, D.P. (2014). *The Positive Case for Negative Campaigning*. Chicago: University of Chicago Press.

Miller, A.H. (1974). Political Issues and Trust in Government: 1964–1970. *American Political Science Review*, *68*(3), 951–72. doi:10.2307/1959140.

Miller, P.R., & Conover, P.J. (2015). Red and Blue States of Mind: Partisan Hostility and Voting in the United States. *Political Research Quarterly*, *68*(2), 225–39. doi:10.1177/1065912915577208.

Moretti, L., Cristofori, I., Zamboni, G., & Sirigu, A. (2012). The Neural Structure of Political Belief. In F. Krueger & J. Grafman (Eds.), *The Neural Basis of Human Belief Systems*. New York: Routledge.

Muddiman, A. (2017). Personal and Public Levels of Political Incivility. *International Journal of Communication*, *11*. https://ijoc.org/index.php/ijoc/article/view/6137.

Mutz, D.C. (2007). The Effects of 'In-Your-Face' Television Discourse on Perceptions of a Legitimate Opposition. *American Political Science Review*, *101*(4), 621–35. doi:10.1017/S000305540707044X.

Mutz, D.C. (2015). *In-Your-Face Politics: The Consequences of Uncivil Media*. Princeton: Princeton University Press.

Mutz, D.C., & Reeves, B. (2005). The New Videomalaise: Effects of Televised Incivility on Political Trust. *American Political Science Review*, *99*(1), 1–15. doi:10.1017/S0003055405051452.

Nelissen, R.M.A., & Zeelenberg, M. (2009). Moral Emotions as Determinants of Third-Party Punishment: Anger, Guilt, and the Functions of Altruistic Sanctions. *Judgment and Decision Making*, *4*, 543–53.

Ng, S.H., & Allen, M.W. (2005). Perception of Economic Distributive Justice: Exploring Leading Theories. *Social Behavior and Personality: An International Journal*, *33*(5), 435–54. doi:10.2224/sbp.2005.33.5.435.

Papacharissi, Z. (2004). Democracy Online: Civility, Politeness, and the Democratic Potential of Online Political Discussion Groups. *New Media & Society*, *6*(2), 259–83. doi:10.1177/1461444804041444.

Persily, N., & Tucker, J.A. (2020). *Social Media and Democracy: The State of the Field, Prospects for Reform*. New York: Cambridge University Press.

Peterson, E., & Kagalwala, A.L.I. (2021). When Unfamiliarity Breeds Contempt: How Partisan Selective Exposure Sustains Oppositional Media Hostility. *American Political Science Review*, *115*(2), 585–98.

Prior, M. (2013). Media and Political Polarization. *Annual Review of Political Science*, *16*, 101–27.

Ryan, T.J. (2012). What Makes Us Click? Demonstrating Incentives for Angry Discourse with Digital-Age Field Experiments. *Journal of Politics*, *74*(4), 1138–52. doi:10.1017/S0022381612000540.

Sampson, T., Maddison, S., & Ellis, D. (2018). *Affect and Social Media: Emotion, Mediation, Anxiety and Contagion*. New York: Rowman & Littlefield.

Sapiro, V. (1999). Considering Political Civility Historically: A Case Study of the United States. *International Society of Political Psychology Annual Scientific Meeting, Amsterdam*.

Scherpenzeel, A., & Toepoel, V. (2012). Recruiting a Probability Sample for an Online Panel: Effects of Contact Mode, Incentives, and Information. *Public Opinion Quarterly*, *76*(3), 470–490. doi:10.1093/poq/nfs037.

Schreiner, M., Fischer, T., & Riedl, R. (2021). Impact of Content Characteristics and Emotion on Behavioral Engagement in Social Media: Literature Review and Research Agenda. *Electronic Commerce Research*, *21*(2), 329–45.

Shannon, V.P. (2000). Norms Are What States Make of Them: The Political Psychology of Norm Violation. *International Studies Quarterly*, *44*(2), 293–316. doi:10.1111/0020-8833.00159.

Shoemaker, P.J. (1996). Hardwired for News: Using Biological and Cultural Evolution to Explain the Surveillance Function. *Journal of Communication*, *46*(3), 32–47. doi:10.1111/j.1460-2466.1996.tb01487.x.

Sidanius, J., & Pratto, F. (1999). *Social Dominance: An Intergroup Theory of Social Hierarchy and Oppression*. New York: Cambridge University Press.

Sigelman, L., & Kugler, M. (2003). Why Is Research on the Effects of Negative Campaigning So Inconclusive? Understanding Citizens' Perceptions of Negativity. *Journal of Politics*, *65*(1), 142–60.

Slater, M.D. (2007). Reinforcing Spirals: The Mutual Influence of Media Selectivity and Media Effects and Their Impact on Individual Behavior and Social Identity. *Communication Theory*, *17*(3), 281–303. doi:10.1111/j.1468-2885.2007.00296.x.

Sobieraj, S., & Berry, J.M. (2011). From Incivility to Outrage: Political Discourse in Blogs, Talk Radio, and Cable News. *Political Communication*, *28*(1), 19–41. doi:10.1080/10584609.2010.542360.

Stephenson, E., & Kahn, C. (2016). Polls Show 'Rigged' Message Resonates. Reuters (October 21).

Sullivan, J.L., Piereson, J.E., & Marcus, G.E. (1982). *Political Tolerance and American Democracy*. Chicago: University of Chicago Press.

Sydnor, E. (2017). The Emotional Consequences of Psychological Conflict Orientation and Political Incivility. *ECPR Joint Session on Political Incivility, University of Nottingham*.

Tabibnia, G., Satpute, A.B., & Lieberman, M.D. (2008). The Sunny Side of Fairness: Preference for Fairness Activates Reward Circuitry (and Disregarding Unfairness Activates Self-Control Circuitry). *Psychological Science*, *19*(4), 339–47. doi:10.1111/j.1467-9280.2008.02091.x.

Tomasky, M. (2015). Very Improbable Candidates. *New York Review of Books*, *62*(17).

Tucker, J.A., Guess, A., Barbera, P., Vaccari, C., Siegel, A., Sanovich, S., Stukal, D., & Nyhan, B. (2018). *Social Media, Political Polarization, and Political Disinformation: A Review of the Scientific Literature*. SSRN working paper.
Tyler, T.R., & Lind, E.A. (1992). A Relational Model of Authority in Groups. *Advances in Experimental Social Psychology*, *25*, 115–91.
Ulbig, S.G. (2008). Voice is Not Enough: The Importance of Influence in Political Trust and Policy Assessments. *Public Opinion Quarterly*, *72*(3), 523–39. doi:10.1093/poq/nfn030.
Valentino, N.A., Brader, T., Groenendyk, E., Gregorowicz, K., & Hutchings, V.L. (2011). Election Night's Alright for Fighting: The Role of Emotions in Political Participation. *Journal of Politics*, *73*(1), 156–70. doi:10.1017/s0022381610000939.
Verba, S., Schlozman, K.L., & Brady, H.E. (1995). *Voice and Equality: Civic Volunteerism in American Politics*. Cambridge: Harvard University Press.
Weismueller, J., Harrigan, P., Coussement, K., & Tessitore, T. (2022). What Makes People Share Political Content on Social Media? The Role of Emotion, Authority and Ideology. *Computers in Human Behavior*, *129*, 107150.
Westfall, J., Van Boven, L., Chambers, J.R., & Judd, C.M. (2015). Perceiving Political Polarization in the United States: Party Identity Strength and Attitude Extremity Exacerbate the Perceived Partisan Divide. *Perspectives on Psychological Science*, *10*(2), 145–58. doi:10.1177/1745691615569849.
Yarchi, M., Baden, C., & Kligler-Vilenchik, N. (2021). Political Polarization on the Digital Sphere: A Cross-Platform, Over-Time Analysis of Interactional, Positional, and Affective Polarization on Social Media. *Political Communication*, *38*(1–2), 98–139.

# 14. Socio-technical and cultural threats to social movements in the Global South: vignettes from Indonesia

*Abdul Rohman*

## INTRODUCTION

Social movements trigger changes in societies. They emerge and resurge as injustice and inequality persist. Activists fight against autocracy, irresponsible governance, and oppression towards minorities and marginalized groups. The activists risk their lives in advocating the ideal world they imagine, as those in power ignore the suffering of those without (Melucci, 1996). The occurrence of a global pandemic such as COVID-19, which had been spiralling out of control in many countries when this chapter was written, is predicted will instil civic unrest, as the incompetence of the powerful in handling the pandemic magnifies existing injustice and inequality (National Intelligence Council, 2021). Thus, activists from different parts of the world rise to fight for justice and equality to become the basis of social governance and to resist tyrannies and authoritarianism.

Digital and social media platforms (hereafter, the platforms) have evidently helped the activists to organize social movements throughout different episodes (Rohman, 2019). During the movements' ascending and peak episodes, the platforms are tools for mobilizing supporters, coordinating, and sharing information (Rohman, Pang, and Pitaloka, 2020). The platforms are then useful for reminiscing about memories the activists shared as the movement descends and enters abeyance (Rohman and Pitaloka, 2020). While whether the affordability of the platforms can cause a movement to emerge remains debatable, their usefulness across different movement episodes is undeniable. Thus, studies that intersect platforms and social movements have been abundant.

That being said, the platforms also bring about new threats to social movements. Major technology companies such as Facebook and Google have been under intense scrutiny in many democratic countries (Romm, 2020) while at the same time dealing with autocratic governments requesting takedowns of content deemed threatening to national security (Amnesty International, 2020). During the first half of 2021, Google Transparency reported that the Vietnamese and Indian governments had respectively requested over 300 and 100 takedowns of content critical of the state and potentially threatening to national security. Globally, upon government requests Google has removed nearly 3 million pieces of content since 2011.[1] Suppressing online discussions considered to be anti-state becomes easier than before as those in power turn the platforms into surveillance tools. Once predicted to be capable of revolutionizing and democratizing societies, the platforms have now become an extension of oppressors as discontent, grievances, and intentions to make change are closely monitored by those who have the superpower to control the access to the platforms (Persily, 2019).

On that basis, this chapter outlines the socio-technical and cultural threats to social movements. To illuminate them, vignettes from Indonesia, the largest democratic, Muslim-predominant, and digitally savvy country in Southeast Asia, is used. This chapter potentially contributes to the existing social movement studies in the Global South, which tend to be digital and social media-centric by showcasing the negative externalities arising from the rapid use of the platforms in multifaceted social spaces.

## WHAT ARE THE SOCIO-TECHNICAL THREATS?

As the usefulness of the platforms becomes central in the organization of social movements, those in power also find ways of using them for cracking down on the movements and activists. Socio-technical threats arise as a result. They revolve around the use of technologies to reduce the efficacy of the platforms for mobilizing resources, creating political opportunities, and maintaining ideologies – three crucial enablers for social movements to emerge and continue. The socio-technical threats are the production of legal infrastructures to legitimate movement crackdowns, state-sponsored hacking, and internet disconnections.

### Legal Infrastructures of Movement Crackdowns

As the deployment of surveillance technologies for controlling societies gains traction, autocratic regimes are in the race to create the infrastructures for legitimizing it (Polyakova and Meserole, 2019). Laws are produced to limit freedom of assembly, expression, and speech, which is essential for social movements to emerge from the ground. The laws shrink the space where activists can freely articulate their discontent, hold perpetrators of social problems and those in power accountable, and call for public support. In this sense, a systemic approach is used to define everything the state considers threatening to national security, economic growth, and social harmony. As a result, citizens who want to support ongoing movements may self-censor their social media posts as fear of being incriminated looms out of the reinforcement of the law.

In practice, the law constrains ordinary citizens and activists from pointing out the inefficacy of state policies and mobilizing support for doing so from a wider audience. While the law may be initially intended to mitigate the undesirable consequences of technologies, it also gives the state an ample opportunity to accuse citizens and activists of defamation and spreading disinformation (DW.com, 2019). In this circumstance, the freedom to opine shrinks as the law instils public fear of being seen as challenging the state. Thus, self-content moderation and a tendency to avoid political conversations or discussions of policies impacting life grow, reducing public participation in protest movements while grievances are shared in private spaces (Strittmatter, 2020).

The legal infrastructure of crackdowns can be seen in the Indonesian Information and Electronic Transactions Law (aka the ITE Law). The law, which was enacted in 2008 and revised in 2016, has been proposed for another revision since 2019 (Oktaviani, 2021). Numerous threats to civil society, media, and activism have arisen as clauses related to defamation and hate speech are used to criminalize dissenters and critics (Prasetyo, 2021). To implement the law, the government issued Ministerial Regulation 5 in 2020, which many social movement organizations (SMOs) demanded to be repealed because of its potential to expand the government's power to silence defenders of freedom of speech (AccessNow, 2021). The law was originally intended for regulating digital information and electronic transactions. However, its ramifications seem to outweigh the benefits since the power to control the internet is centralized to the government. From 2018 to 2019 alone, the law has reportedly been used to criminalize nearly 50 people, ranging from journalists to activists, academics, celebrities, and ordinary citizens (SAFEnet, 2020).

In response, a Twitter account, @pakuite (*Paguyuban Korban* ITE or Association of ITE Victims), emerged in late 2018. As of June 1, 2021, it had 3,186 followers and had tweeted nearly 1,500 times. It aims to raise awareness about the repercussions of the law through sharing relevant news articles and organizing public forums discussing the polemics surrounding it. More importantly, it echoes the voice of the victims and helps them raise funds for financing expenses incurred from the court and other legal matters. @pakuite calls for anyone experiencing digital attacks and harassment to report back by sharing a name and contact details, the types of platforms being attacked (e.g., WhatsApp, website, and Twitter), the chronology and evidence of the attack, and the expected support. This Twitter handle, in general, advocates for a revision of the ambiguous clauses of the ITE Law while simultaneously assisting the victims.

The above vignette from Indonesia suggests that a structural and systemic method to crack down on critics manifests in the formulation of legal infrastructures to limit freedom and widen the state's power to regulate what is appropriate to be communicated in the public sphere. While it is important to maintain social order, the checks-and-balances mechanism over that state's power also needs to be available for justice and equality to prevail. In that sense, the legal infrastructures can be necessary to mitigate uncertainty and chaos arising from the proliferation of internet use (Ang, 2005), but who is advantaged and disadvantaged by the reinforcement is a lingering question. If the legal infrastructures are created only for strengthening the state and weakening the civil society's power, they can be an imminent threat to activism. Unfortunately, the latter seems to be more pronounced as the state prefers making laws to harmonize societies at the expense of dissenters and critiques.

## State-Sponsored Hacking

State-sponsored hacking has become a method to discredit the credibility of activists who criticize government policies and to sow doubt in the information that the activists share (Al-Rawi, 2019). The hacker would attempt to take over the activists' WhatsApp accounts, mobile phones, or social media handles. Detrimental messages to harm the credibility of the activists would be circulated from the hacked accounts, seeding distrust and doubt in the cause that the activists advocate. Later this may lead to malicious campaigns attacking anyone and any entities associated with them. Fabricated tweets, photos, and stories containing innuendos would begin to spread, diverting public attention to the activists' personal credibility. Messages classifiable as disruptive, dangerous, and threatening to social harmony and national security also characterize state-sponsored hacking cases. As such, reasons for arrests and confiscating the activists' gadgets are justified, from which the state can then look for more damaging information. In short, the state-sponsored hacking represents a deliberate attempt to assassinate the character of the activists (Jordan, 2017).

The above assertion is observable in two hacking cases of activists' digital and social media platforms in light of the COVID-19 pandemic in Indonesia. Ravio Patra, a public policy researcher and democracy activist, became an alleged victim of state-sponsored hacking as he actively questioned the government's non-transparent policies about COVID-19 mortality data and the involvement of a presidential staffer in several business solicitations (Rohman, 2021). His WhatsApp account was taken over by unidentified actors on April 22, 2020. A provocation to riot and loot was shared from his WhatsApp account, giving the authority a reason to arrest him as that message was deemed to trigger mass panic and fear. He was released after being detained for more than 30 hours, while the hacker remained unidentified. His legal team believed that the hacking and arrest were orchestrated to criminalize him.

Another alleged state-sponsored hacking case occurred to Pandu Riono, an epidemiologist who actively criticized the government's inconsistent policies to tackle the pandemic and the ineffectiveness of its public health messaging. His Twitter account was hacked on August 19, 2020, and the handle began tweeting photos of him with a woman who was captioned as his mistress and claimed they both were on vacation in Sydney, Australia. In fact, he was in Jakarta and was unaware of the hacking until his friends alerted him. Rather than pursuing legal actions, he created a new Twitter account to inform the public and the new handle seemed to have gained more followers since many found his critiques of the government's pandemic measures credible.

Both cases signify socio-technical threats arising from the state's intent to silence critics through non-transparent deployments of new technologies. Globally, there has been an increase in states' interests to hire hackers for national security reasons (Follis and Fish, 2020). While that may have merit, the public deserves to know whether the hackers are tasked to surveil and silence ordinary citizens and any efforts to hold governments accountable. In the Global North, the scrutiny on the accountability of social media and digital platforms and the state's use of surveillance technologies has been on the rise. At the same time, wealthy autocratic countries such as China and Saudi Arabia have also deployed surveillance technologies on activists. Across Southeast Asia, such technologies have contributed to shrinking freedom of speech and increasing human rights violations in the online sphere (Chandran, 2021; Digital Reach, 2022). In broader terms, different social movements will emerge as a response to social problems, and these state mechanisms gradually shrink the online and offline spheres available for those movements to ascend, peak, and continue.

## Internet Disconnection

As the internet becomes pivotal for mobilizing support and amplifying the movement's immediate goal to a wider audience, disrupting internet access is a powerful move to contain the movement. Debates over who should have control over the internet 'kill switch' have not been resolved yet (Denardis, 2020). In many countries, it is the government that has the power to decide on the fate of the internet during volatile times, in addition to de-platforming and taking down any content they deem unaligned with public and state interests. During a protest, lack of access to an internet connection will at least slow down the circulation of information among the activists and prevent it from reaching the public. Thus, authorities would use any means necessary to keep the protest from spiralling out of control. Internationally, internet shutdowns have become a growing technique of oppressing and disabling rights to make a change (O'Brien and Micek, 2020).

In Indonesia, internet disconnections occurred when protests and civil unrest were happening on one of its eastern islands, Papua. The sectarian conflicts, competitions for gaining control over natural resources, and the politics of inequality between the east and west of Indonesia often trigger protests and violent events. In 2019, the internet was disconnected from August 19 to September 8 in Papua and West Papua and then from September 23 to 29 in Wamena city and parts of Jayapura (SAFEnet, 2020). The national government mentioned that it was an attempt to throttle the spread of mis/disinformation, which, if left unmitigated, would have led to a larger scale of chaos. Conversely, civil society organizations pointed out that such internet disruption violated human rights principles and potentially gave authorities an opportunity to cover up wrongdoings and negligence, and to silence local activists. It became a tool to contain information within Papua and thus make it easier to silence dissent with the safety measures that the government deployed on the ground.

In that case, disconnecting the internet is a contested action. It can be a useful tool to dismantle civil unrest arising from the rapid spread of mis/disinformation and can prevent violent content from spreading to other areas. Disconnecting the internet will help slow down the circulation of false information or any materials deemed to be capable of exacerbating civic unrest, which may, directly and indirectly, affect the safety and security of the public. The questions for consideration are how long the disconnection can last, what conditions are needed to mitigate potential oppressions and crackdowns occurring during the internet disconnection period, and how information flows from and to the disconnected area. Answering these questions can keep the disconnection as a means to govern and regulate potential chaos (Rohman and Ang, 2021).

An inability to clearly answer such questions may lead the internet disconnection to become a tool for oppression (Lim, 2020). The state will have more power to shape narratives over what is happening as the disconnected areas become remote from public attention, thus making it easy to control dissent and unfavourable narratives. Activists are more prone to crackdowns as their online and offline movements wane while state surveillance waxes. The activists may then deploy a guerrilla strategy to survive, as their deliberation spaces shrink when the state tightens surveillance measures. Given that, the internet disconnection is no longer a means to govern as access to the free flow of information is closed, from which potential violations to human rights may follow.

## WHAT ARE THE SOCIO-CULTURAL THREATS?

The socio-cultural threats revolve around detrimental practices arising from internet culture. Different from the socio-technical threats that primarily stem from the state, the socio-cultural threats may originate from social and digital media users, who may or may not be affiliated with the state. The socio-cultural threats flow horizontally as reflected in user behaviours, potentially hindering the emergence and continuity of social movements. This section highlights the phenomena of 'social justice warrior', mob culture, and state-sponsored trolling to exemplify such threats.

### Social Justice Warriors

The internet, on the one hand, allows activists to articulate discontent and grievance immediately as they emerge. On the other hand, it also creates the social justice warrior (SJW) phenomena. The term has been principally assigned to anyone who is politically progressive, inclusive, and pro-feminist on digital and social media platforms (Taylor, 2006). In 2011, its pejorative meaning gained traction on Twitter while progressive views, protests, and other social movements in the Middle East, North and South America, Western Europe, and the Global South populated the news. Since then, it has become a daily expression to label the annoying individuals, particularly the middle-class and urban youths, who use social justice issues for self-serving purposes. In 2015, the Oxford Dictionary included SJW as a new word entry and defined it as an informal, derogatory phrase for 'a person who expresses or promotes socially progressive views' (Ohlheiser, 2015).

Another term related to SJW is 'woke'. The term 'woke' dates back to the early twentieth century but gained traction during the first wave of the Black Lives Matter Movement in 2014 and signified an awareness of racial justice and equality issues. Then, it became teen slang to refer to impulsive and self-righteous responses to social issues (Romano, 2020a). Being woke implies activism without compromises, which to some extent leads to shaming and blaming culture as the belief that the only way of making change is by being excessively judgemental on social media. The former US president Barack Obama once encouraged youths to get rid of such a notion of wokeness (Rueb and Taylor, 2019). Its usage holds the potential to hurt those truly fighting for justice and will largely corrode the noble ideological reason underlying activism works. The negative connotations of being woke gradually create invisible barriers for articulating and supporting social justice issues.

An analysis of 194 comments on a Reddit post titled 'What's your thought about Indonesian SJWs?', published on March 13, 2021, shows that users questioned the motto of SJWs and the noises they were creating on social media platforms, particularly on Twitter. Although the messages that SJWs conveyed were often agreeable, the way they were articulating it online only led to annoyance, which could be detrimental to social justice works in the country. The users seemed to hate the SJWs' self-righteousness and insensitivity to others embedded in their articulation of the messages. In addition, the users also viewed that the Indonesian SJWs tended to grossly follow Western ideological values, which were often unaligned with local situations and practices.

The above discussion exemplifies that a pejorative term such as 'SJW' illuminates the damaging effect of armchair activists on social movements. The excessive wokeness of these armchair activists brings about a negative externality to the movement as negative sentiments are ascribed to anyone expressing progressive views and advocating social justice issues. This may result in a hesitancy to engage in any social movements, particularly in an environment where maintaining harmony and social cohesion is highly important. In other words, 'SJW' gives a bad name to activism, which can then be used to stigmatize activists as agents of social disruptions, noises, and troubles. In an autocratic system, where activist actions have been usually portrayed as unnecessary and dangerous (Wells-Dang, 2012), the negative connotation arising from 'SJW' can bolster that portrayal. This can decrease citizens' inclination to participate in any efforts to bring change to society.

## Online Mob Culture

The rise of 'keyboard ninjas', aka 'keyboard warriors', can threaten the movements as digital and social media users hide behind the privilege of anonymity to collectively attack anyone sharing competing values and beliefs. The anonymity, on the one hand, gives an opportunity for authentically articulating opinions. On the other, it creates an environment where the users overlook others' situations and the context in which the online content is being shared (Christopherson, 2007). The keyboard ninjas misuse the anonymity to eliminate others with different worldviews and mobilize the 'hiveminds' to collectively expose the supposed inaccuracy and falsehood in such worldviews. Activists sharing unpopular opinions are thus susceptible to online mobs as one keyboard ninja may call on another to challenge the 'truth' in such opinions and publicize the activists' personal information.

This may also result in a cancel culture. The fear of being cancelled has made people, particularly public figures, reluctant to share beliefs considered to be contradicting the mainstream (Romano, 2020b). Such fear may instil limits to freedom of speech, which in many cases becomes the foundation for organizing social movements in democratic societies (Tilly, 2004). The argument that the cancel culture can hold people accountable has been weaponized to silence dissenters, thus fuelling popular opinions. To some extent, minority voices contract, as the majority and powerful deem them worth cancelling. The merit of the cancel culture may still hold, but it can fertilize new threats to the freedom to opine under the influence of mob culture.

The effect of mob culture on activists can be observed in the effort to cancel Veronica Koman, an Indonesian activist advocating for the human rights of the Papuan people, in 2020. After government officials demanded that she repay the scholarship she received for graduate school study in Australia, netizens were doubting the credibility of her activism on Twitter. They wondered why she took the scholarship if her stance was against the government's negligence in handling human rights violations in Papua. Those who were opposing her activism for a long time took this as an opportunity to expose her discrepant actions, sowing doubts among those who were initially unaware of her activism. Amid a defence from civil society members and progressive media, Twitter users continued questioning her activism and labelled it as self-serving, particularly given the fact that she had resided in Australia since the completion of her study and had shown little interest in returning to Indonesia.

Online mob culture can reveal the uncommendable actions that activists may commit. The mob find it difficult to move past such actions as they believe that activists should be free from mistakes. This unsympathetic view puts the activists on a pedestal. Thus, when an indication of their mistakes appears, the public believes that they all deserve to be cancelled despite their many prior commendable works. As such, activists in the digital and social media era are walking on eggshells when it comes to communicating their ideas to citizens, who have many opportunities to closely look at the activists' profiles, monitor their behaviours and actions, and track everything they have said online. The online mob culture has made activism liberating no longer as the risk of being stripped and outed is inevitable when the activists unintentionally make mistakes. In this sense, digital and social media platforms have given another layer of burdens to the activists as they must split their focus between making change and maintaining their reputation.

## State-Sponsored Trolling

State-sponsored trolling manifests in the state's attempts to deploy numerous online accounts to harass and silence dissenters, activists, journalists, or anyone considered critical of the state (Nyst and Monaco, 2018). State-sponsored trolls consist of human actors such as social media creators, influencers, and endorsers, and non-human actors such as algorithms and bots. Using the same digital and social media platforms that facilitate social movements around the globe, the trolls promulgate mis/disinformation to potentially damage the reputation of the targeted individuals (Bloomberg, 2018). The state-sponsored trolling phenomenon was evident in the US during

President Donald Trump's administration. It has been pervasive in autocratic regimes such as China and Russia and has gained traction in emerging democratic countries in the Global South such as Indonesia and the Philippines. The trolls are tasked to intimidate dissenters, counter critiques, and incite public doubts in the activists' credibility by manufacturing innuendos and false narratives. In some cases, the state-sponsored trolling can lead to the deaths of the targeted individuals (Monaco, 2019).

This section focuses on the deployment of social media content creators and influencers as trolls. The primary assignment of these groups is to create narratives supporting state agendas by harassing those sharing competing narratives, or derailing online discussions (Kargar and Rauchfleisch, 2019). The trolls mobilize their followers to support one narrative and to discredit the other, thus polishing the credibility of their supporting narrative. The trolls are particularly deployed to endorse the state when critiques spark (Sombatpoonsiri, 2018). This allows the state to step away from responding to the critiques directly or to create an image of supporting freedom of speech through propagating a rhetoric that encourages citizens to engage in public debates, of which the trolls, in fact, have been deployed to steer the direction.

In Indonesia, out of IDR 1.29 trillion (approximately USD 90 million) the national government spent on digital activities from 2014–2020, about IDR 90.45 billion (approximately USD 6 million) had been used to fund social media influencers since 2017. This has become a growing trend among local governments across the country as they expand the total spending on hiring social media influencers (Hidayatullah, 2020). A lack of transparency in the use of influencers in promoting public policies and government programmes threatens the country's democracy, as the public is unable to clearly differentiate the content endorsed by the influencers from those posted by ordinary social media users (Pattisina, 2020). The case will worsen as politicians hire the influencers to organize negative campaigns against rivals during elections and to smear activists and journalists trying to hold those in power accountable. Online harassment of critics and dissenters has been more prevalent as the state has increasingly deployed various digital efforts, including social media creators and influencers, to create a positive public image within the last five years (Hamid and Hermawan, 2020).

In broader terms, while social media creators and influencers can be useful for raising awareness on social issues and public policies, the question lingers around the transparency of the state's intention in hiring them. This potentially becomes a threat to social movements if the state directs them to troll the activists and amplify the state's voice in public spaces at the expense of the activists' voice. That will potentially limit the activists' opportunity to reach a wider audience and impede the audience's ability to differentiate the trolls' content from the activists' voices. Consequently, the messages of change that the activists intend to convey to the public are easily distorted, embellished, and eliminated from public discourse, to systemically constrain movements from attaining their immediate goals.

# CONCLUSION

This chapter has outlined the socio-technical and cultural threats to social movements. They originate from the way in which the powerful deploy digital and social media platforms and emerging surveillance technologies to crack down on the movements, and how such platforms can enable the emergence of behaviours and terms that are detrimental to the movements. Those threats may overlap, lead to one another, or appear independently depending on the ecosystem where the movements occur. They reflect the misuse and abuse of technologies to make the online sphere risky for the activists in promoting change. The threats hinder attempts to organize movements or articulate critiques because they may trigger damaging reactions from the state and public as either or both can directly intervene in any efforts the activists take to make a change.

Thus, future research may investigate the resistance against such threats. The resistance may start at an individual level, which stems from the agency that an activist has to deal with the threats. Questions about the impacts of such threats on the articulation of change and why the activists (dis)continue their activism are worth answering. How the individual resistance can contribute to, or inspire collective resistance, and what infrastructures enable it in tandem with their barriers and mechanisms are a few questions the future research may answer. Both individual and collective resistances are often intertwined as the activists witness that their space for resistance shrinks while the space for repression and oppression expands.

In response to the threats, activists may build social movement infrastructures that are rooted within collective ideologies and goals. The ideologies will strengthen the infrastructures from within by enhancing the activists' common views and ideals as they continue making change despite the presence of various threats. The goals will give the movement's adherents a rational incentive for supporting the change, mobilizing resources, and building alliances for defending the key activists who later become prone to the threats as their public visibilities rise. Framing the ideology and goal of the movement within the context of everyday life holds the potential to make the movement more resonant with both the cultural and rational predispositions of the adherents, primarily when the movement and its key activists are facing threats from multiple directions. Such an approach may gradually attract those who are less interested in social justice issues and enable those living in a politically hostile environment to speak up as they are able to see the change that the movement advocates through their everyday experiences.

# NOTE

1. https://transparencyreport.google.com/government-removals/government-requests?hl=en&lu=country_request_amount&country_request_amount=group_by:reasons.

# REFERENCES


AccessNow (2021) Indonesia: repeal law that imposes harsh intermediary liabilities, risks curtailing expression. https://www.accessnow.org/indonesia-intermediary-liabilities/.

Al-Rawi, A. (2019) Cyberconflict, online political jamming, and hacking in the Gulf Cooperation Council, *International Journal of Communication*, 13, pp. 1301–22.

Amnesty International (2020) *Let Us Breathe! Censorship and Criminalization of Online Expression in Viet Nam*. London: Amnesty International.

Ang, P.H. (2005) *Ordering Chaos: Regulating the Internet*. Singapore: Thomson.

Bloomberg (2018) A global guide to state-sponsored trolling. https://www.bloomberg.com/features/2018-government-sponsored-cyber-militia-cookbook/.

Chandran, R. (2021) Asia's moves to control internet, data raise surveillance fears. Thomson Reuters. https://news.trust.org/item/20210222130914-wsnv8.

Christopherson, K.M. (2007) The positive and negative implications of anonymity in Internet social interactions: 'On the Internet, nobody knows you're a dog', *Computers in Human Behavior*, 23(6), pp. 3038–56. doi:10.1016/j.chb.2006.09.001.

Denardis, L. (2020) *The Internet in Everything*. New Haven: Yale University Press.

Digital Reach (2022) *Digital Rights in Southeast Asia 2021/2022*. N.p.: Digital Reach. https://digitalreach.asia/digital-rights-in-southeast-asia-2021-2022-e-book/.

DW.com (2019) Southeast Asia 'fake news' laws open the door to digital authoritarianism. https://www.dw.com/en/southeast-asia-fake-news-laws-open-the-door-to-digital-authoritarianism/a-50852994.

Follis, L., and Fish, A. (2020) *Hacker States*. Cambridge: MIT Press.

Hamid, U., and Hermawan, A. (2020) Indonesia's shrinking civic space for protests and digital activism. Carnegie Endowment for International Peace. https://carnegieendowment.org/2020/11/17/indonesia-s-shrinking-civic-space-for-protests-and-digital-activism-pub-83250.

Hidayatullah, T. (2020) Pemerintah sering gunakan influencer, kualitas demokrasi jadi pertaruhan. Lokadata. https://lokadata.id/artikel/pemerintah-sering-gunakan-influencer-kualitas-demokrasi-jadi-pertaruhan.

Jordan, T. (2017) A genealogy of hacking, *Convergence*, 23(5), pp. 528–44. doi:10.1177/1354856516640710.

Kargar, S., and Rauchfleisch, A. (2019) State-aligned trolling in Iran and the double-edged affordances of Instagram, *New Media and Society*, 21(7), pp. 1506–27. doi:10.1177/1461444818825133.

Lim, M. (2020) The politics and perils of dis/connection in the Global South, *Media, Culture and Society*, 42(4), pp. 618–25. doi:10.1177/0163443720914032.

Melucci, A. (1996) *Challenging Codes: Collective Action in the Information age*. Cambridge: Cambridge University Press.

Monaco, N. (2019) Troll up your sleeves: Using research to uncover state-sponsored harassment online. Power 3.0. https://www.power3point0.org/2019/01/10/troll-up-your-sleeves-using-research-to-uncover-state-sponsored-harassment-online/.

National Intelligence Council (2021) *Global Trends 2040: A More Contested World*. Washington DC: NIC. https://www.dni.gov/files/ODNI/documents/assessments/GlobalTrends_2040.pdf.

Nyst, C., and Monaco, N. (2018) *State-Sponsored Trolling: How Governments Are Deploying Disinformation as Part of Broader Digital Harassment Campaigns*. Palo Alto: IFTF. https://legacy.iftf.org/statesponsoredtrolling/.

O'Brien, L., and Micek, P. (2020) *Defending Peaceful Assembly and Association in the Digital Age: Takedowns, Shutdowns, and Surveillance*. N.p.: Access Now. https://www.accessnow.org/cms/assets/uploads/2020/07/Defending-Peaceful-Assembly-Association-Digital-Age.pdf.

Ohlheiser, A. (2015) Why 'social justice warrior', a Gamergate insult, is now a dictionary entry. *Washington Post.* https://www.washingtonpost.com/news/the-intersect/wp/2015/10/07/why-social-justice-warrior-a-gamergate-insult-is-now-a-dictionary-entry/.

Oktaviani, Y. (2021) Kronologi Perjalanan Panjang UU ITE. Kompaspedia. https://kompaspedia.kompas.id/baca/infografik/kronologi/kronologi-perjalanan-panjang-uu-ite.

Pattisina, E.C. (2020) 'Influencer' berpotensi merusak demokrasi. Kompaspedia. https://www.kompas.id/baca/polhuk/2020/08/21/influencer-berpotensi-merusak-demokrasi/.

Persily, N. (2019) *The Internet's Challenge to Democracy: Framing the Problem and Assessing Reforms*. Geneva: Kofi Annan Foundation. https://www.kofiannanfoundation.org/app/uploads/2019/02/a6112278-190206_kaf_democracy_internet_persily_single_pages_v3.pdf.

Polyakova, A., and Meserole, C. (2019) *Exporting Digital Authoritarianism: The Russian and Chinese Models*, Policy Brief, Democracy and Disorder Series. Washington DC: Brookings Institution. https://www.brookings.edu/wp-content/uploads/2019/08/FP_20190827_digital_authoritarianism_polyakova_meserole.pdf.

Prasetyo, A. (2021) Polemik UU ITE, ini daftar pasal kontroversi. Hukumonline. https://www.hukumonline.com/berita/baca/lt602b902891fcb/polemik-uu-ite--ini-daftar-pasal-kontroversi?page=all.

Rohman, A. (2019) Persistent connection and participation: New media use in post-peace movement Ambon, Indonesia, *New Media and Society*, 21(8), pp. 1787–1803. doi:10.1177/1461444819831973.

Rohman, A. (2021). *A Fused Resistance Against State-Sponsored Hacking in Indonesia during COVID-19 Pandemic*. SSRN. https://ssrn.com/abstract=4331462 or http://dx.doi.org/10.2139/ssrn.4331462.

Rohman, A., and Ang, P.H. (2021) Disconnection for Protection (D4P): An addition to the disconnection repertoire, *Media, Culture & Society*, 43(6), pp. 1147–57.

Rohman, A., Pang, N., and Pitaloka, D. (2020) The episodes of a Facebook group for information sharing in the Ambon 2011 conflict prevention movement, Indonesia, *Information Communication and Society*, 23(4), pp. 539–54. doi:10.1080/1369118X.2018.1521456.

Rohman, A., and Pitaloka, D. (2020) A blast from the past: Memories, social media, and peace movement, *Communication Review*, 23(3), pp. 203–22. doi:10.1080/10714421.2020.1829304.

Romano, A. (2020a) What is woke: How a Black movement watchword got co-opted in a culture war. Vox. https://www.vox.com/culture/21437879/stay-woke-wokeness-history-origin-evolution-controversy.

Romano, A. (2020b) Why we can't stop fighting about cancel culture. Vox. https://www.vox.com/culture/2019/12/30/20879720/what-is-cancel-culture-explained-history-debate.

Romm, T. (2020) Big tech hearing: Apple, Google, Facebook and Amazon CEOs testified before Congress. *Washington Post*. https://www.washingtonpost.com/technology/2020/07/29/apple-google-facebook-amazon-congress-hearing/.

Rueb, E.S., and Taylor, D.B. (2019) Obama on call-out culture: 'That's not activism'. *New York Times*. https://www.nytimes.com/2019/10/31/us/politics/obama-woke-cancel-culture.html.

SAFEnet (2020) Indonesia digital rights situation report: The rise of digital authoritarian. Denpasar: SAFEnet. https://www.finder.com/digital-wallet-statistics.

Sombatpoonsiri, J. (2018) *Manipulating Civic Space: Cyber Trolling in Thailand and the Philippines – GIGA Focus Asien*. Hamburg: GIGA. https://www.giga-hamburg.de/en/publications/giga-focus/manipulating-civic-space-cyber-trolling-in-thailand-and-the-philippines.

Strittmatter, K. (2020) *We Have Been Harmonized: Life in China's Surveillance State*. London: Custom House.

Taylor, A. (2006) Against activism, *The Baffler*, 30(October), pp. 123–31.

Tilly, C. (2004) *Social Movements, 1768–2004*. Boulder: Paradigm.
Wells-Dang, A. (2012) *Civil Society Networks in China and Vietnam: Informal Pathbreakers in Health and the Environment*. New York: Palgrave Macmillan.

# 15. Strategic public participation in the digital age: the case of the Austrian 'Green Book'

*Noella Edelmann, Valerie Albrecht and Peter Parycek*

## INTRODUCTION

Governments and public administrations have been aware for several years that they must know citizens' needs and changing societal demands in order to develop adequate policies and solutions. Public participation is understood as the direct involvement of citizens and other stakeholders in public administration decision-making processes and the development of innovative public services. All forms and uses of participation support greater interaction between public administration and citizens in order to access new ideas and gain a deeper understanding of the issues, and knowledge also contributes to modernizing the state service. Not only do the public institutions and the stakeholders involved benefit through such collaborative work, but also the private sector, community groups and future users. In public participation processes, social media and digital tools can be used to restructure interactions and support the processes and opportunities for engagement. Digital or e-participation can broaden the basis for decision-making, raise the public's interest in strengthening citizenship, modernize government service delivery, and increase efficiency and quality of the services. Whilst digital advances provide new means and opportunities, the aims and implementation of participation projects cannot be a matter of replacing analogue forms of participation with digital ones, or adding digital components to participation processes. The focus should be on the selection and combination of digital methods and instruments, the instruments that need to be adapted according to the questions set, the topics, the target group, the purpose and objective of the participation processes. Public participation needs to be re-considered in the context of a new 'digital age', and indeed, in recent years, has been characterized by the integration of digital and analogue methods. The COVID-19 pandemic has further supported this development and integration in e-participation.

In Austria, e-participation is defined as 'Interactive administrative processes [that] facilitate participation and citizen involvement. The administration encourages citizens and business to contribute ideas and feedback and to [collaborate] in the organisation of the administrative tasks' (Bundeskanzleramt & Plattform Digitales Österreich, 2017). The *Austrian Digital Roadmap* sees digitalization as involving the public administration, social partners, non-governmental organizations (NGOs), the private sector, political actors, research institutions and civil society

(Bundeskanzleramt & BMWFW, 2016). Here, digitalization is understood as going beyond mere access to new technologies, online information or digital technologies; rather, it is about enabling participation and engagement for all in society. In Austria, e-participation can occur at policy or legislative level, for planning activities, program development or specific projects, and is often triggered top-down by government, political decisions or events such as national elections that facilitate direct contact between citizens and their representatives in parliament (Aichholzer & Allhutter, 2009). There are no legal provisions that specifically focus on e-participation, but an e-participation initiative must fulfil general legal requirements and principles such as the E-Government Act (E-GovG), the Federal Act on electronic signatures and trust services for electronic transactions (SVG), the Data Protection Act (DSG) and the Re-Use of Information Act (IWG), which may impact the way e-participation initiatives are organized. The Austrian Working Group on E-Democracy and E-Participation (2008), with members from across all public administrational levels and a range of other diverse Austrian public sector organizations, suggests that e-participation complements representative democracy and, by fostering civil society participation, can help to achieve the ideal interactive state.

Participation projects have been successfully implemented in Austria for many years, and the projects increasingly use digital technologies. Several guidelines and standards for public participation in Austria are available. In these guidelines, participatory processes should not only be conducted for the purpose of gaining acceptance for policies or decisions, but also in order to make the values and value systems of the participants and their interests and needs visible: 'Public participation means the opportunity for all affected and/or interested persons to represent or raise their interests or concerns in the development of plans, programmes, policies or legal acts' (Bundeskanzleramt & BMNT, 2008). The City of Vienna, for example, was the first municipality in Austria to develop a digitalization strategy on the basis of a multiphasic public participation process (Heissenberger, 2016).

Beside implementation guidelines, participation processes are bound to strategic guidelines such as Austria's IT strategy (Kompetenzzentrum Internetgesellschaft, 2013) or the Smart City framework strategy (Stadt Wien, 2019), but there are also several guides containing recommendations for implementing e-participation. Another dimension that needs to be considered is the results-oriented management system that has been in use in the Austrian federal administration since 2013 and follows the logic of the policy cycle (Bundeskanzleramt & BMASK, 2011). The management system is used for developing and analysing political-administrative processes and evidence-based policy.

This chapter considers digital public participation in Austria and reviews the use of the policy cycle and the impact of digitalization on the design of digital participation projects in Austria that led to the 'Green Book' (Rosenbichler et al., 2020). The Green Book was presented to the Austrian Council of Ministers in 2020 and represents the preparatory step for the development of new guidelines for Austrian public participation projects (BMKÖS & BMK, 2020). This new guideline is designed to help actors and stakeholders at all administrative levels implement high-quality participation projects. This case study considers the participatory process used to collect the data from practitioners and experts from the Austrian federal government, provinces, municipalities, civil society, science, interest groups and the private sector using several different participatory methods and tools. The chapter concludes with a consideration of the case, the impact of this participatory process, future developments and directions for future research.

## PUBLIC PARTICIPATION

'Participation' is a popular term in the political vocabulary, and used in a wide variety of different situations (Pateman, 1970). It requires the involvement of those who are affected, interested and committed to public administrations' decision-making processes (Kurz, 1991), and describes the inclusion of stakeholders through information, consultation, collaboration and empowerment in the decision-making, the design and the implementation of public projects (International Association for Public Participation, 2007b; OECD, 2017). Some functions of public participation are, according to Fisahn (2002), the provision of information either by a public authority or by citizens, ensuring representation and balancing interests, increasing the effectiveness of the administration, gaining acceptance for decisions, and ensuring legal protection and the right to be heard. The European Commission has anchored participation in the environmental sector, and Directive 2003/35/EC of the European Parliament and of the Council (European Parliament, 2003) aims to contribute to preserving, protecting and improving the quality of the environment and protecting human health by public participation. This directive emphasizes the provision of information about the procedure for participation, how the views and opinions expressed by the public are taken into consideration, the decisions taken and the outcome. In this context, the emphasis is on the right the public has to comment and express opinions before decisions are taken on plans and programmes:

> Effective public participation in the taking of decisions enables the public to express, and the decision-maker to take account of, opinions and concerns which may be relevant to those decisions, thereby increasing the accountability and transparency of the decision-making process and contributing to public awareness of environmental issues and support for the decisions taken … Participation, including participation by associations, organisations and groups, in particular non-governmental organisations promoting environmental protection, should accordingly be fostered, including inter alia by promoting environmental education of the public. (European Parliament, 2003, L156/17)

Public participation is a social, communicative and political process based on the inclusion of the stakeholders through mechanisms such as information, consultation, co-operation or co-determination (Parycek & Edelmann, 2009). The International Association for Public Participation's (2007a) core values point out that public participation helps make better decisions which reflect the interests and concerns of those affected. Here, participation includes values such as the right to be involved, recognizes that the public's contribution will influence a decision, recognizes and communicates the needs and interests of those involved and seeks input by the participants in designing the way to participate, and to participate in a meaningful way (International Association for Public Participation, 2007b). All forms of participation, especially where there is no legal obligation to participate, hold numerous potentials. Roberts (2015) points out that the 'active role of citizens is an important ideal [...] it keeps community life vital and public institutions accountable' (p. 3), and this ensures that citizens participate in those decisions (political, technical, legal) that impact them and helps resolve conflict. Further potentials may arise by ensuring greater interaction between public administration and citizens, and greater access to new ideas and know-how, ensuring public benefits through collaborative work, increasing the legitimacy of public decision-making processes and modernizing public service delivery (Parycek, 2020). But, as noted by O'Faircheallaigh (2010), the benefits of public participation are often taken for granted, as the 'underlying rationale for greater public participation is sometimes poorly articulated, making it more difficult to determine how to pursue it effectively' (p. 19). In addition, developments such as the rise of social media, and the use of digital and online technologies and processes, have led to significant changes and innovations in the interaction between public administrations and citizens. Together with the increasing complexity of political-administrative decision-making processes and growing demands for data protection, transparency, diversity, accessibility and equality, they pose major challenges for the design of participatory processes.

In public administration, electronic interaction, and the involvement of citizens using digital technologies and communication tools, is known as 'e-participation'. E-participation dates to the early 2000s and represents one dimension of e-government services (Lee & Kim, 2014). Its developments are based on the collaborative opportunities based on the use of information and communication technologies (ICT), and ICT-based interaction between governments and citizens e-consultations, e-lobbying, e-petitions (Edelmann & Cruickshank, 2012), e-democracy, e-voting (Gibson, Krimmer, Teague & Pomares, 2016), and election campaigns (Hilbert, 2007). E-participation focuses on one- or two-way communication between public decision-makers and citizens and is seen as having the potential to enable, engage and empower civil society (Macintosh, 2004), and to raise the public's interest in public deliberation, engagement and voting (Parycek & Edelmann, 2009; Toots, Kalvet & Krimmer, 2016; Vinkel & Krimmer, 2016). The input and knowledge gained through digital participatory projects is meant to increase the efficacy and quality of the services and to modernize government service delivery (Åkesson & Edvardsson, 2008; Heijlen, Crompvoets, Bouckaert & Chantillon, 2018; Trischler & Scott, 2015; Wiewiora, Keast & Brown, 2016).

Public administrations are increasingly gaining positive experiences with the use of e-participation, and they increasingly encourage its use (Höchtl & Edelmann, 2021; Simonofski, Snoeck, Vanderose, Crompvoets & Habra, 2017). Many countries, cities and municipalities have now created platforms for the digital participation of citizens; for example, the City of Vienna in Austria (Höchtl & Edelmann, 2021).

Yet e-participation initiatives continue to fail because of human error, characteristics of the involved public sector organizations and the political context the e-participation initiative is embedded in, as well as a reliance on the application of a new technology to solve issues related to political disenchantment (Toots, 2019). Toots (2019) suggests that if e-participation is to be successful, there needs to be the provision of information about what to expect from the initiative to the stakeholders, political backing, and a continuous adaptation and alignment of the technology used. Information should highlight the importance and benefits of the participation, and the skills required, reassuring citizens about their capabilities and clarifying the use and implementation of the outcomes obtained, as well as stating a commitment to a transparent process and the results obtained (De Jong, Neulen & Jansma, 2019). The experiences participants have during a process and the quality of the outcomes represent the decisive aspects for successful participation initiatives: 'citizens will ask themselves three questions before deciding to participate: is citizen participation any good, will I be able to contribute, and what is in it for me?' (De Jong et al., 2019, p. 498). Effective public participation processes need to consider the context, identify the purposes of the participation effort, and be iteratively designed and redesigned accordingly (Bryson, Quick, Slotterback & Crosby, 2013).

There have been regular calls for developing guidelines to help design and implement public participation and e-participation projects. Early guidelines aimed to increase the degree of power or involvement provided to the citizens (Arnstein, 1969), for public participation in general (Islam, 2008) or specifically for e-participation (Küstermann, Bittner & Navid, 2019). Some guides highlight evaluation by using acknowledged indicators and success factors (Kubicek & Aichholzer, 2016), others, the goals and outcomes to be achieved by the initiative (Smith, Macintosh & Millard, 2011). This shows that participation is strongly context-dependent (Lee & Kim, 2014; Porwol, Ojo & Breslin, 2016) and that there is no single or uniform solution on how an e-participation initiative is to be designed and implemented.

Participatory processes should not only be conducted for the purpose of gaining acceptance, but to 'make visible the values and value systems of those involved, as well as their interests and needs' (BMLFUW & Bundeskanzleramt, 2011, p. 8), to obtain qualitatively better, robust and sustainable decision-making processes and results in the long term. There is a clear need to consider how public participation can be strategically developed in the digital age.

## ANALOGUE, DIGITAL AND INTEGRATIVE PARTICIPATION

Digitalization has affected many areas of government by transforming traditional or analogue processes into digital ones (Durkiewicz & Janowski, 2018). Whilst the standard understanding of administrational processes, especially in the German and Austrian bureaucracies, is that of a paper-based processing of analogue documents, digitalization has changed the opportunities and formats for new services (Scholl,

2020). Although the need for applying ICT and fostering digital or e-participation is increasing (Lember, Randma-Liiv & Vooglaid, 2022), not all analogue processes must or can be transferred into a digital environment. The use of an integrative participatory design (Wirtz, Daiser & Binkowska, 2018) aims to combine different dimensions from analogue and digital processes and to connect them in the best possible way.

## E-PARTICIPATION IN AUSTRIA

The Austrian constitution includes participation rights and direct democratic procedures, such as petitions, referenda and official opinion polls, but there are no specific policies setting out citizens' rights specifically regarding e-participation. The legal framework to be applied varies according to the design of the e-participation initiative, and constitutional rules and laws, such as the 2018 SVG, the 2001 DSG (amended 2019) and the 2005 IWG (amended 2018; see Höchtl & Lampoltshammer, 2019), impact the way e-participation initiatives are organized.

Several agencies play an important role regarding e-participation in Austria. The 'Platform Digital Austria',[1] created in 2005, represents the Federal Government's coordination and strategy committee for e-Government in Austria; the 'Koop BLSG' (Kooperation Bund-Land-Städte-Gemeinden; Cooperation between federal government, provinces, cities and municipalities)[2] represents the co-operation between the federal level, the provincial level, cities and municipalities, and provides recommendations for IT infrastructure, standards and implementation; and the 'e-Government reference server'[3] provides the joint communication platform for the federal government, provinces, municipalities, communities and partners concerning e-government topics. In addition, the Digitalisation Agency (DIA), established in 2018, coordinates the strategy process and has led to the 'Digital Austria' initiative, which provides an attempt to streamline and harmonize efforts (Hölzl et al., 2019). The Austrian Working Group on E-Democracy and E-Participation, with members from all public administrational levels and external experts, differentiates between different levels of e-participation in terms of information, consultation, co-operation and co-decision. Its white paper on e-democracy and e-participation in Austria (2008) sees e-participation as complementing representative democracy and fostering civil society participation in order to achieve the ideal interactive state.

Central policy documents such as the *Austrian Digital Roadmap* (Bundeskanzleramt & BMWFW, 2016) or *eGovernment in Austria* (European Commission, 2018) describe the Austrian government as committed to the development of a lean, dynamic and strong administration. The *Austrian Digital Roadmap*, for example, points out that digitalization should be more than just access to online information or digital technologies, but also an economic asset useful to businesses, citizens and public institutions, as it drives innovation and reduces the digital divide and encourages participation for all. The eGovernment strategy of Austria (BMDW, 2017) points out the role of digitalization for involvement and participation: 'Interactive administrative processes (that) facilitate participation and citizen involvement. The administration encourages citizens and businesses to contribute ideas and feedback and to collaboration in the organisation of the administrative tasks' (p. 14).

Austrian e-participation projects can be initiated top-down by government or at the same time as political decisions and events; for example, the platform 'wahlkabine.at' (polling booth), which was introduced during the national elections in 2002, or the platform 'meinparlament.at' (My Parliament), developed in 2008 to facilitate direct contact between citizens and their representatives in parliament (Aichholzer & Allhutter, 2009). E-participation initiatives can also be bottom-up, such as the Unibrennt Movement, kick-started in 2009 by students in response to political decisions about higher education (Edelmann, Parycek & Schossböck, 2011). The Ministry for Digital and Economic Affairs emphasizes that a broad range of stakeholders need to be included, such as citizens, interest groups, chambers of commerce, NGOs or social organizations (BMDW, 2020). Recent Austrian e-participation projects show that a broad range of topics and stakeholders at different levels are addressed, such as developing innovative municipal communication platforms,[4] collaborations between schools and the police to develop safe paths for children going to school,[5] and young people developing public transport concepts with their local municipality,[6] but also the digital reform of the Austrian research infrastructure,[7] digital libraries[8] and digital services offered by funeral parlours.[9]

The importance of public participation is reflected in the many guides that have been developed in Austria during the last few years in order to implement different types of participation initiatives. At the local level, participation processes may either follow strategic guidelines such as Austria's IT strategy (Kompetenzzentrum Internetgesellschaft, 2013), or Vienna's Smart City framework strategy (Stadt Wien, 2019). In 2008, the national guide *Standards of Public Participation* (Bundeskanzleramt, 2008) was developed by a ministerial working group, together with interest groups and NGOs. The Austrian 'Standards for Public Participation' public participation is seen as 'the opportunity for all affected and or interested persons to represent or raise their interests or concerns in the development of plans, programmes, policies or legal acts' (Bundeskanzleramt & BMNT, 2008, p. 15). These guidelines, and those that followed them – for example, the supplementary practical guide that followed in 2011 – aim to support the implementation of public participation projects (BMLFUW & Bundeskanzleramt, 2011). Social media, digital technologies, new online tools and digitalized processes have led to significant changes and innovations in the interaction between public administrations and citizens. These guides take into account the use of digital tools, but the relevant digital developments of the past few years need to be incorporated and integrated (Wirtz et al., 2018). There is a clear need for a new strategy to support public participation projects in the digital age.

## THE AUSTRIAN GREEN BOOK

The 'Green Book' (Rosenbichler et al., 2020) presented to the Austrian Council of Ministers in 2020 (BMKÖS & BMK, 2020) represents both a response to digital changes in society and the development of a new guide on participation in Austria: the *Praxisleitfaden: Partizipation im digitalen Zeitalter* (*Practical Guide: Participation in the Digital Age*).[10]

### Designing the Green Book

The Green Book is based on a participatory process based on the introduction of the policy cycle central to the impact-oriented administrative management at the core of the Austrian federal administration (Bundeskanzleramt & BMASK, 2011). The impact-oriented administrative management has been implemented since 1 January 2013 and reflects the logic of the policy cycle, by setting clear goals and developing measures with the aim of having an effect that furthers achieving these goals.

The policy cycle has been used previously for e-participation; for example, in the e-engagement matrix (Macintosh, 2003, cited in Kubicek & Aichholzer, 2016). The model of the policy cycle developed for the Green Book determined the phases of agenda setting, analysis and policy discussion, policy formulation, decision-making, implementation and evaluation on the basis of continuous monitoring. These steps of the policy cycle make it possible to include the more political aspects of agenda setting, which provides the baseline for selecting a theme for the policy by the citizens (Janssen & Helbig, 2018) or larger political issues, which will be analysed and discussed in political fora in the next phase. The strategic or legal aspects will be specified during the phase of policy formulation. What will follow is a decision process on whether and how the formulated policy is to be implemented. The increasing variety of actors influences the implementation of the policy (Höchtl, Parycek & Schöllhammer, 2016), which may occur at all administrational levels and vary widely in scope. The implementation process, its successes and failures will then be evaluated, and leading to the development of new topics. In addition to this evaluation, the actions in all phases of the policy cycle should include reflexivity and continuous monitoring.

The content of the guidelines was developed during a multi-stage participatory process and represents a documentation of the user-centred participatory processes used, current practices, and the findings gained in order to critically assess the conditions and possibilities for an approach that integrates digital and analogue elements in public participation. The Green Book describes the use of the policy cycle to understand participation and approach the design of the guidelines, how the contents were produced and organized, the methods (offline workshops, an online consultation and an online workshop), and the cycle of constant feedback and evaluation of the process and design.

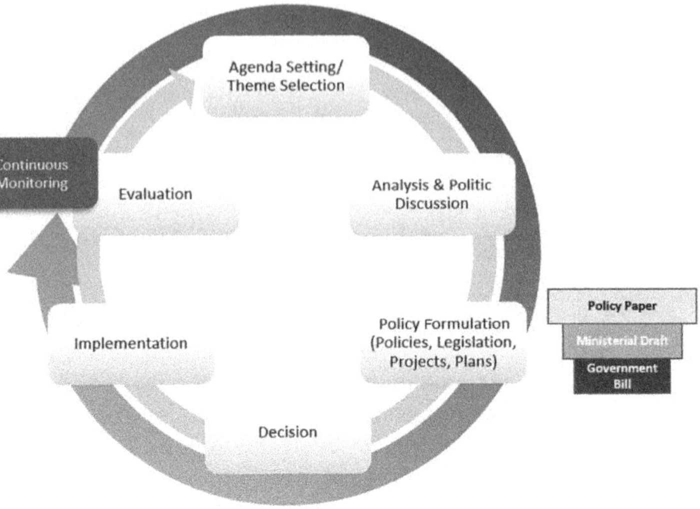


*Source*: Rosenbichler et al., 2020.

*Figure 15.1 The policy cycle in the context of public participation*

Three offline workshops dealt with an aspect of (digital and analogue) public participation in Austria, namely 'Participation in the Policy Cycle', 'Design and Methods', and 'Guiding Principles of the Public Participation'.

1. The first workshop ('Participation in the Policy Cycle') led to an overview of participation within the phases of the policy cycle (see Figure 15.1: These phases are agenda setting, analysis and policy discussion, policy formulation, decision-making, implementation, and evaluation and continuous monitoring). Participation processes can affect a single phase or several phases of the policy cycle, or even the entire policy cycle. Although processes do not always run in a linear fashion, the use of the policy cycle contributes to a clear, precise, goal-oriented view and planning of participation projects in the public sector, and helps implement best practices for each phase of the cycle. All participatory processes must consider the stakeholders, issues, the topics and the decision paths of the participation process.
2. The design of participation processes begins with a definition of the target group and how their involvement influences any decisions. The second workshop, 'Design and Methods', showed how central the careful selection of participatory methods and tools are, as they enable stakeholder participation and ensure useful results for the next phase of the cycle. Important factors for the selection of methods are their functionalities, the range of impact and quality criteria. Consequently, the value of the chosen participatory process, the participation and communication tools need to be evaluated.

3. The application of these methods led to the topics of the third workshop, the 'Guiding Principles of the Participation'. Guiding principles are principles that are valid for all participation projects, should be upheld during every phase of the policy cycle, and always be taken into account. This includes the legal framework, a stakeholder analysis to ensure target-group-oriented communication, the inclusion of diverse stakeholder groups, activation of the participation throughout the entire participation process, and comprehensible and transparent communication during all stages of the participation process. An essential aspect is moderation before, during, and after participation. Moderation should be as neutral as possible, documented and communicated, and be able to deal with emotions and sensitive matters that might arise. Attention must be paid to aspects of gender and diversity.

## Participation in Crisis Situations

During the course of the three workshops, all the contributions were analysed and aggregated by 50 experts. The contents were consolidated and presented to the participants for additional comments using the online platform Discuto.[11] This allowed for the use and assessment of the contents using an additional format, asynchronous online consultation. The results collected during the online consultation were included in the draft version of the Green Book. The draft was made available online to all the participants so that it could be discussed at a final workshop on 15 May 2020.

In addition to the workshops and the results gained from the process up to this point, a final online workshop dealt with the new and unprecedented conditions posed by COVID-19. The workshop topic was adapted to 'Participation in crisis situations'. While the results from the three offline workshops provide a basic framework for public participation in the everyday business of administration, the COVID-19 pandemic reveals that public participation can play a particular role in exceptional or crisis situations (Edelmann & Albrecht, 2021). With the break-out of the pandemic, everybody had to adapt quickly and creatively. The rapid change from analogue processes to digital processes shows the possibilities as well as the necessity of combining and integrating digital and analogue processes into hybrid formats, which will help all organisations act and react quickly in crisis situations. The integration of digital and analogue participation formats allows a broader spectrum of different opinions, diverse experiences and backgrounds.

The Green Book shows that public participation can play a decisive role in long-term processes as well as (crisis) situations that require fast responses and solutions. At the moment digital platforms may still have some limitations, especially with regard to emotional conflicts and complex communication processes. But in everyday life, where analogue contact points are limited, and broad participation of the public is not always possible, digital opportunities are increasingly important for dealing with decision-making processes and crisis situations.

# DIRECTIONS FOR FUTURE RESEARCH IN THE FIELD OF PUBLIC PARTICIPATION

## Impact

Macintosh (2004) and Aichholzer, Kubicek and Torres (2015) show that participation methods can be used in all phases of the policy cycle. In this case, we show that by describing participation processes along the policy cycle, the dimensions of each phase of the cycle become clearer, yet the big picture is not lost. The policy cycle model makes it possible to define interfaces between stakeholder groups and phases precisely, and to support idea generation, information, consultation, decision-making and implementation processes. The responsibilities of the stakeholders involved are clearly defined, can be made transparent and easier to implement. Successful public participation projects are characterized by transparent and clear processes and communication, but digital and technological change increases the complexity of participation. Digital technologies highlight the broad scope of possibilities for public participation in the digital space, and in a crisis, fulfilling the framework conditions and basic principles of participation can ensure security, data protection, transparency, equal treatment and accessibility. Public participation in the context of the policy cycle enables a public administration to be more open to the public, to develop and design new digital processes and services, and to support organizational development.

The COVID-19 pandemic has shown the need to increase the use of these digital tools in all areas of public administration, including participation processes. However, not all aspects of face-to-face communication can be translated into an online format. The COVID-19 crisis has, on the one hand, shown and enabled new potentials, and opened the space for a comprehensive reflection as a driver of both digitalization and public participation. On the other hand, it has made clear the necessity of face-to-face exchanges, and the development of integrative and hybrid models, and future-oriented learning organizations.

Participation in this context is more than just digital participation or the inclusion of analogue methods into digital processes or digital tools in analogue participation. Public participation in the digital age is characterized by the interaction of digital and analogue methods.

## Future Research

It is important to study the implementation of theoretical models, such as the policy cycle, in order to gain the practical evidence and assess its validity in a real context (Rule & John, 2015). The case presented here is an investigation of a phenomenon within its real-life context using multiple sources of evidence and retaining a real-world perspective (Yin, 2014). This allows us to understand the case, and why and how it has worked (Newcomer, Hatry & Wholey, 2015). Different policy cycle models can be found in the literature on participation and e-participation, but in this case, the Green Book uses the policy cycle to address the impact-oriented administrative management central to the Austrian federal administration, which reflects the logic of the policy cycle. The policy cycle is a model based on systemic principles that is useful for the analytical structuring of a political-administrative process. It is also suitable for evidence-based policy-making, monitoring and evaluation, multi-perspective approaches and transparent decision-making processes. In addition, the policy cycle has the advantage of describing the different multi-layered phases of the process, the actors and the content they generate, in a functional and purpose-bound manner. This enables not only a closer analysis of content-related issues within each phase, but also contributes a new perspective on the design and implementation of participation projects in politics, administration and society. In reality, processes do not always run in a linear manner, so the policy cycle contributes to a clear and precise, goal-oriented view and planning of participation projects in the public sector.

E-participation research and practice would benefit from additional insights gained by evaluating the processes and the outcomes of the individual cycle phases and integrating them back into the cycle and the participatory process. The case described here shows how to include citizens in public affairs, but there is a need for future research that considers whether an organization's mission covers participation and whether public managers have the capabilities or want to consider citizens' opinions.

Future research should also analyse the extent to which integrative participatory processes achieve key targets, such as to increase participation, enhance information provision, contribute to better-quality public policies, strengthen public trust, improve and share responsibility for policy-making, and raise public awareness and understanding of policy issues. The outcomes of developing better e-participation initiatives should not only be achieving the key targets, but also the co-creation of public participation processes, the involvement of stakeholders in organizational change, and the modernization of government structures and processes.

Finally, this case study is based in a European country and draws mainly on research in other European countries. It would be particularly useful to study and compare participation processes based on the policy cycle in other, non-European countries with a different political situation, as well as countries that are either at the beginning of a digital integration or are more digitally advanced.

## NOTES

1. https://www.bmdw.gv.at/en/Topics/Digitalisation/In-administration/Platform-Digital-Austria.html.
2. Ibid.
3. Ibid.
4. https://www.innovationshauptplatz.linz.at.
5. https://www.gemeinsamsicher.at/.
6. https://stand-montafon.at/bildung-soziales/jugend/jugendkoordination.
7. https://forschungsinfrastruktur.bmbwf.gv.at.

8. https://www.stadtbibliothek.graz.at/.
9. https://www.friedhoefewien.at
10. https://www.oeffentlicherdienst.gv.at/verwaltungsinnovation/oeffentlichkeitsbeteiligung/DigiPart.html.
11. https://www.discuto.io/de.

# REFERENCES


Aichholzer, G., & Allhutter, D. (2009). *e-Participation in Austria: Trends and public policies*. Institute of Technology Assessment (ITA) Manuscript, No. 09_01.

Aichholzer, G., Kubicek, H., & Torres, L. (2015). *Evaluating E-Participation: Frameworks, Practice, Evidence* (Vol. 19). Springer.

Åkesson, M., & Edvardsson, B. (2008). Effects of e-government on service design as perceived by employees. *Managing Service Quality: An International Journal*(5), 457–78. doi:10.1108/09604520810898839.

Arnstein, S.R. (1969). A ladder of citizen participation. *Journal of the American Institute of Planners*, *35*(4), 216–24.

Austrian Working Group on E-Democracy and E-Participation (2008). *Positionspapier zu E-Democracy und E-Participation in Österreich* (v.1.0.0.0–2008041). e-Government Bund-Länder-Gemeinden. http://reference.e-government.gv.at/uploads/media/EDEM-1-0-0-20080525.pdf.

BMDW (2017). *Administration on the Net: The ABC Guide of eGovernment in Austria*. Bundesministerium für Digitalisierung und Wirtschaft. https://www.bmdw.gv.at/en/E-Government-ABC.html.

BMDW (2020). Beteiligung der Öffentlichkeit. https://www.bmdw.gv.at/Themen/Digitalisierung/Digitales-Oesterreich/Beteiligung-der-Oeffentlichkeit.html.

BMKÖS & BMK (2020). *Vortrag an den Ministerrat - Förderung von Öffentlichkeitsbeteiligung und Open Government – Erstellung „Praxisleitfaden": Partizipation im digitalen Zeitalter*. https://www.bundeskanzleramt.gv.at/dam/jcr:29f2fc43-9389-4505-a1cf-2d944cb860f1/42_23_mrv.pdf.

BMLFUW & Bundeskanzleramt (2011). *Praxisleitfaden zu den Standards der Öffentlichkeitsbeteiligung*. http://partizipation.at/fileadmin/media_data/Downloads/Standards_OeB/praxisleitfaden_2011_72dpi_web.pdf.

Bryson, J.M., Quick, K.S., Slotterback, C.S., & Crosby, B. (2013). Designing public participation processes. *Public Administration Review*, *73*(1), 23–34.

Bundeskanzleramt (2008). *Standards der Öffentlichkeitsbeteiligung: Empfehlungen für die gute Praxis*. https://www.bundeskanzleramt.gv.at/dam/jcr:9507cee7-eaa8-491f-9844-a0c7f136b3ef/60_8BeilageA_tv.pdf.

Bundeskanzleramt & BMASK (2011). *Handbuch Wirkungsorientierte Steuerung*. https://oeffentlicherdienst.gv.at/wirkungsorientierte_verwaltung/berichte_service/Handbuch_Wirkungsorientierte_Steuerung_Mai_2013.pdf?6wd884.

Bundeskanzleramt & BMNT (2008). *Standards der Öffentlichkeitsbeteiligung: Empfehlungen für die gute Praxis*. https://www.partizipation.at/fileadmin/media_data/Downloads/Standards_OeB/standards_der_oeffentlichkeitsbeteiligung_2008_druck.pdf.

Bundeskanzleramt & BMWFW (2016). *Digital Roadmap Austria*. www.digitalroadmap.at.

Bundeskanzleramt & Plattform Digitales Österreich (2017). *Behörden im Netz: das österreichische E-Government ABC*. Bundeskanzleramt, Bereich IKT-Strategie des Bundes. https://www.digitales.oesterreich.gv.at/documents/22124/30428/E-Government-ABC.pdf/b552f453-7ae9-4d12-9608-30da166d710b.

De Jong, M.D.T., Neulen, S., & Jansma, S.R. (2019). Citizens' intentions to participate in governmental co-creation initiatives: Comparing three co-creation configurations. *Government Information Quarterly*, *36*(3), 490–500. doi:10.1016/j.giq.2019.04.003.

Durkiewicz, J., & Janowski, T. (2018). *Is Digitalization Improving Governance Quality? Correlating Analog and Digital Benchmarks*. Paper presented at the 18th European Conference on Digital Government (ECDG).

Edelmann, N., & Albrecht, V. (2021). Is It Valuable to Distinguish Different Stages and Forms of Participation? The Policy Cycle and the Impact of COVID-19 and Digitalisation. Citizen Participation in Times of Crisis EGPA Virtual Workshop.

Edelmann, N., & Cruickshank, P. (2012). Introducing psychological factors into e-participation research. In A. Manoharan & M. Holzer (Eds.), *E-governance and Civic Engagement: Factors and Determinants of E-Democracy* (pp. 338–61). IGI Global.

Edelmann, N., Parycek, P., & Schossböck, J. (2011). The unibrennt movement: A successful case of mobilising lurkers in a public sphere. *International Journal of Electronic Governance*, *4*(1–2), 43–68.

European Commission (2018). *eGovernment in Austria*. https://joinup.ec.europa.eu/sites/default/files/inline-files/eGovernment_in_Austria_2018_vFINAL.pdf.

European Parliament (2003). Directive 2003/35/EC of the European Parliament and of the Council of 26 May 2003 156 C.F.R. (2003).

Federal Act concerning the Protection of Personal Data (DSG) (2001, amended 2019).

Federal Act on Electronic Signatures and Trust Services for Electronic Transactions (Signature and Trust Services Act – SVG) (2018).

Federal Act on Provisions Facilitating Electronic Communications with Public Bodies (E-Government Act – E-GovG), 20003230 C.F.R. (2004).

Fisahn, A. (2002). *Demokratie und Öffentlichkeitsbeteiligung* (Vol. 84). Mohr Siebeck.

Gibson, J.P., Krimmer, R., Teague, V., & Pomares, J. (2016). A review of e-voting: The past, present and future. *Annals of Telecommunications*, *71*(7), 279–86.

Heijlen, R., Crompvoets, J., Bouckaert, G., & Chantillon, M. (2018). Evolving government information processes for service delivery: Identifying types & impact. *Administrative Sciences*, *8*(2). doi:10.3390/admsci8020015.

Heissenberger, S. (2016). *Die partizipative Entwicklung einer digitalen Agenda in einer öffentlichen Verwaltung mit IKT-Unterstützung - Vorgehensempfehlungen für die öffentliche Verwaltung*. Master's Thesis.

Hilbert, M. (2007). *Digital Processes and Democratic Theory: Dynamics, Risks and Opportunities That Arise When Democratic Institutions Meet Digital Information and Communication Technologies*. Martin Hilbert.

Höchtl, B., & Edelmann, N. (2021). A case study of the digital agenda of the City of Vienna: e-participation design and enabling factors. *International Journal of Electronic Government*, forthcoming.

Höchtl, B., & Lampoltshammer, T.J. (2019). Rechtliche Rahmenbedingungen und technische Umsetzung von E-Government in Österreich. In J.E. Stember, W. Eixelsberger, A. Neuroni, A. Spichiger, F.-R. Habbel and M. Wundara (Eds.), *Handbuch E-Government - Technikinduzierte Verwaltungsentwicklung* (pp. 1–27). Springer.

Höchtl, J., Parycek, P., & Schöllhammer, R. (2016). Big data in the policy cycle: Policy decision making in the digital era. *Journal of Organizational Computing Electronic Commerce*, *26*(1–2), 147–69.

Hölzl, W., Bärenthaler-Sieber, S., Bock-Schappelwein, J., Friesenbichler, K., Kügler, A., Reinstaller, A., … Risak, M. (2019). *Digitalisation in Austria: State of Play and Reform Needs*. Final Report, European Union. https://ssrn.com/abstract=3429514.

International Association for Public Participation (2007a). *IAP2 Core Values*. https://cdn.ymaws.com/www.iap2.org/resource/resmgr/pillars/2017_core_values-24x36_iap2_.pdf.

International Association for Public Participation (2007b). *IAP2 Spectrum of Public Participation*. https://cdn.ymaws.com/www.iap2.org/resource/resmgr/pillars/Spectrum_8.5x11_Print.pdf.
Islam, M.S. (2008). Towards a sustainable e-Participation implementation model. *European Journal of ePractice*, *5*(10).
Janssen, M., & Helbig, N. (2018). Innovating and changing the policy-cycle: Policy-makers be prepared! *Government Information Quarterly*, *35*(4), S99–S105. doi:10.1016/j.giq.2015.11.009.
Kompetenzzentrum Internetgesellschaft (2013). *Stand IKT in Österreich*. https://www.kig.gv.at/berichte/IKT-Stand_2013.pdf?6kdmtl.
Kubicek, H., & Aichholzer, G. (2016). Closing the evaluation gap in e-participation research and practice. In G. Aichholzer, H. Kubicek & L. Torres (Eds.), *Evaluating e-Participation* (pp. 11–45). Springer.
Kurz, A. (1991). *Juristische Aspekte der Öffentlichkeitsbeteiligung bei der Planung und Genehmigung umweltrelevanter Großvorhaben*. Deutsches Forschungsinstitut für öffentliche Verwaltung.
Küstermann, G.C., Bittner, E.A.C., & Navid, T. (2019). *Workshop-Based e-Participation: Guidelines and Requirements for Informed Design*. Paper presented at the Americas Conference on Information Systems.
Lee, J., & Kim, S. (2014). *Active Citizen e-Participation in Local Governance: Do Individual Social Capital and e-Participation Management Matter?* Paper presented at the 2014 47th Hawaii International Conference on System Sciences.
Lember, V., Randma-Liiv, T., & Vooglaid, K.M. (2022). Engaging citizens in policy making: The potential and challenges of e-participation. In T. Randma-Liiv & V. Lember (Eds.), *Engaging Citizens in Policy Making* (pp. 1–10). Edward Elgar Publishing.
Macintosh, A. (2004). *Characterizing e-Participation in Policy-Making*. Paper presented at the 37th Annual Hawaii International Conference on System Sciences, 2004.
Mergel, I., Kattel, R., Lember, V., & McBride, K. (2018). *Citizen-Oriented Digital Transformation in the Public Sector*. Paper presented at the Proceedings of the 19th Annual International Conference on Digital Government Research: Governance in the Data Age.
Newcomer, K.E., Hatry, H.P., & Wholey, J.S. (2015). Qualitative data analysis. In K.E. Newcomer, H.P. Hatry, & J.S. Wholey (Eds.), *Handbook of Practical Program Evaluation* (4th Edition) (pp. 561–95). John Wiley & Sons.
OECD (2017). *Recommendation of the Council on Open Government*. https://legalinstruments.oecd.org/en/instruments/OECD-LEGAL-0438.
O'Faircheallaigh, C. (2010). Public participation and environmental impact assessment: Purposes, implications, and lessons for public policy making. *Environmental Impact Assessment Review*, *30*(1), 19–27.
Parycek, P. (2020). *Integrierte Partizipation im Policy Cycle*. Vienna: Impact Hub.
Parycek, P., & Edelmann, N. (2009). *Eparticipation and Edemocracy in Austria: Projects and Tenets for an Edemocracy Strategy*. Paper presented at the 1st International Conference on eGovernment & eGovernance, Ankara.
Pateman, C. (1970). *Participation and Democratic Theory*. Cambridge University Press.
Porwol, L., Ojo, A., & Breslin, J.G. (2016). An ontology for next generation e-participation initiatives. *Government Information Quarterly*, *33*(3), 583–94. doi:10.1016/j.giq.2016.01.007.
Republic of Austria Parliament (2021). The National Council. https://www.parlament.gv.at/ENGL/PERK/NRBRBV/NR/.
Re-Use of Information Act (IWG) (2005).
Roberts, N.C. (2015). *The Age of Direct Citizen Participation*. Routledge.
Rosenbichler, U., Grünwald, A., Kallinger, M., Edelmann, N., Albrecht, V., & Eibl, G. (2020). *Grünbuch: Partizipation im digitalen Zeitalter*. https://www.oeffentlicherdienst.gv.at/ve

rwaltungsinnovation/oeffentlichkeitsbeteiligung/201103_Partizipation_Gruenbuch_A4_BF_1.pdf?7t15d4.

Rule, P., & John, V.M. (2015). A necessary dialogue: Theory in case study research. *International Journal of Qualitative Methods*, *14*(4), 1609406915611575.

Scholl, H.J. (2020). Digital government: Looking back and ahead on a fascinating domain of research and practice. *Digital Government: Research Practice*, *1*(1), 1–12.

Simonofski, A., Snoeck, M., Vanderose, B., Crompvoets, J., & Habra, N. (2017). *Reexamining e-Participation: Systematic Literature Review on Citizen Participation in e-Government Service Delivery*. Paper presented at the 2017 Americas Conference on Information Systems.

Smith, S., Macintosh, A., & Millard, J. (2011). A three-layered framework for evaluating e-participation. *International Journal of Electronic Governance*, *4*(4), 304–21.

Stadt Wien (2019). *Smart City Wien Rahmenstrategie*. https://smartcity.wien.gv.at/wp-content/uploads/sites/3/2019/10/Smart-City-Wien-Rahmenstrategie-2019-2050.pdf.

Toots, M. (2019). Why E-participation systems fail: The case of Estonia's Osale.ee. *Government Information Quarterly*, *36*(3), 546–59. doi:10.1016/j.giq.2019.02.002.

Toots, M., Kalvet, T., & Krimmer, R. (2016). *Success in eVoting – Success in eDemocracy? The Estonian Paradox*. Paper presented at the International Conference on Electronic Participation.

Trischler, J., & Scott, D. R. (2015). Designing public services: The usefulness of three service design methods for identifying user experiences. *Public Management Review*, *18*(5), 718–39. doi:10.1080/14719037.2015.1028017.

Vinkel, P., & Krimmer, R. (2016). *The How and Why to Internet Voting: An Attempt to Explain E-Stonia*. Paper presented at the International Joint Conference on Electronic Voting.

Wiewiora, A., Keast, R., & Brown, K. (2016). Opportunities and challenges in engaging citizens in the co-production of infrastructure-based public services in Australia. *Public Management Review*, *18*(4), 483–507. doi:10.1080/14719037.2014.999820.

Wirtz, B.W., Daiser, P., & Binkowska, B. (2018). E-participation: A strategic framework. *International Journal of Public Administration*, *41*(1), 1–12.

Yin, R.K. (2014). *Case Study Research: Design and Methods* (5th Edition). SAGE.

# PART IV

# RESEARCH METHODS AND PEDAGOGIES

# 16. Big data analytical methods

*Hai Liang*

## INTRODUCTION

Social media are among the most popular sources of big data in contemporary computational social science studies. Social media platforms do not just provide rich data for social sciences; they also raise new research questions regarding the relationships between social media and society. Although different approaches have been developed to answer these questions, big data analytics (and computational methods in general) is the generic method for social media data.

Big data as a concept has been defined in several ways. Originally, it was a technical term referring to data that could not be processed with traditional relational databases (Manovich, 2011). In this sense, big data has been defined according to its volume, variety, and velocity (Laney, 2001; Monroe, 2013). This concrete meaning evolved when the term was adopted by computational social science. Lazer and Radford (2017) have conceptualized big data as the data generated by the digitization of social life. By definition, big data includes all types of digital archives about social life. Social media platforms, such as Twitter and Facebook, are the major sources of such archives and include intrinsically digital human behaviors.

Given the various definitions of big data, there are also different meanings of big data analytics that depend on context. When 'big data' is used as a technical term, 'big data analytics' refers to the tools and methods used to cope with the practical problems related to big data collection, storage, and analysis. In social science, big data analytics is often equivalent to employed computational methods such as text mining, social network analysis, and machine learning. Generally speaking, big data analytics can refer to any computational or statistical model used to solve social science problems with big data.

This chapter outlines big data analytical methods that are widely used for research into social media and society. Specifically, the chapter reviews the different types of big data on social media platforms and summarizes four strategies of big data analysis in social science (i.e., measurement, description, causal inference, and intervention). Finally, the chapter also highlights the challenges and opportunities for future studies.

## SOCIAL MEDIA AS BIG DATA

Various types of data on social media are valuable for social science research. First, the most common form is text data, which include any textual content posted on social media platforms. By leveraging text mining techniques, researchers can extract useful latent variables from texts to answer important questions. For example, King et al. (2013) monitored and analyzed the content of millions of social media posts originating from thousands of platforms in China. Based on this continuous tracking dataset, the authors were able to estimate the volume of censorship; they then classified the content into different topics and automatically detected the sentiment of each statement (criticize or support the state, leaders, or policies) by using text mining. Finally, they compared the censored and uncensored content and found that posts related to collective action were more likely to be censored than other topics, even criticism of the state, policies, or leaders.

Network data are another type of big data commonly used in social science. The 'follow' function on most social media platforms provides unique data for social scientists to study the formation and influence of social networks, which are difficult to collect at a large scale using traditional methods. One of the earliest studies on this type of big data was conducted by Lewis et al. (2012). Based on panel data of Facebook friendship networks and the user profiles of a cohort of college students over four years, the authors used a formal network coevolution model developed by Snijders et al. (2010) to distinguish the effects of social selection (homophily: people are more likely to be friends if they are similar) and social influence (people are more likely to be similar because they are friends) on social networks. Lewis et al. (2012) found that students who share certain tastes in music and movies are likely to befriend one another. However, there is no evidence to support the social influence hypothesis. In addition to the friendship network, other interaction networks, such as the retweeting (reposting) network on Twitter, have been used to measure online fragmentation and echo chambers. Barberá (2015) found that Twitter users primarily retweeted messages from those with similar ideological preferences in the case of political issues but not in many other topic areas.

Behavioral data are usually collected by monitoring user behaviors on social media. The behaviors can be publicly available online or stored privately on web servers. The most accessible behavior data on social media are posting activities, which can be followed over time. Previous studies have found that posting behavior remains constrained by day–night and weekday–weekend schedules (Dodds et al., 2011; Golder & Macy, 2011); there are more posting activities during users' daytimes and on weekdays. Abnormal activities have been used to identify political astroturfing and other computational propaganda strategies (e.g., Keller et al., 2020). Social media activities have also been widely used to track and analyze the patterns of movements and collective action on social media (e.g., González-Bailón et al., 2011). For example, studies have found that peripheral users in online networks are critical for mobilizing participants in large-scale social movements (Jost et al., 2018; Steinert-Threlkeld, 2017). Private behavioral data, such as login and browsing activities, are not directly visible to general users or researchers. Nevertheless, researchers can collaborate with data owners (e.g., Facebook, Twitter) or purchase data from third-party vendors like Alexa, ComScore, and Nelson. For example, Taneja and Wu (2014) used a web browsing dataset from an online ComScore panel to study how cultural proximity, rather than access blockage, shaped online user behavior in China.

Geospatial data include self-reported locations and geo-coordinates embedded in posts such as check-ins on Facebook. Location data are not only useful for marketing purposes but also facilitate large-scale, comparative studies across regions. For example, Liang et al. (2016) randomly sampled 3.3 million Twitter users and identified their country and territory information from the 'location' field. The country information was translated to cultural dimensions (e.g., individualism vs. collectivism), internet penetration, and other aggregate indicators at the country level. Finally, by comparing user behaviors from more than 100 countries, the study found that privacy settings in collectivist societies were more effective at encouraging self-disclosure.

Finally, social media are multimedia platforms including diverse multimedia data, chiefly audio, videos, and still images. Although these data are less popular in social science studies, their potential value has been noticed. For example, Zhang and Pan (2019) used a deep-learning approach to identify collective action events with images from Weibo. This method provides unique benefits in authoritarian regimes because information on protest is usually lacking in other ways.

## BIG DATA ANALYTICS IN CONTEXT

Social media are not merely sources of big data but also the objects of study. Their data can be analyzed to answer a wide range of social questions. Big data analytics can be classified and summarized in different ways, depending on the data type to be analyzed. Methods that process text data are called text mining or computer-assisted content analysis; while social network analysis has been developed to deal with social network data, user behaviors are examined with user analytics, location data are usually processed with spatial models, and image processing is employed to analyze image data. Although this classification is useful for summarizing techniques, it provides little insight into how big data analytics can be incorporated into and facilitate social science research.

Another disadvantage of this typology is that researchers generally employ multiple types of data and analytics in a single study, and it is difficult to separate them in real-world studies. In practice, many studies have incorporated different types of data into a single regression or machine learning framework. For example, machine learning has been adopted to extract variables from and to model social media data, including texts, images, behaviors, locations, and even networks. Like regression models in traditional statistics, machine learning is not one model but a collection of models under the same framework. 'Machine learning' refers to techniques that use an automatic system (i.e., computer algorithms) to learn from past observations to classify new observations or make predictions about future occurrences. In order to teach computers to correctly classify and make predictions, sufficient (usually manually) labeled examples that are presumably correct must be supplied as training data. Computer algorithms are developed and employed to learn the latent patterns in the training data; these learned patterns are then used to make classifications and predictions in a separate test dataset. If those classification or prediction results in the test data are insufficiently accurate, researchers adjust or change the computer algorithms to improve the final model. Training a good model is not the ultimate goal of social science research, which is focused on applying well-trained models to new datasets. Many studies have used pre-trained models (e.g., the SentiStrength model developed by Thelwall et al., 2010) to classify large-scale tweets into positive or negative tones and then use the polarity score as an independent variable to explain other phenomena.

Given the complexity of and disadvantages in the current classification of big data analytics, the present chapter classifies those analytics according to the purposes of their application in empirical social science research. As explained below, empirical studies have used computational methods and social media data to detect and measure key variables (e.g., incivility and political ideology), to describe the prevalence of various social media phenomena (e.g., fake news), to make causal inferences using observational data (e.g., social influence and social selection in network dynamics), and to enable interventions to improve society (e.g., voter mobilization and reducing incivility on social media).

## Measurement

Measurement is the fundamental element in social science research. Detecting and measuring social constructs using big data analytics is one of the most common applications in computational social science. For this purpose, big data analytics are used to detect and measure socially related constructs from social media data so researchers can describe their prevalence at a large scale and relate them to other concepts to investigate relationships. Machine learning suits this purpose very well. For example, Theocharis et al. (2016) detected uncivil comments to politicians on Twitter using machine learning methods and relying only on textual data. They manually coded a random sample of 7,000 tweets according to two dimensions: politeness vs. impoliteness and whether a tweet contained a reference to moral or democratic issues. They selected regularized logistic regression to train the models for the two dimensions separately, eventually achieving an accuracy above 0.80. They then applied the models to classify the rest of the tweets – nearly 800,000 comments to politicians – according to their textual features into different categories. If a tweet was classified as impolite and related to morality or democracy, the tweet was classified as uncivil. Finally, they found that more engaging tweets sent by the politicians were associated with more uncivil tweets received.

It is not only textual data that are used to construct social measures but also other types of social media data. One interesting application is to use network data (e.g., following relationships) to infer the political leanings of online users. The basic assumption of these models is that users are more inclined to interact with other users with similar political leanings on social media platforms by following and liking.

Given the observed interaction networks, the political leanings of the users are considered latent variables and can be estimated statistically. These models have been successfully applied to estimate users' ideologies on Twitter (Barberá, 2015) and Facebook (Bond & Messing, 2015). Other researchers have attempted to combine different types of social media data to measure social concepts using machine learning. Many studies have demonstrated that personality traits can be accurately predicted by combining textual, behavioral, and image data from social media (see Azucar et al., 2018). However, measuring social constructs does not always require advanced methods. For example, without formal models, King et al. (2013) successfully detected online censorship on Chinese websites by continuously monitoring web content and comparing versions over time.

## Description

Big data analytics can be used in social science to estimate and scale up the detailed descriptions of social processes and relationships. Instead of describing trivia or anecdotal phenomena on social media platforms, well-designed descriptive studies can offer deep insights into society. For example, social media have unique advantages to track the information diffusion process in social networks. Anecdotal accounts in viral marketing claim that social media can facilitate information to spread in a viral (person-to-person) manner, in contrast to the broadcast approach that dominated the mass media age. Goel et al. (2016) formally quantified the degree of viral diffusion (i.e., structural virality) by using Twitter data; they found that the broadcast model remains dominant. Furthermore, cascade size (the number of total retweets) has no clear positive relationship with the degree of viral diffusion. On the other hand, by using the measure of structural virality, Vosoughi et al. (2018) found that false news was more likely to spread virally than true news.

In addition to depicting social processes, descriptive statistics related to the prevalence of certain critical phenomena on social media platforms are especially important. In big data studies, researchers have investigated these phenomena, which include ideological segregation and misinformation. In response to the criticism of personalization algorithms and the creation of filter bubbles on social media platforms, Bakshy et al. (2015) examined how 10.1 million US Facebook users interact with socially shared news. In particular, they examined the extent to which heterogenous friends could expose users to cross-cutting content (echo chamber) and the extent to which users encounter diverse content while interacting via Facebook's algorithmically ranked news feed (filter bubble). The results showed that users' choices played a stronger role in limiting exposure to cross-cutting content than algorithmic ranking. The prevalence of 'fake news' is another phenomenon that has been overestimated by the public. By focusing on a sample of registered US voters on Twitter, Grinberg et al. (2019) estimated the composition of each panelist's news exposure from a random sample of tweets posted by their followees. They found that engagement with fake news sources was highly concentrated: only 1 percent of users accounted for 80 percent of fake news exposures, and 0.1 percent accounted for 80 percent of fake news sources shared during the 2016 US presidential election. Similarly, Guess et al. (2019), by linking a survey with respondents' sharing activity recorded in Facebook profile data, found that sharing fake news content was relatively rare on Facebook.

## Causal Inference

Big data analysis was initially focused on correlation (Mayer-Schönberger & Cukier, 2013), as causality and theories would not even matter in industrial and engineering applications. But simple correlation works in certain applications might cause serious problems in both social science and science (Pearl & Mackenzie, 2018), which primarily emphasize causal explanations. Causal inferences are the statistical strategies used to identify whether a variable *X* causes another variable *Y* and, if so, by how much. Researchers have long conducted randomized control experiments to make causal inferences. However, this is less feasible when researching big data on social media. Even before the age of big data and computational social science, several strategies were developed to make causal inferences with observational data in social science. Social media data are usually collected unobtrusively and are thus observational. Researchers can treat social media data with conventional causal inference strategies.

Social media data are usually continuously collected; given this always-on status, interrupted time series (ITS) design is one of the most popular strategies that use social media to make causal inferences. ITS involves tracking a long-term period before and after an intervention to assess the effect of the intervention. If the interruption is generated randomly, the ITS design is a natural experiment design. Salganik (2019) has summarized the strategy as follows: random variation + always-on data = natural experiment. Finally, the treatment effects are estimated by changes in the level and slope trends of the time series. Under the ITS framework, Penney (2016) found that traffic to privacy-sensitive Wikipedia articles, such as those related to terrorism, declined in both level and slope after the US mass surveillance program was leaked by Edward Snowden. This finding supports the findings regarding the chilling effects of online surveillance on internet use. Using a similar design, Hobbs and Roberts (2018) found a gateway effect that the sudden blocking of Instagram in China increased the use of Facebook and Twitter (both of which had previously been blocked) by Chinese netizens.

Causal treatment effects can also be estimated by matching, which controls for confounding factors that are observable and measured. The goal of matching is to find one or more non-treated units for every treated unit with similar observable characteristics. In this way, the treated and non-treated groups are fairly comparable, and any difference is thus an estimation of the treatment effect. If the observed characteristics for matching are sufficient to account for all confounding factors, the treatment effect will be estimated unbiasedly. Social media data, as big data, provide massive cases for researchers to find matched samples, which is difficult using traditional methods. For example, in order to study the effects of auction starting price on the probability of a sale and sale price, Einav et al. (2015) found hundreds of thousands of matched cases (the same products with different starting prices but similar other characteristics) from the massive logs of eBay.

Although social media provide many cases for matching, the data usually have limited variables. Nevertheless, as mentioned above, text is the most common data format on social media platforms and could yield many variables using text mining techniques. Roberts et al. (2020) proposed a method to adjust for confounding with text matching. The assumption is that the latent variables extracted from texts are sufficient to block confounding. For example, to examine how the experience of being censored affects their future online experience (e.g., being censored again and posting less), researchers need to block the confounding effects of the content posted by the users. Certain types of content may be associated with both users' likelihood of being censored and future behaviors. By matching the content features between censored and uncensored posts, the authors found that being censored increased the likelihood of being censored in the future but did not decrease posting rates.

Instrumental variable (IV) estimation has long been employed in econometrics to estimate causal relationships when random experiments are not feasible. To estimate the causal effect of *X* on *Y*, an ideal IV is supposed to be highly correlated with *X* but have no direct effect on *Y*. Theoretically, random assignment in controlled experiments determines *X* – which condition to be assigned – in its entirety but has no direct relationship with *Y* and thus is a perfect IV. As long as IVs are found, estimators such as the two-stage least squares model can be used to estimate causal effects. The IV approach not only solves the problems caused by omitted confounding variables in many observational studies but also situations involving reverse causation, where *Y* causes *X*.

In social network analysis, the reciprocal relationship between homophily and social influence is a well-known problem in explaining many social behaviors in social networks. For example, happiness and other emotions are correlated between socially connected individuals both online and offline, such that the friends of happy individuals are also happy. However, it is difficult to ascertain whether this clustering phenomenon is caused by social influence (emotions spread to individuals from their friends) or by choosing social contacts with similar emotions. Coviello et al. (2014) employed the IV approach to solving the problem by collecting network and text data from millions of Facebook users. To estimate the causal effects of social connections (Facebook friends) on emotional similarity (expressing similar emotions in Facebook statuses), the authors proposed rainfall as an IV; the dependent variable was an individual's emotion, and the independent variable was that individual's friends' emotions. Rainfall outside the individual's city may negatively influence the emotional expressions of the individual's friends where it is raining but would not influence that individual's emotion directly. The authors found that rainfall outside an individual's city is correlated with the individual's emotional expression, indicating the existence of an emotional contagion effect.

While panel data are difficult to collect using traditional methods, they are relatively easy to collect from social media platforms. Panel data help social scientists observe changes and make causal inferences by tracking individual users, known as panelists, over the long term. Different models are available to work with panel data. The fixed-effects model controls for all variables, whether or not they are observed, as long as they remain constant within individual users over time. The underlying logic is that causal effects could be evaluated by within-individual variation since it would be possible to control for all confounding variables at the individual level. A special type of fixed-effects model is the difference-in-differences (DID) model, which is conditioned on a group-level rather than an individual-level effect. DID assumes that the outcomes of the treated and control group units would have evolved in a parallel way in the absence of the treatment. Therefore, the difference between the observed and assumed values is the treatment effect. For example, Zhang (2016) used geo-located posts from Weibo to construct treated groups who were physically close to one of the protests in Hong Kong when they occurred, whereas the control groups were those who were also close to those locations but had left Hong Kong before the protests occurred. The authors then used DID estimators and found that witnessing protests had a significant causal impact on civic engagement.

In addition to these classic causal inference strategies, special methods have been developed to make causal inferences with network data. Currently, the most sophisticated model is the stochastic actor-based model for network dynamics (see Snijders et al., 2010). The model adopts a causal mechanical explanation approach and assumes that the network evolves as a stochastic process driven by the actors. Various influences (e.g., the tendencies of popularity, reciprocity, and transitivity) on network changes could be modeled and estimated within this model. More recently, machine learning has also been incorporated into the estimation of causal effects, especially to estimate heterogeneous treatment effects and to deal with high-dimensional variables (see Grimmer et al., 2021).

## Intervention

Although it is not always feasible for social scientists, field experiments are increasingly conducted on popular social media platforms. Field experiments are randomized control experiments conducted in natural settings and can involve more representative participants than laboratory experiments. Field experiments are generally thought to have better external validity and a stronger basis for causal inferences than other methods. However, conducting field experiments in offline conditions is technically difficult and expensive. By comparison, implementing randomization on social media platforms is more realistic and less obtrusive because the interventions might not be noticed by the participants. Field experiments on social media are usually referred to as digital field experiments. They have been employed to examine the causal relationships between social influence and the unpredictability of the success of cultural products (Salganik et al., 2006) and between social networks and political mobilization (Bond et al., 2012) and emotional contagions (Kramer et al., 2014); see Salganik (2019) for more examples.

In addition to establishing causal relationships by conducting digital field experiments, social scientists can leverage interventions to 'solve' notable social problems on social media, such as political incivility and polarization. Munger (2017) conducted a digital field experiment on Twitter to reduce the use of anti-black racist slurs by white men. The author collected a sample of Twitter users who had harassed other users by automatic keyword searching (using the word 'n****r'). The sampled users were randomly assigned to the treatment conditions, where the harassers received sanction messages from researcher-controlled accounts known as Twitter bots. The study shows that even simple interventions can be effective at reducing uncivil behaviors. Bail et al. (2018) designed a large-scale experiment on Twitter to examine whether exposure to opposing views could reduce polarization. They surveyed a large sample of Democratic and Republican Twitter users; then, some of the Republican (Democratic) users were randomly assigned to the treatment conditions, where they were encouraged to follow a liberal (conservative) Twitter bot for a month. The results were not encouraging: Republicans (not liberals) who followed the liberal bot became significantly more conservative, indicating that exposure to cross-cutting views might actually increase political polarization.

## CHALLENGES AND OPPORTUNITIES

Big data analytics studies have demonstrated that social media data can facilitate and advance research into social media and society. Despite numerous studies having been published, many problems are unsolved, and new challenges are emerging. The first major challenge involves data quality, which is also related to data access, ethics, and privacy. Although social media data are pervasive in computational social science studies, by considering social media as big data sources, a few theoretical and methodological assumptions are usually implicit in empirical studies. Computational social scientists, unlike computer scientists, usually have to assume a parallel universe on social media to generalize their findings (Lazer & Radford, 2017). In most cases, this is not a major problem for engineering purposes. A good recommender system on Amazon works well even if it does not work at all on other platforms. On the contrary, generalizability is a core requirement in social science research. However, substantial differences between online and offline behaviors and across online platforms have been reported in previous studies (see Golder & Macy, 2014).

Theoretically speaking, bridging datasets online and offline (e.g., combining Twitter data with surveys) and from different platforms (e.g., combining Facebook and Twitter data) will improve the generalizability of big data studies. Nevertheless, the reality is that much of the most valuable social media data are controlled by a few social media companies, and those data are either inaccessible or only accessible by researchers with high status (Edelmann et al., 2020). Even when ideal datasets are accessible, linking datasets across sources can cause additional ethical problems. In addition, despite the richness of social media data, important data related to psychological states are lacking. Even if certain variables like personality and emotion can be predicted using machine learning methods with social media data, many others, such as motivation (especially for inactive social media users), are difficult to predict. Furthermore, many social media studies are not conducted based on representative samples, even though some random sampling methods have been proposed for social media data collection (Liang & Zhu, 2017).

The second challenge is that existing big data analytics are mostly descriptive. It is relatively straightforward to use big data analytics for measuring social concepts and incorporating them into conventional models. Although descriptive studies are essential for social sciences, as mentioned above, many other strategies are available and should be strengthened in future studies. In particular, social media data provide unique benefits for causal influences, given their key features: big, unobtrusive, and always on (Salganik, 2019). In order to make causal inferences using social media data, researchers need to be active in research design instead of relying on purely data-driven approaches. Even though the data are already there, in a carefully designed study, it remains necessary to think about what data should be collected and how to analyze the data in order to make valid inferences. For example, in a panel design, sampling users is far more appropriate than sampling that uses keyword searching. If researchers need to estimate influences in a network using the stochastic actor-based model, a whole network (instead of ego networks) should be collected.

Intervention in big data studies, though not as common as other methods, is increasingly important to promote a more 'solution-oriented approach' in social science (Watts, 2017). Digital field experiments have enormous potential to develop solution-oriented social science. In this kind of research design, concrete interventions are usually required to solve certain practical, important, and pervasive social problems on social media platforms. If an intervention is not concrete and practical, it is unlikely that researchers could implement the experiment on an appropriately large scale or observe meaningful consequences. However, as long as an intervention is demonstrated to be effective, it could be applied directly to the real world. The outcomes should also be practical and pervasive social problems, such as political motivation, online polarization, incivility, and the diffusion of misinformation. Otherwise, it might be difficult to recruit enough qualified participants. The solution-oriented approach should be different from traditional applied research or solving engineering problems for specific social media platforms. For example, thousands of A/B tests that provide different interfaces are conducted every day on the leading social media platforms to optimize usability and revenues. Solution-oriented social science would be equally concerned with the advancement of social theories. As in the examples mentioned above, by reducing uncivil comments using Twitter bots, researchers also know more about the role of norms in political deliberation (Munger, 2017). By increasing the likelihood of voting using Facebook networks, researchers have demonstrated how social networks can influence human behaviors (Bond et al., 2012).

Finally, since many social scientists emphasize the advancement of theories over data and methods, researchers using big data analytics are inevitably required to answer the question of how big data analytical methods could contribute to the development of (novel) social theories. First, big data has been used to revisit long-standing social theories or hypotheses that were once thought impossible to test. For example, the availability of social network data and the development of large-scale computational network analytics have enabled the formal examination of network formation dynamics and the impacts of social networks on human behaviors (e.g., Lewis et al., 2012). Leveraging large-scale text mining, Liang and Fu (2019) were able to test the enduring assumption in social network theories that structural redundancy is positively correlated with information redundancy. In addition to testing pre-existing theories, big data analytics provide new opportunities for exploratory studies and, therefore, the development of new theories. Nelson (2020) proposed a methodological framework for theory development using computational methods, which she calls a computational grounded theory. More specifically, computational methods (especially unsupervised methods) could help researchers detect novel patterns in big data; those patterns can be refined through an interpretive engagement with data and finally confirmed using further computational models.

## REFERENCES


Azucar, D., Marengo, D., & Settanni, M. (2018). Predicting the big 5 personality traits from digital footprints on social media: A meta-analysis. *Personality and Individual Differences*, *124*, 150–159. https://doi.org/10.1016/j.paid.2017.12.018.

Bail, C.A., Argyle, L.P., Brown, T.W., Bumpus, J.P., Chen, H.H., Hunzaker, M.B.F., Lee, J., Mann, M., Merhout, F., & Volfovsky, A. (2018). Exposure to opposing views on social media can increase political polarization. *Proceedings of the National Academy of Sciences of the United States of America*, *115*(37), 9216–21. https://doi.org/10.1073/pnas.1804840115.

Bakshy, E., Messing, S., & Adamic, L.A. (2015). Exposure to ideologically diverse news and opinion on Facebook. *Science*, *348*(6239), 1130–1132. https://doi.org/10.1126/science.aaa1160.

Barberá, P. (2015). Birds of the same feather tweet together: Bayesian ideal point estimation using Twitter data. *Political Analysis*, *23*(1), 76–91. https://doi.org/10.1093/pan/mpu011.

Bond, R., & Messing, S. (2015). Quantifying social media's political space: Estimating ideology from publicly revealed preferences on Facebook. *American Political Science Review*, *109*(1), 62–78. https://doi.org/10.1017/S0003055414000525.

Bond, R.M., Fariss, C.J., Jones, J.J., Kramer, A.I., Marlow, C., Settle, J.E., & Fowler, J.H. (2012). A 61-million-person experiment in social influence and political mobilization. *Nature*, *489*(7415), 295–98. https://doi.org/10.1038/nature11421.

Coviello, L., Sohn, Y., Kramer, A.D.I., Marlow, C., Franceschetti, M., Christakis, N.A., & Fowler, J.H. (2014). Detecting emotional contagion in massive social networks. *Plos One*, *9*(3), e90315. https://doi.org/10.1371/journal.pone.0090315.

Dodds, P.S., Harris, K.D., Kloumann, I.M., Bliss, C.A., & Danforth, C.M. (2011). Temporal patterns of happiness and information in a global social network: Hedonometrics and Twitter. *Plos One*, *6*(12), e26752. https://doi.org/10.1371/journal.pone.0026752.

Edelmann, A., Wolff, T., Montagne, D., & Bail, C.A. (2020). Computational social science and sociology. *Annual Review of Sociology*, *46*, 61–81. https://doi.org/10.1146/annurev-soc-121919-054621.

Einav, L., Kuchler, T., Levin, J., & Sundaresan, N. (2015). Assessing sale strategies in online markets using matched listings. *American Economic Journal: Microeconomics*, *7*(2), 215–47. https://doi.org/10.1257/mic.20130046.

Goel, S., Anderson, A., Hofman, J., & Watts, D.J. (2016). The structural virality of online diffusion. *Management Science*, *62*(1), 180–196. https://doi.org/10.1287/mnsc.2015.2158.

Golder, S.A., & Macy, M.W. (2011). Diurnal and seasonal mood vary with work, sleep, and daylength across diverse cultures. *Science*, *333*(6051), 1878–81. https://doi.org/10.1126/science.1202775.

Golder, S.A., & Macy, M.W. (2014). Digital footprints: Opportunities and challenges for online social research. *Annual Review of Sociology*, *40*, 129–52. https://doi.org/10.1146/annurev-soc-071913-043145.

González-Bailón, S., Borge-Holthoefer, J., Rivero, A., & Moreno, Y. (2011). The dynamics of protest recruitment through an online network. *Scientific Reports*, *1*, Article 197. https://doi.org/10.1038/srep00197.

Grimmer, J., Roberts, M.E., & Stewart, B.M. (2021). Machine learning for social science: An agnostic approach. *Annual Review of Political Science*, *24*(1), 395–419. https://doi.org/10.1146/annurev-polisci-053119-015921.

Grinberg, N., Joseph, K., Friedland, L., Swire-Thompson, B., & Lazer, D. (2019). Fake news on Twitter during the 2016 US presidential election. *Science*, *363*(6425), 374–78. https://doi.org/10.1126/science.aau2706.

Guess, A., Nagler, J., & Tucker, J. (2019). Less than you think: Prevalence and predictors of fake news dissemination on Facebook. *Science Advances*, *5*(1). https://doi.org/10.1126/sciadv.aau4586.

Hobbs, W.R., & Roberts, M.E. (2018). How sudden censorship can increase access to information. *American Political Science Review*, *112*(3), 621–36. https://doi.org/10.1017/S0003055418000084.

Jost, J.T., Barberá, P., Bonneau, R., Langer, M., Metzger, M., Nagler, J., Sterling, J., & Tucker, J.A. (2018). How social media facilitates political protest: Information, motivation, and social networks. *Political Psychology*, *39*, 85–118. https://doi.org/10.1111/pops.12478.

Keller, F.B., Schoch, D., Stier, S., & Yang, J. (2020). Political astroturfing on Twitter: How to coordinate a disinformation campaign. *Political Communication*, *37*(2), 256–80. https://doi.org/10.1080/10584609.2019.1661888.

King, G., Pan, J., & Roberts, M.E. (2013). How censorship in China allows government criticism but silences collective expression. *American Political Science Review*, *107*(2), 326–43. https://doi.org/10.1017/S0003055413000014.

Kramer, A.D.I., Guillory, J.E., & Hancock, J.T. (2014). Experimental evidence of massive-scale emotional contagion through social networks. *Proceedings of the National Academy of Sciences of the United States of America*, *111*(24), 8788–90. https://doi.org/10.1073/pnas.1320040111.

Laney, D. (2001). 3D data management: Controlling data volume, velocity and variety. *META Group Research Note*, *6*(70), 1.

Lazer, D., & Radford, J. (2017). Data ex machina: Introduction to big data. *Annual Review of Sociology*, *43*, 19–39. https://doi.org/10.1146/annurev-soc-060116-053457.

Lewis, K., Gonzalez, M., & Kaufman, J. (2012). Social selection and peer influence in an online social network. *Proceedings of the National Academy of Sciences of the United States of America*, *109*(1), 68–72. https://doi.org/10.1073/pnas.1109739109.

Liang, H., & Fu, K.W. (2019). Network redundancy and information diffusion: The impacts of information redundancy, similarity, and tie strength. *Communication Research*, *46*(2), 250–272. https://doi.org/10.1177/0093650216682900.

Liang, H., Shen, F., & Fu, K.W. (2016). Privacy protection and self-disclosure across societies: A study of global Twitter users. *New Media & Society*, *19*(9), 1476–97. https://doi.org/10.1177/1461444816642210.

Liang, H., & Zhu, J.J.H. (2017). Big data, collection of (social media, harvesting). In J. Matthes, C.S. Davis, & R.F. Potter (Eds.), *The International Encyclopedia of Communication Research Methods*. Wiley Press.

Manovich, L. (2011). Trending: The promises and the challenges of big social data. In M.K. Gold (Ed.), *Debates in the Digital Humanities* (Vol. 2, pp. 460–475). University of Minnesota Press.

Mayer-Schönberger, V., & Cukier, K. (2013). *Big Data: A Revolution That Will Transform How We Live, Work, and Think*. Houghton Mifflin Harcourt.

Monroe, B.L. (2013). The five Vs of big data political science: Introduction to the virtual issue on big data in political science political analysis. *Political Analysis*, *21*(V5), 1–9. https://doi.org/10.1017/S1047198700014315.

Munger, K. (2017). Tweetment effects on the tweeted: Experimentally reducing racist harassment. *Political Behavior*, *39*(3), 629–49. https://doi.org/10.1007/s11109-016-9373-5.

Nelson, L.K. (2020). Computational grounded theory: A methodological framework. *Sociological Methods & Research*, *49*(1), 3–42. https://doi.org/10.1177/0049124117729703.

Pearl, J., & Mackenzie, D. (2018). *The Book of Why: The New Science of Cause and Effect*. Basic Books.

Penney, J.W. (2016). Chilling effects: Online surveillance and Wikipedia use. *Berkeley Technology Law Journal*, *31*(1), 117–82. http://www.jstor.org/stable/43917620.

Roberts, M.E., Stewart, B.M., & Nielsen, R.A. (2020). Adjusting for confounding with text matching. *American Journal of Political Science*, *64*(4), 887–903. https://doi.org/10.1111/ajps.12526.

Salganik, M.J. (2019). *Bit by Bit: Social Research in the Digital Age*. Princeton University Press.

Salganik, M.J., Dodds, P.S., & Watts, D.J. (2006). Experimental study of inequality and unpredictability in an artificial cultural market. *Science*, *311*(5762), 854–6. https://doi.org/10.1126/science.1121066.

Snijders, T.A.B., Van de Bunt, G.G., & Steglich, C.E.G. (2010). Introduction to stochastic actor-based models for network dynamics. *Social Networks*, *32*(1), 44–60. https://doi.org/10.1016/j.socnet.2009.02.004.

Steinert-Threlkeld, Z.C. (2017). Spontaneous collective action: Peripheral mobilization during the Arab Spring. *American Political Science Review*, *111*(2), 379–403. https://doi.org/10.1017/S0003055416000769.

Taneja, H., & Wu, A.X. (2014). Does the Great Firewall really isolate the Chinese? Integrating access blockage with cultural factors to explain web user behavior. *Information Society*, *30*(5), 297–309. https://doi.org/10.1080/01972243.2014.944728.

Thelwall, M., Buckley, K., Paltoglou, G., Cai, D., & Kappas, A. (2010). Sentiment in short strength detection informal text. *Journal of the American Society for Information Science and Technology*, *61*(12), 2544–58. https://doi.org/10.1002/asi.21416.

Theocharis, Y., Barberá, P., Fazekas, Z., Popa, S.A., & Parnet, O. (2016). A bad workman blames his tweets: The consequences of citizens' uncivil Twitter use when interacting with party candidates. *Journal of Communication*, *66*(6), 1007–31. https://doi.org/10.1111/jcom.12259.

Vosoughi, S., Roy, D., & Aral, S. (2018). The spread of true and false news online. *Science*, *359*(6380), 1146–51. https://doi.org/10.1126/science.aap9559.

Watts, D.J. (2017). Should social science be more solution-oriented? *Nature Human Behaviour*, *1*(1), Article 15. https://doi.org/10.1038/s41562-016-0015.

Zhang, H. (2016). *Causal Effect of Witnessing Political Protest on Civic Engagement*. SSRN. https://papers.ssrn.com/abstract=2647222.

Zhang, H., & Pan, J. (2019). CASM: A deep-learning approach for identifying collective action events with text and image data from social media. *Sociological Methodology*, *49*, 1–57. https://doi.org/10.1177/0081175019874760.

# 17. Public opinion analytics with social media

*Kokil Jaidka*

## INTRODUCTION

The etymology of public opinion suggests a link between the private *opinions*, ideas, and preferences of individuals and the collective welfare of the *public* (Krippendorff, 2005). Over the centuries, public opinion has played an essential role in picking political successors, pushing policy changes, protesting proposed legislation, partisan politics, and opposing authoritarian regimes. The traditional conceptualization of public opinion suggested it to be a simple aggregation of individual views (Price, 1992), and mass media was the irrefutable source of what the public wanted, which issues they thought about, and how they thought about them, conveyed through polls, news stories, and interviews.

In recent years the use of social media in political processes has necessitated a reconsideration of how public opinion is understood and how it is measured. Social media allow for a variety of ways to participate in politics. For example, social media users self-identify as supporters of a political party, interact with their representatives, mobilize support for political and social causes, and debate issues with other citizens (for a review of recent work, see Boulianne, 2015). In addition, they offer a platform for mediated deliberation (Rinke, 2016), where citizens can access political information and commentary directly from the media and their representatives. In the context of opinion formation, citizens can access mass media and interpersonal conversations together as they read about topics of public interest and the individual opinions of other citizens in the form of comments and user-generated posts.

Consequently, with the emergence of social media, political opinion mining is increasingly helpful in understanding how public opinion is constructed as the emergent product of debate and dissent. Public opinion is now understood to be irreducible to the opinions of the individuals (Neubaum & Krämer, 2017) because of how it is co-constructed by *networked publics*: the intersection of the people and the practices they engage in (boyd, 2010). Networked publics represent a collection of people who share a common understanding of the world or a shared identity. Social media platforms are a form of networked publics because they constitute spaces constructed through network technologies but imagined through the interactions of the people and communities on them. The notion of imagined communities on social media is central to its role as a shared 'public sphere' for reasoned dissent and the formation of public opinion (Rinke, 2016).

Social media analytics offers many benefits to the researcher looking to understand and model public opinion. Social media support the 'News Finds Me' paradigm (Gil de Zúñiga & Diehl, 2019), engaging even politically apathetic users to consider and form an opinion on the salient issues of the day. In addition, exposure to cross-cutting views and ideologies may help users recalibrate their perception of the majority opinion (Neubaum & Krämer, 2017). However, social media are not simply fertile grounds for forming and developing informed opinions: they are also ideal for studying public opinion. Thus far, four main approaches have emerged that mine public opinion from social media posts. First, *volumetric* approaches examine the sheer volume of posts as a signal of public opinion. Second, *semantic* approaches examine the topics under discussion. Third, *sentiment analysis* approaches examine the affective tone of messages. Finally, *social network* approaches examine the structural features of the communities engaging in online discussions. Subsequently, dynamic measurements of the volume, topics, sentiments, and networks can enable social scientists to understand how the public makes sense of developing events and allow pollsters to forecast future trends and election outcomes.

Social media data offers a rich resource for understanding how the general public feels and thinks. However, there are caveats, as social media data comprises unavoidable systemic and demographic biases (Salganik, 2019) due to social media platforms' technological design and programming limitations. This chapter describes the main opportunities, approaches, and pitfalls of using social media data for public opinion analytics and related work. Finally, we discuss potential avenues for future research.

## BACKGROUND

In the run-up to the 2008 US presidential election, more than half of the entire adult population of the United States were 'online political users' because they went online to take part in or get news and information about the presidential campaign. Therefore, social media offer an opportunity for political parties to mobilize support via a direct, interactive medium (Smith, 2009).

Social media-based political analyses offer a richer understanding of social phenomena because they allow researchers to consider political opinions in people's daily lives, and their networks of friendship and influence, and at different points across time and geographies. They also capture a wide range of signals about human attitudes and behaviors, including the content of people's conversations, their browsing patterns and content preferences, and the structure of their social networks. The use of social media as a social sensor for political analysis has four main advantages over traditional polls.

The first is the ability to have dynamic measurements of public opinion during an ongoing event rather than relying on extrapolations from previously collected survey data. Among the first instances of this was an analysis of Twitter posts ('tweets') during the 2008 US presidential debate (Diakopoulos & Shamma, 2010; Shamma et al., 2009), which helped identify important topics and associated public reactions through Twitter trends. Other studies have demonstrated how social media data, event data, and audiovisual data can be combined to predict public volume, sentiment, and opinion change during ongoing political events (Khosla et al., 2019; Shah et al., 2015).

The second advantage is to allow a non-uniform treatment of opinions to distinguish opinion leaders, who may have an inordinate influence on other citizens' opinions. Thus, for example, social media trends help identify majoritarian and emerging views put forth by 'the politically active internet users (who) act like opinion-makers' and 'who are able to influence (or to "anticipate") the preference of a wider audience' (Ceron et al., 2014, p. 345). In contrast, traditional polling would consider everyone to represent a single vote, absent their sociocultural influence.

The third advantage is collecting political opinion 'in situ' in the affective and social context in which it is expressed. Political opinions are formed through discussions and debates, some of which may occur on social media. There is thus reason to believe that public opinion is more than the sum of the parts, reflecting an 'ongoing product of conversation, embedded in social relationship' (Anstead & O'Loughlin, 2015, p. 215). Instead, a survey interview represents an artificial situation that may pose a false dichotomy to the participant: absent any contextual information, would they vote for a candidate or not?

The fourth advantage of social media-based opinion analytics is examining the process of opinion formation over time rather than the opinions at any given point. A longitudinal analysis of a panel of social media users may also facilitate more precise forecasting to overcome some of the systematic biases involved in collecting and forecasting based on social media data alone.

Therefore, scholars have custom-built panels of social media users based on their voter registration records (An & Joseph, 2021; Grinberg et al., 2019; Radford et al., 2017) or survey responses (Ahmed et al., 2021; Eady et al., 2019) to describe how citizens engage with political representatives (An & Joseph, 2021), consume social media posts (Barberá, 2015; Eady et al., 2019), and share fake news (Grinberg et al., 2019). These research designs are also helpful in triangulating findings from traditional social science methods, such as surveys and public opinion polls.

In summary, the data from online social settings, such as those facilitated by social media, are invaluable in understanding how public opinion evolves and drifts over time. Because of the pervasiveness of social media, many studies have examined their utility in mining public opinion and forecasting elections for different countries in Europe, including the United Kingdom, France, Netherlands, Denmark, and Germany; the Asia-Pacific, including India, Pakistan, Singapore, Malaysia, and Australia; Africa, including Kenya; and South America, including Chile and Argentina. For a review of recent work in social media-based predictions, see Rousidis et al. (2020). In the following sections, I will examine social media from a technological and methodological lens to better understand its importance for the field of computational social science.

# KEY CONCEPTS

Social media platforms comprise a set of standard features that allow users to articulate their identities and ideas, associate with other users, and navigate these connections and control information flows. The following paragraphs review how the primary features of social media allow social scientists to describe and model public opinion formation.

## Profiles

People 'write themselves into being' in their social media profiles (boyd, 2010). Furthermore, the content in a social media profile is often not simply limited to an individual's name, identity, or demographic markers but also comprises their conversations with others. Therefore, profiles can be as dynamic as the social media feed and are co-created from conversations, discussions, and contributions by a user's network.

Social media profiles constitute the core unit of measurement in social media-based public opinion mining. On social media, key opinion leaders can also influence other users in their network to behave a certain way (Bakshy et al., 2011). The study of how users curate their personal and social identities offers clues into their psychological and political personalities. According to the Social Identity Deindividuation (SIDE) model, greater personal anonymity and salient group identity are typically associated with greater group conformity (Postmes et al., 2001). Users' profile cues may also determine how they behave towards in-group and out-group members (Iyengar et al., 2012; Suhay et al., 2018) and the messages they post on social media (Rathje et al., 2021).

## Networks

Social media platforms are sites for 'networking,' where individuals articulate ties with others. These networks appear to flatten offline hierarchies since they can be directly connected to (or 'follow') celebrities, elites, and political representatives. On the other hand, in some social media platforms, these ties may be bidirectional – that is, they represent 'friendships' as they must be mutually confirmed by both individuals to be displayed. Network features are also helpful in characterizing individuals according to their implicit political ideology preference (Barberá, 2015) and their influence on their social network (Bakshy et al., 2011).

On the other hand, network features are also helpful in understanding how a community can mobilize social media users at its periphery into political action; e.g., protest action. More decentralized networks are expected to have greater outreach than dense, tightly knit networks (Barberá et al., 2015). Social network structures are also helpful for testing assumptions about the strength of weak ties in political participation (Valenzuela et al., 2018). Granovetter's argument about the 'strength of weak ties' suggested that less intimate social connections provide an efficient venue for spreading information (Granovetter, 1973). Valenzuela et al. (2018) suggested that weak ties explain the potential of platforms such as Twitter to mobilize protest action among Chilean youth. Other studies have suggested that weak ties only offer a form of 'bridging' social capital in exposing people to new ideas and opportunities (Burke & Kraut, 2013).

### The Public Feed

A feature that is increasingly important to the role of social media platforms in the formation and maintenance of networked publics is the 'stream of consciousness' public feed as the live, ever-scrolling narrative of personal expression, delivered as posts, and comments, trending topics, and events. Of course, each user is privy to only a sliver of the social media pulse, which social media platforms have algorithmically curated based on the profiles they follow, the topics they consume, and the links they click (Gadde & Beykpour, 2018). Nevertheless, the sense of belonging to a collective is reinforced through their witnessing of the single, public feed common to everyone on the social media platform and the common experience and understanding of the present time, emphasized by how most platforms timestamp content relative to the current moment ('2 minutes ago'), instead of when the content was posted (Leaver et al., 2020).

The dynamics of public feeds help one understand how information (and consequently, public opinion) spreads on social media (Vosoughi et al., 2018; Zhang et al., 2017), which can be modeled similar to viral diffusion, as person-to-person rather than a one-to-many contagion (Liang, 2018). Moreover, they describe shifts in opinion related to developing events (Khosla et al., 2019) and the divergent discourse of counternarratives (Gallagher et al., 2018). They are also invaluable in modeling how exogenous events can affect online discourse, such as the emotions of political discourse (Ahmed et al., 2017).

These critical features of social media reiterate its distinctive position at the intersection of identity, technology, and information. Moreover, they facilitate the technologically mediated mobilization of individual expressions into many social phenomena, such as the formation of public opinion and the emergence of offline protest action. I will discuss the major methodological approaches social scientists follow to describe and characterize these and other political phenomena in the following sections.

## MAIN APPROACHES FOR MEASUREMENT

The analysis of social media trends for public opinion mining involves volumetric, semantic, sentiment, and structural measurements of the communities involved in discussing a specific topic of political relevance.

In the following paragraphs, I discuss the main approaches relevant to public opinion analytics from social media. Each approach has its share of strengths and limitations.

## Volumetric Approaches

Volumetric analysis can measure the proportional share of party mentions in a set of social media posts for a given time. Prior work applying volumetric shares (Gaurav et al., 2013; Jaidka et al., 2019) demonstrated the utility of normalizing volume shares according to specific mentions and unique authors to obtain a more accurate measure of attention by reducing the impact of heavy social media users. In addition, volumetric analysis creates opportunities to cross-reference social media trends with other data sources and observe possible cause-and-effect relationships. For instance, Wells et al. (2020) examined the relationship between Twitter attention and news media to establish how candidates can potentially leverage social media attention to trigger news coverage.

Volumetric analyses are sensitive to dynamic changes and are an appropriate metric for live monitoring of opinion changes. However, they are easy to manipulate, as they will often revolve around ongoing political events and politicians in the news. Volume-based counts are unreliable in countries with high internet inequality or limited social media use. Tweets may mention more than one party, which would inflate party-level estimates. Tweet volume can be gamed by astroturfing or heavy users. Studies have demonstrated how political parties can potentially manufacture public opinion and organic popularity (De Cristofaro et al., 2014; Ratkiewicz et al., 2011). Many new, unique social media accounts are seen to post the same content in a short period to get a topic or point of view to trend (Jakesch et al., 2021).

## Semantic Approaches

Semantic approaches highlight the topics being discussed on social media. Automated content analysis methods often rely on simple natural language processing techniques to identify the words, phrases, and concepts (co-occurring words and phrases) characteristic of the public discourse. The frequent keywords and phrases mentioned in social media posts can be identified through volumetric measures (term frequencies) and through uniqueness measures (inverse-document frequencies), which together highlight the most prominent words and phrases that are more important in individual texts while mathematically eliminating the words that are generally common in the English language.

Prior studies have used such approaches to characterize protest discourse and its shifts over time (Gallagher et al., 2018; Lukito et al., 2021). Simple content-analytic methods can also be applied to compare the semantic trends in social media against those in other textual sources. For instance, prior research has used semantic methods to highlight the differences between how social conflicts are framed by the mainstream media versus individual citizens on social media (Ahmed et al., 2019). A comparative approach offers the opportunity to reevaluate the role played by mass media in shaping the public's attitudes about important issues in an increasingly dynamic and fragmented online environment (Baum & Potter, 2008; Wells et al., 2020).

However, a word-and-phrase-based approach may not identify distinct themes when the dataset is already narrowly focused on a topic, issue, or political party. A more sophisticated approach involves using topic modeling techniques to identify conceptual topics characterized by many co-occurring words and phrases. One such technique is Latent Dirichlet Association, or LDA (Blei et al., 2003), which has recently been valuable in characterizing vaccine discourse from Russian Twitter accounts (Walter et al., 2020). Even more sophisticated approaches train machine learning models to learn the association between word frequencies or news consumption behaviors, which can then, given a new dataset of posts or behaviors, be applied to predict the ideology (Preoţiuc-Pietro et al., 2017), stance (Ng & Carley, 2022) or future voting behavior (Guess, 2021). More recently, research suggests that without further training, large language models (LLMs), which are pretrained on massive datasets comprising books, articles speeches, social media posts, and websites, can be used to infer ideology (Wu et al., 2023), although other researchers caution that these methods may exaggerate interpersonal political differences in opinion (Bisbee et al., 2023), and others caution that LLMs operate out of a pro-environmental, left-libertarian bias (Hartmann, Schwenzow, & Witte, 2023). Other research suggests that LLMs, when applied in complement with network-based measures, may even offer more accurate estimates of the public opinions of the silent majority than otherwise (Sun et al., 2023).

## Sentiment Approaches

Sentiment-based measurements yield the proportional share of party mentions that are positive or negative. The automatic content analysis approach followed to yield sentiment measurements can rely on a standard 'unsupervised' method to look up words in the social media posts in a standard sentiment dictionary and then score the overall post for the presence of positive and negative sentiment. On the other hand, a supervised approach would first 'learn' the words that predict sentiment in a smaller hand-labeled dataset of social media posts. Then, the remaining posts would again be scored for positive and negative sentiment based on this newly learned dictionary of sentiment words.

Prior work has suggested that in political contexts, supervised methods for sentiment measurement regularly outperform unsupervised methods (González-Bailón et al., 2012; Jaidka et al., 2019; Monti et al., 2013; Skoric et al., 2020). However, according to O'Connor et al. (2010), 'text sentiment is volatile … it is best used to detect long-term trends.' Sentiment analysis with lexica like Subjectivity Lexicon and SentiWordNet may have poor coverage in a dataset discussing politics (Chung & Mustafaraj, 2011; Jaidka et al., 2019). Furthermore, sentiment is often expressed as a reaction to immediate events and is hard to disambiguate from actual preferences (Bermingham & Smeaton, 2011). Other disadvantages include the need for natural language resources (pre-trained sentiment models) or techniques (domain transfer, machine translation) from high-resource languages to languages with few resources for processing, parsing, or modeling. Domain transfer may even be necessary when using English sentiment models in new contexts. A detailed discussion of the limitations of sentiment analysis-based methods of electoral prediction is covered in Skoric et al. (2020).

## Network Approaches

Social network analysis models the influence of social media accounts based on their connections to other users. Simple approaches to social network analysis often border on volumetric approaches, and much depends on how the authors calculate and interpret the metrics. For example, while the number of followers of a political party's social media account reflects the attention it has achieved (a volumetric measure), the opportunity to extrapolate the follower network to a two-hop network and measure the potential reach of the political party constitutes a network measure (Cameron et al., 2016). More recently, in a large research project spanning hundreds of thousands of users, and combining web tracking and survey data from the same set of users (Munzert et al., 2023), network approaches have been applied to examine how people consume and share news (Guess et al., 2023a; Nyhan et al., 2023), and their exposure to like-minded, cross-cutting, or untrustworthy news (Guess et al., 2023b; González-Bailón et al., 2023), as well as the implications this may have on their political opinions. The authors report mixed or marginal findings on the effects on attitudes or public opinion and recommend further research to understand external confounds, as well as the group-level factors that better characterize the findings (González-Bailón et al., 2023; González-Bailón & Lazer, 2023).

Social network measures can focus on the influence of a political party and its candidates within the online sphere. They offer an understanding of whether these accounts occupy central positions and whether they control the information flow in the online social network. Social network measures are a function of the incoming, outgoing, or bidirectional links to social media accounts (Jaidka et al., 2019; Livne et al., 2011). While these are often relatively stable over time, the dynamic measures of a political party's network effects can be based on the interaction and engagement around the content about or posted by these accounts, such as the number of shares, impressions, and comments they receive (Pimenta et al., 2013). These signals can be used to iteratively update the PageRank metric and thereby predict election outcomes, as has been done in Sweden (Dokoohaki et al., 2015), or to update the hub-authority metrics relating to propaganda or political campaigning (Guarino et al., 2020), thereby offering a way to track online influence dynamically.

Network measures are often more stable than volumetric or sentiment features and help dampen the estimation effects associated with national parties overrepresented on social media or regional parties that may be popular online. A meta-analysis of 74 published studies in social media-based electoral prediction also reflects the theoretical importance of interactions in the formation of public opinion (Skoric et al., 2020). Combining structural features and machine learning-based sentiment features reported the most accurate predictions among all the individual approaches considered.

A limitation of using network-based approaches is that these approaches can get computationally expensive at an exponential rate. Bot accounts can also game more straightforward social network-based measurements which consider how users mention each other.

## CONCLUSION

The social media landscape offers many opportunities to understand voters and their relationship with political candidates. First, however, researchers should consider how the importance of online political spaces – and their predictive ability for offline consequences – rely heavily on the social and democratic context in which they are used. For instance, studies of social media use in Russia (Beissinger, 2017) and Reuter and Szakonyi (2015) suggest that 'virtual civil societies' may be disconnected from the majority population. According to a recent study, this may explain why removing tweets from election candidates reduces the prediction biases in social media-based electoral predictions for Russia while increasing the errors for the United States (Aibassova, 2022).

Early aggregate measurements of social media trends suffered from certain limitations, such as those raised by Jungherr et al. (2012) and Metaxas et al. (2011) in criticizing early studies. Social media data collections and measurements are known to have low replicability (González-Bailón et al., 2014) and are likely not to be fully representative of the voter demographic (Dimitrova & Matthes, 2018); nevertheless, scholars have supported their use for public opinion mining (Ceron et al., 2014). Other scholars have also raised their concerns about the replication crises that arise when research projects are designed based on partial data and data decisions are contingent on many, somewhat arbitrary, exogenous variables (Bermingham & Smeaton, 2011; O'Connor et al., 2010). Subsequently, studies involving social media data with predictive models involve a more precise research design, which is increasingly pre-registered to maintain integrity and scientific rigor. Models for analysis include sophisticated inputs about social media trends' semantic and structural characteristics.

The social media ecology has changed in the past decade in terms of the evolution of online spaces and their features for interaction and engagement. There is, therefore, an emerging need to reevaluate the frameworks used for the collection and analysis of social media data. While this chapter has focused on and reviewed the research from text-based platforms for electoral predictions, new social media platforms offer individuals and political parties new opportunities for political participation, propaganda, and outreach. While a fundamental understanding of volumetric, semantic, sentiment, and social network approaches would aid scholars in designing studies for inter-platform, inter-group, and perhaps cross-platform comparisons, the changes in the social media ecology prompt the need to design new analytical frameworks for public opinion mining. These are spurred by the increasingly critical role of stakeholders and algorithms in determining how social media data is viewed, used, censored, or shared for profit. I highlight three reasons why this may be necessary:

- Evolution: Social media platforms have evolved, and the features and algorithms underlying profiles, networks, and public feeds have changed. Many classic public opinion studies are increasingly hard to replicate. For example, Instagram is increasingly important as a platform for political parties to connect with a younger voter demographic (for a review, see Boulianne & Hoffmann, 2022). Political parties are looking beyond text and image content to connect with their constituencies through live view feeds (Zulli & Towner, 2021) and even TikTok dance videos (Becker, 2021; Medina Serrano et al., 2020). On the other hand, the social media ecology is increasingly becoming unsocial. A shift to instant-message-based, non-public, encrypted platforms implies that predicting election outcomes based on self-expression is now nearly impossible. Furthermore, the social media environment is increasingly fragmented. For instance, in the United States, many subcommunities from Twitter or Reddit have migrated to new platforms such as Gab or Truth Social, based solely on their partisan preferences. These shifts imply that as partisan communities no longer share the same online space, it is no longer possible to compare the electoral effects of one party with another.
- Ephemerality: Social media data is disappearing, either because of privacy concerns, bot accounts, API (Application Programming Interface) restrictions, or the built-in ephemerality of messages. Information collected at one point in time may no longer be available later. Social media posts are also increasingly being censored. Censorship at the platform level implies that specific posts, topics, or accounts are suspended, banned, or temporarily suppressed from reaching a wider audience. Alternatively, the reasons for censorship and exclusion can often be political. It is concerning that the resultant social media corpora may be less representative of the range of voices and perspectives that exist within any society, particularly those of a more radical nature.
- Ethics: More restrictive data protection policies (e.g., the General Data Protection Regulation, or GDPR, adopted in the European Union) severely limit data use. Scholars are also encouraged to consider how social media data for public opinion has broader ethical implications, such as the discussion by Chancellor et al. (2019). Users, too, have a different perception of how their data is and should be used (Fiesler & Proferes, 2018; Hallinan et al., 2020), which can formulate the recommended best practices for ethical decision-making.

The many challenges associated with data access and measurement suggest the need to interpret all research findings regarding data provision, provenance, and processing methodologies. An emerging trend in studies employing social media analysis is the uptake in open science practices related to pre-registering analysis plans

(Bakker et al., 2021), data collection (Bender & Friedman, 2018; Gebru et al., 2021), hypothesis testing (Aczel et al., 2020) and model building (Mitchell et al., 2019), and considering the associated risks for marginalized populations (Mohammad, 2021). Scholars employing these practices can support more responsible, replicable, and ethical social media studies for understanding and forecasting political opinion.

## REFERENCES

Aczel, B., Szaszi, B., Sarafoglou, A., Kekecs, Z., Kucharský, Š., Benjamin, D., ... Wagenmakers, E.J. (2020). A consensus-based transparency checklist. *Nature Human Behaviour*, *4*(1), 4–6.

Ahmed, S., Chen, V.H.H., Jaidka, K., Hooi, R., & Chib, A. (2021). Social media use and anti-immigrant attitudes: Evidence from a survey and automated linguistic analysis of Facebook posts. *Asian Journal of Communication*, *31*(4), 1–23.

Ahmed, S., Cho, J., & Jaidka, K. (2019). Framing social conflicts in news coverage and social media: A multicountry comparative study. *International Communication Gazette*, *81*(4), 346–71.

Ahmed, S., Jaidka, K., & Cho, J. (2017). Tweeting India's Nirbhaya protest: A study of emotional dynamics in an online social movement. *Social Movement Studies*, *16* (4), 447–65.

Aibassova, A. (2022). *Predicting Election Results Using Online Sentiments in Russia and the US* (Unpublished Master's thesis). Nazarbayev University, Kazakhstan.

An, Z., & Joseph, K. (2021). An analysis of replies to Trump's tweets. In *Proceedings of the International AAAI Conference on Web and Social Media* (Vol. 15, pp. 49–60). AAAI.

Anstead, N., & O'Loughlin, B. (2015). Social media analysis and public opinion: The 2010 UK General Election. *Journal of Computer-Mediated Communication*, *20*(2), 204–20.

Bakker, B.N., Kokil, J., Dörr, T., Fasching, N., & Lelkes, Y. (2021). Questionable and open research practices: Attitudes and perceptions among quantitative communication researchers. *Journal of Communication, 71*(5), 715–38.

Bakshy, E., Hofman, J.M., Mason, W.A., & Watts, D.J. (2011). Everyone's an influencer: Quantifying influence on Twitter. In *Proceedings of the Fourth ACM International Conference on Web Search and Data Mining* (pp. 65–74). ACM.

Barberá, P. (2015). Birds of the same feather tweet together: Bayesian ideal point estimation using Twitter data. *Political Analysis*, *23*(1), 76–91.

Barberá, P., Wang, N., Bonneau, R., Jost, J.T., Nagler, J., Tucker, J., & González-Bailón, S. (2015). The critical periphery in the growth of social protests. *PloS One*, *10*(11), e0143611.

Baum, M.A., & Potter, P.B. (2008). The relationships between mass media, public opinion, and foreign policy: Toward a theoretical synthesis. *Annual Review of Political Science*, *11*, 39–65.

Becker, A.B. (2021). Getting out the vote on Twitter with Mandy Patinkin: Celebrity authenticity, TikTok, and the couple you actually want at Thanksgiving dinner ... or your Passover Seder. *International Journal of Communication*, *15*, 3580–3599.

Beissinger, M.R. (2017). 'Conventional' and 'virtual' civil societies in autocratic regimes. *Comparative Politics*, *49*(3), 351–71.

Bender, E.M., & Friedman, B. (2018). Data statements for natural language processing: Toward mitigating system bias and enabling better science. *Transactions of the Association for Computational Linguistics*, *6*, 587–604.

Bermingham, A., & Smeaton, A. (2011). On using Twitter to monitor political sentiment and predict election results. In *Proceedings of the Workshop on Sentiment Analysis where AI meets Psychology (SAAIP 2011)* (pp. 2–10). Asian Federation of Natural Language Processing.

Bisbee, J., Clinton, J., Dorff, C., Kenkel, B., & Larson, J. (2023). Synthetic replacements for human survey data? The perils of Large Language Models. Available at OSF: https://doi.org/10.31235/osf.io/5ecfa.

Blei, D.M., Ng, A.Y., & Jordan, M.I. (2003). Latent Dirichlet allocation. *Journal of Machine Learning Research*, *3*, 993–1022.

Boulianne, S. (2015). Social media use and participation: A meta-analysis of current research. *Information, Communication & Society*, *18* (5), 524–38.

Boulianne, S., & Hoffmann, C.P. (2022). The social, civic, and political uses of Instagram in four countries. *Journal of Quantitative Description: Digital Media*, *2*. https://doi.org/10.51685/jqd.2022.001.

boyd, d. (2010). Social network sites as networked publics: Affordances, dynamics, and implications. In Z. Papacharissi (Ed.), *A Networked Self* (pp. 47–66). Routledge.

Burke, M., & Kraut, R. (2013). Using Facebook after losing a job: Differential benefits of strong and weak ties. In *Proceedings of the 2013 Conference on Computer Supported Cooperative Work* (pp. 1419–30). Association for Computing Machinery.

Cameron, M.P., Barrett, P., & Stewardson, B. (2016). Can social media predict election results? Evidence from New Zealand. *Journal of Political Marketing*, *15*(4), 416–32.

Ceron, A., Curini, L., Iacus, S.M., & Porro, G. (2014). Every tweet counts? How sentiment analysis of social media can improve our knowledge of citizens' political preferences with an application to Italy and France. *New Media & Society*, *16*(2), 340–358.

Chancellor, S., Birnbaum, M.L., Caine, E.D., Silenzio, V.M., & De Choudhury, M. (2019). A taxonomy of ethical tensions in inferring mental health states from social media. In *Proceedings of the Conference on Fairness, Accountability, and Transparency (FAccT)* (pp. 79–88). Association for Computing Machinery.

Chung, J., & Mustafaraj, E. (2011, August). Can collective sentiment expressed on Twitter predict political elections? In *Proceedings of the AAAI Conference on Artificial Intelligence* (pp. 1770–1771). AAAI.

De Cristofaro, E., Friedman, A., Jourjon, G., Kaafar, M.A., & Shafiq, M.Z. (2014). Paying for likes? Understanding Facebook like fraud using honeypots. In *Proceedings of the 2014 Internet Measurement Conference* (pp. 129–36). Association for Computing Machinery.

Diakopoulos, N.A., & Shamma, D.A. (2010). Characterizing debate performance via aggregated Twitter sentiment. In *Proceedings of the SIGCHI Conference on Human Factors in Computing Systems* (pp. 1195–8). Association for Computing Machinery.

Dimitrova, D.V., & Matthes, J. (2018). Social media in political campaigning around the world: Theoretical and methodological challenges. *Journalism & Mass Communication Quarterly*, *95*(2), 333–42.

Dokoohaki, N., Zikou, F., Gillblad, D., & Matskin, M. (2015, August). Predicting Swedish elections with Twitter: A case for stochastic link structure analysis. In *Proceedings of the 2015 IEEE/ACM International Conference on Advances in Social Networks Analysis and Mining* (pp. 1269–76). Association for Computing Machinery.

Eady, G., Nagler, J., Guess, A., Zilinsky, J., & Tucker, J.A. (2019). How many people live in political bubbles on social media? Evidence from linked survey and Twitter data. *Sage Open*, *9*(1), 2158244019832705.

Fiesler, C., & Proferes, N. (2018). 'Participant' perceptions of Twitter research ethics. *Social Media + Society*, *4*(1), 2056305118763366.

Gadde, V., & Beykpour, K. (2018). Setting the record straight on shadow banning. *Twitter Blog*. https://blog.twitter.com/official/en-us/topics/company/2018/Setting-the-record-straight-on-shadow-banning.html.

Gallagher, R.J., Reagan, A.J., Danforth, C.M., & Dodds, P.S. (2018). Divergent discourse between protests and counter-protests: #blacklivesmatter and #alllivesmatter. *PloS One*, *13*(4), e0195644.

Gaurav, M., Srivastava, A., Kumar, A., & Miller, S. (2013). Leveraging candidate popularity on Twitter to predict election outcome. In *Proceedings of the 7th Workshop on Social Network Mining and Analysis* (pp. 1–8). Association for Computing Machinery.

Gebru, T., Morgenstern, J., Vecchione, B., Vaughan, J.W., Wallach, H., Iii, H.D., & Crawford, K. (2021). Datasheets for datasets. *Communications of the ACM*, *64*(12), 86–92.

Gil de Zúñiga, H., & Diehl, T. (2019). News finds me perception and democracy: Effects on political knowledge, political interest, and voting. *New Media & Society*, *21*(6), 1253–71.

González-Bailón, S., Banchs, R.E., & Kaltenbrunner, A. (2012). Emotions, public opinion, and US presidential approval rates: A 5-year analysis of online political discussions. *Human Communication Research*, *38*(2), 121–43.

González-Bailón, S., & Lazer, D. (2023). Are algorithmic bias claims supported?—Response. *Science*, *381*(6665), 1420–1420.

González-Bailón, S., Lazer, D., Barberá, P., Zhang, M., Allcott, H., Brown, T., ... & Tucker, J.A. (2023). Asymmetric ideological segregation in exposure to political news on Facebook. *Science*, *381*(6656), 392–398.

González-Bailón, S, Wang, N., Rivero, A., Borge-Holthoefer, J., & Moreno, Y. (2014). Assessing the bias in samples of large online networks. *Social Networks*, *38*, 16–27.

Granovetter, M.S. (1973). The strength of weak ties. *American Journal of Sociology*, *78*(6), 1360–1380.

Grinberg, N., Joseph, K., Friedland, L., Swire-Thompson, B., & Lazer, D. (2019). Fake news on Twitter during the 2016 US presidential election. *Science*, *363* (6425), 374–8.

Guarino, S., Trino, N., Celestini, A., Chessa, A., & Riotta, G. (2020). Characterizing networks of propaganda on Twitter: A case study. *Applied Network Science*, *5*(1), 1–22.

Guess, A.M. (2021). (Almost) Everything in Moderation: New Evidence on Americans' Online Media Diets. *American Journal of Political Science*, *65*(4), 1007–1022.

Guess, A.M., Malhotra, N., Pan, J., Barberá, P., Allcott, H., Brown, T., ... & Tucker, J.A. (2023a). Reshares on social media amplify political news but do not detectably affect beliefs or opinions. *Science*, *381*(6656), 404–408.

Guess, A. M., Malhotra, N., Pan, J., Barberá, P., Allcott, H., Brown, T., ... & Tucker, J.A. (2023b). How do social media feed algorithms affect attitudes and behavior in an election campaign?. *Science*, *381*(6656), 398–404.

Hallinan, B., Brubaker, J.R., & Fiesler, C. (2020). Unexpected expectations: Public reaction to the Facebook emotional contagion study. *New Media & Society*, *22*(6), 1076–94.

Hartmann, J., Schwenzow, J., & Witte, M. (2023). The political ideology of conversational AI: Converging evidence on ChatGPT's pro-environmental, left-libertarian orientation. Available at SSRN: http://dx.doi.org/10.2139/ssrn.4316084.

Iyengar, S., Sood, G., & Lelkes, Y. (2012). Affect, not ideology: A social identity perspective on polarization. *Public Opinion Quarterly*, *76* (3), 405–31. https://doi.org/10.1093/poq/nfs038.

Jaidka, K., Ahmed, S., Skoric, M., & Hilbert, M. (2019). Predicting elections from social media: A three-country, three-method comparative study. *Asian Journal of Communication*, *29*(3), 252–73.

Jakesch, M., Garimella, K., Eckles, D., & Naaman, M. (2021). Trend alert: How a cross-platform organization manipulated Twitter trends in the Indian general election. arXiv e-prints, arXiv-2104.

Jungherr, A., Jürgens, P., & Schoen, H. (2012). Why the Pirate Party won the German election of 2009 or the trouble with predictions: A response to Tumasjan, A., Sprenger, T.O., Sander, P.G., & Welpe, I.M. 'Predicting Elections with Twitter: What 140 Characters Reveal About Political Sentiment.' *Social Science Computer Review*, *30*(2), 229–34.

Khosla, S., Chhaya, N., Jindal, S., Saha, O., & Srivastava, M. (2019). Do events change opinions on social media? Studying the 2016 US presidential debates. In *Proceedings of the International Conference on Social Informatics* (pp. 287–97). Springer.

Krippendorff, K. (2005). The social construction of public opinion. In E. Wienand, J. Westerbarkey & A. Scholl (Eds.), *Kommunikation uber kommunikation* (pp. 129–49). VS Verlag für Sozialwissenschaften.
Leaver, T., Highfield, T., & Abidin, C. (2020). *Instagram: Visual Social Media Cultures*. John Wiley & Sons.
Liang, H. (2018). Broadcast versus viral spreading: The structure of diffusion cascades and selective sharing on social media. *Journal of Communication*, *68*(3), 525–46.
Livne, A., Simmons, M., Adar, E., & Adamic, L. (2011). The party is over here: Structure and content in the 2010 election. In *Proceedings of the International AAAI Conference on Web and Social Media* (Vol. 5, No. 1, pp. 201–8). AAAI.
Lukito, J., Sarma, P., Foley, J., Abhishek, A., Bucy, E., Doroshenko, L., Sun, Z., Pevehouse, J., Sethares, W., & Shah, D. (2021). Resonant moments in media events: Discursive shifts, agenda control, and Twitter dynamics in the first Clinton-Trump debate. *Journal of Quantitative Description: Digital Media, 1*. https://doi.org/10.51685/jqd.2021.019.
Medina Serrano, J.C., Papakyriakopoulos, O., & Hegelich, S. (2020, July). Dancing to the partisan beat: A first analysis of political communication on TikTok. In *Proceedings of the 12th ACM Conference on Web Science* (pp. 257–66). Association for Computing Machinery.
Metaxas, P.T., Mustafaraj, E., & Gayo-Avello, D. (2011). How (not) to predict elections. In *Proceedings of the 2011 IEEE Third International Conference on Privacy, Security, Risk and Trust and 2011 IEEE Third International Conference on Social Computing* (pp. 165–71). IEEE.
Mitchell, M., Wu, S., Zaldivar, A., Barnes, P., Vasserman, L., Hutchinson, B., Spitzer, E., Raji, I.D., & Gebru, T. (2019). Model cards for model reporting. In *Proceedings of the Conference on Fairness, Accountability, and Transparency (FAccT)* (pp. 220–229). Association for Computing Machinery.
Mohammad, S.M. (2021). Ethics sheets for AI tasks. arXiv preprint, arXiv:2107.01183.
Monti, C., Rozza, A., Zappella, G., Zignani, M., Arvidsson, A., & Colleoni, E. (2013). Modelling political disaffection from Twitter data. In *Proceedings of the 2nd International Workshop on Issues of Sentiment Discovery and Opinion Mining* (pp. 1–9). Association for Computing Machinery.
Munzert, S., Ramirez-Ruiz, S., Watteler, O., Breuer, J., Batzdorfer, V., Eder, C., ... & Yang, J. (2023). Publishing combined web tracking and survey data. Available at OSF: https://doi.org/10.31219/osf.io/y4v8z.
Neubaum, G., & Krämer, N.C. (2017). Monitoring the opinion of the crowd: Psychological mechanisms underlying public opinion perceptions on social media. *Media Psychology*, *20*(3), 502–31.
Ng, L.H.X., & Carley, K.M. (2022). Is my stance the same as your stance? A cross validation study of stance detection datasets. *Information Processing & Management*, *59*(6), 103070.
Nyhan, B., Settle, J., Thorson, E., Wojcieszak, M., Barberá, P., Chen, A.Y., ... & Tucker, J.A. (2023). Like-minded sources on Facebook are prevalent but not polarizing. *Nature*, *620*(7972), 137–144.
O'Connor, B., Balasubramanyan, R., Routledge, B., & Smith, N. (2010, May). From tweets to polls: Linking text sentiment to public opinion time series. In *Proceedings of the International AAAI Conference on Web and Social Media* (Vol. 4, No. 1). AAAI.
Pimenta, F., Obradovic, D., & Dengel, A. (2013). A comparative study of social media prediction potential in the 2012 US Republican presidential preelections. In *Proceedings of the 2013 International Conference on Cloud and Green Computing* (pp. 226–32). IEEE.
Postmes, T., Spears, R., Sakhel, K., & de Groot, D. (2001). Social influence in computer-mediated communication: The effects of anonymity on group behavior. *Personality and Social Psychology Bulletin*, *27*(10), 1243–54. https://doi.org/10.1177/01461672012710001.

Preoţiuc-Pietro, D., Liu, Y., Hopkins, D., & Ungar, L. (2017, July). Beyond binary labels: Political ideology prediction of Twitter users. In *Proceedings of the 55th annual meeting of the association for computational linguistics* (Vol. 1: long papers) (pp. 729–740). ACL.
Price, V. (1992). *Public Opinion* (Vol. 4). SAGE.
Radford, J., Horgan, L., & Lazer, D. (2017). Baselines for demographic inference on a new gold standard Twitter corpus. In *Proceedings of the 2017 IEEE International Conference on Big Data (Big Data)* (pp. 4822–3). IEEE.
Rathje, S., Van Bavel, J.J., & Van der Linden, S. (2021). Out-group animosity drives engagement on social media. *Proceedings of the National Academy of Sciences*, *118*(26), e2024292118.
Ratkiewicz, J., Conover, M., Meiss, M., Gonçalves, B., Patil, S., Flammini, A., & Menczer, F. (2011). Truthy: Mapping the spread of astroturf in microblog streams. In *Proceedings of the 20th International Conference Companion on World Wide Web* (pp. 249–52). Association for Computing Machinery.
Reuter, O.J., & Szakonyi, D. (2015). Online social media and political awareness in authoritarian regimes. *British Journal of Political Science*, *45*(1), 29–51.
Rinke, E.M. (2015). Mediated Deliberation. In G. Mazzoleni (Ed.), *International Encyclopedia of Political Communication*. Wiley.
Rinke, E.M. (2016). Mediated Deliberation. In G. Mazzoleni, K.G. Barnhurst, K. Ikeda, R.C. M. Maia & H. Wessler (Eds.), *The International Encyclopedia of Political Communication* (Vol. 2, pp. 813–26). Wiley-Blackwell.
Rousidis, D., Koukaras, P., & Tjortjis, C. (2020). Social media prediction: A literature review. *Multimedia Tools and Applications*, *79*(9), 6279–6311.
Salganik, M.J. (2019). *Bit by Bit: Social Research in the Digital Age*. Princeton University Press.
Shah, D.V., Hanna, A., Bucy, E.P., Wells, C., & Quevedo, V. (2015). The power of television images in a social media age: Linking biobehavioral and computational approaches via the second screen. *Annals of the American Academy of Political and Social Science*, *659*(1), 225–45.
Shamma, D.A., Kennedy, L., & Churchill, E.F. (2009). Tweet the debates: Understanding community annotation of uncollected sources. In *Proceedings of the First SIGMM Workshop on Social Media* (pp. 3–10). Association for Computing Machinery.
Skoric, M., Liu, J., & Jaidka, K. (2020). Electoral and public opinion forecasts with social media data: A meta-analysis. *Information*, *11*(4), 187.
Smith, A. (2009). *The Internet's Role in Campaign 2008* (Vol. 15). Pew Internet & American Life Project.
Suhay, E., Bello-Pardo, E., & Maurer, B. (2018). The polarizing effects of online partisan criticism: Evidence from two experiments. *International Journal of Press/Politics*, *23*(1), 95–115.https://doi.org/10.1177/1940161217740697.
Sun, C., Li, J., Fung, Y., Chan, H.P., Abdelzaher, T., Zhai, C., & Ji, H. (Forthcoming). Decoding the silent majority: Inducing belief augmented social graph with Large Language Model for response forecasting. In *Proceedings of the 2023 Conference on Empirical Methods in Natural Language Processing* (EMNLP).
Valenzuela, S., Correa, T., & Gil de Zúñiga, H. (2018). Ties, likes, and tweets: Using strong and weak ties to explain differences in protest participation across Facebook and Twitter use. *Political Communication*, *35*(1), 117–34.
Vosoughi, S., Roy, D., & Aral, S. (2018). The spread of true and false news online. *Science*, *359*(6380), 1146–51.
Walter, D., Ophir, Y., & Jamieson, K.H. (2020). Russian Twitter accounts and the partisan polarization of vaccine discourse, 2015–2017. *American Journal of Public Health*, *110*(5), 718–24.

Wells, C., Shah, D., Lukito, J., Pelled, A., Pevehouse, J.C., & Yang, J. (2020). Trump, Twitter, and news media responsiveness: A media systems approach. *New Media & Society, 22*(4), 659–82.

Wu, P.Y., Tucker, J.A., Nagler, J., & Messing, S. (2023). Large Language Models can be used to estimate the ideologies of politicians in a zero-shot learning setting. Available at arXiv: https://doi.org/10.48550/arXiv.2303.12057.

Zhang, Y., Moe, W.W., & Schweidel, D.A. (2017). Modeling the role of message content and influencers in social media rebroadcasting. *International Journal of Research in Marketing, 34*(1), 100–119.

Zulli, D., & Towner, T.L. (2021). The effects of 'live,' authentic, and emotional Instagram images on Congressional candidate evaluations. *Social Media + Society*, 7(4), 20563051211062917.

# 18. Ethnographic approaches to digital folklore

*Gabriele de Seta*

## 'YOU CAN WRITE A DISSERTATION ABOUT STUFF LIKE THIS?'

I started doing research about Chinese digital folklore during my doctorate, almost a decade before drafting this chapter. At times, my pursuit of this topic has been a meandering search of ways of conceptualizing the very same phenomenon I was interested in; at other times, it has been a thrilling ride along the online trajectories of a dazzling variety of digital content. Over the years, I have witnessed new jargon terms and even new Chinese characters emerge and become current across a country with a billion internet users; I have followed the unpredictable journeys of stylized emoticons as users edited them and combined them into intricately layered semiotic resources; and I have tracked the developments of messaging software, social networking websites and video-sharing platforms, accompanied by the rising and falling fortunes of local online celebrities and trending topics. My fieldwork, conducted across Chinese cities and online spaces, combined the participant observation of internet use in everyday life contexts and face-to-face interactions with the digital ethnography developed by media anthropologists. Despite its apparent coherence, this combination of research subject and methodology – studying digital folklore ethnographically – has consistently proved to be a puzzling one, not only for me and my academic colleagues, but also for the people I was talking to.

This shared puzzlement was evident from the beginning of my research, as documented by a fieldnote written in early January 2014 during my first week in Wuhan, one of the cities I visited during my fieldwork. Still adjusting to the sudden loss of access to non-Chinese social media because of nationwide internet restrictions, I stayed with a friend who was teaching at a local university, and ended up hanging out with some of his students who shared a flat near the campus. Huddled in our jackets because of the lack of heating in the humid winter night, sitting in front of a couple of desks placed alongside a wall of the students' shared bedroom, we took turns at showing each other videos on Bilibili, a Chinese video streaming platform, on two laptops sitting between power extenders, bottles of water, USB cables, a chocolate bar, oranges, video game-branded mousepads, cheap audio speakers and packs of cigarettes. After I shared a funny mashup of Chinese TV celebrity Ge Pao which everyone had seen before, one of the students showed me one of their favourite videos: the Adolf Hitler meltdown scene from the movie *Downfall*, dubbed with Chinese subtitles making up nonsensical and hilarious transliterations of his German lines. For the first time in the field, I ventured in explaining my interest in this kind of online content for my academic research project. The response was a disbelief that I would then encounter several more times throughout my fieldwork: 'Really? You can write a dissertation about stuff like this?!'

Of course, the puzzlement was a matter of both scope and distinction. How to explain that I was not only interested in this specific kind of video, nor in the entire Bilibili website, but in various genres of user-generated content circulating online in different forms? How to communicate why I wanted to trace and understand precisely the kinds of creative practices that users deemed to be most trivial? I spent months trying to figure out the most appropriate Chinese terms to talk about digital folklore – was it *egao*, or 'making bad' parodies, that I was looking for? Or was *wangluo wenhua*, 'internet culture', a better term for it? Luckily, terminological discussions were the order of the day: even on that same night, we shifted from watching funny video mashups to debating the definitions of jargon terms like *tuhao* (uncultured nouveau riche), *gaofushuai* (tall, rich and handsome) and *diaosi* (loser), recently popularized stereotypes about socioeconomic status. As one of the students concluded, 'These terms are *kouyu* [spoken vernacular], we use them among friends' – digital folklore circulated throughout the country via online interactions, but was also pervasive in everyday social contexts. Moreover, these repertoires of slang terms, humorous sayings, images and audiovisual parodies did not emerge from a generalized cyberspace, but were intricately connected to situated sociotechnical contexts of everyday use – in the case of my time in Wuhan, they circulated among complaints about unreliable internet access on campus, gaming laptops lugged to classes to play video games on the local wi-fi network, and e-commerce smartphone apps scoured for special offers during school breaks.

Eventually, I did 'write a dissertation about stuff like this', but not without struggling to define what digital folklore is, reflecting about why it is a relevant topic for media anthropology, and figuring out productive ways of studying it ethnographically. In this chapter, I briefly summarize different disciplinary theorizations of digital folklore, proposing a definition that captures its relevance for research on digital media use, and connect it to digital ethnography as a valuable methodological approach to this topic. Digital ethnography has been extensively discussed and fine-tuned for different kinds of research areas, but I argue that there has not yet been a specific discussion of practical ways to use digital ethnography to study the repertories of vernacular content that emerge and circulate on digital media. For this reason, I describe some heuristics for identifying, collecting, interpreting and writing about digital folklore. The central section of this chapter offers a toolbox of practical ways to study digital folklore, four strategies responding to various aspects of this fuzzy concept: first, following its circulation as a repertoire of semiotic resources; second, participating in its creation and sharing practices; third, analysing its vernacular aesthetics; and fourth, archiving it as both preservation and knowledge-production. These four strategies build on long-standing debates in media anthropology, enriching the toolbox of digital ethnography with specialized heuristics for the study of digital folklore. As I argue in the conclusion, researching digital folklore will remain an important task for media anthropologists regardless of what form digital media will take in the future.

## DIGITAL FOLKLORE, DIGITAL ETHNOGRAPHY

Users of digital media likely have some intuitive sense of what digital folklore is: e-mail account holders might have received chain messages or jokes and sent them to their own contacts; many users of instant messaging apps have at some point encountered funny images, videos or texts copy-pasted across chat conversations; members of discussion forums or social networking websites are familiar with genres of in-group humour that are often obscure to outsiders; users of social media platforms like Facebook, Twitter, Sina Weibo or VK regularly share stickers, animated GIFs and reaction images with intricate referents and convoluted backstories; video game players are expert in specialized jargons and shared knowledges about in-game events. Early scholarship exploring human interactions in cyberspace called this sort of content 'internet culture' (Porter, 1997), while more recent analyses of specific genres like internet memes relate them to a pervasive and globalized 'digital culture' (Shifman, 2014). Anthropologists are familiar with the problematic implications of the overdetermined and generalizing concept of culture (Abu-Lughod, 1991; Clifford, 1986; Hobart, 2000), many of which persist when a culture is identified as emerging on, and characterizing, entire technological assemblages such as the internet (Ardevol, 2005) or even the global ecosystems of new media at large (Jenkins, 2006) – but what alternatives are there?

The less totalizing and perhaps outmoded concept of folklore offers a less generalizing way to account for this sort of digital media content. Folklorists have been among the earliest researchers to notice the emergence of peculiar creative practices around new technologies like Xerox machines (Preston, 1974), office computers (Dundes & Pagter, 1975) and bulletin boards (Dorst, 1990). With the popularization of communication technologies, folklore scholars recognized their discipline's need to include this 'electronic vernacular' (Kirschenblatt-Gimblett, 1996, 1998) into its scope, a call that was heeded by a wave of analyses of 'cyber folk art' (Foote, 2007), 'vernacular webs' (R.G. Howard, 2008), 'newslore' (Frank, 2011), and other examples of the 'folklore of the internet' (Blank, 2009; Kõiva & Vesik, 2009). At the same time, researchers across disciplines have drawn similar connections between vernacular modes of expression and new media technologies; for example, Henry Jenkins identifies a 'new vernacular culture' (Jenkins, 2006, p. 132), Jean Burgess explores the digital remediation of 'vernacular creativity' (Burgess, 2007) and Limor Shifman describes memes as '(post)modern folklore' (Shifman, 2014, p. 15). In my own overview of these creative practices, I borrow the term 'digital folklore' from internet artists Olia Lialina and Dragan Espenschied, who have thoroughly theorized it as 'the most important, beautiful and widely misunderstood language of New Media' (2009), and I propose the following definition:

> Existing at the crossroads of anthropology and folkloristics, media and cultural studies, aesthetics and design, art history, and communication studies [...] digital folklore is the folklore of the Internet, a vernacular emerging from below and a folk art created by users for users, coalescing into repertoires of jokes, memes, and other genres of digital content. (de Seta, 2020, p. 180)

Having settled on a definition, albeit fuzzy and provisional, of digital folklore, the question remains: how to study it? Anthropologists have been researching media ethnographically for decades (Bräuchler & Postill, 2010; Ginsburg et al., 2002), and yet the majority of studies of digital folklore approach it through interpretive or quantitative methods, relying on the visual or textual analysis of specific genres of content to advance arguments about discourses and representations. The lack of ethnographic engagement is surprising, firstly because of the long-standing anthropological interest in folklore (Blank, 2012, p. 3), and secondly because, as Gabriella Coleman notes, ethnography is in fact optimally suited to investigate the vernacular cultures and prosaic practices of digital media (2010, p. 188). Moreover, digital media are by no means new grounds for ethnographic research. Since the mid-1990s, anthropologists have been articulating proposals to adapt ethnographic methodologies to the study of human–computer interaction and networked communication (Baym, 1994; Ito, 1996). Pioneering anthropological studies of the internet in everyday life contexts (D. Miller & Slater, 2000) have been complemented by numerous methodological frameworks, including 'virtual ethnography' (Hine, 2000), 'network ethnography' (P.N. Howard, 2002), 'cyberethnography' (Kuntsman, 2004) or 'netnography' (Kozinets, 2010), each denoting its own specific epistemological angle by augmenting ethnography with technical terms and industry buzzwords (Abidin & de Seta, 2020).

Among the countless terminological variations, 'digital ethnography' has prevailed as an umbrella term for the application of ethnographic methodologies to the study of digital media. Whether it is adopted to investigate them as tools, places or ways of being (A. Markham, 2004, p. 360), digital ethnography allows one to account for the ubiquity of digital media in everyday life (Hine, 2013) and their role in shaping the very notion of the human (D. Miller & Horst, 2012, p. 4). And while prolonged debates revolve around the balancing between face-to-face interaction and mediated co-presence (Murthy, 2008) or the definition of the field as it is expanded by sociotechnical networks (Burrell, 2009), a growing and interdisciplinary community of researchers have contributed to establishing digital ethnography as a highly specialized methodology for the study of a wide variety of media technologies (Pink et al., 2016). As the forty-four chapters of the recent *Routledge Companion to Digital Ethnography* make clear, this methodological approach is suitable for research on data and infrastructures, politics and social movements, sociality and relationships, materiality and consumption, space and mobility, play and design, as well as their yet uncharted future developments (Hjorth et al., 2017). Digital folklore, or the vernacular content sustained by the creative practices of digital media users, sits squarely at the intersection of many of these areas, and is evidently a prime topic for digital ethnographic research.

# FOUR STRATEGIES: A TOOLBOX FOR DIGITAL FOLKLORISTS

Digital ethnography is an obvious methodological choice for studying digital folklore. As hinted in the previous section, the concept of digital folklore allows one to approach vernacular content on digital media without resorting to the overdetermining framework of culture, while also offering a broad enough category to encompass heterogeneous repertoires of semiotic resources and media practices ranging from emoticons and reaction images to video game jargons and short video trends. With its focus on sustained participation and dialogic engagement across different media and their contexts of use, ethnography is particularly suited for this sort of research topic. This section details four strategies to implement digital ethnography when researching digital folklore. These strategies build on the rich methodological debates highlighted above, and aim at fine-tuning the existing frameworks of digital ethnography for the study of vernacular content and practices emerging on digital media. As with any other toolbox, this one invites experimentation and personalization: rather than offering a comprehensive methodological guide, the following subsections have the less ambitious goal of providing aspiring digital folklorists with practical suggestions for the identification, collection, interpretation and representation of this intuitive yet puzzling category of vernacular creativity.

## Follow the Circulation

A defining characteristic of folklore is performance – jokes are cracked, lullabies are sung, tales are narrated. Digital folklore, conversely, relies on the inscriptive affordances of computational media: it exists in a variety of data formats, and is stored across devices and networks. As in the case of pre-digital technological folklores, this medium-specific materiality is one of its key traits (Roemer, 1994). From this it follows that the main practices through which users sustain digital folklore are practices of sharing, rather than of performance (Buccitelli, 2012) – texts are copy-pasted into chat boxes, images are downloaded and reuploaded on social media, videos are streamed and embedded on platforms, and so on. The dispersed nature of these inscriptions, which are customarily scattered across different information systems and communication technologies, easily escapes the focused attention of traditional fieldwork; for this reason, 'multi-sited ethnography' (Marcus, 1995) is often adopted as a way to get hold of content and practices ricocheting between different media and contexts. The central strategy of multi-sited ethnography is that of 'following' one's objects of study as they move between settings (1995, p. 106). In the case of digital folklore, rather than people, things, metaphors, plots, lives, conflicts or even networks (Burrell, 2009), what the ethnographer needs to follow is circulation itself. As they share content of various formats through different technologies, digital media users inscribe traces which in turn can be followed to understand how digital folklore circulates (Geiger & Ribes, 2011). The advantage of following the circulation of digital folklore is that it allows one not only to maintain consistency across dispersed sites of interest, but also to gather insights into its changes across time – in this way, digital ethnography is not only multi-sited but also 'multi-timed' (Postill, 2017).

In my own research, developing this strategy was necessary to make sense of the dazzling variety of digital folklore I encountered on Chinese social media. Before traveling to China to observe digital media use in everyday contexts and talk to users about their practices, I spent several months familiarizing myself with different social media platforms and apps; even just by interacting with a few contacts online and browsing a selection of web-based resources, I was confronted with unmanageable quantities of content in different media formats. Taking screenshots, saving representative samples of digital folklore and trying to interpret them in fieldnotes was neither productive nor sustainable. After deciding to focus on humorous images, I developed a process to follow their circulation backwards from my encounter with them. After finding a piece of digital folklore that seemed relevant to my research – either because it was widely shared, or had some striking detail or existed in multiple versions – I would download it in its original format, record its provenance and try to figure out its origins. Almost always, the user sharing it was not the original creator, and establishing authorship required following social media traces like links, reshares or watermarks. In many cases, simply browsing was not enough, and I eventually resorted to using Google's reverse image search function to try to pinpoint other web-based locations of a certain image. Given China's internet restrictions, a similar function offered by local search engine Baidu turned out to be a much better choice, which helped me find several other locations where an individual image had been shared, often enriched by additional paratexts or metadata.

Following the circulation of a specific image not only helped me gather information on its context of use and backstory, but also revealed details about its history and dissemination, and minor changes it accrued as it was uploaded and downloaded across different websites or social media platforms. Moreover, this strategy also prompted me to understand how specific kinds of content were categorized by users: from my point of view, many of these images would have been 'memes', but Chinese users sharing them online referred to them through a variety of specialized terms such as *egao* ('making bad', parody) or *gaoxiaotu* (funny images). Beyond this specific example, following the circulation of digital folklore allows researchers to move beyond the immediacy of a specific encounter with a piece of content and to contextualize its trajectory across time. The optimal process to follow content largely depends on its format: search engines can obviously be queried for textual content, and many of them offer increasingly accurate ways of searching for images by similarity or relatedness. Metadata and other platform-specific information can also point to useful details about circulation: upload dates, watermarks, links, authorship and tags can all contribute to clarify where a specific piece of content came from, how it changed through time, and why it was shared in different contexts. The driving principle of this strategy is that of digital methods – repurposing digital media functions and affordances as research tools (Rogers, 2013, p. 5) – and its main objective is to help researchers make sense of unwieldy quantities of heterogeneous data, narrowing them down into more manageable categories such as genres (Crowston & Williams,

2000; Wiggins & Bowers, 2015) or repertoires (Orlikowski & Yates, 1994) that can then be investigated ethnographically.

## Participate Beyond Observation

Digital folklore is, for the most part, vernacular digital media content, and following its circulation unravels its structuring in genres and repertoires. But circulation is sustained by the everyday practices of digital media users, which include various modes of sharing, but also creating, editing, commenting, remixing, and so on. All these practices involve creativity: as already observed by Mary J. Hatch and Michael O. Jones in their analysis of the 'photocopylore' circulating in modern offices, individual creative acts all contribute to larger vernacular repertoires that socialize people into communities of meaning (1997, p. 284). This remains true in the case of digital folklore, as even the smallest act – repeating a slang term, liking a social media post or suggesting a funny video to a friend – contributes to the circulation of vernacular creativity. Whether it is sharing gameplay experiences with other *Grand Theft Auto* players (K. Miller, 2008), uploading parody remixes of a Hitler scene from *Downfall* (Gilbert, 2013), or conversing in a shared jargon with Papua New Guineans on Facebook (Dalsgaard, 2016, p. 100), digital folklore is mediated through user practices. After focusing on a specific repertoire or genre of interest, researchers can further narrow down their field of inquiry by looking at these practices, since they offer important details about the sociotechnical networks and assemblages that sustain the circulation of digital folklore. Who is sharing these hilarious GIF animations, and who created them in the first place? Which communities are appropriating a certain nostalgic song, and which platforms are banning videos featuring it? Where do users encounter a specific jargon term, and how do both hashtags and algorithmic feeds shape its dissemination?

Following circulation is not enough to answer these questions, and participation becomes crucial to understand how digital folklore is sustained by media practices. I have attempted to participate in the practice of vernacular creativity, more or less successfully, during various research projects about Chinese digital folklore. Most recently, I investigated a popular repertoire of *huanlian* ('face-changing', deepfake) content and traced it back to video-sharing platform Bilibili. Hundreds of relevant videos were accessible to any website visitor, but in order to understand the creative practices behind these video manipulations I had to figure out ways to look beyond the content and determine how it was created, shared and interpreted. After obtaining an account on Bilibili, I started experiencing the platform's main functions – bookmarking videos of interest through the 'Like' button, commenting on some of them alongside hundreds of other users, and contacting some creators by following them and then sending private messages. While some replied to my queries, many ignored them. Faced with a clear barrier between creators and viewers, I watched some tutorials about creating *huanlian* videos, and applied my rudimentary coding skills to produce a few passable ones, which I then uploaded on the platform, tagging them and categorizing them so that they would become part of the same repertoire of content I was interested in. Becoming a *huanlian* creator myself (albeit an extremely amateur one) was useful in multiple ways: first, it forced me to consult the same materials through which Bilibili users learned to create deepfakes, experiencing the same trial-and-error creative processes; second, it helped me understand how video repertoires are constructed and curated through tags and categories; and third, it signalled my aspiration to belong to a community of creators, making my private queries to other Bilibili users more fruitful.

Where following the circulation of digital folklore is useful to narrow down heterogenous content into more manageable repertoires, participating beyond observation allows researchers to further put their ethnographic field into focus. Regardless of genre and format, all digital folklore exists because it is practiced, and practice is the nexus at which processes of creation, dissemination and interpretation are articulated (A.M. Peck, 2014). After having identified a field where ethnographic participation is possible – an online community, a website, a discussion forum, a social media page, a microblogging hashtag, a chat group, a video game server, and so on – it is necessary to move beyond observation and experience the relevant media practices. These practices can vary from ordinary (like sharing or liking a link) to specialized (like Photoshopping or creating a deepfake video), might require the researcher to acquire local knowledges (learning slang terms or how to use software) and potentially confront them with cultural or ethical thresholds (community gatekeeping, encounters with harmful content). In all these cases, participating in the practices that sustain a repertoire of digital folklore allows the ethnographer to experience circulation first-hand, understand the dynamics of content and map how different practices contribute to its trajectories. The key tools of this strategy are already at the core of ethnography: observation, participation and experiential engagement with research participants. Interviews and group discussions with users are an ideal occasion to inquire about practices in depth, but might not be easy to arrange depending on the context of mediation; other kinds of interaction, such as private chat exchanges, requests for help or collaborative activities can all be fruitful entry points into a dialogic understanding of vernacular creativity.

## Probe Vernacular Aesthetics

If circulation is sustained by variegated media practices, the content of digital folklore repertoires is characterized by specific aesthetics often obscure to community outsiders and observers unfamiliar with specific genres. These vernacular aesthetics are not generalizable to digital media or to the internet at large, and are often highly contextual and medium-specific, depending on the content's format, the platforms where it circulates, and the tools used to create it. Vernacular aesthetics are also what grants digital folklore its distinctiveness and recognizability – the early home computing culture and amateur homepage-making practices painstakingly investigated by Olia Lialina, for example, are inextricably tied to the Comic Sans font, starry night backgrounds and 'Under Construction' signs (2009, p. 22). Similarly, early text-based virtual reality environments were characterized by the linguistic and interactional aesthetics of spamming, spoofing or lurking (Marvin, 1995), while the political images shared by US conservatives via e-mail drew on shared cultural referents to cement a group identity (Duffy et al., 2012). More recently, the rage comics popularized on image boards share an 'ugly aesthetic' (Douglas, 2014) of messiness and coarseness, and users of the r/MemeEconomy subreddit appraise pieces of digital folklore as if they were investment-worthy assets (Literat & Van den Berg, 2017). Every genre and repertoire of digital folklore is articulated through specific aesthetic vocabularies, and probing how vernacular aesthetics are negotiated and interpreted is a central task of ethnographic inquiry, as it pushes researchers beyond the 'what' and 'how' questions that can be answered by looking at circulation and practice, and allows them to understand why digital folklore is created and shared in the first place.

After returning from my doctoral fieldwork in China, I had many of these questions left to answer. One of them, for example, was related to a specific repertoire of humorous images featuring the faces of some celebrities superimposed on stylized human figures holding cartoony swords and engaging in various antics. Most of these images had textual captions and were shared on different digital media platforms ranging from discussion boards and microblogging websites to instant messaging software like QQ and WeChat; and yet, neither reading the captions nor observing their use in context was enough to understand what these images meant, why they were funny, and how different visual and textual elements played against one another. As Christina Xu notes, this genre of content is formally similar to internet memes, but their Chinese name *biaoqing* ('expressions', emoticons) points to a different set of referents that have more to do with expressivity and affect than with spreadability and virality (2016). In order to understand these *biaoqing*, I started posting them myself on Chinese social media platforms and using them in instant messaging applications, trying to observe how they were received or directly asking for some interpretive assistance. This helped, and I at least managed to figure out the main slang terms used in many of the captions. But the overall composition of this genre of *biaoqing* remained obscure, and eventually I relied on the unfailing expertise of Baisong, one of my research participants, who was kind enough to oblige my endless questioning about different versions of an image, dissect its composition into design elements with peculiar backstories, and even share with me his creative process as he experimented with image-editing software to make his own versions (de Seta, 2016).

Probing vernacular aesthetics contributes to the ethnographic study of digital folklore in two ways: first, it pushes inquiry beyond the identification of a repertoire and the mapping of creative practices, toward a dialogic understanding of signification; second, it challenges the widespread interpretative approaches to vernacular content that tend to rely on the researcher's own preconceptions. Even when studying familiar genres of digital folklore, analyses of content and discourse are always at risk of confirmation biases and misinterpretations: interrogating vernacular aesthetics in dialogue with the users who articulate them is often conducive to unsettle the ethnographer's presuppositions. While the example above was centred on visual content, it is possible to probe the vernacular aesthetics of any genre of digital folklore, from group jargons and emoji compositions to dance routines on short video apps.

This strategy is also useful, more generally, to understand how users conceptualize broader aesthetic categories such as the social effervescence around certain kinds of content (Coates, 2017), or how they negotiate aesthetic decisions through collaborative yet uncoordinated processes (A. Peck, 2015). Ethnography is again already well equipped to probe vernacular aesthetics: after having identified a repertoire and having participated in the practices that sustain it, engaging fellow users in discussions about its compositional elements and stylistic vocabularies should be easier and less daunting. Besides asking users why a certain genre of digital folklore is funny, disturbing, popular or outmoded, or seeking help in interpreting a specific piece of content, it is also possible to test one's understanding of vernacular aesthetics first-hand, by creating digital folklore and sharing it, experiencing its reception and afterlife, verifying hypotheses or learning from failures. Just like the use of cultural probes in design or art probes in experimental ethnography (Willim, 2013), this strategy deploys the object of research as a lure to 'evoke and provoke' (p. 83) reactions and responses.

## Archive, Preserve, Curate

An important implication of the materiality of digital folklore is that its traces persist as data that is often dispersed and unstructured. Some vernacular content is exchanged synchronously, such as chat messages or livestreaming comments, but most users encounter digital folklore asynchronously, and some of them contribute to its preservation by saving, collecting, archiving or otherwise organizing repertories in some form. Just like office workers collected photocopied vignettes and bureaucratic spoofs (Hatch & Jones, 1997, p. 279), social media users save their favourite reaction images or animated GIFs for later use, and short video app viewers compile 'best of' selections to be reuploaded on other platforms. Pioneering anthropologists of computer-mediated communication recognized that these new affordances of digital media make possible 'inexpensively collecting, organizing, and exploring digital data' (Paccagnella, 1997), although it is also necessary to approach these practices critically and self-reflexively, since the 'fragmented archive' of digital cultures (Doueihi, 2011, p. 122) tends to be shaped by asymmetries in agency over data and questions of interoperability. Regardless, collecting and organizing digital folklore are central components of ethnographic research on vernacular creativity, both as practices shared with other users and as ways to preserve data for future historical analysis (Brügger, 2011). As Annette Markham suggests, the impulse to automate data collection and archive massive quantities of data is not necessarily conducive to qualitative insight, while an ethnographic approach sensitive to situated practices of curation can help make sense of content that is 'tangled in a dense network of unfathomably meaningful data trails' (2013, p. 441).

I have adopted strategies to archive, preserve and curate vernacular content in various research projects investigating Chinese digital folklore. During my graduate studies, I regularly collected visual content from Chinese social media as part of digital ethnographic work, and I developed a process to archive it in a way that was useful for me in the long term. After saving images and videos on my devices in their original format, I would trace them back to their source through reverse image searches, organize them chronologically in file folders and then upload them, alongside additional information and tags, on a dedicated Tumblr blog. This created an archive that was browsable online and searchable by tag or textual query, and which proved useful in multiple ways: as a repository of content for further analysis, as a source for elicitation prompts during interviews and as a public front for my research project. At the time of writing, this specific archive is still available online, but it was not specifically designed with the purpose of preservation. For another research project, I collaborated with the Geocities Research Institute and retrieved a large sample of early Chinese homepages from their archived server data. In this case, a preservation project became the starting point to conduct ethnographic fieldwork on materials created two decades in the past; besides analysing the coding and design of amateur Chinese webpages from the mid-1990s, I was able to track down some of their creators and talk to them about their memories of the early web. On other occasions, especially when working with contemporary art institutions and exhibitions, I curated selections of content from these same archives in order to produce artworks or texts outside of established academic formats.

These are only some of the possibilities opened up by archiving, preserving and curating repertoires of digital folklore. Informed by insights into the circulation of content, the media practices sustaining it, and the vernacular aesthetics that characterize it, collecting data becomes not just a technical matter but an ethnographic effort in its own right. The key concept of this strategy is again inspired by digital methods: interrogating the medium of choice through its own affordances, formats and related practices. How do different digital media encourage (or discourage) the archiving, preservation and curation of content? How do users collect and organize digital folklore, and what can ethnographers learn from these practices? This strategy can be applied in several ways depending on the digital media that is being studied: uploading and tagging content, creating webpages or social media repositories or even bespoke archival platforms are all productive ways to approach data collection and organization according to different logics. There are also many options to create archives, ranging from basic file systems and textual documentation to preservation-oriented tools such as the Internet Archive, a US-based digital library which allows the saving of web content to a public repository, or Webrecorder (now Conifer), which is designed to preserve social media content and dynamic websites (Espenschied, 2016). Some of these tools can be automated to varying degrees, and every project requires devising an optimal strategy for data collection and organization. Alongside the three other strategies outlined in the preceding sections, archiving, preserving and curating digital folklore is an integral part of the ethnographic approach to vernacular creativity, as it produces primary data for analysis while also drawing the researcher into the same practices through which users collect and organize this sort of content.

## CONCLUSION: ETHNOGRAPHIES OF DIGITAL FOLKLORE AFTER THE INTERNET

Given the long tradition of studying folklore anthropologically, approaching digital folklore through ethnography seems an obvious choice. And yet, the scope, variety and rapid changes of vernacular content and creative practices can make this a methodologically puzzling endeavour. As I argued in this chapter, digital folklore has been a consistent presence in the history of computation and networked communications; digital ethnography, specifically developed by media anthropologists with the purpose of researching these new technologies, is an approach well suited to these mediated forms of vernacular creativity. Despite a rich body of methodological literature, I identified a lack of specific discussions of how to study digital folklore ethnographically. For this reason, this chapter outlines four strategies: following the circulation; participating beyond observation; probing vernacular aesthetics; and archiving, preserving and curating digital folklore. These four strategies, distilled from my own research experience and that of many other scholars, are offered as a toolbox: as with any other assortment of tools, they can be picked up and utilized in different combinations, experimented with or repurposed for different uses. Digital folklore existed before the World Wide Web, before e-mails and before graphical interfaces; it thrived among programmers, amateur web designers and image board users, and circulates today on social media apps and content platforms; in the near future, it will likely continue to exist, as new digital media, content formats and creative practices become popular on local and global scales.

At the time of writing, the platformization of cultural production, the rise of algorithmic media and the advancement of machine learning techniques are already shaping digital folklore in new and unexpected ways. Social media platforms are designed to encourage user participation and facilitate the circulation of specific types of content in order to maximize engagement metrics like views, shares and likes. As platforms tailor their content formats to emerging genres of vernacular creativity, their affordances channel the circulation of digital folklore into proprietary ecosystems while users find new ways to work around these constraints. Similarly, the widespread use of algorithmic personalization shapes social media feeds and confronts users with more opaque and less controllable decisions about what is visible to whom. Algorithmic curation directly impacts how repertoires of digital folklore are constructed and made sense of by users, foregrounding new kinds of non-human agency that participate in the co-production of vernacular content. Finally, machine learning plays an increasingly important role in several aspects of this process – from creation through circulation to curation – adding another layer of computational agency into the mix. User-friendly tools like image filters, object tracking, face recognition and natural language processing models facilitate the production of audiovisual content, and various genres of synthetic media like deepfakes, and enter the repertoire of digital folklore as users experiment with their potentials and limitations. Whatever form digital folklore takes in the post-internet, post-algorithmic, distributed or cooperative metaverses to come, the strategies outlined in this chapter will hopefully remain useful to understand the puzzling mediations of vernacular creativity.

## REFERENCES

Abidin, C., & de Seta, G. (2020). Private messages from the field: Confessions on digital ethnography and its discomforts. *Journal of Digital Social Research*, *2*(1), 1–19. https://doi.org/10.33621/jdsr.v2i1.35.

Abu-Lughod, L. (1991). Writing against culture. In R.G. Fox (Ed.), *Recapturing Anthropology: Working in the Present* (pp. 137–62). School of American Research Press.

Ardevol, E. (2005). Cyberculture: Anthropological perspectives of the Internet. Using Anthropological Theory to Understand Media Forms and Practices Workshop.

Baym, N.K. (1994). From practice to culture on Usenet. *Sociological Review*, *42*(S1), 29–52.

Blank, T.J. (Ed.) (2009). *Folklore and the Internet: Vernacular Expression in a Digital World*. Utah State University Press.

Blank, T.J. (2012). Introduction: Pattern in the virtual folk culture of computer-mediated communication. In T.J. Blank (Ed.), *Folk Culture in the Digital Age: The Emergent Dynamics of Human Interaction* (pp. 1–24). Utah State University Press.

Bräuchler, B., & Postill, J. (Eds.) (2010). *Theorising Media and Practice*. Berghahn Books.

Brügger, N. (2011). Web archiving – Between past, present, and future. In M. Consalvo & C. Ess (Eds.), *The Handbook of Internet Studies* (pp. 24–42). Wiley-Blackwell.

Buccitelli, A.B. (2012). Performance 2.0: Observations toward a theory of the digital performance of folklore. In T.J. Blank (Ed.), *Folk Culture in the Digital Age: The Emergent Dynamics of Human Interaction* (pp. 60–84). Utah State University Press.

Burgess, J. (2007). *Vernacular Creativity and New Media* [PhD Thesis, Queensland University of Technology]. https://eprints.qut.edu.au/16378/1/Jean_Burgess_Thesis.pdf.

Burrell, J. (2009). The field site as a network: A strategy for locating ethnographic research. *Field Methods*, *21*(2), 181–99. https://doi.org/10.1177/1525822X08329699.

Clifford, J. (1986). Introduction: Partial truths. In J. Clifford & G.E. Marcus (Eds.), *Writing Culture: The Poetics and Politics of Ethnography* (pp. 1–26). University of California Press.

Coates, J. (2017). So 'hot' right now: Reflections on virality and sociality from transnational digital China. *Digital Culture & Society*, *3*(2), 77–98. https://doi.org/10.14361/dcs-2017-0206.

Coleman, E.G. (2010). Ethnographic approaches to digital media. *Annual Review of Anthropology*, *39*(1), 487–505. https://doi.org/10.1146/annurev.anthro.012809.104945.

Crowston, K., & Williams, M. (2000). Reproduced and emergent genres of communication on the World Wide Web. *Information Society*, *16*(3), 201–15. https://doi.org/10.1080/01972240050133652.

Dalsgaard, S. (2016). The ethnographic use of Facebook in everyday life. *Anthropological Forum*, *26*(1), 96–114. https://doi.org/10.1080/00664677.2016.1148011.

De Seta, G. (2016). Neither meme nor viral: The circulationist semiotics of vernacular content. *Lexia. Rivista Di Semiotica*, *25–26*, 463–86. https://doi.org/10.4399/97888255031 5926.

De Seta, G. (2020). Digital folklore. In J. Hunsinger, L. Klastrup & M.M. Allen (Eds.), *Second International Handbook of Internet Research* (pp. 167–80). Springer. https://doi.org/10.1007/978-94-024-1202-4_36-1.

Dorst, J. (1990). Tags and burners, cycles and networks: Folklore in the telectronic age. *Journal of Folklore Research*, *27*(3), 179–90.

Doueihi, M. (2011). *Digital Cultures*. Harvard University Press.

Douglas, N. (2014). It's supposed to look like shit: The Internet ugly aesthetic. *Journal of Visual Culture*, *13*(3), 314–39.

Duffy, M., Page, J.T., & Young, R. (2012). Obama as anti-American: Visual folklore in right-wing forwarded e-mails and construction of conservative social identity. *Journal of American Folklore*, *125*(496), 177–203. https://doi.org/10.5406/jamerfolk.125.496.0177.

Dundes, A., & Pagter, C.R. (1975). *Work Hard and You Shall Be Rewarded: Urban Folklore from the Paperwork Empire*. Wayne State University Press.

Espenschied, D. (2016, August 9). Rhizome releases first public version of Webrecorder. Rhizome. http://rhizome.org/editorial/2016/aug/09/rhizome-releases-first-public-version-of-webrecorder/.

Foote, M. (2007). Userpicks: Cyber folk art in the early 21st century. *Folklore Forum*, *37*(1), 27–38.

Frank, R. (2011). *Newslore: Contemporary Folklore on the Internet*. University Press of Mississippi.

Geiger, R.S., & Ribes, D. (2011). Trace ethnography: Following coordination through documentary practices. *2014 47th Hawaii International Conference on System Sciences*, 1–10. https://doi.org/10.1109/HICSS.2011.455.

Gilbert, C.J. (2013). Playing with Hitler: *Downfall* and its ludic uptake. *Critical Studies in Media Communication*, *30*(5), 407–24. https://doi.org/10.1080/15295036.2012.755052.

Ginsburg, F.D., Abu-Lughod, L., & Larkin, B. (Eds.) (2002). *Media Worlds: Anthropology on New Terrain*. University of California Press.

Hatch, M.J., & Jones, M.O. (1997). Photocopylore at work: Aesthetics, collective creativity and the social construction of organizations. *Studies in Cultures, Organizations and Societies*, *3*(2), 263–87. https://doi.org/10.1080/10245289708523498.

Hine, C. (2000). *Virtual Ethnography*. SAGE.

Hine, C. (2013). *The Internet*. Oxford University Press.

Hjorth, L., Horst, H., Galloway, A., & Bell, G. (Eds.) (2017). *The Routledge Companion to Digital Ethnography*. Routledge.

Hobart, M. (2000). *After Culture: Anthropology as Radical Metaphysical Critique*. Duta Wacana University Press.

Howard, P.N. (2002). Network ethnography and the hypermedia organization: New media, new organizations, new methods. *New Media & Society*, *4*(4), 550–574. https://doi.org/10.1177/146144402321466813.

Howard, R.G. (2008). Electronic hybridity: The persistent processes of the vernacular web. *Journal of American Folklore*, *121*(480), 192–218.

Ito, M. (1996). Theory, method, and design in anthropologies of the Internet. *Social Science Computer Review*, *14*(1), 24–6.

Jenkins, H. (2006). *Convergence Culture: Where Old and New Media Collide*. New York University Press.

Kirschenblatt-Gimblett, B. (1996). The electronic vernacular. In G.E. Marcus (Ed.), *Connected: Engagements with Media* (pp. 21–65). University of Chicago Press.

Kirschenblatt-Gimblett, B. (1998). Folklore's crisis. *Journal of American Folklore*, *111*(441), 281–327.

Kõiva, M., & Vesik, L. (2009). Contemporary folklore, Internet and communities at the beginning of the 21st Century. In M. Kõiva (Ed.), *Media & Folklore: Contemporary Folklore IV* (pp. 97–117). ELM Scholarly Press.

Kozinets, R.V. (2010). *Netnography: Doing Ethnographic Research Online*. SAGE.

Kuntsman, A. (2004). Cyberethnography as home-work. *Anthropology Matters Journal*, *6*(2). http://www.anthropologymatters.com/index.php/anth_matters/article/view/97/191.

Lialina, O. (2009). A vernacular web. In O. Lialina & D. Espenschied (Eds.), *Digital Folklore* (pp. 19–33). Merz & Solitude.

Lialina, O., & Espenschied, D. (Eds.) (2009). *Digital Folklore*. Merz & Solitude.

Literat, I., & Van den Berg, S. (2017). Buy memes low, sell memes high: Vernacular criticism and collective negotiations of value on Reddit's MemeEconomy. *Information, Communication & Society*, *22*(2), 232–49. https://doi.org/10.1080/1369118X.2017.1366540.

Marcus, G.E. (1995). Ethnography in/of the world system: The emergence of multi-sited ethnography. *Annual Review of Anthropology*, *24*, 95–117.

Markham, A. (2004). The Internet as research context. In C. Seale, G. Gobo, J.F. Gubrium & D. Silverman (Eds.), *Qualitative Research Practice* (pp. 358–74). SAGE.

Markham, A.N. (2013). Fieldwork in social media: What would Malinowski do? *Qualitative Communication Research*, *2*(4), 434–46. https://doi.org/10.1525/qcr.2013.2.4.434.

Marvin, L.-E. (1995). Spoof, spam, lurk, and lag: The aesthetics of text-based virtual realities. *Journal of Computer-Mediated Communication*, *1*(2). https://doi.org/10.1111/j.1083-6101.1995.tb00324.x.

Miller, D., & Horst, H.A. (2012). The digital and the human: A prospectus for digital anthropology. In H.A. Horst & D. Miller (Eds.), *Digital Anthropology* (pp. 3–35). Berg.

Miller, D., & Slater, D. (2000). *The Internet: An Ethnographic Approach*. Berg.

Miller, K. (2008). Grove Street Grimm: *Grand Theft Auto* and digital folklore. *Journal of American Folklore*, *121*(481), 255–85. https://doi.org/10.2307/20487609.

Murthy, D. (2008). Digital ethnography: An examination of the use of new technologies for social research. *Sociology*, *42*(5), 837–55. https://doi.org/10.1177/0038038508094565.

Orlikowski, W.J., & Yates, J. (1994). Genre repertoire: The structuring of communicative practices in organizations. *Administrative Science Quarterly*, *39*(4), 541–74.

Paccagnella, L. (1997). Getting the seats of your pants dirty: Strategies for ethnographic research on virtual communities. *Journal of Computer-Mediated Communication*, *3*(1). https://doi.org/10.1111/j.1083-6101.1997.tb00065.x.

Peck, A. (2015). Tall, dark, and loathsome: The emergence of a legend cycle in the digital age. *Journal of American Folklore*, *128*(509), 333–48. https://doi.org/10.5406/jamerfolk.128.509.0333.

Peck, A.M. (2014). A laugh riot: Photoshopping as vernacular discursive practice. *International Journal of Communication*, *8*, 1638–62.

Pink, S., Horst, H., Postill, J., Hjorth, L., Lewis, T., & Tacchi, J. (2016). *Digital Ethnography: Principles and Practice*. SAGE.

Porter, D. (Ed.) (1997). *Internet Culture*. Routledge.

Postill, J. (2017). The diachronic ethnography of media: From social changing to actual social changes. *Moment Journal*, *4*(1), 19–43. https://doi.org/10.17572/mj2017.1.1943.

Preston, M.J. (1974). Xerox-lore. *Keystone Folklore*, *19*(1), 11–26.

Roemer, D.M. (1994). Photocopy lore and the naturalization of the corporate body. *Journal of American Folklore*, *107*(423), 121–38. https://doi.org/10.2307/541076.

Rogers, R. (2013). *Digital Methods*. MIT Press.

Shifman, L. (2014). *Memes in Digital Culture*. MIT Press.

Wiggins, B.E., & Bowers, G.B. (2015). Memes as genre: A structurational analysis of the memescape. *New Media & Society*, *17*(11), 1886–1906. https://doi.org/10.1177/1461444814535194.

Willim, R. (2013). Out of hand: Reflections on elsewhereness. In A. Schneider & C. Wright (Eds.), *Anthropology and Art Practice* (pp. 81–88). Bloomsbury.

Xu, C. (2016, August 1). A field guide to China's most indispensable meme. *Motherboard*. http://motherboard.vice.com/read/china-meme-face-a-biaoqing-field-guide.

# 19. Looking back on the scroll back: reflections on the social media scroll back method

*Claire Moran, Elianne Renaud, Taylor Annabell, Fan Yang and Brady Robards*

## INTRODUCTION

As much of our lives are recorded on, organized through, and reflected upon via social media, these channels of communication, news, and social connection come to serve as important digital traces of lives. With their widespread uptake, platforms like Facebook, Instagram, Twitter, Reddit, Snapchat, and TikTok have also become important research sites to understand politics, identity, belonging, the flow of information, and history.

The 'social media scroll back' method (Robards & Lincoln, 2017) is a qualitative research method, usually undertaken during one-on-one interviews,[1] where a researcher and participant 'scroll back' through the participant's social media together, to collaboratively make sense of social media in a research context. The 'scroll back' can be used to scroll through a profile on Instagram or a newsfeed on Facebook or a comment history on Reddit, with the participant in control (on a computer or smartphone, for instance). The researcher and participant become 'co-analysts' of the digital traces inscribed on social media by the participant, with the researcher prompting and asking questions, while the participant reflects, interprets, and provides context. The scroll back puts the participants in the 'driver's seat' of the interview, allowing them to take the researcher in different directions, as they can choose to dwell on and explain or scroll past the digital traces that make up their profiles and feeds. Participants give context to the content that is scrolled through, providing deeper meanings and 'shaping the matter that comes to matter' (Robards & Lincoln, 2017, p. 716).

In this chapter, we seek to extend understandings and applications of the social media scroll back method developed by Robards and Lincoln (2017, 2019), as influenced by Ferreday and Lock (2007), Dobson (2012), and Marwick and boyd (2014). To do this, we present four case studies on how the social media scroll back method has been advanced and extended in four separate research projects, by: Moran, in a study on the social media experiences of African young people in Australia; Renaud, in a study on the use of Instagram by queer femmes in Australia and North America; Annabell, in a study on the use of Instagram and Facebook by young women in London; and Yang, in a study on the use of WeChat Official Accounts by Chinese Australian media professionals. The chapter is co-authored with each of these researchers, who provide reflections on their use of this approach in separate case studies.

Our case studies cover a range of different research topics (national identity, race, sexuality, gender, and media industries), groups of participants (migrants, women, queer femmes, and media workers), different social media platforms (Facebook, Instagram, Snapchat, and WeChat), and a variety of modes of engaging with participants (in-person, via video conferencing, synchronously, and asynchronously). Throughout this chapter, we seek to provide a set of examples of how the social media scroll back method might work in different research contexts. We engage with challenges and opportunities, as well as ethical dilemmas, limitations, and possibilities for future research.

## BACKGROUND: DEVELOPING THE SCROLL BACK METHOD

Scrolling is a key part of the social media experience and describes both the physical act of touching a screen, mouse, or trackpad to move through content and also the cognitive processes of filtering, interpreting, and making sense of what we see on social media. The action of 'scrolling together' elicits a dialogue between the researcher and the participant that, while grounded in the digital traces of the participant, allows the participant to reflect on experiences beyond the screen, like what is left unsaid or later erased. For example, a photo of a couch might remind someone about a period of homelessness and staying with friends; a photo of an ex-partner might remind someone of a break-up; a post about travelling might prompt reflection on new experiences, new friendships, and new perspectives on the world. Participants can reflect on their memories of life events, detail their friendships and discuss the things that matter most to them as related to the research topic. Prompts from the researcher can include: 'What was the story behind that status update?', 'Who are the friends in those photos?', and 'Can you tell me more about this post?' Social media disclosures come to serve as prompts for reflection, memory work, and discussion. This is perhaps a key advantage of incorporating the scroll back method compared to a traditional interview, as it allows researchers to see the overall picture as participants work through and piece together the different parts of their life-worlds prompted by their own digital traces.

Inspired by previous research – such as Ferreday and Lock's (2007) use of participants' blogs to explore gender identity, Dobson's (2012) research on Myspace profiles as sites of self-determination, and Duguay's (2014) work incorporating Facebook into interviews as a form of photo-elicitation – Robards and Lincoln (2017) developed the scroll back method to study young people's use of Facebook. It was initially used to attend more closely to the longitudinal nature of digital traces inscribed through the Facebook 'Timelines' feature and to centre the participant as a co-analyst in understanding and contextualizing these digital traces (see Robards

& Lincoln, 2017, for a longer discussion). By focusing on participants' sustained use of Facebook, the scroll back captured how disclosure practices (what people say and post; see Vitak & Kim, 2014) changed over time and how participants 'grew up' through the lens of Facebook's archival functions. Robards and Lincoln (2017) suggest this method could replicate some aspects of longitudinal qualitative research, as researchers sit with and 'see' participants grow and change over potentially several years of social media use, within a single interview. In this 'long form' of the scroll back, which typically takes place during a one-on-one, one-hour interview, the researcher asks the participant to scroll in chronological order through their social media timeline, from the moment they first joined the site to the time of the interview. Participants are encouraged to reflect on the digital content that they come across, which may include their profile pictures, status updates, comment histories, event check-ins, and photo albums. These digital traces are incredibly rich, longitudinal, and organic (not collected as part of research) and therefore act as participants' personal (and often intimate) records of their lives, allowing researchers to elicit participants' reflections on their complex life histories and personal narratives.

More recently, the scroll back method has been adapted to a 'short form', where it is used to elicit participant disclosures about targeted topics. In this approach researchers may ask participants to scroll back through their social media timelines to find posts that document specific events or subject matter. For example, a study by Roberts et al. (2019) asked participants to scroll back through their social media profiles to find a post that documented, reflected on, or anticipated an event where alcohol consumption was present. These posts became prompts that participants used to recall specific drinking events and to discuss their alcohol consumption. In this short form of the scroll back, participants were encouraged to send screenshots of their social media posts to the research team so that visual records of participants' social media profiles could be captured and analysed alongside their interview transcriptions. The short form of the scroll back may be particularly useful when researchers have limited time with participants, or when the scroll back is being employed alongside other data collection methods; for example, focus groups or ethnographic observations. For more about the long form and short form of the scroll back method, see Robards and Lincoln (2019).

The scroll back method has been adapted by researchers across different topics and platforms, such as: the use of Twitter by people with young-onset dementia (Talbot et al., 2021), women's safety in online–offline fitness spaces (Toffoletti et al., 2021), the relationship between algorithms and gender on Netflix (Siles et al., 2021), social media and youth identity (Theodoridis, 2020), instances of support in Facebook groups by donor-conceived people (Newton, 2020), the management of LGBTQI+ identities on social media (Talbot et al., 2020), parenting culture in Finland (Lehto & Paasonen, 2021), digitally mediated martyrdom and social justice movements (Lewis, 2020), exploring men's risky drinking cultures on Instagram and Facebook (Roberts et al., 2019), and preteens' use of the social media platform Musical.ly (Savic & McCosker, 2018).

In the following sections, we examine four separate case studies of research projects where the social media scroll back method has been used and advanced. In each case study, the lead researcher reflects on the opportunities and challenges associated with this kind of qualitative method in order to map out how this method might be adapted and advanced in future research.

## SCROLLING BACK WITH AFRICAN AUSTRALIAN YOUTH

The social media scroll back method was employed in a study by Moran that explored the social media experiences of African young people (aged 16–25) in Australia. In this study, I (Moran) aimed to situate Afrocentric youth perspectives of social media, with a particular focus on understanding the potential of digital spaces to create and foster inclusivity. The scroll back method was used alongside six months of social media ethnography, which involved friending and/or following participants ($n = 15$) on their main social media platforms (most often this included Instagram, Snapchat, and Facebook) and documenting their engagement in these spaces. The scroll back interview was conducted at the beginning of the six-month-long social media observation, providing an important 'starting point' for the researcher and participant to discuss the social media practices that the participants are engaged in and to reflect on the significant role that these spaces played in their everyday lives. The benefits and challenges of using these two methods concurrently have been discussed in depth elsewhere (see Moran & Robards, 2020).

The scroll back method produced novel insights into the social media practices of the African young people who participated in the project. For the majority of participants ($n = 12$), the scroll back interview was conducted face-to-face; for others ($n = 3$), it was conducted via digital video conferencing or phone. In the face-to-face interviews, participants held their devices and scrolled through their different social media accounts, as they chose the platforms they wanted to show the researcher (often they started with their 'favourite'), and periodically paused their scrolling to narrate the posts they came across. The researcher sat alongside the participant, observing the content they scrolled through and occasionally prompting them to reflect more critically on certain aspects of their profile, such as their profile picture, biographical information, and social networks. Prompts from the researcher included questions like: 'Why did you choose that image as your profile photo?' and 'Who is included in your "close friends" group?' In particular, participants' reflections on their profile pictures and avatars – like the Snapchat Bitmoji – produced unique insights into how they used their social media platforms to represent their racialized bodies and identities. The following discussion will focus on this, using an extract from one participant interview (King, 18 years old, self-identifying as South Sudanese), to demonstrate how the scroll back interview captured data that illustrate the significant way race and racialized experiences factored into the 'presentation of self' (Goffman, 1959) on social media.

King spoke about the design of his Snapchat Bitmoji in relation to the media stereotypes of 'African gangs' that have been prominent within the immigration and crime discourse in Australia, particularly among Melbourne African youth since the Moomba riots in 2016 (for further details of the impact of 'African gangs' media coverage, see Blaustein et al., 2019). King described his Bitmoji in the following way:

King: I mean, I don't look intimidating or anything like that. I look nice … and friendly.
Claire: Someone would say you're intimidating?
King: Yeah.
Claire: Why would they say that?
King: Because of my … [*long pause*] being South Sudanese. People sometimes just look at your profile and they think you're a bad person or a bad influence based on your picture. They'll assume that you're like other Black people they've seen in their life, they'll assume you're the same person.
Claire: Why would they think that?
King: People mostly view Africans in general as violent or criminals. There are only a few people doing it [criminal activities] but they generalize the whole population.
Claire: Who do you mean when you say "they"?
King: Channel 7, for example. I follow them on social media, so it comes up in my Facebook feed.
Claire: So you have intentionally tried to present yourself as not intimidating?
King: Yeah, I usually put something that's not intimidating to someone or rude in any way.

Here, the scroll back method has elicited King's reflection on his Bitmoji, where he draws direct connections between the 'African gangs' narrative and his social media practices. He describes the impact of this narrative, which has stereotyped the African migrant population in Australia as 'violent' and 'criminal', and explains that in the creation of his Bitmoji, he has deliberately attempted to disassociate himself from this stereotype. In doing so, he has ensured that his Bitmoji is perceived as not 'intimidating'. King wants to avoid being judged as a 'bad person' or 'bad influence' by people who view his profile. He refers specifically to Channel 7, an Australian commercial television channel, whose news and current affairs broadcast team have been found to have amplified this moral panic through inaccurate and misleading statements (see ACMA, 2019). King designed his Bitmoji to set himself apart from these stereotypes, describing his Bitmoji as 'nice' and 'friendly'. We can see this by looking at his Bitmoji, which is smiling and waving. King concluded the interview by reflecting on the importance of social media in his life, stating that it allowed people to 'see the person that I am'. These insights, elicited by the scroll back interview, allow us to grasp the complex factors that influence participation in digital spaces for racialized young people.

There are many challenges in 'doing' digital research, and we should be critical of the limitations of different digital methods. The scroll back interview also did have its limitations when employed in this study. Most significant was the difficulty in scrolling through participants' ephemeral content on social media platforms such as Snapchat. During some interviews, although participants spoke about their constant use of Snapchat, they could not share any Snapchat 'stories' with the researcher because the content had disappeared when it was viewed. In some cases, participants were able to share their 'saved' content, but in the majority of interviews, participants could only describe the types of content they would send and receive, rather than share specific examples with the researcher. This is where the social media ethnography was a complementary method to the scroll back as data was continually captured for six months. Beyond the interview, the researcher could continually stay immersed in the digital spaces of the participants, capturing data that was not achievable during the scroll back interview.

## SCROLLING BACK WITH QUEER FEMMES IN AUSTRALIA AND NORTH AMERICA

The scroll back interview was adapted by Renaud in a research project that explored the self-image-making practices ('selfies') of queer femmes in Australia and North America. The study sought to understand how selfie practices enable ideas and enactments of femininity to be expanded, reclaimed and critiqued, and how these digital negotiations may render new subjectivities and alternative imaginings around femininity. The primary method used for this study was semi-structured interviews that I (Renaud) undertook with 13 self-identified queer femmes from Australia and North America, who are engaged in curating and sharing selfies on Instagram (or other social media spaces). Participants were recruited through social media feeds and online networks and interviewed via Zoom. Given the study's focus on selfies, there was an emphasis on using a mixed method or 'remixed' design (see Markham, 2013) to effectively capture the digital and visual data, relative to the social media spaces occupied by the queer femme participants. As such, the scroll back method was adapted into interviews whereby participants could (if they wished) 'scroll back' during the semi-structured interview to select selfies from their social media platforms to illustrate or expand their verbal responses to interview questions. This allowed participants to draw on their Instagram profile as a type of digital archive during their interview. This was intended to encourage participant reflexivity and co-analysis as participants could draw on concrete examples as 'a prompt, and as a primary text of analysis' (Robards & Lincoln, 2017, p. 719).

Participants were informed during the scheduling and at the commencement of the interview that they would be able to use their Instagram posts to offer examples of selfies for the discussion. There were no scripted interview questions that specifically focused on eliciting examples via scroll back for co-analysis with participants. The option to use their Instagram profile for examples was taken up by eight participants during the interview sessions. In these cases, the opportunity to revisit their own archive of selfies typically produced vivid participant accounts of their personal selfie practices. This included explanation and some co-analysis of the practical aspects of selfie curation, as well as the cultural, affective, and symbolic properties of selfie making and sharing. These insights shed light on the significance of selfies to queer femme visibility and recognition and the relationship between social media and participants' intimate, subjective practices around identity. For example, Gayle said:

> My most recent picture that I posted just this last weekend, my caption is "fat, gay and thriving" and so I feel like that the idea of fat, gay and thriving for me really encapsulates what I'm trying to show for my Instagram … a queer femme who's not afraid of femininity, and at the same time while being feminine is strong is confident can wear whatever the fuck she wants. Be whoever the fuck she wants, go wherever the fuck she wants … and then as like a fat queer femme can sit with my belly out if I want, I can eat ice cream if I want, and fuck you for all of these things you're saying about me. And so I think it's really … Instagram in particular, curating my Instagram feed is really about pushing back on what people kind of want to see in their feed.

However, the way in which the scroll back method was adapted in this study also produced some limitations. The informal approach whereby participants were voluntarily invited to revisit posts was not always effective in drawing out examples or nurturing the role of participants as 'co-analysts of their own digital traces', as intended by Robards and Lincoln (2017, p. 721). At times, participants seemed ambivalent when invited to share or discuss an example from their Instagram profile. There was also a sense of uncertainty around what type of examples the interviewer was looking for or would find most valuable for the study. In these cases, discussions arising from these examples seemed cursory or stilted in analysis. In retrospect, the informality around the purpose and use of examples may have inadvertently constituted ambiguity for some participants. This could have been circumvented if there was a more structured framework for scrolling back included in the study design that: (a) provided greater context and clarity in advance of the interview to the type of examples that would be useful for participants to consider for the discussion (i.e., a selfie that best expresses your queer femininity), and (b) included a specific sub-set of questions designed to probe participant examples (i.e., what specific intertextual elements of this example do you feel actualize your queer femininity? How/why?). This more systematic approach would inform participants of the types of examples that would be of value for discussion and, through direct intentional questioning, provide a greater opportunity for meaningful co-analysis during the interview session.

The overall effectiveness of the scroll back method as adapted in this study was also impacted by the physical separation of the interviewer and participant. In Robards and Lincoln (2017) and Moran's case studies, interviewers were mostly co-located with participants as they scrolled back. However, in this study, interviews were predominantly conducted online via Zoom. This meant that the interviewer could only view the content selected by the participant when it was held up to their web camera. This made the content less visually readable and reduced the amount of co-analysis time with the participant. While participants were still able to provide good narrative accounts of their images, the video setting seemed to constrain opportunities to probe deeper into the content and ask further questions relevant to the selected examples, particularly around intertextual components (such as hashtags and captions). This was further impeded by Renaud's limited access to participants' Instagram accounts which was solely observational, resulting in findings that were constrained to the analysis of examples shared by participants during the interview.

As such, it is useful for researchers who wish to follow a similar approach to consider these limitations and build contingent approaches into their project design to ensure rich opportunities for meaningful co-analysis with participants. This would primarily involve more clear and deliberate framing around the scroll back process in all interviews, a set of questions built into the interview schedule to structure the scroll back, and engaging in screen-sharing or screen-shotting in a more deliberate way for interviews conducted via Zoom (as Annabell discusses below). This would help the participant and researcher see profiles and examples together, and dwell on them when the participant chooses to.

## SCROLLING BACK ON INSTAGRAM AND FACEBOOK WITH YOUNG WOMEN IN LONDON

The scroll back method was part of a study conducted by Annabell, examining digital memory work on Instagram and Facebook. The research project examined how young women labour to remember their (gendered) selves on platforms, grappling with the distributed agency between humans and non-humans in the remembering process and the interplay of personal expectations and cultural norms that shapes the ongoing assessment of how the past should be remembered in digital traces. Due to the timing of the fieldwork, the research also explored how young women responded to and reflected on personal and social change associated with COVID-19 and Black Lives Matter in their digital memory work.

Like Moran and Renaud, I (Annabell) carried out the scroll back method as part of a semi-structured interview with young women (aged 18–21) living in London. This interview marked the beginning of a six-month-long observation in which I followed participants ($n = 16$) on Instagram and Facebook, echoing the ethnographic research design of Moran and Robards (2020). Participants were also invited to follow-up interviews and to reflect collectively on my interpretations of the data in focus groups. These overlapping methods generated rich data about how digital memories work as part of the everyday lives of a small group of young women and endeavoured to position participants as 'co-analysts' (Robards & Lincoln, 2017, p. 721) throughout the research process.

Interviews were conducted face-to-face ($n = 8$) and online ($n = 8$) due to COVID-19 restrictions. The online interviews were conducted using the screen-sharing method on Zoom for the scroll back. This helped overcome the issue Renaud encountered where participants had to show the researcher their phone screens via a webcam, which produced stilted sharing and insufficient time to dwell and reflect together. When interviews need to be conducted via Zoom or similar platforms, screen-sharing can be an excellent way for both the researcher to clearly see the content that the participant is scrolling through, and it also allows the researcher to query, prompt, and invite the participant to pause or dwell as needed.

Reinforcing the reflections of Deakin and Wakefield (2014), the change in the interview setting did not seem to affect the quality of the conversation or, in this instance, the opportunity to observe digital memory work in action. Young women in both mediated environments were afforded the agency to decide what digital traces to tell stories about. For example, Chloe identified particular digital traces as being mnemonically significant for managing her mood and feelings in the present:

> Especially this section of my feed is my favourite ever … My final month in Australia and it just has so many good memories … And a lot of meaningful words and captions that are really long, not all of them, but just things that remind me of the good times and it's a time in my life that I really miss. So if I'm ever feeling sad then it is like I'll go automatically back to this kind of stage and be like aww Australia is so beautiful and this is how I felt.

Like other young women in this study, Chloe indicates how she pursues her own past digital traces to be 'made happy', following Ahmed's (2010) notion of happiness as a form of orientation towards objects. Crucially, this relationship between emotion and digital memory work is more complex than what she described during the traditional part of the interview, in which she primarily focused on the prioritization of happy sharing and remembering and the need to interject moments of 'reality' into her digital traces.

While Chloe chose to identify parts of her profile to narrate and paused to elaborate on her digital memory work as exemplified in the excerpt, Yasmin scrolled through 10 years' worth of sharing, telling short stories about most traces for over one and a half hours. Significantly, the scroll back method is flexible and responsive to the interests of the individual as it prioritises their interests while rendering comparisons between scroll backs (including across mediated environments) is less useful because of how the participant guides this interaction. Yasmin's repeated concern, during the scroll back, of making the researcher 'bored' was as revealing as the way she chose to engage in remembering. It speaks to a cultural devaluing of social media activities and the opportunity for researchers to take young women seriously as cultural producers and labourers (Dobson, 2015) to the extent that they should be involved in the research process.

In reflecting on the scroll back method in this study, it is interesting to consider how interviews 'felt' in the online space – following Longhurst's (2016) reflective rather than comparative approach – compared to face-to-face scroll back interviews. For example, in a Zoom interview, participant Arianna scrolled through 43 posts on her Instagram account in a matter of seconds, thematically categorizing them quickly. She then paused to discuss the continuous presence of her ex-boyfriend, which led to further scrolling and an apology: ‘sorry I’m scrolling really fast I forgot that you can see this’. This raises an important ethical concern about the visibility of the researcher online, in which the researcher’s body no longer acts as a reminder of their observing presence because they are invisible during the screen-share. Due to the COVID-19 pandemic, scroll back interviews were unexpectedly shifted to an online setting. During these interviews, participants expressed that remembering their past digital traces brought a sense of comfort, especially during the pandemic. This research method then may have felt familiar and enjoyable in a time of uncertainty and also contributed to the way that participants spent an average of 20 percent longer time than face-to-face interviews. In addition, participants may have felt more at ease with the researcher observing their navigations through a digital interface instead of physically sitting next to them looking at their device. This change in mediated environment has thus raised the question of how bodies and embodiment are part of the scroll back method and the need to think further about the ethical implications of bodily presence in this type of research, which is by its nature tied to intimacy.

## SCROLLING BACK ON WECHAT WITH CHINESE AUSTRALIAN MEDIA PROFESSIONALS

This project concerns the emergent Chinese ethnic media industry on ‘WeChat Official Accounts’ (WOAs), where I (Yang) scrolled back with Chinese Australian media professionals ($n$ = 24) through their WeChat accounts to better understand their use of this platform and to extend understandings of ‘back-end’ uses of social media. WOAs are an information-broadcasting ‘subplatform’ residing within messaging and social media platform WeChat and are situated between WeChat and individual users. Whereas individual, everyday WeChat users have the most limited access to the platform’s API (application programming interface), WeChat affords WOAs access to the back-end interface of the WOA system through which WOA operators can change the elements displayed on the WOA user’s front-end interface. This gives these WOAs a greater level of access and control within the platform when compared to everyday WeChat users.

Since August 2012, with the launch of the WOA function, Chinese migrant entrepreneurs have been engaging with this information-broadcasting feature to produce and circulate news stories among Chinese migrants in Australia and beyond. I dubbed this specific use of the platform feature ‘news-focused WOAs’ (Yang & Martin, 2020). This project addresses the media practice within the news-focused WOAs in Australia, whose daily operation is configured and continually reconfigured by the WOA system.

The methodological design of this project was guided by Bruno Latour’s (1994) epistemology of technology as the mediation of power, in which the ‘black-boxed’ operation and power dynamics of social media, in particular, are hidden. In light of this, the project proposed and implemented an innovative use of the scroll back method (Robards & Lincoln, 2017) by combining the method with the platform-based walkthrough method (Light et al., 2018) and the media go-along method (Jørgensen, 2016). Combining aspects of these three methods allowed me to understand the interaction between users and the 'front end' interface and opened opportunities for studying the hidden 'back-end' interface.

Twenty-four Chinese Australian media professionals in news-focused WOAs participated in the project. The participant cohort was constituted by ten content producers, three chief editors, four marketers, six account directors, and one IT operator. During the interviews, participants were invited to scroll back through their published articles on the news-focused WOAs, walk through the front-end interface of the WOA on their mobile phones by tapping each feature with the researcher, and recall how the change of the platform algorithm, policy, and the WOA feature structured their professional media practices. This request did not intend to involve any revelation of participants' personal information on WeChat as the platform is known for its extensive use among diverse social and professional contexts (Chen et al., 2018). When participants offered me a departure point on the transformation of the WOA front-end interface and their navigation, I delved into a further exploration after the fieldwork to confirm and specify the change. For example, I traced the WOA's recurring (dis)engagement with using algorithms to curate and present the content based on participants' mentioning of their constant manoeuvring of publication timings.

The back-end interface was exclusively accessed by the media professionals at the senior managerial level, and the relevant update remains inaccessible to the public. For the informants with access to the back-end interface, I asked them to take me through the publication procedure of a typical article, their daily monitoring and interactions with their readers and subscribers, and their navigation with the changing platform affordance from the back-end system. As with Moran, Renaud, and Taylor, this took place in the middle of the interview after establishing rapport and trust between the researcher and account managers. In the end, three account managers agreed to take me through the back-end of the WOA feature. During the process, I observed the publication procedure, took photos and screenshots (with consent) of the back-end system of the WOA and the platform announcements, and wrote down notes on the key interface features to facilitate later analysis. I also invited the three participants to recollect the change from the back end that shaped their media practices.

The combined use of the scroll back, walkthrough, and media go-along methods (see Møller & Robards, 2019) allowed me to understand how WOAs were used by media professionals, from both the front and back ends. These approaches helped to mitigate some of the ethical concerns derived from the researcher–participant collaboration oriented to understand users' personal and subjective experiences with platforms in the past or at present, as the project was only concerned with the professional use of the WOA feature. However, the extended deployment of the three methods in the back-end WOA system produced new ethical concerns. The basic information of account subscribers and readers, including name, profile picture, location, identified gender, their interactions with the news-focused WOAs (if any), and possibly the confidential statistics of the accounts, were displayed in the back-end system. As neither the reader group nor the subscriber base was the subject of this research, the researcher did not intend to view or include their profiles in the study. Any revelation of the account's statistics had required approval from the participant before they were incorporated into the analysis. Thus, while scrolling back through these accounts and interfaces with my participants did allow me to access information that I otherwise could not have achieved, it also raises new challenges around treating this greater level of access and insight with sensitivity and care.

## CONCLUSION

The different case studies presented in this chapter highlight several benefits of utilizing the scroll back interview method to study a broad range of social phenomena including African young people's experiences of belonging in Australia, the enactment of femininity by queer femmes through selfies, the digitally mediated memory work of young women in London, and the Chinese ethnic media industry on WOAs.

As identified in the case studies by Moran, Renaud, Annabell, and Yang, the scroll back method can be employed effectively alongside other methods (such as social media ethnography, the walkthrough method, the media go-along method, and as part of traditional interviews), demonstrating the flexibility of the scroll back method to be utilized in mixed-methods studies. However, as each of the researchers in this chapter has explained, these kinds of research methods also require careful planning, framing in advance prior to interviews with participants, the establishment of trust and rapport during interviews, and deliberate but flexible guidance of participants through the scroll back process. Whereas some research participants might think of scrolling back through their social media histories as banal or boring (as with Annabell's participant), others have thought a lot about the nuance and intended impressions given off by their profiles (such as with Moran's participant), differently modulated by their subject positions and experiences. While some aspects of social media can be largely public and open (like profile photos or some entire accounts), others are highly sensitive, ephemeral or restricted, like the 'back end' of the media account on WeChat in Yang's project or the Snapchat stories in Moran's project. Thus, each researcher employing this kind of method must reflect critically on the potential sensitivities and limitations around scrolling back through social media with research participants in advance but must also remain open to negotiating this process with participants as the research unfolds, expecting and accommodating variations and detours.

The case studies in this chapter have also drawn attention to some of the challenges of using the scroll back method, particularly in the context of COVID-19, during which the scroll back interviews had to be moved from a face-to-face setting to web conferencing platforms like Zoom. As Renaud's case study made clear, this can be challenging when you are not physically co-present and not able to see the screens along with your participants in order to prompt reflection, probe, and invite participants to dwell or explain. Annabell's solution with screen-sharing via Zoom, for instance, did allow more effective sharing and co-analysis, but also presented new challenges around the absence of physical bodies as a reminder that the researcher was watching.

To end, we encourage other researchers to test, adapt, and expand the scroll back method in their own projects. As we have demonstrated, there are numerous benefits to be gained from utilizing this method to study a variety of phenomena related to social media use and communication, but also identity, memory, cultural practices, experiences of belonging, community, news sharing and news production, and more. There is a potential for the scroll back method to be remixed, modified, and propelled into new formulations and imaginings as social media continues to be an important site of research but also a channel of identity, culture, and life. This seems particularly imperative as social media platforms continually introduce and expand ephemeral or semi-private features (like Instagram 'stories' and 'close friends' groups) which have seen significant user engagement and uptake. As such, the scroll back method may become less focused on scrolling *back* through social media timelines (with less of a focus on the longitudinal digital traces of participants), and instead be used to scroll *through* the different features of platforms that participants routinely utilize. For example, asking participants to scroll through the 'explore' page on Instagram to elicit reflections on the type of algorithmic driven content that the platform recommends to them. 'Explore' is a heavily used feature of Instagram (Instagram, 2018) and given its 'personalization' to each user could reveal significant insights into a participant's interests and digitally mediated connections. Researchers could also ask participants to scroll *through* their 'saved', 'archived', 'blocked', 'muted', or 'hidden' content to understand how participants employ the different affordances of social media platforms to cultivate their social media experiences. For example, this could be used to elicit participants' reflections on how they manage their safety on digital platforms, which could be particularly insightful for specific groups of users who face high levels of abuse and harassment in digital spaces, such as women or LGBTQI+ or Indigenous users. Ultimately, the adoption and remodification of the scroll back method will depend on the research questions, participants or communities of study, and the social media platforms that researchers utilize, and we would encourage the method to be adapted to reflect these individual research needs.

## NOTE

1. All interviewees within this chapter have been anonymized.

## REFERENCES

ACMA (Australian Communications and Media Authority) (2019). Channel Seven 'African gangs' claim breaches accuracy requirements, press release, March 26. https://www

.acma.gov.au/articles/2019-03/channel-seven-african-gangs-claim-breaches-accuracy-requirements.
Ahmed, S. (2010). *The Promise of Happiness*. Durham, NC: Duke University Press.
Blaustein, J., Benier, K., & Maher, S. (2019). Voices of reason: youth South Sudanese Australians have their say, *Monash Lens*, May 21. https://lens.monash.edu/@politics-society/2019/05/21/1374964/young-south-sudanese-australians-have-their-say.
Chen, J.Y., Mao, Z., & Qiu, J.L. (2018). *Super-Sticky WeChat and Chinese Society*. Bingley: Emerald.
Deakin, H., & Wakefield, K. (2014). Skype interviewing: Reflections of two PhD researchers. *Qualitative Research*, *14*(5), 603–16.
Dobson, A.S. (2012). 'Individuality is everything': 'Autonomous' femininity in MySpace mottos and self-descriptions. *Continuum Journal of Media & Cultural Studies*, *26*(3), 371–83.
Dobson, A.S. (2015). *Postfeminist Digital Cultures: Femininity, Social Media, and Self-Representation*. New York, NY: Palgrave Macmillan.
Duguay, S. (2014). 'He has a way gayer Facebook than I do': Investigating sexual identity disclosure and context collapse on a social networking site. *New Media & Society*, *18*(6), 891–907.
Ferreday, D., & Lock, S. (2007). Computer Cross-Dressing: Queering the Virtual Subject. In K. O'Riordan & D.J. Phillips (Eds.), *Queer Online: Media, Technology, and Sexuality* (pp. 155–76). New York, NY: Peter Lang.
Goffman, E. (1959). *The Presentation of Self in Everyday Life*. Harmondsworth: Penguin.
Instagram (2018). Ads in Explore. https://business.instagram.com/igb/a/ads-in-explore.
Jørgensen, K.M. (2016). The media go-along: Researching mobilities with media at hand. *MedieKultur: Journal of Media and Communication Research*, *32*(60), 32–49.
Latour, B. (1994). On technical mediation: Philosophy, sociology, genealogy. *Common Knowledge*, *3*(2), 29–64.
Lehto, M., & Paasonen, S. (2021). 'I feel the irritation and frustration all over the body': Affective ambiguities in networked parenting culture. *International Journal of Cultural Studies*, *24*(5), 811–26. https://doi.org/10.1177/13678779211003584.
Lewis, K. (2020). *Digitally Mediated Martyrdom: The Visual Politics of Posthumous Images in the Popular Struggle for Social Justice*. PhD Thesis, Digital Media Research Centre, Creative Industry Faculty, Queensland University of Technology.
Light, B., Burgess, J., & Duguay, S. (2018). The walkthrough method: An approach to the study of apps. *New Media & Society*, *20*(3), 881–900.
Longhurst, R. (2016). *Skype: Bodies, Screens, Space*. London: Routledge.
Markham, A. (2013). Remix Culture, Remix Methods: Reframing Qualitative Inquiry for Social Media Contexts. In N. Denzin & M. Giardina (Eds.), *Global Dimensions of Qualitative Inquiry* (pp. 63–81). Walnut Creek, CA: Left Coast Press.
Marwick, A., & boyd, d. (2014). Networked privacy: How teenagers negotiate context in social media. *New Media and Society*, *16*, 1051–67. https://doi.org/10.1177/1461444814543995.
Møller, K., & Robards, B. (2019). Walking through, going along and scrolling back: Ephemeral mobilities in digital ethnography. *Nordicom Review*, 40(S1), 95–109.
Moran, C., & Robards, B. (2020). Researching connected African youth in Australia through a social media ethnography and scroll back interviews. *African Journalism Studies*, *41*(4), 83–102.
Newton, G. (2020). The 'Search-for method': Examining instances of support in Facebook groups for donor-conceived people. *Selected Papers of #AoIR2020, The 21st Annual Conference of the Association of Internet Researchers*, virtual event, October 27–31, 2020.
Robards, B., & Lincoln, S. (2017). Uncovering longitudinal life narratives: Scrolling back on Facebook. *Qualitative Research*, *17*(6), 715–30.

Robards, B., & Lincoln, S. (2019). Social Media Scroll Back Method. In P. Atkinson, S. Delamont, A. Cernat, J.W. Sakshaug & R.A. Williams (Eds.), *SAGE Research Methods: Foundations*. Thousand Oaks, CA: SAGE. https://dx.doi.org/10.4135/9781526421036851495.

Roberts, S., Ralph, B., Elliott, K., Robards, B., Lindsay, J., O'Brien, K., Savir, M. & Lubman, D. (2019). *Exploring Men's Risky Drinking Cultures*. VicHealth and Monash University. Melbourne: Victorian Health Promotion Foundation. https://www.vichealth.vic.gov.au/-/media/ResourceCentre/PublicationsandResources/alcohol%20misuse/MensRiskyDrinking/Mens%20risky%20drinking%20final%20report.pdf.

Savic, M., & McCosker, A. (2018, May 23). *Circumventing Social Media Restrictions: Preteens' Use of Musical.ly*. Paper presented at ICA Preconference 2018: Trust, Control and Privacy: Mediatisation of Childhood and Adolescence in the Digital Age. Prague: International Communication Association.

Siles, I., Martinez-Toledo, Y., & Meléndez-Moran, A. (2021). *Streaming the Romance: Gendered Algorithmic Interpellation on Netflix*. Paper presented at 71st Annual International Communication Association Conference, May 27–31.

Talbot, C., O'Dwyer, S.T., Clare, L., & Heaton, J. (2021). The use of Twitter by people with young-onset dementia: A qualitative analysis of narratives and identity formation in the age of social media. *Dementia*, *20*(7), 2542–57.

Talbot, C., Talbot, A., Roe, D., & Briggs, P (2020). The management of LGBTQ+ identities on social media: A student perspective. *New Media & Society*, *24*(8), 1729–50.

Theodoridis, K. (2020). *'There's Just Nothing Stable Anymore': A Sociological Examination of the Relationship between Social Media Consumption and Youth Identity in an Age of Uncertainty*. PhD Thesis, Department of Sociology, Manchester Metropolitan University.

Toffoletti, K., Thorpe, H., Pavlidis, A., Olive, R., and Moran, C. (2021). Visibility and vulnerability on Instagram: Negotiating safety in women's online-offline fitness spaces. *Leisure Sciences*, *45*(8), 705–23. https://doi.org/10.1080/01490400.2021.1884628.

Vitak, J., & Kim, J. (2014). You can't block people offline: Examining how Facebook's affordances shape the disclosure process. In *Proceedings of the 17th ACM Conference on Computer Supported Cooperative Work & Social Computing* (pp. 461–74). New York, NY: Association for Computing Machinery. https://doi.org/10.1145/2531602.2531672.

Yang, F., & Martin, F. (2020). The 2019 Australian federal election on WeChat Official Accounts: Right-wing dominance and disinformation. *Melbourne Asia Review*. https://doi.org/10.37839/MAR2652-550X5.8.

# 20. A critical review of media and communications scholarship on messaging apps

*Emma Baulch, Amelia Johns and Ariadna Matamoros-Fernández*

## INTRODUCTION

The past decade has seen the rising popularity of mobile messaging apps for commercial transactions, everyday communication and political communication. Over the course of the 2010s, WeChat, WhatsApp, Telegram, Signal, Line and Discord have begun to occupy a prominent place in the social media landscapes encountered by individuals across the globe. The most widely used mobile messaging apps, such as WhatsApp, WeChat, Facebook Messenger and Telegram, were all established in the last ten years and have experienced considerable growth in that period. WhatsApp, owned by Meta, has grown from 10 million users after its establishment in 2009 to 2 billion users in February 2020 (Dean, 2022a). Facebook Messenger, established as a standalone app in 2011, has a user base that has grown from 200,000 recorded in 2014 to 1.3 billion in 2020. WeChat, established in 2011 and owned by Chinese tech company Tencent, has a user base that rivals Facebook Messenger with 1.24 billion users as of 2021 (Iqbal, 2022). Telegram, established in 2013 by Russian entrepreneurs Nikolai and Pavel Durov, grew steadily over the period March 2014 (35 million users) to July 2021 (550 million users) (Dean, 2022b). Media reports of significant increases in Telegram's user base after WhatsApp announced changes to its data privacy policy are not borne out by the statistics (Chee & Wong, 2021). The biggest increase in Telegram's user base took place in the 14 months between December 2014 and February 2016 (200 per cent increase); the user base increased by 34 per cent in the period before and after the WhatsApp announcement (Dean, 2022b).

The expansion of messaging apps' user base has been most pronounced globally in the last decade. It was in this period that we saw the establishment and extraordinary growth of the current crop of messaging platforms, which some writers have referred to as the 'third wave' of messaging after SMS (short message/messaging service; the first wave), and Blackberry Messenger and Skype (second wave) (Devaney, 2016). The pronounced uptake of messaging since the 2010s can be linked to a combination of factors. First is the increasing number of people with the means by which to acquire and use apps; i.e., a smartphone and a mobile internet connection. Between 2012 and 2020, smartphone penetration worldwide nearly quadrupled, increasing from 1.06 billion to 3.8 billion users (Statista, 2020), and internet users grew from

2.5 billion to 4 billion people (ITU, 2020). The second factor is the ease of using messaging apps to communicate for those with patchy internet connections, especially those in the Global South, where increases in smartphone ownership and internet penetration over the last decade have been most pronounced. As Treré (2020) writes of WhatsApp: 'Its simplicity, reliability and accessibility are some of its core selling points, especially for people in the Global South where online services are accessed mainly through cell phones and several connectivity and bandwidth issues are often thwarting a rapid and fluid digital experience.' According to the International Telecommunication Union (ITU), the number of internet users in the developed world increased by only 22 per cent between 2012 and 2020, but it increased by 82 per cent in the developing world. Over the same period, broadband mobile users in the developed world increased by 94 per cent, but the developing world recorded a 480 per cent increase (ITU, 2020).

In this chapter, we survey the literature in the field of media and communications pertaining to online messaging, with a particular focus on the so-called 'third wave', or messaging apps specifically. Therefore, the body of work only includes studies published after 2009. By undertaking this survey of existing literature, the chapter aims to guide researchers interested in positioning their work within a broader field of scholarship, designing methodologies to study this important development in digital communications, and addressing gaps and unanswered questions. The body of work was compiled using a library database (EBSCOHost), searching for the keyword 'instant messaging' in abstracts, titles and keywords. The search was limited to 2010–2021, English-language and full-text peer-reviewed journal articles in media and communications journals. We then conducted a similar search in 12 hand-selected, top-tier, Q1 journals across regions of key interest in the instant messaging scholarship to capture articles that the database search failed to identify, and that addressed our research questions (RQs). The journals were: *Communication and the Public*; *Communication Theory*; *New Media & Society*; *Asian Journal of Communication*; *Mobile Media & Communication*; *Information, Communication & Society*; *International Journal of Communication*; *Journal of Communication*; *Media, Culture & Society*; *Chinese Journal of Communication*; *Convergence*; and *Multimodal Communication*. We found that the studies of instant messaging published in these journals had already been identified in our database search.

We collected relevant works (URL and abstract) in a Zotero library, then eliminated duplications and excluded studies that did not match our aims (i.e., to address the research questions). The resulting body comprised 77 journal articles and one book.

In what follows, we identify patterns and variations in the body of work in terms of how messaging apps are being conceptualized, the geographic objects of focus for messaging apps' scholarship and methods employed to study messaging apps. We do so by addressing the following questions:

1. How have media/communications scholars perceived the societal and historical implications of the growth of online messaging?

2. Which geographical contexts and messaging apps do researchers engage with in studies of online messaging/messaging apps?
3. What are the methodological and ethical challenges of researching messaging apps?

We then conclude the chapter by identifying gaps in the existing media and communications scholarship on messaging apps, by addressing a final question:

4. What are the limitations of the existing body of media/communications work on online messaging and how might these limitations be addressed in future research?

## RQ 1: HOW HAVE MEDIA/COMMUNICATIONS SCHOLARS PERCEIVED THE SOCIETAL AND HISTORICAL IMPLICATIONS OF THE GROWTH OF ONLINE MESSAGING?

In order to address this research question, we categorized the works in two stages. Firstly, we identified eight *topics* (objects of research): political participation, everyday uses, journalism, business models, health and wellbeing, migration, ethics and methods of researching mobile messaging apps. Secondly, we identified four broader *themes*: participation, mobility, literacy and governance. The first mode of categorization points to the fields of social practice deemed (by media and communications scholarship) to be most affected by mobile messaging apps. The second mode of categorization (into themes) points to the different fields of study informing media and communications scholarship on messaging apps: citizenship studies and journalism studies ('publics' and 'the citizen' as key terms), mobile media studies (with 'spatio-temporal' as a key term), discourse studies (with 'multimodality' as a key term), and platform studies (with 'platformization' and 'infrastructuralization' as key terms).

### Topics

The corpus was heavily dominated by studies of everyday uses ($n = 24$; see Figure 20.1). Articles grouped under this topic studied everyday social interactions (Elareshi et al., 2020; Wang and Sandner, 2019); networks, ties and trust (Shen and Gong, 2019; Zeng Skovhøj, 2021); cyberbullying (Aizenkot and Kashy-Rosenbaum, 2019); adoption and use patterns (Dhir et al., 2020; Huang and Zhang, 2017; Jin and Yoon, 2016; Lin and Li, 2014; Matassi et al., 2019; Montag et al., 2015; Yan and Schroeder, 2020); racism (Matamoros-Fernández, 2020); changing conversational norms (Choe, 2018; Cui, 2016; Dogruel and Schnauber-Stockmann, 2021; He and Tan, 2021; Schwarz, 2011); and disconnection tactics (Gangneux, 2021; Huang and Miao, 2021; Mannell, 2019).

We also categorized a relatively high number of articles ($n = 21$) as studies of political participation. These works examine attitudes and practices surrounding misinformation (Gill and Rojas, 2020; Kwak et al., 2020), the uses of messaging apps to stage protest actions (Gil de Zúñiga and Goyanes, 2021), for election campaigning (Moura and Michelson, 2017; Sun and Yu, 2020; Tapsell, 2018), for political discussion (Caetano et al., 2018; Gil de Zúñiga et al., 2021; Guo, 2017; Kligler-Vilenchik and Tenenboim, 2020; Valeriani and Vaccari, 2018; Velasquez et al., 2021; Vermeer et al., 2021; Yang and Men, 2020), and for social movements (Al Zidjaly, 2014; Johns, 2020; Johns and Cheong, 2019; Milan and Barbosa, 2020; Treré, 2015, 2018, 2020).

The works categorized studies of journalism ($n = 12$) as examining practices involving the use of chat apps for: (1) news gathering, news-making and news distribution; and (2) consumption, discussion and sharing of news. A number of articles examine journalists' use of mobile messaging apps to identify and interact with sources, and inquire into its implications for interpreting evidence from sources, and safeguarding their identities (Agur, 2019; Belair-Gagnon et al., 2017, 2018; Dodds, 2019). Others consider whether the increasing importance of mobile messaging apps for news distribution has changed the ways news organizations curate their content for online distribution (Boczek and Koppers, 2020). Some examine how mobile messaging group chats can play a role in setting the news agenda (Kligler-Vilenchik and Tenenboim, 2020; Su and Xiao, 2021). The works studying news consumption note changes in the ways people interact with news as they do so increasingly on mobile devices. Some study the uses and gratifications of 'news snacking' on mobile messaging apps (Lou et al., 2021) and of reposting and sharing news (Wei et al., 2018), while others examine the dynamics of chat groups that lend themselves to the discussion of news (Swart et al., 2018) or compare the demographic characteristics of those who share news on messaging apps in different cultural contexts (Kalogeropoulos, 2021).

Works categorized as studies of business models ($n = 9$) consider the evolution of individual messaging apps in order to understand their ability to pervade everyday life, often seamlessly. Plantin and de Seta (2019), Luqiu and Kang (2021) and Harwit (2017) discuss how techno-nationalism, or Chinese state policies, support the development of WeChat as a key infrastructure connecting all Chinese citizens and offering them up for surveillance. Chen et al. (2018), Peng (2017), Harwit (2017) and Steinberg (2020) consider how WeChat and Line have become 'sticky' by examining how user practice co-evolves with platform architecture, making the app difficult to leave as everyday social practices become enmeshed with it.

Two of the works categorized as studies of migration ($n = 3$) examine how family dynamics play out when members use messaging apps to interact with one another over a distance. Yu et al. (2017) consider how parents use messaging apps to transmit 'traditional Chinese' values to their children who are studying overseas. They discuss the use of WeChat by parents to monitor their children's behaviours from a distance and how children respond by 'performing' traditional Chinese values in their interactions with parents on messaging apps. Alinejad (2019) studies the repertoires of social media employed by Dutch Turkish people to keep in contact with family and finds that these migrants use WhatsApp selectively to maintain intimacy and enact emotional care (see also Borkert et al., 2018; Ju et al., 2019).

Two of the works categorized as studies of health and wellbeing ($n$ = 4) discuss how mobile messaging chat groups serve as a collective, democratic space where health service users engage in peer learning as they share and critique medical expertise relating to their conditions (Baxter, 2018; Lyons, 2020). One study focuses on the relationship between WeChat use and the psychological wellbeing of older people (Rui et al., 2019), while another explores how WhatsApp groups provide a constant, unwavering presence, shoring up the emotional wellbeing of people living in conflict zones (Roitman and Yeshua-Katz, 2021; see also Malka et al., 2015).

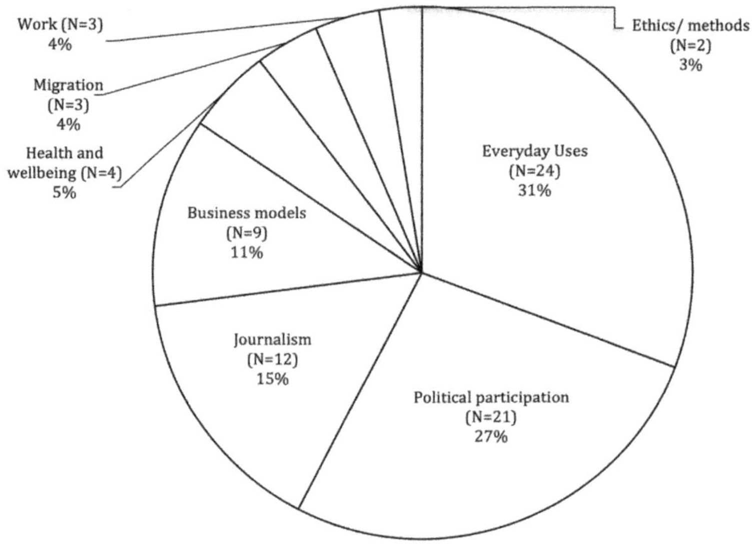


*Figure 20.1 Distribution by topic*

## Themes

As mentioned above, the four themes identified – participation, mobility, literacy and governance – reveal the different fields of study informing media and communications scholarship on messaging apps. They also point to four main lines of inquiry into messaging apps' historical development concerning their relationship to: (1) publics and the citizens, (2) spatio-temporal orders, (3) language and (4) state and corporate power.

The works grouped under the theme of participation can be associated with citizenship studies' and journalism studies' approaches to studying media. Most of the studies in our corpus ($n$ = 39) fell into this category (see Figure 20.2). They included works on the topics of journalism, political participation, everyday uses, and health and wellbeing. They examined the relationships between messaging apps and everyday social connections, as well as questions surrounding messaging apps' capacities to shape the qualities of public discourse by providing new tools for news gathering, dissemination and consumption, for social movements and for political discussion.

Works grouped under the theme of mobility ($n = 19$) can be associated with mobile media studies and consider the spatio-temporal changes that come about with the widespread use of messaging apps.

Many of the studies build on Licoppe's (2004) seminal article discussing the temporal convergence of communication with absent parties and those that involve physical co-presence, as a result of the spread of personal mobile communication devices. Licoppe describes this as 'connected presence … where co-present interaction and mediated communication seem woven in a seamless web' (2004, p. 135). Some of the articles in this sub-corpus consider the implications of such convergence for communicative etiquette (Dogruel and Schnauber-Stockmann, 2021). Others consider the implications for user agency, by way of strategies of disconnection to 'limit availability to and through mobile messaging … as [it] becomes ever more deeply embedded in daily life' (Mannell, 2019, p. 76; see also Gangneux, 2021, and Ju et al., 2019). Others still consider implications for work, now a precarious time/space increasingly polluted by the leisure/work melange that flows through messaging apps (Cho et al., 2019; Huang and Zhang, 2019). And finally, there are those that consider implications for the ways news organizations curate and disseminate news, with the demise of a dedicated time/space for doing so, and the rise of mobile-mediated 'news snacking' (Boczek and Koppers, 2020).

Works grouped under the theme of literacy ($n = 8$) consider how unique languages or grammars are evolving on mobile messaging apps due to their technical features, which combine mobility and privacy with multimodality. Cui (2016) argues that scholarship privileging messaging apps' mobility tends to depict them as devices that primarily afford synchronous communication between physically distanced interlocutors, and this overlooks the importance of multimodality in the ways people engage messaging apps (see also Krishnan and Hunt, 2021). Matamoros-Fernández (2020) considers how WhatsApp harbours unique visual grammars that inflict racist harm. Caetano et al. (2018) identify different forms of expression among political and non-political groups on WhatsApp (whereby non-political groups make great use of multimodality). Choe (2018) discusses how KakaoTalk users make use of the app's linguistic resources to indicate listenership. Baxter (2018) analyses the linguistic possibilities of WhatsApp for constructing support and solidarity in a group of cancer patients.

Works grouped under the theme of governance ($n = 8$) consider how messaging apps' design and evolution highlight the development of platforms and point to corporate and state control of public discourse. The role messaging apps play in the processes of platformization and infrastructuralization is a key question within this theme. Helmond describes platformization as a process involving 'the extension of … platforms into the web and their drive to make external web data platforms ready' (2015, p. 1). Nieborg and Poell identify Amazon, Google, Microsoft and Facebook as prime drivers of platformization 'in the West' (2018, p. 4276) and argue that it introduces a platform logic into the production of cultural commodities, whereby such commodities become contingent upon business models of platforms in order to gain visibility, to circulate and be transacted. Therefore, platformization describes a process whereby the *business logic* of platforms infuses and shapes processes of cultural production. Infrastructuralization describes a process whereby the *technical capacities* of platforms enable them to operate as 'ubiquitous utilities' (Nieborg and Helmond, 2019, p. 191) and whereby the access to platforms increasingly defines membership in a society.

Many of the works categorized under the theme of governance consider how mobile messaging apps are implicated in these processes of infrastructuralization and platformization, although not all make use of these terms. Steinberg (2020) studies sticker production on the Line messaging app as an example of the platformization of cultural production, and Nieborg and Helmond (2019) describe Facebook Messenger as a platform that plays a significant role in Facebook's platformizing. Chen et al. (2018), Harwit (2017), Luqiu and Kang (2021), Pan (2020), Peng (2017) and Plantin and de Seta (2019) study WeChat, and in particular the business logic and technical features that make the platform so central to many aspects of daily life in China, and the implications of such for state surveillance of discourse. The absence of studies of WhatsApp's role in infrastructuralization and platformization represents a notable gap.

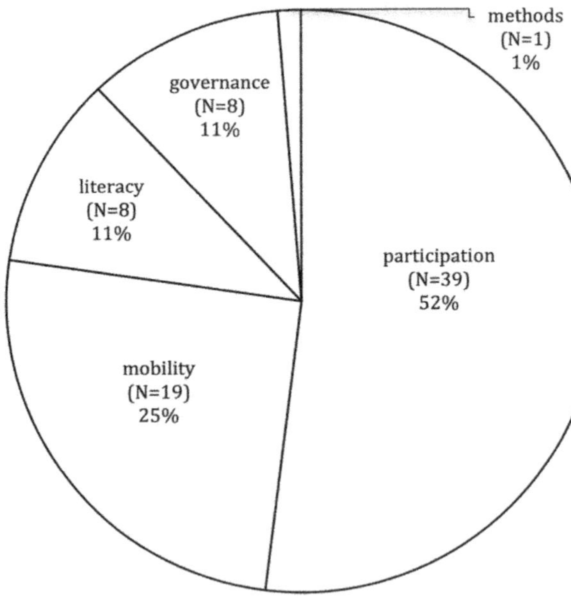


*Figure 20.2 Distribution by theme*

## RQ 2: WHICH GEOGRAPHICAL CONTEXTS AND MESSAGING APPS DO RESEARCHERS ENGAGE WITH IN STUDIES OF ONLINE MESSAGING/MESSAGING APPS?

When the corpus is broken down in terms of messaging apps studied (see Figure 20.3), WhatsApp emerges as the clear leader, with 42 per cent of papers focusing on the app, followed by WeChat (33 per cent of papers). A smaller number of studies of mobile messaging apps do not specify particular apps (13 per cent), and single-case studies focused on KakaoTalk, Line, Telegram and Facebook Messenger. Many of the studies of WeChat ($n$ = 11) in our corpus were published in the *Chinese Journal of Communication*, and we posit that the rich scholarship on WeChat may be partly attributed to the presence of a journal dedicated to studying media and communications in China. The dearth of scholarship examining Facebook Messenger represents a notable gap, considering the high numbers of monthly active users of this app globally (second to WhatsApp).

When the corpus is broken down in terms of countries studied, China emerges as the leader (see Figure 20.4). The corpus includes case studies from 20 countries across all continents of the globe, except Africa (where WhatsApp is an important feature of the communicative landscape). Some studies of African countries were

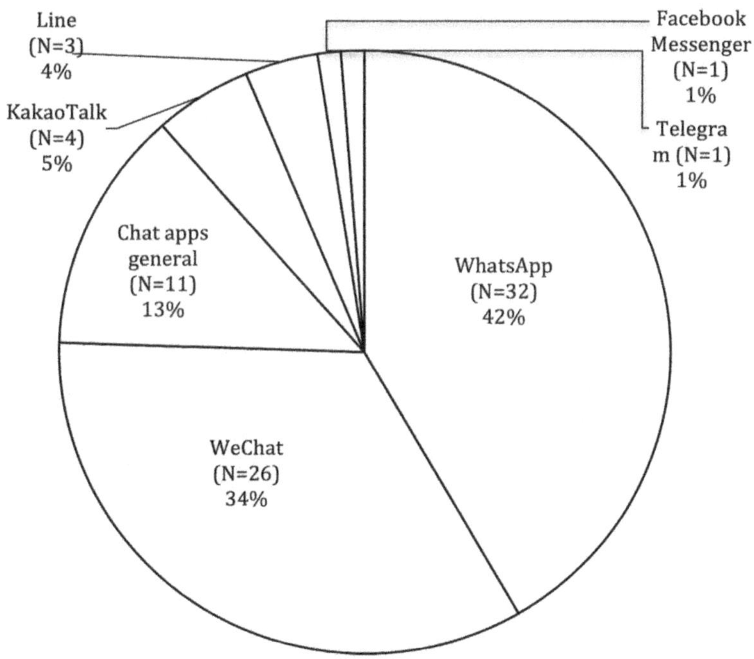


*Figure 20.3 Distribution by messaging app studied*

eliminated from the corpus because they were not published in media and communications journals.

When broken down in terms of geographic regions, the corpus shows a strong bias towards China, followed by Europe, East Asia and the Middle East, Southeast Asia and Latin America (see Figure 20.5). Again, the absence of Africa is notable, as is the relatively large size of the corpus studying Western Europe. The small number of studies of North American messaging app landscapes is also notable, considering the important role US-based studies have played in the development of internet studies.

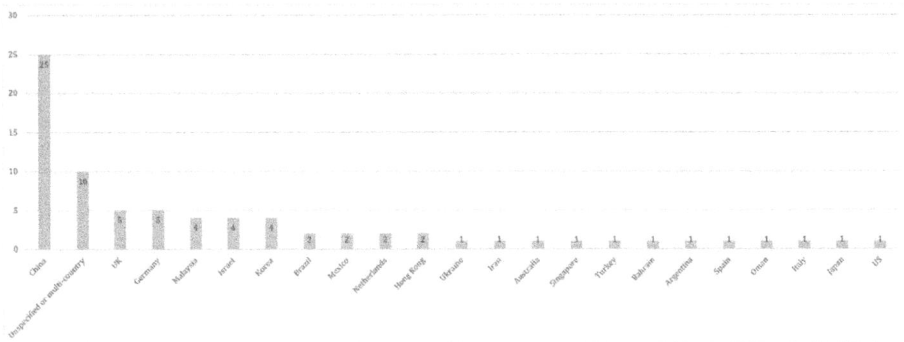


*Figure 20.4 Articles by country studied*

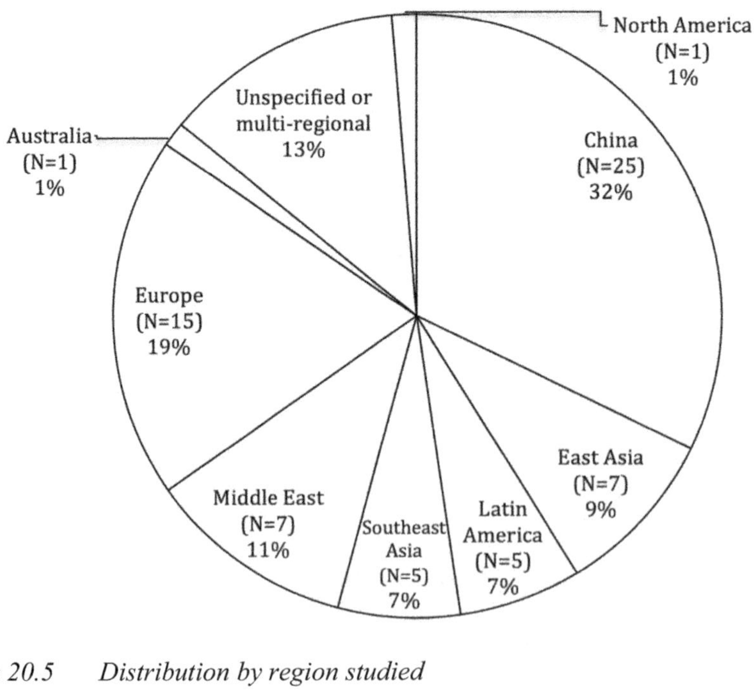


*Figure 20.5 Distribution by region studied*

## RQ 3: WHAT ARE THE METHODOLOGICAL AND ETHICAL CHALLENGES OF RESEARCHING MESSAGING APPS?

Messaging apps' often closed architectures due to encryption present unique challenges for researchers. On open social media platforms, user practices can be examined by accessing data through the platform's application programming interface (API) or scraping, enabling big data studies to be performed using quantitative and computational analysis. Public user accounts and comments can also be accessed by qualitative researchers. Messaging app practices by individuals and groups are much more diffuse and closed, invisible to the outside observer. For this reason, messaging apps research thus far has relied heavily on various self-reporting methods, including interviews, focus group discussions (FGD), surveys, user diaries and logs. In addition, observational methods are used to analyse mobile chat groups, including public, web-searchable groups and private groups, for which the researcher must gain ethical clearance to access and observe.

Most of the studies in our corpus ($n$ = 30) relied on interviews or FGD for data collection. Three of these studies also used diaries or communicative behaviour logs, which participants completed and submitted to the researcher (Schwarz, 2011; Yu et al., 2017; Zeng Skovhøj, 2021) (see Figure 20.6). A large number of studies ($n$ = 20) used a combination of surveys and statistical analysis to study adoption and use (Boczek and Koppers, 2020; Dhir et al., 2020; Huang and Zhang, 2017; Lin and Li, 2014; Soliman and Salem, 2014), or to study the relationships between mobile messaging apps use and other topics, such as news literacy, political participation or political identity, work burnout, or social connectivity and wellbeing (Cho et al., 2019; Dogruel and Schnauber-Stockmann, 2021; Gil de Zúñiga and Goyanes, 2021; Gill and Rojas, 2020; Kwak et al., 2020; Rui et al., 2019; Shen and Gong, 2019; Valeriani and Vaccari, 2018; Velasquez et al., 2021; Yang and Men, 2020). A small number of studies ($n$ = 4) analysed messaging apps by tracing their 'biographies' to consider their changing social, political and economic implications as they evolve (Chen et al., 2018; Harwit, 2017; Nieborg and Helmond, 2019; Steinberg, 2020). Two were applied field experiments (Moura and Michelson, 2017; Vermeer et al., 2021) and one was a systematic literature review (Pang and Woo, 2020).

## CONCLUSION

This review has attempted to map the field of messaging apps studies by locating this body of work as a subfield within media and communications studies. There are limitations associated with this approach that could be addressed in subsequent reviews. As mentioned above, the body of work we reviewed revealed that in the field of media communications, messaging apps are considered historically significant because they affect important shifts in mobility, citizenship, political communication and journalism. Therefore, we may expect to find studies of messaging apps published in journals dedicated to those fields. Such studies were not captured by

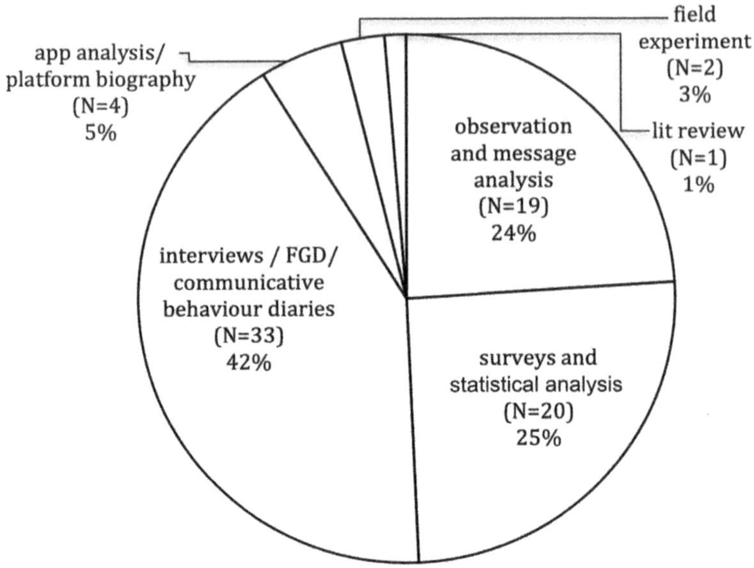


*Figure 20.6 Distribution by method applied*

our search, which was limited to media and communications journals. Moreover, our criteria for selecting studies to include in the corpus was simple, and did not undergo the rigorous considerations of inclusion and exclusion that would be expected of a systematic review (which our review is not).

In conclusion, we seek to highlight two important gaps to be addressed in future research. The first relates to the lack of critical studies of mobile messaging apps that can help to understand how emerging user practices relate to platform power and how scholarship on processes of platformization and infrastructuralization taking place through the spread of mobile messaging is still in its infancy. The second relates to the need to experiment with and chronicle methods of studying messaging apps that would enable researchers to directly observe user practice as it unfolds.

## Critical Messaging Apps Studies

The corpus displays a strong bias towards studies of the relationship between mobile messaging apps and participation in public discourse, through news gathering, distribution and consumption, rumour and misinformation sharing, and the creation of community on chat groups. Conversely, there is a dearth of work on governance that considers the implications of mobile instant messaging (MIM) for extending state and corporate power. As a result, the corpus provides quite a detailed picture of the group and individual users' motivations for using mobile messaging apps, what they use them for and the gratifications they draw from such uses. But it lacks a thorough account of how political and social arrangements of power and existing ideologies and logic are being encoded in messaging apps by the corporate institutions that own them and how such ideologies may permeate the social practices and the meanings individual users attribute to mobile messaging apps. In other words, the critical body of work that can help us understand how platform power may be shaping perceptions of use, social practices and cultures of use, or how activists and everyday users may be resisting these logic, is still very much underdeveloped. Only one work in our corpus addresses this question (Santos and Faure, 2018).

Similarly, work on how the design and architecture of messaging (that which marks them as a distinct genre of online communication media) advances the core business of platforms – i.e. data extraction, via platformization and infrastructuralization – is under-studied. Most of the works ($n = 6$) grouped under the governance theme attend to this question (Chen et al., 2018; Harwit, 2017; Luqiu and Kang, 2021; Nieborg and Helmond, 2019; Peng, 2017; Plantin and de Seta, 2019; Steinberg, 2020). However, five of these works study WeChat, highlighting a strong interest in how that platform operationalizes state and corporate power in ways that undermine public discourse. This is far from matched by similar studies of other platforms. Considering that studies of WhatsApp dominate the corpus as a whole, and in view of its importance within the mobile messaging landscape globally, the dearth of critical work on WhatsApp is notable.

## New Methods for Studying Mobile Messaging

The corpus displays a heavy reliance on user self-reporting via surveys, interviews and focus groups, and direct observations of user practice skew towards the observation of group interactions. As a result, we know much about the dynamics of group interactions and much less about the repertoires of relationships and communicative practices that individual users develop on the platform. For example, interacting with groups is only one of messaging apps' many uses. They are also used for one-on-one communication, with friends and family members, but also for commercial transactions. Moreover, there is an urgent need for work that chronicles in detail methods for researching messaging apps, and their respective limitations. The corpus tends to overlook the limitations of particular methods, such as how reliance on self-reporting works to circumscribe the field of observation in particular ways. It also fails to consider how the survey, interview and FGD data might be verified or contextualized through direct observation of users' practices. Creative methods to 'get at' user practices, such as data donations (Matamoros-Fernández and Estrada-Grajales, 2019), scroll back interviews (Robards and Lincoln, 2019) or mapping exercises, are under-represented. These methods offer researchers ways to observe user practices as they unfold, and can help to address the limitations of methods that rely on users' testimonies (which can conflict with what users actually do).

## REFERENCES

Agur, C. (2019). Insularized connectedness: Mobile chat applications and news production. *Media and Communication*, 7(1), 179–88. https://doi.org/10.17645/mac.v7i1.1802.

Aizenkot, D., & Kashy-Rosenbaum, G. (2019). Cyberbullying victimization in WhatsApp classmate groups among Israeli elementary, middle, and high school students. *Journal of Interpersonal Violence*, 36(15–16), NP8498–NP8519. https://doi.org/10.1177/0886260519842860.

Alinejad, D. (2019). Careful co-presence: The transnational mediation of emotional intimacy. *Social Media + Society*, 5(2), 2056305119854222. https://doi.org/10.1177/2056305119854222.

Al Zidjaly, N. (2014). WhatsApp Omani teachers: Social media and the question of social change. *Multimodal Communication*, 3(1), 107–30. https://doi.org/10.1515/mc-2014-0007.

Baxter, J. (2018). 'Keep strong, remember everything you have learnt': Constructing support and solidarity through online interaction within a UK cancer support group. *Discourse & Society*, 29(4), 363–79. https://doi.org/10.1177/0957926518754414.

Belair-Gagnon, V., Agur, C., & Frisch, N. (2017). The changing physical and social environment of newsgathering: A case study of foreign correspondents using chat apps during unrest. *Social Media + Society*, 3(1), 205630511770116. https://doi.org/10.1177/2056305117701163.

Belair-Gagnon, V., Agur, C., & Frisch, N. (2018). Mobile sourcing: A case study of journalistic norms and usage of chat apps. *Mobile Media & Communication*, 6(1), 53–70. https://doi.org/10.1177/2050157917725549.

Boczek, K., & Koppers, L. (2020). What's new about WhatsApp for news? A mixed-method study on news outlets' strategies for using WhatsApp. *Digital Journalism*, 8(1), 126–44. https://doi.org/10.1080/21670811.2019.1692685.

Borkert, M., Fisher, K.E., & Yafi, E. (2018). The best, the worst, and the hardest to find: How people, mobiles, and social media connect migrants in(to) Europe. *Social Media + Society*, 4(1), 205630511876442. https://doi.org/10.1177/2056305118764428.

Caetano, J.A., de Oliveira, J.F., Lima, H.S., Marques-Neto, H.T., Magno, G., Meira, W., Jr., & Almeida, V.A.F. (2018). Analyzing and characterizing political discussions in WhatsApp public groups. *ArXiv*, 10.

Chee, K., & Wong, C. (2021, October 5). WhatsApp fights back over privacy concerns as users jump to Telegram, Signal. *Straits Times*. https://www.straitstimes.com/tech/whatsapp-stresses-privacy-as-users-flock-to-rivals.

Chen, Y., Mao, Z., & Qiu, J. L. (2018). *Super Sticky Wechat and Chinese Society*. Emerald.

Cho, J., Lee, H.E., & Kim, H. (2019). Effects of communication-oriented overload in mobile instant messaging on role stressors, burnout, and turnover intention in the workplace. *International Journal of Communication*, 13, 21. https://ijoc.org/index.php/ijoc/article/view/9290.

Choe, H. (2018). Type your listenership: An exploration of listenership in instant messages. *Discourse Studies*, 20(6), 703–25. https://doi.org/10.1177/1461445618770471.

Cui, D. (2016). Beyond 'connected presence': Multimedia mobile instant messaging in close relationship management. *Mobile Media & Communication*, 4(1), 19–36. https://doi.org/10.1177/2050157915583925.

Dean, B. (2022a). WhatsApp 2022 user statistics: How many people use WhatsApp? *Backlinko*. https://backlinko.com/whatsapp-users.

Dean, B. (2022b). How many people use Telegram in 2022? 55 Telegram stats. *Backlinko*. https://backlinko.com/telegram-users.

Devaney, E. (2016). The 3 waves of 1:1 messaging software & why marketers need to adapt. *Drift*, July 21. https://www.drift.com/blog/3-waves-of-messaging-software/.

Dhir, A., Kaur, P., & Rajala, R. (2020). Continued use of mobile instant messaging apps: A new perspective on theories of consumption, flow, and planned behavior. *Social Science Computer Review*, 38(2), 147–69. https://doi.org/10.1177/0894439318806853.

Dodds, T. (2019). Reporting with WhatsApp: Mobile chat applications' impact on journalistic practices. *Digital Journalism*, 7(6), 725–45. https://doi.org/10.1080/21670811.2019.1592693.

Dogruel, L., & Schnauber-Stockmann, A. (2021). What determines instant messaging communication? Examining the impact of person- and situation-level factors on IM responsiveness. *Mobile Media & Communication*, 9(2), 210–228. https://doi.org/10.1177/2050157920943926.

Elareshi, M., Ziani, A.-K., & Al Shami, A. (2020). Deep learning analysis of social media content used by Bahraini women: WhatsApp in focus. *Convergence*, 27(2), 472–90. https://doi.org/10.1177/1354856520966914.

Gangneux, J. (2021). Tactical agency? Young people's (dis)engagement with WhatsApp and Facebook Messenger. *Convergence*, 27(2), 458–71. https://doi.org/10.1177/1354856520918987.

Gil de Zúñiga, H., Ardèvol-Abreu, A., & Casero-Ripollés, A. (2021). WhatsApp political discussion, conventional participation and activism: Exploring direct, indirect and generational effects. *Information, Communication & Society*, 24(2), 201–18. https://doi.org/10.1080/1369118X.2019.1642933.

Gil de Zúñiga, H., & Goyanes, M. (2021). Fueling civil disobedience in democracy: WhatsApp news use, political knowledge, and illegal political protest. *New Media & Society*, 146144482110478. https://doi.org/10.1177/14614448211047850.

Gill, H., & Rojas, H. (2020). Chatting in a mobile chamber: Effects of instant messenger use on tolerance toward political misinformation among South Koreans. *Asian Journal of Communication*, 30(6), 470–493. https://doi.org/10.1080/01292986.2020.1825757.

Guo, L. (2017). WeChat as a semipublic alternative sphere: Exploring the use of WeChat among Chinese older adults. *International Journal of Communication*, *11*, 408–28.

Harwit, E. (2017). WeChat: Social and political development of China's dominant messaging app. *Chinese Journal of Communication*, 10(3), 312–27. https://doi.org/10.1080/17544750.2016.1213757.

He, H., & Tan, C.K.K. (2021). Strangers in the borderlands: WeChat and ethical ambiguity in Yunnan, China. *Chinese Journal of Communication*, 14(2), 123–38. https://doi.org/10.1080/17544750.2020.1769701.

Helmond, A. (2015). The platformization of the web: Making web data platform ready. *Social Media + Society*, 1(2), 205630511560308. https://doi.org/10.1177/2056305115603080.

Huang, H., & Zhang, X. (2017). The adoption and use of WeChat among middle-aged residents in urban China. *Chinese Journal of Communication*, 10(2), 134–56. https://doi.org/10.1080/17544750.2016.1211545.

Huang, L.V., & Zhang, K. (2019). Engagement, formality, and visibility: Managing paradoxes of using mobile instant messaging for work. *International Journal of Communication*, 13, 1919–38.

Huang, Y., & Miao, W. (2021). Re-domesticating social media when it becomes disruptive: Evidence from China's 'super app' WeChat. *Mobile Media & Communication*, 9(2), 177–94. https://doi.org/10.1177/2050157920940765.

Iqbal, M. (2022). WeChat revenue and statistics 2022. Business of Apps. https://www.businessofapps.com/data/wechat-statistics/.

ITU (2020). Statistics. https://www.itu.int/en/ITU-D/Statistics/Pages/stat/default.aspx.

Jin, D.Y., & Yoon, K. (2016). Reimagining smartphones in a local mediascape: A cultural analysis of young KakaoTalk users in Korea. *Convergence*, 22(5), 510–523. https://doi.org/10.1177/1354856514560316.

Johns, A. (2020). 'This will be the WhatsApp election': Crypto-publics and digital citizenship in Malaysia's GE14 election. *First Monday*. https://doi.org/10.5210/fm.v25i12.10381.
Johns, A., & Cheong, N. (2019). Feeling the chill: Bersih 2.0, state censorship, and 'networked affect' on Malaysian social media 2012–2018. *Social Media + Society*, 5(2), 205630511882180. https://doi.org/10.1177/2056305118821801.
Ju, B., Sandel, T.L., & Thinyane, H. (2019). WeChat use of mainland Chinese dual migrants in daily border crossing. *Chinese Journal of Communication*, 12(4), 377–94. https://doi.org/10.1080/17544750.2019.1593207.
Kalogeropoulos, A. (2021). Who shares news on mobile messaging applications, why and in what ways? A cross-national analysis. *Mobile Media & Communication*, 9(2), 336–52. https://doi.org/10.1177/2050157920958442.
Kligler-Vilenchik, N., & Tenenboim, O. (2020). Sustained journalist–audience reciprocity in a meso news-space: The case of a journalistic WhatsApp group. *New Media & Society*, 22(2), 264–82. https://doi.org/10.1177/1461444819856917.
Krishnan, A., & Hunt, D.S. (2021). TTYL :-) … Nonverbal cues and perceptions of personality and homophily in synchronous mediated communication. *Information, Communication & Society*, 24(1), 85–101. https://doi.org/10.1080/1369118X.2019.1635183.
Kwak, N., Lane, D.S., Qinfeng Zhu, Lee, S.S., & Weeks, B.E. (2020). Political rumor communication on instant messaging platforms: Relationships with political participation and knowledge. *International Journal of Communication*, 14, 5663–85.
Licoppe, C. (2004). 'Connected' presence: The emergence of a new repertoire for managing social relationships in a changing communication technoscape. *Environment and Planning D: Society and Space*, 22(1), 135–56. https://doi.org/10.1068/d323t.
Lin, T.T.C., & Li, L. (2014). Perceived characteristics, perceived popularity, and playfulness: Youth adoption of mobile instant messaging in China. *China Media Research*, 10(2), 60–71.
Lou, C., Tandoc, E., Hong, L., Pong, X., Lye, W., & Sng, N. (2021). When motivations meet affordances: News consumption of Telegram. *Journalism Studies*, 22(7), 934–52.
Luqiu, L.R., & Kang, Y. (2021). Loyalty to WeChat beyond national borders: A perspective of media system dependency theory on techno-nationalism. *Chinese Journal of Communication*, 14(4), 451–68. https://doi.org/10.1080/17544750.2021.1921820.
Lyons, A. (2020). Negotiating the expertise paradox in new mothers' WhatsApp group interactions. *Discourse, Context & Media*, 37, 100427. https://doi.org/10.1016/j.dcm.2020.100427.
Malka, V., Ariel, Y., & Avidar, R. (2015). Fighting, worrying and sharing: Operation 'Protective Edge' as the first WhatsApp war. *Media, War & Conflict*, 8(3), 329–44. https://doi.org/10.1177/1750635215611610.
Mannell, K. (2019). A typology of mobile messaging's disconnective affordances. *Mobile Media & Communication*, 7(1), 76–93. https://doi.org/10.1177/2050157918772864.
Matamoros-Fernández, A. (2020). 'El Negro de WhatsApp' meme, digital blackface, and racism on social media. *First Monday*. https://doi.org/10.5210/fm.v25i12.10420.
Matamoros-Fernández, A., & Estrada-Grajales, C. (2019). Misogyny on WhatsApp: Examining the metaphor of 'dirt' in memes about Venezuelan migrant women in Colombia. In K. Lewis, H. Berents, D. Myles, E.C. Cabalquinto, A. Matamoros-Fernández & C. Estrada-Grajales (2019). *Performing (In)justice: The Contentious Politics of Digitally Mediated Visuals*. AoIR Selected Papers of Internet Research, 2019. https://doi.org/10.5210/spir.v2019i0.10972.
Matassi, M., Boczkowski, P.J., & Mitchelstein, E. (2019). Domesticating WhatsApp: Family, friends, work, and study in everyday communication. *New Media & Society*, 21(10), 2183–2200. https://doi.org/10.1177/1461444819841890.
Milan, S., & Barbosa, S. (2020). Enter the WhatsApper: Reinventing digital activism at the time of chat apps. *First Monday*. https://doi.org/10.5210/fm.v25i12.10414.

Montag, C., Błaszkiewicz, K., Sariyska, R., Lachmann, B., Andone, I., Trendafilov, B., Eibes, M., & Markowetz, A. (2015). Smartphone usage in the 21st century: Who is active on WhatsApp? *BMC Research Notes*, 8(1), 331. https://doi.org/10.1186/s13104-015-1280-z.

Moura, M., & Michelson, M.R. (2017). WhatsApp in Brazil: Mobilising voters through door-to-door and personal messages. *Internet Policy Review*, 6(4). https://doi.org/10.14763/2017.4.775.

Nieborg, D.B., & Helmond, A. (2019). The political economy of Facebook's platformization in the mobile ecosystem: Facebook Messenger as a platform instance. *Media, Culture & Society*, 41(2), 196–218. https://doi.org/10.1177/0163443718818384.

Nieborg, D.B., & Poell, T. (2018). The platformization of cultural production: Theorizing the contingent cultural commodity. *New Media & Society*, 20(11), 4275–92. https://doi.org/10.1177/1461444818769694.

Pan, J. (2020). Temporality alignment: How WeChat transforms government communication in Chinese cities. *Chinese Journal of Communication*, 13(3), 241–57. https://doi.org/10.1080/17544750.2019.1679855.

Pang, N., & Woo, Y.T. (2020). What about WhatsApp? A systematic review of WhatsApp and its role in civic and political engagement. *First Monday*. https://doi.org/10.5210/fm.v25i12.10417.

Peng, Y. (2017). Affective networks: How WeChat enhances Tencent's digital business governance. *Chinese Journal of Communication*, 10(3), 264–78. https://doi.org/10.1080/17544750.2017.1306573.

Plantin, J.-C., & de Seta, G. (2019). WeChat as infrastructure: The techno-nationalist shaping of Chinese digital platforms. *Chinese Journal of Communication*, *12*(3), 257–73. https://doi.org/10.1080/17544750.2019.1572633.

Robards, B., & Lincoln, S. (2019). Social media scroll back method. In P. Atkinson, S. Delamont, A. Cernat, J.W. Sakshaug, & R.A. Williams (Eds.), *SAGE Research Methods: Foundations*. https://dx.doi.org/10.4135/9781526421036851495.

Roitman, Y., & Yeshua-Katz, D. (2021). WhatsApp group as a shared resource for coping with political violence: The case of mothers living in an ongoing conflict area. *Mobile Media & Communication*, 205015792110214. https://doi.org/10.1177/20501579211021455.

Rui, J.R., Yu, N., Xu, Q., & Cui, X. (2019). Getting connected while aging: The effects of WeChat network characteristics on the well-being of Chinese mature adults. *Chinese Journal of Communication*, 12(1), 25–43. https://doi.org/10.1080/17544750.2018.1530270.

Santos, M., & Faure, A. (2018). Affordance is power: Contradictions between communications and technical dimensions of WhatsApp's end-to-end encryption. *Social Media and Society*, 4(3). https://doi.org/10.1177/2056305118795876.

Schwarz, O. (2011). Who moved my conversation? Instant messaging, intertextuality and new regimes of intimacy and truth. *Media, Culture & Society*, 33(1), 71–87. https://doi.org/10.1177/0163443710385501.

Shen, C., & Gong, H. (2019). Personal ties, group ties and latent ties: Connecting network size to diversity and trust in the mobile social network WeChat. *Asian Journal of Communication*, 29(1), 18–34. https://doi.org/10.1080/01292986.2018.1504976.

Soliman, A., & Salem, M. (2014). Investigating intention to use mobile instant messenger: The influence of sociability, self-expressiveness, and enjoyment. *Journal of American Academy of Business*, 19, 286–93.

Statista (2020, December 10). Smartphone users worldwide 2016–2021. https://www.statista.com/statistics/330695/number-of-smartphone-users-worldwide/.

Steinberg, M. (2020). LINE as super app: Platformization in East Asia. *Social Media + Society*, 6(2), 205630512093328. https://doi.org/10.1177/2056305120933285.

Su, Y., & Xiao, X. (2021). From WeChat to 'We set': Exploring the intermedia agenda-setting effects across WeChat public accounts, party newspaper and metropolitan newspapers

in China. *Chinese Journal of Communication*, 14(3), 278–96. https://doi.org/10.1080/17544750.2020.1839777.
Sun, W., & Yu, H. (2020). WeChatting the Australian election: Mandarin-speaking migrants and the teaching of new citizenship practices. *Social Media + Society*, 6(1), 205630512090344. https://doi.org/10.1177/2056305120903441.
Swart, J., Peters, C., & Broersma, M. (2018). Shedding light on the dark social: The connective role of news and journalism in social media communities. *New Media & Society*, 20(11), 4329–45.
Tapsell, R. (2018). The smartphone as the 'weapon of the weak': Assessing the role of communication technologies in Malaysia's regime change. *Journal of Current Southeast Asian Affairs*, 37(3), 9–29. https://doi.org/10.1177/186810341803700302.
Treré, E. (2015). Reclaiming, proclaiming and maintaining collective identity in the #YoSoy 132 Movement in Mexico: An examination of digital frontstage and backstage activism through social media and instant messaging platforms. *Information, Communication & Society* 18(8), 901–15. https://doi.org/10.1080/1369118X.2015.1043744.
Treré, E. (2018). The sublime of digital activism: Hybrid media ecologies and the new grammar of protest. *Journalism & Communication Monographs*, 20(2), 137–48. https://doi.org/10.1177/1522637918770435.
Treré, E. (2020). The banality of WhatsApp: On the everyday politics of backstage activism in Mexico and Spain. *First Monday*. https://doi.org/10.5210/fm.v25i12.10404.
Valeriani, A., & Vaccari, C. (2018). Political talk on mobile instant messaging services: A comparative analysis of Germany, Italy, and the UK. *Information, Communication & Society*, 21(11), 1715–31. https://doi.org/10.1080/1369118X.2017.1350730.
Velasquez, A., Quenette, A.M., & Rojas, H. (2021). WhatsApp political expression and political participation: The role of ethnic minorities' group solidarity and political talk ethnic heterogeneity. *International Journal of Communication*, 15, 22.
Vermeer, S.A.M., Kruikemeier, S., Trilling, D., & de Vreese, C.H. (2021). WhatsApp with politics?! Examining the effects of interpersonal political discussion in instant messaging apps. *International Journal of Press/Politics*, 26(2), 410–437. https://doi.org/10.1177/1940161220925020.
Wang, Y., & Sandner, J. (2019). Like a 'frog in a well'? An ethnographic study of Chinese rural women's social media practices through the WeChat platform. *Chinese Journal of Communication*, 12(3), 324–39. https://doi.org/10.1080/17544750.2019.1583677.
Wei, R., Huang, J., & Zheng, P. (2018). Use of mobile social apps for public communication in China: Gratifications as antecedents of reposting articles from WeChat public accounts. *Mobile Media & Communication*, 6(1), 108–26. https://doi.org/10.1177/2050157917728100.
Yan, P., & Schroeder, R. (2020). Variations in the adoption and use of mobile social apps in everyday lives in urban and rural China. *Mobile Media & Communication*, 8(3), 318–41. https://doi.org/10.1177/2050157919884718.
Yang, A., & Men, L.R. (2020). Political information use on WeChat and political discussion in China: Toward a networked political discussion model. *Chinese Journal of Communication*, 13(2), 129–47. https://doi.org/10.1080/17544750.2019.1618354.
Yu, Q., Huang, P., & Liu, L. (2017). From 'connected presence' to 'panoptic presence': Reframing the parent–child relationship on mobile instant messaging uses in the Chinese translocal context. *Mobile Media & Communication*, 5(2), 123–38. https://doi.org/10.1177/2050157916688348.
Zeng Skovhøj, F.H. (2021). Managing everyday communication with strong, weak, and latent ties via WeChat: Availability, visibility, and reciprocal engagement. *Mobile Media & Communication*, 9(3), 513–30. https://doi.org/10.1177/2050157920982322.

# 21. How can we take advantage of students' social media skills in the classroom? An international exploration

*Maria-Jose Masanet and Carlos A. Scolari*

## INTRODUCTION

This was an actual dialogue between one of the authors of this chapter and his then 10-year-old son a decade ago:

| | |
|---|---|
| Author | What video game are you playing now? |
| Son | *Call of Duty*. |
| Author | What's it about? |
| Son | It's set in World War II. This week I was fighting to get to Berlin before the Russians, but they arrived before the Allied troops. "We" moved fast forward after the Normandy landing … |
| Author | D-Day? |
| Son | Yes, on June 6, 1944. At first, we advanced quickly, but the Germans got strong in the Rhine with their tanks, and the Russians, who were advancing through Poland, reached Berlin earlier. |
| Author | One question … Do you know who Napoleon was? |
| Son | … He was French, wasn't he? |
| Author | You don't know who Napoleon was? |
| Son | No. They should make a game about him. |

This kind of intergenerational dialogue was at the base of the original formulation of the Transmedia Literacy project (2015–18); for full details of the project, see Scolari (2018). It could be said that the combination of social media and mobile devices has radically transformed the production, circulation, and consumption of media content. Today, sharing photos, videos, audio files, memes, and comments through platforms like Instagram, YouTube, and TikTok is part of the everyday life of millions of teenagers and young people around the world. Teenagers upload their own contents, handle them using the filters or editing tools, and 'comment', 'like', and 'share' the photos and videos of others. Social media are also a place where teenagers follow the lives and interactions of celebrities, peers, and even people they do not know. When tweens do all these online activities, they are acquiring and improving a broad spectrum of media skills, from content creation and manipulation to storytelling. In some cases, in these informal environments, they even gain professionally relevant skills (Masanet et al., 2020); for example, managing contents or communities or constructing a personal brand.

Formal education has made great efforts to adapt to these new socio-technical conditions, especially in the past two decades, with the aim of getting closer to the life and interests of teenagers and children. But the general perception is that the social life of tweens is built up around a set of digital technologies and new practices and actors (YouTubers and Instagrammers, among others) that are frequently very far from the educational protocols and the mechanisms and ways of doing in schools (Scolari, 2018). Researchers like Manuel Castells have highlighted the existence of a cultural and technological gap between today's adolescents' lives and a school system that has not evolved along with society and the digital environment:

> The idea that today a young person must load a backpack of boring textbooks set by ministerial bureaucrats, and must remain closed in a classroom to support an irrelevant speech in the name of his/her future, is simply absurd (Castells, 2007, p. 25).

Although many educators reject these online practices or rule out getting closer and using them in their daily practice, the philosophy proposed in the present text is the opposite. In other words, the main objective of this chapter is to explore tweens' social media skills and practices with the purpose of introducing and taking advantage of these skills in the classroom through innovative activities and teaching dynamics. That is, the intention is to reduce the aforementioned gap between adolescents' media practices and uses and the school system.

Although the research was carried out before the COVID-19 pandemic and lockdown, the situation experienced on a global scale during 2020–21 confirmed the importance of the skills and practices developed by young people in informal learning settings like social media: in many families it was these tweens who taught adults how to use communication platforms during the lockdown. At the same time, in contradiction to those who believed that young people only had a life online, the lockdown showed precisely the opposite: their lives, like the lives of adults, unfolded in a hybrid environment that fluctuated between 'virtual' and 'real' spaces.

The H2020 Transmedia Literacy project was an international research project oriented towards answering a series of questions: What are tweens doing with media? What skills are they developing in these informal learning environments? How do they learn (and share) these skills? What informal learning strategies do they apply? The next section will introduce the research project and its theoretical and methodological background. Thereafter, we will focus on part of the outcomes of the research: the social media skills and practices detected during the fieldwork in seven countries in Latin America and Europe and in Australia. Before concluding the chapter, the final section is dedicated to the activities that could be applied in formal settings to 'exploit' the social media skills that tweens develop in informal learning environments.

## TOWARDS A MAP OF TRANSMEDIA LITERACIES

Although it is almost impossible to process the many existing definitions of 'media literacy', scholars like Potter (2005, 2010) have tried to organize, classify and synthesize the different conceptions. According to Potter, the basic principles and proposals of media literacy are:

- Mass media have the capacity to exert a wide range of potentially negative effects on individuals;
- The purpose of media literacy is to help people to protect themselves from the potentially negative effects;
- Media literacy is a continuum where subjects occupy a personal position that depends on their knowledge structures, skills, and experiences;
- Media literacy is a multidimensional space that involves cognitive, emotional, aesthetic, and moral domains.

Potter's conception of media literacy is strongly anchored in a theory of negative media effects. In this context, the aim of media literacy is 'to target a potential negative media effect and to either inoculate people against such an effect occurring or to counter the already negative effect' (Potter, 2010, p. 685). The Transmedia Literacy project took a more nuanced approach to media literacy. Following scholars like Buckingham (2003), the research team adopted a production-centred approach. According to Buckingham and Domaille (2009), the more contemporary definition of media literacy 'seems to be based on notions such as "critical awareness", "democratic participation" and even "enjoyment" of the media' (p. 23). This approach, also known as 'media education', entails a more active, student-centred, participatory pedagogy.

The above-mentioned changes in the media ecology unlocked the debate about the pertinence of traditional definitions of media literacy (mostly based on the idea of 'inoculation' and considering young people as 'victims' of media) and led to the emergence of new literacies. The research team also considered that media literacy could no longer be limited to the critical analysis of media contents or the acquisition of skills inside the formal education system. In this context, transmedia literacy could be understood as a set of skills, practices, values, priorities, sensibilities, and learning/sharing strategies developed and applied in the context of the new participatory cultures. If traditional literacy was book-centred or, in the case of media literacy, mostly television-centred, then multimodal literacy places digital networks and interactive media experiences at the centre of its analytical and practical experience (Scolari, 2018, p. 15).

Traditional forms of literacy generally treated the subject as illiterate, while media literacy focused on the consumer as a passive spectator. However, transmedia literacy considers the subject to be an active agent and sometimes even a *prosumer* (a concept introduced by Toffler, 1980) or *participatory creator* (Meyers et al., 2013). As many tweens are now developing their transmedia skills outside the school environments, on YouTube, online forums, social media and blogs, among others, these informal learning spaces are a key component of transmedia literacy research and strategies. Table 21.1 presents a comparative vision of traditional, media, and transmedia literacy.

*Table 21.1 Literacy, media literacy, and transmedia literacy (Scolari, 2018)*

| | Literacy | Media literacy | Transmedia literacy |
|---|---|---|---|
| Media semiotics (language) | Verbal text (write/read) | Multimodal | Multimodal |
| Media supports | Books and printed texts | Printed, audio-visual and digital | Digital networks, interactive media, transmedia |
| Aim of the action | To develop critical readers and writers | To develop critical consumers and producers | To develop critical prosumers |
| Subject interpellation | As an illiterate | As a passive media consumer | As a prosumer |
| Direction of the action | Top-down | 1. Top-down<br>2. Bottom-up | 1. Bottom-up<br>2. Top-down |
| Learning environment | Formal (schools) | Formal (schools), informal and non-formal | From informal to formal (schools) |
| Role of the teacher | Knowledge authority – Mediator student/text | Knowledge mediator – Creator of learning experiences with the media | Knowledge facilitator – Cultural translator |
| Theoretical references | Linguistics | Media studies (Theory of media effects) – Cultural studies | Media studies (Media ecology – Transmedia storytelling) – Cultural studies |

Therefore, as mentioned in the introduction of this chapter, in the Transmedia Literacy project the team focused on exploring media skills, practices, and learning strategies developed by young people in informal settings. In order to do this, the team applied an ethnographic approach, following the precepts of short-term ethnography (Pink & Morgan, 2013). This kind of methodology allowed the team to carry out the research in a shorter time period than traditional ethnography since the researchers had the opportunity to create different contexts and situations in a more interventional way. The objective was to design a methodology able to involve participants in a meaningful context and go deeper into the research objectives. Indeed, the team needed to create a context (inside the schools) that allowed the exploration of practices that usually take place outside the schools. A set of participatory-creative workshops on video games, participatory culture, and social media was designed and developed so that the team could explore and observe direct interactions between tweens and media in the context of collaborative participation. The project design followed five steps (Scolari et al., 2020): (a) management of ethical and data protection protocols, (b) questionnaires (survey), (c) participatory-creative workshops, (d) in-depth interviews, and (e) online observation of different significant communities (Figure 21.1).

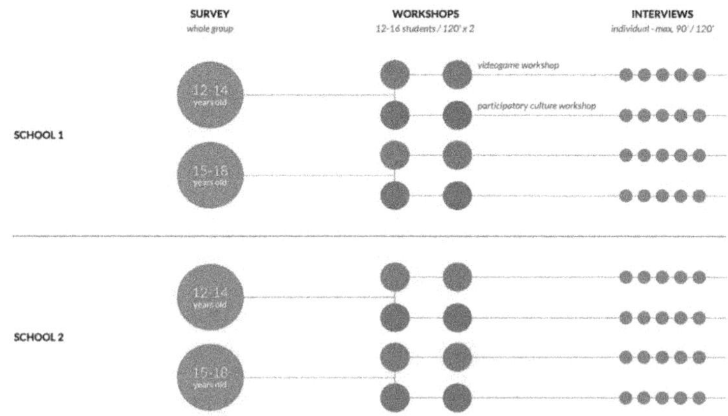


*Source:* Scolari (2018)

*Figure 21.1 Data-gathering techniques: survey, workshops, and interviews*

This chapter will specifically focus on the data that emerged from the workshops and interviews. The team worked with tweens from 12 to 18 years old, and between two and four schools from each country participated in the research.

As the research was carried out in eight countries, the final objective of the project was to obtain data from a broad-spectrum international context in order to create a complex and extensive map of skills and informal learning strategies. In other words, more than a comparative analysis between countries, the objective was to develop a general view of what tweens are doing with media in different contexts and settings to 'feed' a database of transmedia skills. For this reason, the team focused on detecting similarities, while the differences observed during the fieldwork were identified as future lines of research.

Finally, the project constructed a map of transmedia skills and informal learning strategies. This map distributed the skills into nine dimensions: production, risk prevention, performance, social management, individual management, content management, media and technology, ideology and ethics, and narrative and aesthetics. These dimensions included 44 main skills and 190 specific skills (Scolari et al., 2018). Six main areas were detected in relation to informal learning strategies: learning by doing, problem solving, imitating/simulating, playing, evaluating, and teaching (see Figure 21.2).

As this chapter focuses on the use of social media in the classroom, the analysis will centre on exploring the skills closely related to them. Although the skills related to the use of social media span across all the dimensions detected in the project, they are more predominant in some of them, such as in production or social, individual, and content management. The following section will be dedicated to these skills.

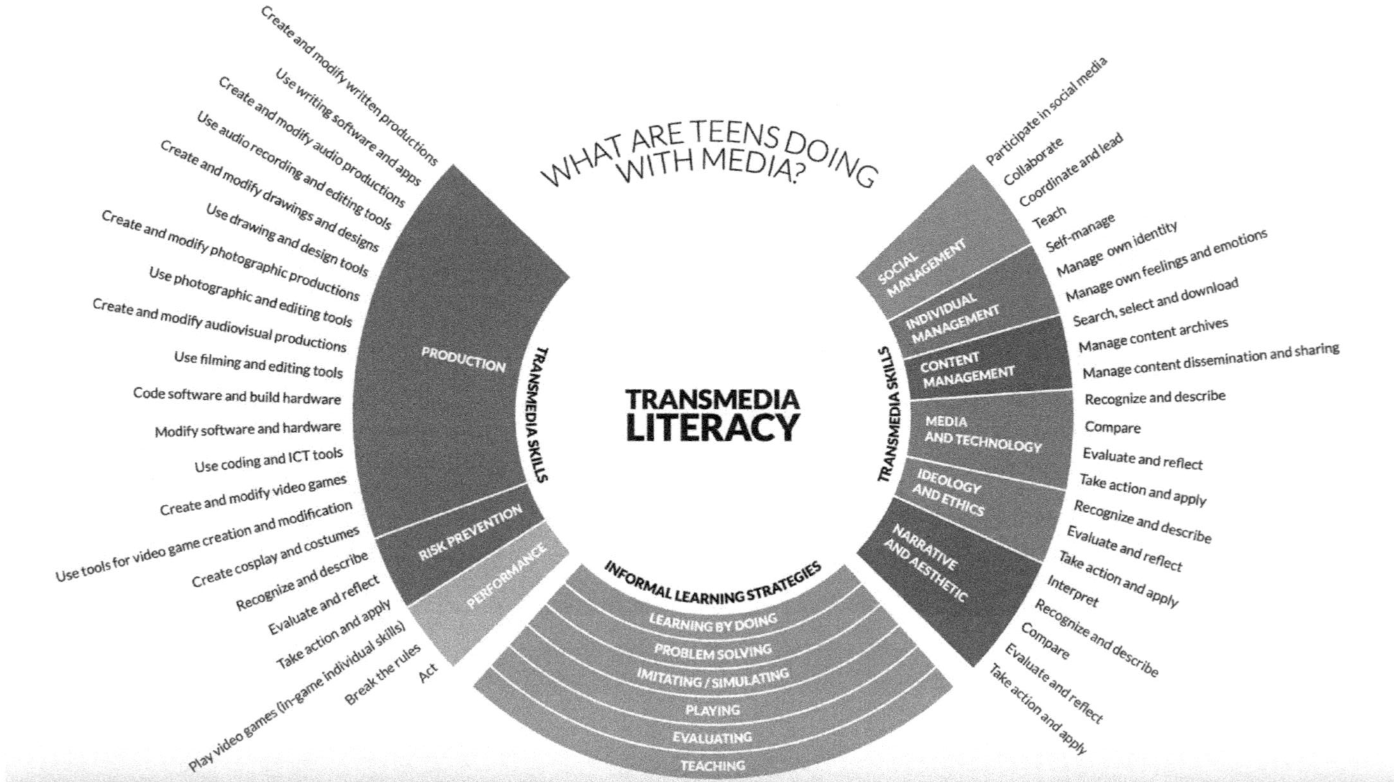


*Source*: Scolari (2018)

*Figure 21.2 Map of transmedia skills and informal learning strategies*

## SOCIAL MEDIA SKILLS

During the fieldwork, the research team observed that tweens made complex and varied use of social media. Although, as already mentioned, the research was not intended to compare the situation in different countries, some data may serve to better frame youth media practices. The study showed that the use of social media varied in the different contexts studied, and also that social media use differed due to gender (Masanet et al., 2021). For example, in South American countries, the most used networks were Facebook and YouTube, with around 90 per cent, while in Europe, they were YouTube, with almost 100 per cent, and WhatsApp, with around 90 per cent. In Australia, on the other hand, the use of YouTube stood out, with around 80 per cent, along with Instagram (around 70 per cent). The girls proved to be more intense users of Instagram and Snapchat in all contexts, while boys used YouTube more intensely (except in South American countries).

As can be seen, practically all tweens have access to and use social media where they follow content producers or create their own content; however, the practices and skills they develop in these environments can be very varied and uneven. Most tweens make basic use of social networks and in the context of the project, these users were defined as 'casual'. However, others make a more sophisticated or professional use, and in the project, these users were defined as 'aspirational' or 'expert' (Guerrero-Pico et al., 2019). The team, therefore, observed an unequal use of social media in terms of distribution, intensity, and complexity (Pereira et al., 2018). There were tweens who focused their activity mainly on the 'consumption' of content, while others were powerful 'creators'. Many of the tweens that participated in the research followed celebrities (mainly YouTubers and Instagrammers). Some, on the other hand, have become 'proto-celebrities' themselves and, through the process of constructing a celebrity profile and personal brand linked to it, have developed skills typical of marketing and advertising professionals (Masanet et al., 2020). This variety of practices, uses, and dynamics is reflected in a wide range of skills. This section will present a selection of the most common skills and a few of the less common skills that are pertinent to the argument of the chapter.

### Creating Content for Social Media: From Writing Texts to Fanvids

Adolescents create different content for social media, from the most basic, such as the written text of a private Telegram message, to more complex content, such as fanvids, memes, or collages. In social media limited to a close circle of people, such as WhatsApp, it is observed that the creation of content tends to follow a more spontaneous process. However, on other platforms with a more social nature, such as YouTube, the process tends to be more planned (Pereira et al., 2018). In both cases, different skills are observed, which are related to planning and creating photos, videos, and graphic design. It is in the planned processes that the most sophisticated practices and skills emerge. For example, the research team came across tweens who carried out semi-professional processes when they prepared and created content for

YouTube channels, such as locating scenes for recording, preparing a video entry mask and a logo (brand), or editing the content with software such as Photoshop.

Table 21.2 presents a synthesis of the image, video, and text production skills detected during the fieldwork when the participants created content for their social media accounts. The team detected skills related to the conception and planning of the product and production process, and post-production and product review skills, as shown in Table 21.2. The researchers also detected skills related to the re-appropriation of content from other users. Some tweens, for example, created memes and other content from textual materials already available on social media. In this case, they appropriated materials and reinterpreted them to generate new materials of their own. As can be seen, the content that adolescents share on social networks can be very varied and rich in diversity, from selfies and videos to drawings, paintings, and graphic designs. Obviously, what predominates is written text, photos, and videos. It is also important to note that, in all these phases, we can find skills related to narrative and aesthetic construction. This area can run through all the others, from the process of conceiving the idea to the editing.

There is an area of skills related to creation processes that cannot be left out of this section: social management skills. Tweens create content for social media, sometimes individually and sometimes collectively, depending on the context, environment, and motivations. During the fieldwork, the research team observed that through the collective creation process the tweens also acquire competencies related to coordination, collaboration, and teaching. For example, some adolescents showed coordination and leadership skills when they created a video collaboratively. They also showed skills in creating internal rules for the operation and organization of the group itself. Finally, the team also found teenagers who together created profiles on social networks. For example, they created a YouTube profile to share their collective works. Through this practice, they also acquired social media management and promotion skills.

As can be seen, there are multiple content creation skills. Table 21.2 includes a list of skills that spans from the most basic to the most complex and sophisticated competencies. The level of complexity of the skills varies depending on each tween, but the most basic skills (for example, taking photos/selfies) tend to be very widespread among tweens, and therefore these skills can be easily used in the classroom.

## Managing and Participating in Social Networks: Content, Digital Identity, Feelings, and Emotions

The other large area of skills that emerged from the tweens' social media use is related to the management of and participation in social networks. In this case, the skills detected can be divided into four main areas (Table 21.3): participating in social media, content management, management of personal digital identity construction, and management of feelings and emotions. Similar to the previous case, both simpler and more complex skills were detected.

*Table 21.2 Social media skills related to photo, audio-visual, and textual productions*

| Dimension | Social media skills | Examples |
|---|---|---|
| Conception and planning | • Conceiving<br>• Planning | 'Look, I follow Tumblr blogs and things like that. They are of girls who give loads of ideas on how to make pictures. And well, sometimes you try and say, "Oh that's a nice pic", and sometimes you say, "This sucks."' |
| Production | • Taking photos/selfies<br>• Filming/directing<br>• Creating text<br>• Designing a logo<br>• Designing graphic art for video pieces<br>• Drawing and painting | *[Q: What have you downloaded?]*<br>'We have downloaded some apps.'<br>'Action, which is a recorder to capture how we play, and then video editors.'<br>'We created a sort of logo, we put it at the beginning of the video along with music, and then the video started.' |
| Post-production & review | • Editing<br>• Reviewing | 'Well, we made a video and we edited it with an app we had, and we cut it into parts.' |
| Re-appropriation to generate a new content | • Modifying | 'We took "Gangnam Style", changed the lyrics and made a sort of music video.' |
| Narrative and aesthetic | • Considering aesthetic and narrative values when producing content | *[Q: Do you put a filter on them?]*<br>'Yes, I upload them … I put a filter or something like that, a frame, whatever, like in black and white.' |
| Social management when creating content: collaborate, coordinate and teach | • Creating collaboratively<br>• Coordinating and leading a group of people when creating contents<br>• Teaching others in their content creation<br>• Creating social rules when producing contents collaboratively<br>• Collaboratively creating, managing, and promoting social media and networking | 'Nobody talks when we are farming [a *Minecraft* term].'<br>*[In a workshop]* One group explains that they have created a YouTube channel to share their gameplays. |

The most popular dimension in this area is participation in social media. Practically all tweens who participated in the research applied many of these skills. Some competencies are very simple and could be defined as 'common'. Others are more complex and, in some cases, 'semi-professional' since they mimic and are close to the skills of professional profiles in the field of marketing and advertising (Masanet et al., 2020). The most common skills are implemented in daily practice, such as 'liking', 'following', and 'sharing'. Tweens not only follow their peers and acquaintances, but also celebrities (Instagrammers and YouTubers) or people and profiles with whom they share tastes or interests.

Many participants affirmed that they give importance to 'likes' and even automate their use since some claimed to 'like' everything without discrimination. Therefore, 'like' becomes a key element in the participation dynamics in social networks. Similarly, 'share' also becomes a common dynamic, as many tweens share content they like with friends and family on a regular basis. Skills like 'commenting', 'tagging', and 'chatting' are also common practices but require more effort to develop. Some tweens tag other profiles in their creations and/or posts to get more likes and increase their visibility. They are therefore applying a promotion strategy. Likewise, chatting or commenting implies an evaluation or review of content or topics and the creation of more textual content.

On the other hand, the skills that could be defined as 'semi-professional' are not very common and were only developed by specific tweens in the study. In this case, the research team found skills related to the ability to participate in and manage fan communities, such as 'engaging in fan communities' and 'coordinating/leading online communities'. Semi-professional skills related to the generation, positioning, and management of a personal brand in social media also emerged during the fieldwork. An example of this could be found in tweens who distribute and share content in the time slots in which the content can have the greatest impact, or when they tag influencers with shared interests and who can give visibility to their content, etc. The team detected two skills in this regard: 'positioning a personal brand' and 'actively performing social media marketing strategies.'

*Table 21.3 Social media skills related to management and participation in social media*

| Dimension | Social media skills | Example |
|---|---|---|
| Participating in social media | • Liking<br>• Following<br>• Commenting<br>• Tagging<br>• Sharing<br>• Chatting<br>• Engaging in fan communities<br>• Positioning a personal brand<br>• Actively performing social media marketing strategies<br>• Recognizing and describing the rules or terms of use within an online community<br>• Coordinating/leading in online communities | 'They can like the picture, and they can share it themselves if they want to.'<br>'Yes, for example in the official forum, once I reported having issues with a bug.'<br>*[Q: Have you noticed an increase in followers since you made your account public?]*<br>'I got a notification for me to explore other people's pictures that are usually the ones with the most likes, you know? So they come up and I guess that's how they saw me and they like it.' |
| Content management | • Searching, selecting, and downloading<br>• Managing content dissemination and sharing | 'So there's pages on Facebook about video games and that, and I follow them because perhaps they say something interesting.' |

| Dimension | Social media skills | Example |
|---|---|---|
| Management of their own digital identity construction | • Expressing one's personality through the production of social media content<br>• Reflecting on personal identity construction | |
| Management of feelings and emotions | • Being empathetic and open to experiencing different emotions<br>• Being resilient and adaptive | 'I'm not really good at art. I'm not really the artistic type, so I wouldn't be able to do other things like game designing.' |

Regarding the 'content management' dimension, the research team detected that the tweens manage different contents when they use social media. These contents could be produced by themselves or by others. When teens use social media, they look for and select both individual profiles and contents. In specific cases, they even download some of these contents. When tweens carry out these activities, they develop and apply skills related to the 'search, selection, and download' of content, but they also disseminate and share their own content. In this case, the skill they develop and apply is 'managing content dissemination and sharing'.

Finally, many of the tweens who make use of social media end up acquiring skills related to constructing and managing their digital identity and managing feelings and emotions. When a user creates content for their personal profile and manages interactions with other users, in one way or another, they are building their digital identity. In some cases, the team found that it is not only about personal expression through creating content but that the identity-building process may also involve a reflection or even criticism of themselves and the way they show themselves on social media. Through all these processes and practices, naturally, skills related to the management of feelings and emotions are also developed. When, for example, tweens do not receive the expected feedback or reception of the content shared on social networks, they must, in one way or another, learn to manage their emotions and feelings in order to deal with the situation.

As in the previous case, the research team detected varied skills with different levels of complexity, which are not developed by all tweens in the same way. Again, the team found some basic skills that practically all tweens apply and that could be incorporated in the classroom in a simple way.

## HOW TO EXPLOIT SOCIAL MEDIA SKILLS IN THE CLASSROOM

This section presents three examples of activities that can be applied in formal learning environments and some of the skills that can be developed in informal settings. These activities can be easily adapted to different contexts and classroom dynamics.

## Synt-Class: Extracting Meaningful Content from a Class through Social Media

The objective of this activity is to synthesize the content worked on in a class through the language of different social media, such as Instagram, YouTube, Twitter, or TikTok. This activity helps not only to organize the content and detect and extract the most relevant information, but also to create a repository with the contents developed in the classroom. It is an activity that can be applied in any subject, from mathematics to art, and can be used occasionally in a specific class or throughout the entire course.

The dynamics of the activity are simple and seek to implement some of the skills presented in the previous section, such as those related to producing, participating in, and managing social media. The activity is divided into five phases:

- Introduction (30 minutes). The teacher explains the dynamics to be carried out in the session: the students must synthesize the content of the class through social media and be able to create all kinds of content: text, images, video, etc. Before beginning the process, the teacher and the students agree on which social media will be used and create collective profiles for the class group. They all share the passwords and usernames of the social media profiles. They also stipulate a series of rules on the use and management of the profiles (privacy, copyright, type of language to be used, etc.). Finally, the teacher explains whether it is a specific activity or whether it will be ongoing throughout the course.
- Organization (5 mins). The class is divided into groups of between two and four students, and each group assigns roles to its members to carry out the activity.
- Development in the classroom (duration depends on activity). The teacher explains the task or activity planned for the session.
- Development at home (30–90 mins). Once the class is over, the group meets and discusses the most important issues they have detected during the session. They then design the content and choose the most suitable platform(s) for its dissemination. Finally, this content is shared on the class's social media accounts.
- Closing (10–15 mins). In the next class, the teacher retrieves the content that the students have uploaded to their social media and discusses it with them.

This activity can be evaluated or not. If it is evaluated, teachers are recommended to take into account a series of items such as the capacity for synthesis, coherence and clarity, and the adaptation of the content created to the specific language of each social media. In addition, the ability of teams to generate interaction in networks and to plan and organize teamwork should be considered.

## Creating Educational Content with YouTube: Learning through Teaching

The objective of this activity is to internalize and understand concepts and contents worked on in the classroom by creating videos for YouTube. It is an activity that can be applied to any subject. Students must prepare a YouTube video in which they explain to students in lower grades of the centre (or classmates) the concept or content worked on in class in a clear and friendly way. With this activity, students are not only internalizing and understanding specific contents in depth, but they are also re-elaborating and transmitting them through their own didactic methods and approaches, using YouTube's own language. The videos created through the activity, as in the previous one, can be used to create a repository of YouTube educational materials for other students.

With this activity, the students implement different skills related to the content creation process: conception and planning, production, post-production and review, narrative and aesthetics, and social management. They also apply some skills related to managing and participating in social networks, such as content management skills. The activity is divided into four phases:

- Introduction (30–45 mins). The teacher explains to the students the dynamics to be carried out in the session: he or she explains some contents of the subject (for example, an experiment in a science class or a literary genre in a language class) to the students, who then create an educational YouTube video in which they explain these same contents to students of lower courses of the centre. To motivate the students, before starting with the explanation of the contents, the teacher shows them YouTube videos in which similar contents are explained.
- Organization (5–10 mins). The class is divided into groups of between three and five students, and each group assigns roles to its members to carry out the activity.
- Development (55–110 mins). First, students conceive and plan the video (structure, script, performance, shots, etc.). Second, the students film and edit the video. The teacher supports them throughout the preparation of the video, giving them instructions when the content is not clear and helping them resolve their doubts (always related to the subject content they are working with). If students do not have time to finish the videos during the class sessions planned for this activity, they should finish them at home.
- Presentations (30–55 mins). Students present their videos to their classmates. During the presentations, they have to explain the decisions they made, the structure of the video and the production process, the possible problems that have arisen during the process, etc. The teacher and the rest of the students comment on the presentations and videos.

This activity is designed to be evaluated. Some of the items to consider in the evaluation are: the planning and organization of the work team, the ability to design and plan the video, the ability to clearly convey specific content, the ability to choose one's own methods and didactic approaches to teach others, the richness of the complementary sources used during the process, and the capacity for synthesis and verbal expression.

### Memetorics: Learning Rhetorical Figures by Creating Memes

This activity has a very specific and focused objective: to introduce the different rhetorical figures to the students. In order to do this, a dynamic based on creating memes is proposed. At the end of the activity, students should know what a rhetorical figure is, what they are useful for, and how to use them for communication. However, they will also explore and debate other areas, such as viral communication or the concept of the meme itself.

In this activity, the students mainly put into practice production, narrative, and aesthetic skills. The activity is divided into five phases:

- Preparation (20–30 mins). At home, students read a list of rhetorical figures (prepared by the teacher) that includes a description of each figure and examples from literature and journalism.
- Introduction (10–20 mins). The teacher explains the main rhetorical figures on the list and shows some graphic examples (photographs, audio-visuals, etc.). Once the presentation is finished, the teacher explains the activity to be carried out: the students must produce memes that reproduce different rhetorical figures by combining text and image.
- Organization (5 mins). The class is divided into groups of between two and four students.
- Development (25–35 mins). Students design and prepare their memes. The teacher explains to the students that there are many websites and apps that allow users to create and download memes, and advises them to use these resources.
- Presentation (10–25 mins). The activity ends with an exhibition of the productions created by the class and a final debate on the circulation of viral information and rhetoric.

This activity can be evaluated or not. If it is evaluated, it is recommended as a final co-evaluation activity: all the memes are printed and distributed among the different groups. Each group must evaluate a meme based on different criteria such as the correct use of the rhetorical figure, the coherence between image and text, creativity, etc.

## CONCLUSION

When the media practices of tweens are analysed from the perspective of transmedia literacy, by interpellating young people not as media 'victims' but as active agents and 'prosumers', a series of skills developed in informal settings begins to emerge. Far from the mythology of the 'digital native' (Masanet et al., 2019; Scolari, 2018), the research team of the H2020 Transmedia Literacy project found a very complex reality in which the new generations must confront a media ecology that is in the process of mutation. Tweens' experiences on social media are very varied, and researchers must consider a wide range of practices. The map of transmedia skills presented in this chapter has one characteristic: these skills are distributed in society in a very uneven way (no young person or adult can master all of these competencies!). In this context, rather than repressing or expelling these experiences from the school environment, formal education should empower them and help democratize them.

This chapter only includes a very small selection of the activities that can be used to 'exploit' these skills inside the classroom. As can be seen, these are simple activities that apply the aforementioned social media skills.[1] These activities can be adapted to different contexts, tempos, and evaluations. The main idea is to create activities that take advantage of the skills that adolescents develop informally and bring the school closer to the tweens' media practices. In addition, through these activities, the very sophisticated skills, normally carried out by a smaller proportion of adolescents, could be extended to all the students. The proposed activities can help create peer learning dynamics in which transmedia skills are shared and learned in the classroom as well (for example, those tweens who know how to edit a video can teach other students who do not know). In other words, the final objective of these actions is to democratize knowledge and to reduce the distance between informal and formal learning.

Obviously, the logic of 'transmedia literacy' does not have to be exclusive to the secondary education context: suitably adapted, it can also be applied in primary or higher education. In the specific case of the authors of this chapter, they have successfully exploited the productive transmedia skills that students had already acquired outside the university within their own undergraduate courses, for example, to produce videos and podcasts featuring theoretical content. In essence, this shift from user-generated to 'student-generated content' is at the centre of the transmedia literacy philosophy.

Regarding the H2020 Transmedia Literacy project, it allowed the implementation of participatory ethnographic methods that, by emphasizing creativity and content production, made working with adolescents easier. In short, teenagers were not passive subjects of the research but rather active participants as they were encouraged to produce media content and debate on the processes of media creation, consumption, and use. The rapid evolution of the media ecosystem and the migration between platforms should be mentioned among the limitations of the study. Between 2015 and 2018 the most important social media platforms among young people were Instagram, WhatsApp, YouTube, and, to a lesser extent, Snapchat, but today, tweens' 'media diet' shows a strong presence of TikTok and Twitch. It can be affirmed, then, that any study on the media practices of young people is always limited to a relatively short time period. Therefore, these kinds of inquiries should be repeated periodically to have a better picture of tweens' transmedia practices through time.

## NOTE

1. More activities can be found in the Teacher's Kit of the Transmedia Literacy project: http://transmedialiteracy.upf.edu/.

## REFERENCES


Buckingham, D. (2003). *Media Education: Literacy, Learning and Contemporary Culture*. Cambridge: Polity.

Buckingham, D., & Domaille, F. (2009). Making Media Education Happen: A Global View. In: C.-K. Cheung (ed.) *Media Education in Asia*. London: Springer, pp. 19–30.

Castells, M. (2007). Estudiar, ¿para qué? (To study, What for?). *La Vanguardia*, November 24.

Guerrero-Pico, M., Masanet, M.-J., & Scolari, C.A. (2019). Toward a typology of young produsers: Teenagers' transmedia skills, media production, and narrative and aesthetic appreciation. *New Media and Society*, *21*(2), 336–53. https://doi.org/10.1177/1461444818796470.

Masanet, M.-J., Guerrero-Pico, M., & Establés, M.-J. (2019). From digital native to digital apprentice: A case study of the transmedia skills and informal learning strategies of adolescents in Spain. *Learning, Media and Technology*, *44*(4), 403–13. https://doi.org/10.1080/17439884.2019.1641513.

Masanet, M.-J., Márquez, I., Pires, F., & Lanzeni, D. (2020).Teens and digital image creation on social media: Informal learning, transmedia skills and professional profiles. *BiD: Textos Universitaris de Biblioteconomia i Documentació*, *45*. https://dx.doi.org/10.1344/BiD2020.45.11.

Masanet, M.-J., Pires, F., & Gómez-Puertas, L. (2021). Riesgos de la brecha digital de género entre los y las adolescentes. *Profesional de La Información*, *30*, e300112. https://doi.org/10.3145/epi.2021.ene.12.

Meyers, E., Erickson, I., & Small, R. (2013). Digital literacy and informal learning environments: An introduction. *Learning, Media and Technology*, *38*(4), 355–67.

Pereira, S., Moura, P., Masanet, M.-J., Taddeo, G., & Tirocchi, S. (2018). Media uses and production practices: Case study with teens from Portugal, Spain and Italy. *Comunicación y Sociedad*, *33*, 89–114. https://doi.org/10.32870/cys.v0i33.7091.

Pink, S., & Morgan, J. (2013). Short-term ethnography: Intense routes to knowing. *Symbolic Interaction*, *36*(3), 351–61. https://doi.org/10.1002/symb.66.

Potter, W.J. (2005). *Media Literacy*. Thousand Oaks, CA: SAGE.

Potter, W.J. (2010). The state of media literacy. *Journal of Broadcasting and Electronic Media*, *54*(4), 675–96.

Scolari, C.A. (ed.) (2018). *Teens, Media and Collaborative Cultures: Exploiting Teens' Transmedia Skills in the Classroom*. Transmedia Literacy. Barcelona: H2020 Research and Innovation Action/Universitat Pompeu Fabra.

Scolari, C.A., Ardèvol, E., Pérez-Latorre, Ò., Masanet, M.-J., & Lugo Rodríguez, N. (2020). What are teens doing with media? An ethnographic approach for identifying transmedia skills and informal learning strategies. *Digital Education Review*, *37*, 269–87. https://doi.org/https://doi.org/10.1344/der.2020.37.265-283.

Scolari, C.A., Masanet, M.-J., Guerrero-Pico, M., & Establés, M.-J. (2018). Transmedia literacy in the new media ecology: Teens' transmedia skills and informal learning strategies. *Profesional de La Información*, *27*(4), 801–12. https://doi.org/10.3145/epi.2018.jul.09.

Toffler, A. (1980). *The Third Wave*. New York, NY: Bantam Books.

# Index